IMPERFECT DEMOCRACIES

IMPERFECT DEMOCRACIES
The Democratic Deficit in Canada and the United States

Edited by Patti Tamara Lenard and Richard Simeon

UBCPress · Vancouver · Toronto

© UBC Press 2012

All rights reserved. No part of this publication may be reproduced, stored in a retrieval system, or transmitted, in any form or by any means, without prior written permission of the publisher, or, in Canada, in the case of photocopying or other reprographic copying, a licence from Access Copyright, www.accesscopyright.ca.

21 20 19 18 17 16 15 14 13 12   5 4 3 2 1

Printed in Canada on FSC-certified ancient-forest-free paper
(100% post-consumer recycled) that is processed chlorine- and acid-free.

Library and Archives Canada Cataloguing in Publication

Imperfect democracies: the democratic deficit in Canada and the United States / edited by Patti Tamara Lenard and Richard Simeon.

Includes bibliographical references and index.
Also issued in electronic format.
ISBN 978-0-7748-2376-0 (bound); ISBN 978-0-7748-2377-7 (pbk.)

    1. Democracy – Canada. 2. Democracy – United States. 3. Canada – Politics and government – 21st century. 4. United States – Politics and government – 21st century. 5. Comparative government. I. Lenard, Patti Tamara, 1975- II. Simeon, Richard, 1943-

| JL75.I46 2012 | 320.97109'051 | C2012-904687-6 |

Canada

UBC Press gratefully acknowledges the financial support for our publishing program of the Government of Canada (through the Canada Book Fund), the Canada Council for the Arts, and the British Columbia Arts Council.

This book has been published with the help of a grant from the Canadian Federation for the Humanities and Social Sciences, through the Awards to Scholarly Publications Program, using funds provided by the Social Sciences and Humanities Research Council of Canada.

Printed and bound in Canada by Friesens
Set in Futura Condensed and Warnock by Artegraphica Design Co. Ltd.
Copy editor: Joanne Richardson
Proofreader: Sara Chang
Indexer: Annette Lorek

UBC Press
The University of British Columbia
2029 West Mall
Vancouver, BC V6T 1Z2
www.ubcpress.ca

Contents

Acknowledgments / vii

Introduction / 1
PATTI TAMARA LENARD AND RICHARD SIMEON

1 The Democratic Deficit: Canada and the United States in Comparative Perspective / 23
PIPPA NORRIS

2 Citizen Expectations and Democratic Performance: The Sources and Consequences of Democratic Deficits from the Bottom Up / 51
NEIL NEVITTE AND STEPHEN WHITE

3 Defining and Identifying a Democratic Deficit / 76
DAVID BEETHAM

4 Democracy in American Elections / 91
MICHAEL McDONALD

5 Can Canada's Past Electoral Reforms Help Us to Understand the Debate over Its Method of Election? / 111
JOHN C. COURTNEY

6 Regulating Political Finance in Canada: Contributions to Democracy? / 138
LISA YOUNG

7 Campaign Finance Reform in the United States / 161
ROBERT G. BOATRIGHT

8 Imperfect Legislatures / 181
DAVID C. DOCHERTY

9 Democracy's Wartime Deficits: The Prerogative Presidency and Liberal Democracy in the United States / 204
DANIEL J. TICHENOR

10 The "Centre" of the Democratic Deficit: Power and Influence in Canadian Political Executives / 226
GRAHAM WHITE

11 Extending the Franchise to Non-Citizen Residents in Canada and the United States: How Bad Is the Democratic Deficit? / 248
PATTI TAMARA LENARD AND DANIEL MUNRO

12 Citizen Representation and the American Jury / 269
ETHAN J. LEIB AND DAVID L. PONET

13 Supplementary Democracy? Democratic Deficits and Citizens' Assemblies / 291
AMY LANG AND MARK E. WARREN

14 Reflections on the Democratic Deficit in Canada and the United States / 315
SIMONE CHAMBERS AND PATTI TAMARA LENARD

Contributors / 330

Index / 334

Acknowledgments

First, we would like to thank the contributors for allowing us to include their work in *Imperfect Democracies*. All our contributors have been conscientious and responsive to our many requests, and, as a result, they have made our editorial work easy.

This volume has its origins in a conference we ran with the support of the Weatherhead Center for International Affairs at Harvard University. We would like to thank the center for its financial support and Helen Clayton for her support in organizing this workshop. We would like to thank the many commentators we invited to contribute their thoughts on the papers presented at this workshop: Karim Bardeesy, Joseph Fishkin, Jason Kaufman, Ofrit Liviatan, Daniel Nadler, Eleanor Neff Powell, Thomas Ponniah, James Snider, and Robert Vipond. Their work contributed immensely to the quality of the final chapters published in this volume.

We would also like to thank Emily Andrew at UBC Press for her ongoing support of and enthusiasm for this volume, and the anonymous reviewers whose comments on individual chapters were tremendously valuable. Finally, we would like to thank Katherine Wood, who stepped in at the last minute to aid in preparing the final manuscript.

IMPERFECT DEMOCRACIES

Introduction

PATTI TAMARA LENARD AND RICHARD SIMEON

Take a look at nearly every attempt to rank countries according to their democratic credentials and one finds that both Canada and the United States consistently place among the most democratic countries in the world. World Audit's democracy ranking places Canada in eighth place and the United States in fifteenth, for example, and Global Democracy places the United States in twelfth place and Canada in fifteenth.[1] Freedom House and Transparency International give similarly positive ratings. By international standards, in other words, one would be hard pressed to complain about the "democraticness," or, more elegantly, the quality of democracy in either of these countries. Despite ongoing contestation about the results of the 2000 American presidential race, about district boundaries and campaign finance in the United States, or large gaps between votes and seats won in Canada, or perhaps excessive partisanship in both countries, few seriously consider the democratic institutions and practices of these countries to be in real jeopardy. They are imperfect, as the title of our volume suggests, but they are not at risk of being overthrown or even seriously undermined.

Yet there is a paradox here. Even as both countries are confident in their status as democracies, voices expressing concern about the quality of Canadian and American democracy have become louder and more insistent.[2] It is increasingly proclaimed that they suffer from "a democratic deficit" and that this deficit raises questions about the legitimacy and effectiveness of their democratic institutions.³ There is increasingly, it seems, a gap between the theory and ideal of democracy and its gritty, messy practice in both countries. Ideally democracies are characterized by the collective self-determination of their citizens, with the latter feeling that they have the opportunity to control, or at least to influence, the direction of public policy. This, for many, means more than the opportunity to vote in free and fair elections. It also suggests inclusion and representation (everyone has a voice); political equality (everyone's voice counts equally); citizen engagement in community political life; and effectiveness, responsiveness, and accountability on the part of elected governments. Yet citizens report an ever-increasing dissatisfaction with their democratic institutions along all these dimensions. This dissatisfaction is reflected in well known, and frequently reported, statistics showing the decline of trust in political leaders and the decline in confidence in the effectiveness of democratic institutions.⁴ Citizens are increasingly confident not in their ability but, rather, in their *inability* to influence the political direction of their country. They are no longer, we might say, confident in the "quality" of their democracies. Susan Pharr and Robert Putnam's volume *Disaffected Democracy* observes, for example, a "disillusionment" with their governments among both Canadians and Americans as well as increases in reports of political alienation; and Richard Nadeau and Thierry Giasson observe increasing reports of "democratic malaise" among Canadians.⁵ These reports are by no means unique. In *Imperfect Democracies,* we compare and contrast the democratic deficit debates in Canada and the United States. But we also hope to contribute to a wider comparative discussion that will help to clarify the concept of the democratic deficit: how we measure it, how we assess its dimensions, and what kinds of solutions might be implemented to remedy it.

It is of course difficult to say, concretely, what is meant by the quality of democracy, and it is by no means clear how we might measure it.⁶ In part, the difficulty stems from the awareness that all democracies will be "imperfect" in some sense. Although, according to Ian Shapiro, "democrats expect much of democracy, in reality, democracy often disappoints. Both in its operation and its consequences it fails to live up to the promise people associate with it ... At best we can perhaps say that the democratic ideal lives in adaptive tension with the political realities in most so-called democracies."⁷ In other words, it is a mistake to believe that democracy will live up to its ideal in the first place. At best, we can say that the extent to which a democracy meets its ideal "is a matter of degree: of the extent to which democratic principles and mediating values are realised in practice ... for the moment, it is sufficient to emphasise that democracy is a continuum, and that it is always a work in progress."[8] Democracy can be more, or less, but never complete.

These complications suggest the deep challenge in offering a clear definition of democratic quality. We follow Jorge Vargas Cullell in assessing the quality of a democracy by "the extent to which political life and institutional performance in a country (or part of it) with a democratic regime coincide with the democratic aspirations of its citizens."[9] We refer to the gap between the reality of democratic life and citizens' aspirations as the "democratic deficit." In so far as Canadians and Americans demand more responsiveness from their democratic institutions, and in so far as they feel themselves incapable of exercising political control over them, we have reason to worry about the quality of democratic practice and its associated democratic deficit. As the contributors to this volume illustrate, however, we also have reason to be optimistic: there are multiple possible solutions to the democratic deficit, and we can be hopeful that they will be implemented.

Imperfect Democracies brings together Canadian and American scholars to compare and contrast the democratic deficit and to evaluate recommended solutions. Those versed in the politics of both countries know that there are tremendous similarities in their democratic systems and in the ways in which their citizens interpret the working of their politics. Both fall squarely into the category of liberal democracies. We offer a *most similar* systems comparison in that we compare two advanced liberal democracies. Yet the *specific* concerns expressed in the two countries are in many ways distinct: while Canadians have traditionally been concerned with executive dominance and the unrepresentative nature of the electoral system (in which votes do not translate, proportionally, into seats), Americans have paid more attention to the role of special interests and money in political life. That said, there is much to be gained by a sustained comparison of democratic practice, and the democratic deficits, in both countries. In this volume, the contributors focus on three questions in particular:

- Why are we talking about a democratic deficit in the first place? Why, in other words, are Canadians and Americans expressing concern about the quality of their respective democracies? And why are they doing so now?
- What is the location of the deficit? In what ways, specifically, are the Canadian and American democracies falling short? In what ways can we "measure" the extent of the democratic deficit?

- What can we do to mitigate the deficit? What moves, if any, have already been made to reform it? Are the reforms "cautious" or "aggressive"?[10] Are there parallels in the ways that Canadians and Americans have proposed to reform the deficit? Does either country suggest unique mechanisms by which to reform it? What can each country learn from the experiences of the other?

The inspiration for *Imperfect Democracies* lies in recent efforts to generate an effective system for auditing democratic practice. The International Institute for Democracy and Electoral Assistance (IDEA) has developed a comprehensive methodology to allow for context-specific democratic audits. Led by Professor David Beetham, it is perhaps best known for its audits of many developing countries and for its *Democratic Assessment Questionnaire*, designed to help citizens assess their own country's democratic performance. It is as relevant to advanced democracies like those considered here as it is to newly formed democracies. A democratic audit, writes Beetham, "is undertaken as a domestic project by citizens of the country being assessed, as part of an internal debate about the character of its political institutions and public life."[11] By allowing the citizens who are auditing their own democracy to have input into the precise aspects of democracy that matter to them – in large part by enabling them not only to shape the questions that drive the audit but also to select what they consider the most important from among those developed by IDEA – the democratic audit permits citizens to "differentiate between those aspects of a country's life which are more satisfactory from a democratic point of view and those which give cause for concern."[12]

This strategy allows democracy assessors to confront an obstacle that challenges all attempts to evaluate democratic practice: there is more than one – indeed, there are many more than one – democratic ideal.[13] As any scholar of democracy knows, for example, an emphasis on a minimalist democracy suggests a commitment to one set of ideals (competitive elections and formal equality, as exemplified by Robert Dahl's concept of polyarchy); a commitment to more participatory democracy suggests an alternative set of ideals (political participation and civic education); and a commitment to representative democracy suggests a commitment to yet another set of ideals (adequate representation and effective accountability).[14] Fully deliberative democracy that replaces competitive, representative, majoritarian democracy with reasoned discussion leading to consensual decisions sets an ever higher and more difficult standard.[15] The variations of ideal-type democracies are not infinite, of course, but they are sufficiently numerous and varied that we run the risk of evaluating a country – in which citizens are committed to the ideals of participatory democracy – as democratic (i.e., as not suffering from a deficit) when their institutions only satisfy the minimum requirements. A democratic audit – by allowing citizens to define their own democratic priorities – overcomes this risk by offering a way to audit a country that is consistent with the democratic aspirations of its own citizens. Note that the claim is not that there are no defining features of democratic institutions: to be democratic in the first place, democratic institutions must protect the basic political equality of all citizens – that is, their right to participate in the institutions that produce the legislation that governs their lives. The claim is simply that the specific institutions that protect the political equality of citizens can vary tremendously in form.

Thus, before we can measure the quality of a democracy, we must recognize that "every democratic country must make an inherently value-laden choice about what *kind* of democracy it wishes to be."[16] Democracies must be able to choose the criteria for judgment that best suits them: they can focus on whether their country is performing better or worse in comparison to, for example, neighbouring countries, or they can assess their own democratic practice over time with a view to evaluating whether the trend is towards enhanced or reduced democracy. The quality of democracy can thus be evaluated against some ideal standard (are we as good as we could be?), comparatively (are we better or worse than others?), or over time (are we getting better or worse?). Additionally, we must recognize that the instantiation of some democratic ideals may be incompatible with the instantiation of others. We must therefore adopt a "pluralist notion of democratic quality," according to which "there are not only dense linkages but also trade-offs and tensions among the various dimensions of democratic quality; and democracies will differ in the normative weights they place on various dimensions (for example, freedom versus responsiveness; or majority rule versus minority rights). There is no objective way of deriving a single framework of democratic quality, right and true for all societies."[17] This is also true of Canada and the United States: we should not assume that when their citizens call for greater democracy, they are necessarily calling for the same thing either within the two countries or between them.

Many countries, not least of which is Canada, have recently engaged in democratic audits inspired directly or indirectly by IDEA's pioneering work.[18] The Canadian Democratic Audit, led by Professor William Cross, wished to respond, in particular, to the dissatisfaction Canadians express with their political system.[19] Voter participation in Canada has dropped; Canadians believe their political representatives are increasingly unresponsive to their needs and demands; and they are increasingly dissatisfied with the performance of their democratic institutions.[20] In response, the Canadian Audit engaged in a full-scale review of Canada's central political institutions in an attempt to identify more clearly the source of Canadian malaise and to offer specific suggestions for reform. Cross describes the purposes of the Canadian Audit as follows: "to examine the way Canadian democracy functions, to listen to what others have to say about the operation of Canadian democracy, to assess its strengths and weaknesses, to consider where there are opportunities for advancement, and to evaluate potential reforms."[21] The audit produced nine volumes, each of which focuses on a specific institution, and the authors of many of these volumes contribute their analyses to this book.

The terms "democratic deficit" and "democratic audit" do not appear to be as widely used in American political discourse as they are in Canadian political discourse. But the issues and concerns reflected in the Canadian debate abound in the United States as well – in political argument, in popular and scholarly literature, in the work of NGOs from Common Cause to MoveOn.org, and, perhaps most obviously, in the Obama administration's Open Government Initiative, about which he wrote the following: "My administration is committed to creating an unprecedented level of openness in Government. We will work together to ensure the public trust and establish a system of transparency, public participation, and collaboration. Openness will strengthen our democracy and promote efficiency and effectiveness in Government."[22] Whether the Obama administration meets these goals or not, Obama's public avowal of them suggests recognition that citizens believe that democracy is, in important ways, failing them.

The Uniqueness of Our Approach

Imperfect Democracies evaluates the Canadian and American democracies, and the nature of their respective democratic deficits, in comparative perspective. It includes contributions from Canadian and American scholars who focus on a set of democratic institutions – the executive, the legislative, and the electoral system – in order to evaluate the ways in which these institutions do or do not live up to democratic ideals of popular sovereignty and political equality. One of our contributors, Pippa Norris, observes that, in global comparative focus, there seems to be little to complain about, democratically, in the United States and Canada. Many – if not most – countries in the world are doing worse, democratically speaking, in comparison to them. Yet, as William Cross notes in some remarks on the results produced by the Canadian Democratic Audit, "it is hard to know what to make of the knowledge that Canada is 100 places ahead of Chad" according to standard checklist models of democracy assessment (and readers who wondered whether in fact Canada's ranking – fifteenth – by Global Democracy suggested room for improvement rather than democratic satisfaction might feel the same). By comparing two mature democracies, then, we can generate many helpful insights into the nature of the democratic deficit and how citizens perceive it.

On the one hand, there are significant institutional differences between Canada and the United States. Canada has a strong though increasingly fragmented multi-party system, characterized by strong party discipline; the American two-party system is much looser. Canada has a strong tradition of executive dominance; in the United States, power tends to shift between strong executives (the "imperial presidency") and a strong Congress (the "imperial Congress"), but, compared to Canada's, the American legislature is far more powerful. Authority tends to be more concentrated in Canada and more dispersed in the United States. The United States is a presidential/congressional system; Canada is a parliamentary/cabinet system based on the British Westminster model. The United States is a national federation centred in Washington; Canada is a highly regional, decentralized, and multinational federation. American political culture is deeply inspired by its revolutionary history and the resulting emphasis on liberty, individualism, and limited government. Canada has a more conservative tradition, with a greater emphasis on collective values and "peace order and good government."[23] These and other cultural and institutional differences (not to mention the status of the United States as a hegemonic power in the world and Canada as a middle power) suggest that the issues raised, the discourse within which they are debated, and the institutions that are singled out for reform are likely to differ between the two countries. For example, faced with powerful cabinets and first ministers, Canadian reformers often seek to enhance the role of Parliament and parliamentarians – more "free votes," better-staffed committees, fixed terms for Parliament, and so on. Faced with widely dispersed authority, multiple veto points associated with checks and balances, and "divided government," Americans have often argued for more disciplined and responsible parties.

Yet similarities also emerge when we focus on citizens and their perceptions of the qualities of their respective democracies. In both countries, citizens express dissatisfaction with the quality of their democratic institutions. As we note above, Canadians and Americans both report decreased trust in their political representatives and decreased confidence in their political institutions. Both countries employ majoritarian political systems, which maximize the number of losers in any given election and therefore tend to generate more disaffection than do systems of proportional representation.[24]

Several contributors to *Imperfect Democracies* wonder whether the shared, negative attitudes towards the effectiveness of their democratic institutions result from a trend that plagues other Western democratic countries as well.[25] Perhaps we need to consider, they suggest, that democratic citizens of mature democracies in general – Canada and the United States included – have become more demanding. It may well be that it is their rising expectations about what democracy ought to provide, rather than the emergence of new weaknesses in their democratic institutions, that is driving dissatisfaction among democratic citizens. As Pippa Norris notes, citizens are increasingly critical of their democratic institutions, even as it remains unclear whether this new critical attitude emerges from rising expectations or reduced democratic performance in response, for example, to globalizing trends that move certain decisions from the domestic, democratic environment to transnational environments.[26] It is not clear whether the problem is citizens' increasing expectations, or the declining performance of existing institutions and elites, or both. Thus, we must assess whether the democratic deficit should be seen primarily as a *citizen deficit* (citizens are unengaged, uninformed, and uninterested) or as an *institutional deficit* (political institutions are non-inclusive, unresponsive, unaccountable, etc.). Reform proposals will, obviously, differ depending on the diagnosis along both these dimensions; the former might call for better civic education, for example, and the latter for the reform of institutions. Which element of the deficit is most important will shape the proposals for reform.

As readers will see, the authors draw strikingly different conclusions about the circumstances that ought to be held responsible for causing the perception of a deficit. Yet there is one broad observation that can be made: a comparison between Canada and the United States illustrates no clear democratic winner. In a three-way comparison of a variety of democratic institutions in Canada, the United States, and Mexico, Robert Pastor observes that "the United States nearly always comes in third place." But we find in this book that there are dimensions along which Canada is more democratic and others along which the United States is more democratic. And there are yet others along which they fare similarly. For example, although consensus among our contributors suggests that the Canadian electoral process is superior to the American process (particularly since the election officer in Canada is non-partisan), both countries do seem to be facing declines in political participation. In the ongoing competition between Canada and the United States (which often seems more vivid on the Canadian side), there seems to be no broad winner in the race to have the highest-quality democracy. The smugness sometimes voiced by commentators on both sides of the border is unjustified.

In addition to its comparative structure, *Imperfect Democracies* offers another distinctive feature – namely, a focus on both institutional and normative questions. Our analysis of institutions and practices is predicated on a normative commitment to the value of democracy. In Ian Shapiro's words, whereas "it might be going too far to say that democracy is all things to all people ... it is fair to say that there is a strong propensity to associate democracy with a wide array of activities and outcomes that people value."[27] In this volume, we display a commitment to the normative superiority of democracy, even as we recognize that certain institutions are better able to deliver democratic goods than are others. Thus, we heed the warning, which opens a recent evaluation of Latin American democracies, to guard "against the temptation of drawing false conclusions from the correct observation that democracy's normative superiority is a sufficient argument to justify its existence."[28] A normative commitment to democracy, as well as the awareness that, however democratic the institutions, improvements will always be required, underpins this volume. Any democracy – the Canadian and the American models included – can more or less instantiate democratic ideals, and the purpose of *Imperfect Democracies* is to clarify the ways in which these ideals remain uninstantiated and, then, to consider some solutions.

It is the widespread perception among citizens, to which we have already referred several times in this introduction, that, however mature their democracies, they are failing their citizens in important ways. It is the institutions that, it seems, succeed or fail with regard to delivering democratic goods – yet it is the citizens who are able to provide feedback with respect to whether these goods are being delivered. We rely on citizens' responses to signal dimensions about which we, as committed democrats, should be worried. In other words, there is an important relationship between citizens' subjective opinions with respect to democracy and the ways in which the institutions function in practice, and we need to pay attention to this relationship (even if, as Pippa Norris, Neil Nevitte, and Stephen White would have it, the difficulty is rising expectations and not newly failing institutions).

What matters, we might say following Patti Tamara Lenard and Daniel Munro, is the *salience* of the democratic deficit. It may be that democratic institutions do fail (perhaps necessarily so) to live up to ideal democratic values, but what matters is how salient this deficit is to the citizens who must live and interact, politically and socially, in an imperfect democracy.

Of course, historically, political participation – especially in democracies – has nearly always been imbued with a normative status. From Ancient Greek democratic theory through to contemporary accounts of the normative status of democratic theory, political participation is nearly always viewed as a moral good, in which citizens are morally obligated to engage or are at least praised for doing so.[29] Although in practice we may no longer view political participation as a moral good that should be prized above other possible human activities, many of us continue to believe that voting is a civic duty.[30]

We would be remiss if we did not observe – with Neil Nevitte and Stephen White – the considerable controversy, especially in American political science, concerning whether the evidence does indeed reveal a decline in overall political participation. Even as this debate remains unresolved, however, there is a consequence to reports of declining satisfaction in democratic institutions even if it is true that political participation has remained relatively constant over time. This is the concern that occupies, for example, Russell J. Dalton in *Democratic Challenges, Democratic Choices*, in which he worries that the consequences of decreased satisfaction are that democratic institutions may well suffer with respect to the willingness of citizens to comply (relatively) voluntarily with democratic legislation. He writes:

> Democratic polities are based on the presumption that citizens will voluntarily comply with the laws. If political distrust increases, this may lower voluntary compliance in areas such as tax laws and acceptance of government regulation ... These examples highlight a general feature of democracy: democracy functions with minimal coercive force because of the legitimacy of the system and the voluntary compliance of the public. Declining feelings of political trust and political support can undermine this relationship, and thus the workings of democratic government.[31]

In other words, even if citizens continue to participate in political activity, their willingness to comply with burdensome democratic legislation may decline enough to threaten the ability of political actors to implement democratic legislation with the expectation of compliance.

The solutions proposed in *Imperfect Democracies* recognize not only the danger that undemocratic institutions will increasingly shut citizens out (formally or informally) from the democratic process but also the danger that this will threaten legitimate democratic institutions, which are essential to protecting the trust that underpins widespread voluntary compliance with democratic legislation. These dangers may encourage, at best, a dissatisfaction with democratic political performance and, at worst, a more general disaffection that suggests that the legitimacy of the democratic system is in peril.[32]

Three Themes

As we note earlier, our contributors engage with the democratic deficit in Canada and the United States along three dimensions: the sources of the democratic deficit, its location, and possible reforms.

The Sources of the Democratic Deficit

We wonder whether we should attribute these declining positive evaluations of democratic institutions to an increase in citizen expectations or to an increasing inability of democratic institutions to keep up with the demands of citizens. Why, when "democratic values have been snowballing through so much of the world," is it that "many of the Western countries that spawned those values are confronting failings of democratic legitimacy"?[33]

In her chapter, Pippa Norris questions the benefits of focusing on the democratic deficit in Canada and the United States. Both countries, she notes, are consistently at the top of rankings of democratic countries. Norris compares and contrasts many of the methods by which we rank countries according to their democratic credentials – some of which employ minimalist standards and others of which employ more demanding standards – and observes that, whatever the methodology, the central indicators employed tend to correlate with one another. A country that is ranked as highly democratic by one standard is likely to be ranked as highly democratic by the others. These indicators, Norris suggests, can be valuable in providing a preliminary analysis of democratic health. But, she observes, for the most democratic of countries – including Canada and the United States – we reach a kind of "ceiling" effect, after which we must turn to more detailed analyses of a country's democratic health.

In their contribution, Neil Nevitte and Stephen White ask whether the 2005-6 World Values Survey is able to shed light on the disjuncture between our entrenched democratic institutions and our perception that they are not functioning effectively. Their results reveal, unsurprisingly, that Canadians and Americans are strongly committed to democracy, even as they express differing views with respect to its central components. In particular, Americans are less likely to believe that distributive equality is a core democratic value, even as low-income Americans express a higher than average dissatisfaction with the results of their democratic institutions. Nevitte and White speculate about the possible causes of this dissatisfaction – the unrepresentativeness of political actors, worries that democracies are unable to deal with the proliferation of citizen-driven demands – and observe that a dominant effect has to do with one's sense of what democracy is meant to provide. That is, one's own ideal of democracy shapes how one responds to the type of democracy on offer. Paradoxically, moreover, they find that those who are dissatisfied with their democracy are *more* rather than less likely to be engaged in political activity.

In other words, dissatisfied democrats cannot be counted on to disengage from political activity (and so we do not have an adequate explanation of the reasons for decreasing voter turnout and political participation more generally), even as they continue to express doubt about the effectiveness of the institutions with which they engage. In some sense, we might even say that dissatisfied democrats are our ideal democratic citizens: they are informed, aware, and politically active. They engage the political system because they believe that we can do better. These are citizens who are empowered by high levels of education as well as by competence with new technologies that speed the flow of information and facilitate political participation. These dissatisfied democrats, however, must be distinguished from those we term "disaffected." Disaffected citizens have disengaged from political activity. These are citizens who believe their governments have been effectively disempowered by the forces of globalization and the now pervasive neoliberal ideology, both of which appear to weaken the capacity of government to act to protect the interests of citizens. Additionally, they no longer believe that they can influence the political process in a meaningful way. Especially among the lower classes, disaffection is exacerbated by stagnating or declining incomes, increased inequality, and the erosion of the welfare state.

Locating the Democratic Deficit
One obvious place to look for a democratic deficit is in the electoral system since the vote (combined with competitive elections, of course, because turnout numbers without supporting democratic institutions are meaningless,

as Norris observes) is perhaps the sine qua non of democratic politics. In Canada, especially, complaints are regularly made about the failure of votes to translate into seats. For example, recently, Sujit Choudry and Michael Pal made headlines with research that suggested that visible minority votes were especially diluted in Canada as a result of the indirectly representative nature of the Canadian electoral system.[34]

Challenges abound in both Canadian and American electoral systems. Michael McDonald's contribution assesses the challenges posed by the "two-tier" voting process in the United States. Unlike in most electoral democracies, where the government is responsible for maintaining updated voter lists, Americans are officially required to register in advance of voting day. Many Americans are effectively disenfranchised by the complicated rules, and early deadlines, that attend registration. Making voting more "convenient," suggests McDonald, is not a "cure-all" for the ills that face democratic politics in the United States; but data suggest that it would increase voter participation by a noticeable margin. The challenges to easing the process of voting, however, are frequently mired in partisan politics.

As John Courtney notes, one significant advantage of Canada's electoral system is its commitment to a nonpartisan election administration (though he is circumspect about its capacity to be effective in all national environments). In his chapter, Courtney traces the progress of electoral reform in Canada, one element of which is the adoption of a fully nonpartisan national election administration. Courtney suggests a variety of reasons why Canadians have been motivated to implement electoral reform in the past: progressively more tolerant social values, successful advocacy group campaigns, dissatisfaction with brazen electoral manipulation, and so on. Electoral reform in Canada is on the agenda again, but it bears little resemblance to previous movements for reform. Unlike in the past, present-day demands for electoral reform emerge from the confluence of many different events: front-burner elections (elections that signal major shifts in the party system), provincial attempts to modify electoral systems, evidence that other democratic countries (New Zealand, Scotland, Italy, etc.) can change their electoral system, and, of course, heightened concerns about a democratic deficit. Of special importance, writes Courtney, is that present debates about electoral reform are bringing to the fore the various ways in which citizens understand the role of elections and their individual status as voters. As voters, they are making increased demands on a democratic system that may require electoral reform (i.e., changes in how votes are distributed among parties, changes in the representative relationship between citizens and their representatives, etc.) in order for them to be met.

Debates about electoral reform involve not only the very important question of the relationship between the vote and the eventual outcome in terms of representatives (and their representativeness) but also the rules surrounding electoral campaigns. The worry here is that these rules restrict all but the most wealthy from running for office, that they permit far too much special-interest input into electoral campaigns (especially by way of donations), and that the campaigns themselves do not adhere to the democratic principles of equality and popular control.

With respect to campaign finance reform, Canada and the United States offer especially interesting comparative insights. Both countries engaged in reforms in the 1970s and are presently again engaging in reforms, and both implemented these reforms to deal with perceived corruption and unfairness – that is, to ensure that inequality in the market did not replicate itself in the public sphere. Both sets of reforms (in both countries) aimed to increase the transparency of the electoral system more generally, and the most recent reforms emphasize redressing the imbalance between large collective donations and smaller donors so as to increase the political participation of the latter. While Canadians express anxiety about the *result* of the process (and so measure success in terms of political output), Americans express anxiety about the front end of the process.[35]

While Lisa Young emphasizes the relatively benign role of political finance in Canadian politics and the relative unimportance of these issues in Canada, Robert Boatright emphasizes how campaign finance reform debates in the United States are framed around the trust and confidence they might (re)engender in the American democratic system. According to Young, recent changes in campaign finance rules render them better able to meet democratic ideals (although recently one of these incentives – that parties would be financially rewarded for the overall number of citizens who voted for them, regardless of their electoral success more generally – has recently been revoked). On the other hand, Boatright expresses scepticism concerning the "evidence" that suggests a relationship between reformed campaign finance regulations and increases in political trust (though the impact of the Supreme Court's recent decision to allow unlimited corporate donations has already become evident in the unregulated role of multi-million-dollar PACs). He does observe, though, that it may be useful to view campaign contributions as an important form of political participation and that, if we do, then there are a range of options we might employ to encourage political participation of this kind: tax credits for campaign contributions (which exist in Canada), matching funds, and so on. Canada has made more fundamental reforms to election finance than has the United States (including stricter contribution limits and limits on third-party advertising), in part because of court decisions that stress individual freedom of speech in the United States and collective values of fairness in Canada.

In democratic political theory, there has been a decided move towards evaluating the extent to which one's *vote* does or does not translate into genuine political influence, or *voice*. As we see in the next section, in which we outline the suggested reforms, there has been a move away from a minimalist, and even a strictly representative, democracy towards more participatory and deliberative forms of democracy. These latter forms, it is suggested, are better able to meet the spirit of the democratic ideals to which we are committed. However, the debates about electoral reform suggest that the question of *vote* is not itself resolved.[36]

Patti Tamara Lenard and Daniel Munro suggest that one locus of the democratic deficit lies in the failure of Canada and the United States to extend the franchise to non-citizen permanent residents. In these tremendously diverse countries, the proportion of non-citizen residents, with the legal right to abode and who are on the path to citizenship, is high. Yet there is a variety of reasons to worry that the process by which these individuals attain citizenship, and thereby the right to vote, is such that many will remain without the franchise for many years. According to Lenard and Munro, if we believe that voting is among the most important ways in which one can ensure that one's interests are taken into account in the political environment, we ought to consider extending the right to vote to permanent residents, at least at the local level (where their interests are affected in a direct and clear way). Although the salience of the democratic deficit as it relates to the inability of permanent residents to vote is relatively low (moreover, the primary concern of non-citizen residents is not the right to vote but, rather, their relatively low socio-economic status) and, therefore, not necessarily worth working towards given other priorities, Lenard and Munro note that liberal democratic principle leans towards extending the vote to permanent residents, at least at the municipal level.

How then do votes translate into representation in the legislature? David Docherty offers a comparative evaluation of the extent to which American and Canadian legislatures live up to the democratic ideals they are meant to embody. In his estimation, the Canadian legislature has much work to do to persuade Canadians of its relevance (especially given the history of executive dominance in Canada). For Docherty, the adversarial nature of the Canadian legislature is such that it undercuts the confidence Canadians might have in it. Even as we deem Question Period to be a success – it is an effective system of oversight and scrutiny – we must recognize that it serves, in part, to undermine the legislature's work. There are tremendous obstacles to reforming the legislature in Canada – for example, party discipline is getting stronger and campaigns have become much more leader-centred – but we need to focus on solutions. Docherty advocates enlarging the House of Commons and establishing more powerful committees, even as he notes that the American system contains both of these and that the result is not reassuring, at least with regard to resolving the democratic deficit.

What is fascinating here is that there is a clear democratic deficit in both the American and Canadian legislatures, but it takes diametrically opposite forms. In Canada, the problem is powerless and ineffective legislatures paralyzed by executive dominance and party discipline; in the United States, it is powerful legislatures with widely dispersed power and influence that can lead to gridlock, lowest common-denominator solutions, and undue influence for lobbyists and parochial interests. Here, as with debates about the electoral system, institutional differences between the two countries lead to quite distinct manifestations of the democratic deficit and, consequently, to quite different solutions.

Both Graham White (Canada) and Daniel Tichenor (the United States) continue this analysis, exploring the relationship between democracy and executive power. Here again the institutional differences, which are linked to historical political culture, are critical. From the beginning, the United States has been committed to limited government and has feared the concentration of power – hence, a strong system of checks and balances and the separation of powers are central to the American political system. Canada has traditionally been more committed to a strong, effective executive, played out in Westminster parliamentary government. As Tichenor notes in his introduction, "committed democrats like Thomas Paine have long viewed executive leadership with dread since it has a tendency to make citizens passive, dependent, and deferential – qualities decidedly ill-suited for self-government."[37] Recent debate in Canada has focused on the dominance of the prime minister and premiers (first minister government) and the weakening not only of parliaments but also of cabinets. Yet, in his chapter, Graham White questions the conventional wisdom of executive dominance in Canada, observing that there is far too little analysis to support this claim. There is, White argues, no real benchmark by which to evaluate prime ministerial strength. But his analysis suggests that there is little evidence that the prime minister makes autocratic decisions as often as is claimed; rather, in general, decisions are made in a deliberative and, therefore, democratic manner among senior cabinet members rather than imposed from above. Even if there is a democratic deficit at the executive level, it is not as significant as has been claimed. Daniel Tichenor explores the exercise of prerogative powers by the presidency in the United States, with a view to exploring its compatibility with democracy. His assessment shows us that, historically, the dominant understanding of political representation has a tremendous influence on the perceived (legitimate) prerogatives of executive power. His timely chapter evaluates the relationship between concepts of political representation and the perceived role of executive leadership by comparing the actions of wartime presidents. He argues, in particular, that George W. Bush's administration's approach to executive leadership, criticized around the world, was in fact a logical outgrowth of historical developments in the trajectories of executive prerogatives in the United States.

This discussion also illustrates how debates about the democratic deficit can vary both between parties and over short periods of time. In the United States, the Nixon and Johnson presidencies led to a large literature condemning the "imperial presidency." When Congress sought to rein in presidential power, another literature complained about the "imperial Congress," which was frustrating decisive action on important issues. Parties out of power protest against executive power; once in office, they seek to protect it.

Resolving the Democratic Deficit

Earlier we introduced a distinction between cautious reforms and aggressive reforms. The cautious approach is incremental and recommends that "institutional change should be employed sparingly and only after careful reflection."[38] Because institutional change may well have unintended consequences, and because democratic institutions are necessarily interrelated such that a reform to one may well affect others, we must take care in advocating for change. The aggressive approach recommends "major changes," and its advocates worry considerably less than do advocates of the cautious approach about unintended consequences. As Allan Tupper explains, "they have a longer-term perspective and ultimately want to change attitudes as a catalyst to major reforms."[39] This distinction allows us to capture the differences in the kinds of proposed institutional reforms.[40] Here, we employ an additional distinction between reform and innovation. The set of suggestions to resolve the democratic deficit that emerges from those working within a particular institution are characterized as reforms. As readers will see, the chapters in Part 2 ("Reforming the Institutions of Democratic Governance") offer such suggestions. David Docherty argues, for example, for an enlarged House of Commons and increasingly powerful committees as a way to improve the likelihood that elected representatives will be able to do their constituents' bidding; and Robert Boatright argues for tax credits for campaign contributions on the grounds that they may serve to increase political participation among poorer Americans.

However, our contributors do not restrict themselves to suggestions of the kind that demand the reform of existing institutions. Contributors to Part 3 ("New Directions for Deepening Democracy") consider institutional *innovation* – that is, they suggest what Amy Lang and Mark Warren call "supplemental institutions" as a way of ameliorating the democratic deficit. They consider the recent attempt to institute electoral reform in British Columbia (later emulated by Ontario) by relying on a randomly selected citizens' assembly to consider the merits of alternative electoral systems. The citizens' assembly, they argue, can "supplement our received institutions in ways that redress democratic deficits."[41] It was designed as a mechanism to inoculate the reform process against the vested interests of incumbent politicians and to give the final voice to the people through a referendum. The citizens' assembly model is no "cure-all," the authors concede, but they nevertheless conclude that it has "strengths in precisely those areas in which Canadian and American political institutions are weak ... inclusive representation, sustained deliberation focused on public interests, and accountability."[42]

Ethan Leib and David Ponet also consider mechanisms through which citizens might have a more direct hand in policy formation or, at least, in consultations. They argue that most proposals to offer citizens a way to have more influence fail to consider the ways in which consulted citizens "represent" citizens at large. A focus on how "citizen representatives" are able to adequately represent the views of citizens more generally leads Leib and Ponet to consider lessons offered by the representative principles employed in American jury systems. Their evaluation of juries reveals several principles by which we can measure the representativeness of citizen representatives. In this way, they argue, the normative insights developed from within the field of representation theory can best be applied to new institutions, like the citizens' assembly, in such a way that citizen representatives are, in fact, genuinely representative of society at large.

It is of course not clear whether we need to turn to "supplemental" institutions or whether the democratic resources our received institutions can provide are sufficient to remedy the democratic deficit. One clear difference between these institutional reforms, however, and the institutional "supplements" that Lang and Warren recommend is their emphasis on citizens' agency. The reforms we list above are tremendously important mechanisms by which we can improve certain key aspects of democratic practice: they serve to move us closer to meeting democratic ideals. They may serve, in particular, to alter citizens' perceptions of the effectiveness of the democratic institutions under which they live. But their emphasis is mainly on *institutional* change and the impact this change will have on the effectiveness, and the perception of the effectiveness, of democratic institutions. What these supplemental institutions add is a focus on the agency of citizens. They take account of democratic citizens in their capacity as democratic actors and, in doing so, focus on empowering citizens to effect democratic change themselves rather than reducing them to the mere recipients of democratic change. Since the democratic deficit is reflected in citizens' perceived lack of agency with respect to political influence, an emphasis on institutional change of the kind that generates a sense of agency may be the direction to pursue.

However, before enthusiastically proposing a radical course of action, it is worth observing the possibility that new "democracy-deepening" institutions may not have the desired effect if that effect is understood simply in terms of reversing trends in survey data that reveal dissatisfaction. It is possible that "asking for more opportunities for citizen input into the system may not be a panacea for perceived inadequacies of democratic governance."[43] One reason to think that we will not see the benefits of new and more democratic institutions in survey data involves the now frequently observed claim that citizens' expectations of democratic governance have increased as democratic institutions have become more entrenched. For example, according to Dalton, "the same individuals who are critical of how politicians and political institutions are functioning today also have high aspirations for democratic process."[44] It may even be that citizens' expectations have increased at a higher rate than have the capacities of democratic institutional performance to meet them. But these rising expectations may be cause to celebrate, rather than to worry about, the state of democratic institutions. We should perhaps focus, at least in part, not on the fact that dissatisfied democrats are dissatisfied but, rather, on how they are now, more than ever, *democrats*. It may be that a "deepening commitment to democratic principles" is one of the central "factors contributing to the dissatisfaction with contemporary governments."[45] If this is so, then the solution to democratic dissatisfaction is – as our contributors suggest, and even if we are never rewarded with survey data reporting decreasing rather than increasing rates of dissatisfaction – after all, more democracy.

NOTES

1 See http://www.worldaudit.org/ and http://www.democracyranking.org/, respectively.
2 A quick Google search in June 2008 yielded 397,000 references to the "democratic deficit" in the United States, and 208,000 in Canada.
3 The term "democratic deficit" originated in the European Union, reflecting concern about the elitism and bureaucracy of community decision making as well as the weakness of the elected European Parliament.
4 John R. Alford, "We're All in This Together: The Decline of Trust in Government, 1958-1996," in *What Is It about Government that Americans Dislike?*, ed. John R. Hibbing and Elizabeth Theiss-Morse (Cambridge: Cambridge University Press, 2001); Ronald Inglehart, "Trust, Well-Being and Democracy," in *Democracy and Trust*, ed. Mark Warren (Cambridge: Cambridge University Press, 1999); Pippa Norris, ed., *Critical Citizens: Global Support for Democratic Governance* (Oxford: Oxford University Press, 1999).
5 R.D. Putnam, S.J. Pharr, and R.J. Dalton, "Introduction: What's Troubling the Trilateral Democracies?," in *Disaffected Democracies: What's Troubling the Trilateral Democracies?*, ed. S.J. Pharr and R.D. Putnam (Princeton: Princeton University Press, 2000), 9-11; Richard Nadeau and Thierry Giasson, "Canada's Democratic Malaise: Are the Media to Blame?" *IRPP Choices* 9, 1 (2003): 229-67.
6 For attempts, see the essays collected in David Beetham, ed., *Defining and Measuring Democracy: Institutional versus Socioeconomic Factors* (New York: Sage Publications, 1994); Alex Inkeles, ed., *On Measuring Democracy* (New Brunswick, NJ: Transaction Publishers, 1991).
7 Ian Shapiro and Casiano Hacker-Cordon, "Promises and Disappointments: Reconsidering Democracy's Value," in *Democracy's Values*, ed. Ian Shapiro and Casiano Hacker-Cordon (Cambridge: Cambridge University Press, 1999), 1.
8 David Beetham, ed., *International IDEA Handbook on Democracy Assessment* (Leiden: Kluwer Law International, 2002), 17.
9 Jorge Vargas Cullell, "Democracy and the Quality of Democracy: Empirical Findings and Methodological and Theoretical Issues Drawn from the Citizen Audit of the Quality of Democracy in Costa Rica," in *The Quality of Democracy: Theory and Applications*, ed. Guillermo O'Donnell, Jorge Vargas Cullell, and Osvaldo M. Iazetta (Notre Dame: University of Notre Dame Press, 2004), 96.

10 We borrow the terms "cautious' and "aggressive" to describe reform proposals from Allan Tupper, "Auditing the Auditors: The Canadian Democratic Audit," *Canadian Public Administration* 50, 4 (2007): 635-53.
11 David Beetham, "The Idea of a Democratic Audit in Comparative Perspective," *Parliamentary Affairs* 52, 4 (1999): 568.
12 Ibid.
13 David Held, *Models of Democracy* (Oxford: Polity Press, 1996).
14 For example, see Robert Dahl, *Polyarchy: Participation and Opposition* (New Haven: Yale University Press, 1971); Carole Pateman, *Participation and Democratic Theory* (Cambridge: Cambridge University Press, 1976); Nadia Urbinati, *Representative Democracy: Principles and Genealogy* (Chicago: University of Chicago Press, 2006).
15 For example, see John Dryzek, *Deliberative Democracy and Beyond: Liberals, Critics, Contestations* (Oxford: Oxford University Press, 2000); Jon Elster, ed., *Deliberative Democracy* (Cambridge: Cambridge University Press, 1998); Samantha Beson and José Luis Martí, eds., *Deliberative Democracy and Its Discontents* (Vermont: Ashgate Press, 2006); Ethan Leib, *Deliberative Democracy in America: A Proposal for a Popular Branch of Government* (University Park: Penn State Press, 2005).
16 Larry Diamond and Leonardo Morlino, "The Quality of Democracy: An Overview," *Journal of Democracy* 15, 4 (2004): 21.
17 Ibid., 22.
18 Examples include the Costa Rican Democratic Audit, which is evaluated in O'Donnell, Vargas Cullell, and Iazzetta, *The Quality of Democracy*; and the Australian Democratic Audit (http://www.arts.anu.edu.au/democraticaudit/).
19 According to William Cross, the Canadian Democratic Audit was in fact inspired mainly by the Danish Power and Democracy Study (1998). See this website for more information: http://www.ps.au.dk/. For an evaluation and interpretation of the results, see Peter Munk Christiansen and Lise Togeby, "Power and Democracy in Denmark: Still a Viable Democracy," *Scandinavian Political Studies* 29, 1 (2006): 1-24.
20 William Cross, "Canada Today: A Democratic Audit," *Canadian Parliamentary Review* 24, 4 (2001-2): 37-55.
21 Ibid.
22 Open Government Initiative, http://www.whitehouse.gov/.
23 Seymour Martin Lipset, *Continental Divide: The Values and Institutions of the United States and Canada* (New York: Routledge, 1990); Michael Henry Adams, *Fire and Ice: The United States and Canada and the Myth of Converging Values* (Toronto: Penguin Group, 2004).
24 Christopher J. Anderson, André Blais, Shaun Bowler, Todd Donovan, and Ola Listhaug, *Losers' Consent: Elections and Democratic Legitimacy* (Oxford: Oxford University Press, 2005).
25 Putnam, Pharr, and Dalton, "Introduction."
26 Norris, *Critical Citizens*.
27 Shapiro and Hacker-Cordon, "Promises and Disappointments," 2.
28 Osvaldo M. Iazzetta, "Introduction," in O'Donnell, Vargas Cullell, and Iazzetta, *The Quality of Democracy*, 3.

29 Not *all* accounts of democracy prize democratic political participation as a moral good, of course. The most commonly cited example of a democratic theorist who does not prize political participation as a good is Joseph Schumpeter, in his *Capitalism, Socialism and Democracy* (New York: Harper, 1950).
30 Stephen Knack, "Civic Norms, Social Sanctions and Turnout," *Rationality and Society* 4, 2 (1992): 133-52.
31 Russell J. Dalton, *Democratic Challenges, Democratic Choices: The Erosion of Political Support in Advanced Industrial Democracies* (Oxford: Oxford University Press, 2004), 12.
32 We owe the distinction between "disaffection" and "dissatisfaction" to Simone Chambers.
33 Ian Shapiro, *Democracy's Place* (Ithaca: Cornell University Press, 1996), 2.
34 Michael Pal and Sujit Choudhry, "Is Every Ballot Equal? Visible Minority Vote Dilution in Canada," *IRPP Choices* 13, 1 (2007), http://papers.ssrn.com/.
35 We owe this way of framing the debate about campaign finance reform to Robert Vipond.
36 We owe this way of articulating the distinction between "vote" and "voice" to Simone Chambers.
37 Tichenor, this volume, 207.
38 Tupper, "Auditing the Auditors," 644. It is also worth noting that today, after years of failed discussion, Canadians are wary of debating constitutional reform. The bar to constitutional change is at least as high in the United States.
39 Ibid., 645.
40 Tupper employs the distinction to good effect to distinguish, for example, John Courtney's reluctance to propose additional (significant) electoral reform from David Docherty's attempts to revitalize the Canadian legislature.
41 Lang and Warren, this volume, 291.
42 Ibid., 299.
43 Anderson et al., *Losers' Consent*, 189.
44 Dalton, *Democratic Challenges*, 195.
45 Ibid., 191.

1

The Democratic Deficit
Canada and the United States in Comparative Perspective

PIPPA NORRIS

Imperfect Democracies focuses upon the quality of contemporary democracy in Canada and the United States. The list of symptoms highlighted by the Canadian Democratic Audit highlights issues of low and eroding voter turnout, widespread disaffection with political parties, and weak linkages connecting citizens and the state.[1] William Cross summarizes the initial motivation to establish the audit:

> Much was written in the 1990s and early years of the 21st century concerning a "democratic deficit" and "democratic malaise" in Canada. There was substantial evidence that many Canadians were dissatisfied with the state of their democratic practices and institutions. The Canadian party system was in the midst of significant upheaval, voter turnout rates had reached a record low and public confidence in democratic institutions was in significant decline. At the same time, new phenomena such as increased pressures of globalization and changing communications technologies were posing new challenges to Canadian democracy.[2]

Before looking in detail at Canada and the United States, however, it is useful to reflect more generally upon broader comparisons, not least with regard to what concepts and benchmarks underlie any attempt to evaluate the quality of democratic governance. Developments in North America can best be understood by comparing them with a wide range of established democracies in Western Europe. Observers in many Western European and Anglo-American states echo similar concerns to those expressed in Canada.[3]

The longitudinal evidence available within the United States and Western Europe challenges conventional claims that an inevitable downward spiral of public disenchantment with politics has occurred across all established democracies. Confidence in political institutions and satisfaction with democracy usually displays a pattern of trendless fluctuations over time rather than any simple erosion. Nevertheless, a broader perspective suggests that a democratic deficit – reflecting a sizeable and persistent gap between citizens' aspirations for democracy and their evaluations of the performance of democratic governance – is also evident in many societies.[4] The notion of a "democratic deficit" first arose in debates about the legitimacy of the European Union. Some commentators have regarded the core decision-making institutions in the European Union as falling well short of the standards of democratic accountability and transparency that exists at the national level within each of the member states.[5] The original idea was to judge the legitimacy of decision-making processes within the European Union against the democratic standards of European nation-states. But this useful idea is not confined to this context: it can be applied wherever the perceived democratic performance fails to meet public expectations, whether concerning a specific public-sector agency or institution, the collective regime or constitutional arrangements governing the nation-state, or the agencies of global governance and multilateral organizations, including the United Nations.[6] The idea of a democratic deficit also builds upon work, developed more than a decade ago, that first identified the phenomenon of "critical citizens."[7] This group of citizens holds democracy to be the ideal form of government, yet, at the same time, it remains deeply sceptical when evaluating how democracy works in its own country. As David Beetham interprets this phenomenon (Chapter 3, this volume), any deficit raises concern about the failure of democratic governance to meet public expectations of democracy.

Logically, any deficits between public aspirations and evaluations of democratic performance may arise due to rising public expectations, the role of the news media as the key intermediary, or the failure of governments to perform as expected.[8] The democratic deficit is a matter of concern as it is thought to have important consequences, including for political protest, for allied forms of political behaviour and rule of law and, ultimately, for processes of democratization. A leaking reservoir of political trust is seen as tying policy makers' hands and limiting voluntary compliance with government authority.[9] Dissatisfaction with democratic performance is also usually regarded, at least implicitly, as an important cause of civic disengagement, encouraging an erosion of conventional participation among citizens. At worst, fragile regimes lacking a broad and deep foundation of legitimacy among the mass public are widely believed to face a serious risk of instability and even breakdown.[10] Whether deficits become politically salient among citizens, whether they spur expressions of activism such as protest politics, whether they subsequently trigger institutional reforms in the public policy agenda, and whether they even catalyze regime transitions, however, depends upon multiple conditions. No simple and straightforward line connects democratic deficits with contemporary phenomena such as the "Occupy Canada" movement, the rise of the Tea Party, or thousands of protestors' rallying against austerity measures and corporate greed on the streets of Athens, Madrid, Rome, and Brussels.

The assumption that the general public in Canada, the United States, and European democracies has become deeply disillusioned with government and politics is so pervasive today that many accounts jump straight into the discussion of consequences and solutions without critically questioning the evidence for the trends and causes of disaffection. To understand these claims, in the first section I summarize what is known about system support from the previous research literature, which indicates that concern over trust and confidence in governing institutions has usually waxed and waned over the years, reflecting the impact of contemporary political events, real politik, and global waves of democratization. In the second section I set out the framework used to describe and interpret trends in citizens' orientations, emphasizing the importance of paying close attention to the "when," "where," and "what" of change.

In this chapter I focus upon comparing established democracies, as it is for them that the longest and richest time-series survey data are available. Longitudinal trends are documented in the United States and the nation-states of Western Europe, all affluent societies with extensive historical experience of democracy. My analysis compliments that in other chapters in this volume, which focus upon trends in the Canadian evidence. Using an expanded version of the Eastonian framework of system support, I first compare developments in the most specific levels of support, including attitudes towards particular government agencies, and then move upwards to consider more diffuse indicators of satisfaction with the general performance of democratic regimes and the strength of core attachments to the nation-state.

The trend evidence available in the United States and Western Europe demonstrates that, when changes in system support do occur, it is usually far more common to observe fluctuations over time in successive surveys rather than straightforward linear or uniform decline. Some cross-national changes in system support do occasionally occur simultaneously – symbolized by the events of 9/11, after which support for government appears to peak simultaneously across many countries – but these are the exception, not the rule. In terms of "where" changes occur, persistent cultural differences can be observed over many years, even among relatively similar nations (e.g., contrasting levels of confidence in government in Italy and Spain, different levels of trust in parties in the Netherlands and Belgium, and diverse patterns of national pride in Germany and France). During the last decade, a few established democracies (notably the United Kingdom and Portugal) experienced a rising tide of mistrust of government institutions, which should raise concern; yet, during the same period, Belgium and Finland experienced the reverse.[11] Last, with regard to "what" changes occur, instead of a uniform general pattern, contrasts in public attitudes towards different branches of government are apparent within each country, including the United States, and are exemplified by different levels of trust and confidence in the legislature and in the courts. Perhaps most important for an accurate diagnosis, at the most diffuse level, public satisfaction with the general performance of democracy in Western Europe has usually strengthened over time, not weakened. Affective attachments to the nation-state remain strong and stable.

Theories of Eroding Public Trust and Confidence in Government

The earliest surveys of American public opinion towards government were conducted during the decade after the end of the Second World War, at a time when the role and functions of the federal government had expanded greatly under the New Deal Roosevelt administration and when the United States had recently emerged as victorious and economically dominant in the world. It was often assumed that, during this era, American public opinion was relatively favourable towards the role of government. Rather than a "golden age," however, the earliest studies conducted by Hyman and Sheatsley in 1954, McClosky in 1958, and Mitchell in 1959 describe American postwar attitudes as ambivalent towards government. Public opinion typically expressed pride in American democracy and yet considerable scepticism about the morality and honesty of elected politicians. The American,

Mitchell concluded, "tends to expect the worst in politics but hopes for the best."[12]

Systematic comparative work on public opinion towards government originated during the late 1950s and early 1960s, with Almond and Verba's landmark study entitled *The Civic Culture*. The theoretical impetus for this work reflected contemporary concern to understand the underlying causes of regime instability during the second great reverse wave of democracy.[13] The context involved the rise of Nazi Germany and Italian fascism and the global disruption of the Second World War as well as the 1960s collapse of fledgling parliamentary democracies in many newly independent African states emerging from colonial rule and the checkered political experience of Latin America due to a succession of military coups, populist dictators, and communist revolutions.[14] The central message emerging from *The Civic Culture* emphasizes that political stability requires congruence between culture and structure. Almond and Verba argue that the democratic public needs to be finely balanced between the dangers of either an excessively deferential, apathetic, and disengaged citizenry, on the one hand, and an overly agitated, disenchanted, and heated citizenry, on the other. They posit an optimal level of political trust in stable democratic states, such as Britain and the United States, where active and watchful citizens check the powerful without succumbing to the destabilizing forces of either excessive loyalty and deference or excessive disaffection and alienation. The idea that societies differ in their political culture is hardly novel; indeed, it has been the subject of philosophical speculation from Montesquieu to de Tocqueville. But one of the more radical aspects of Almond and Verba's work is the way that they derive support for their theory from a path-breaking cross-national opinion survey, thus demonstrating that citizens' orientations could be examined empirically. They analyze the mass publics in Mexico, the United States, Italy, Britain, and Germany during the late-1950s.

Almond and Verba conclude that the United States (and, to a lesser extent, Britain) exemplifies their notion of a *civic* culture:

> Respondents in the United States, compared with those in the other four nations, are very frequently exposed to politics. They report political discussion and involvement in political affairs, a sense of obligation to take an active part in the community, and a sense of competence to influence the government. They are frequently active members of voluntary associations. Furthermore, they tend to be affectively involved in the political system:

they report emotional involvement during election campaigns, and they have a high degree of pride in the political system. And their attachment to the political system includes both generalized system affect as well as satisfaction with specific government performance.[15]

By contrast, Italy (and, to a lesser extent, Mexico) exemplifies an *alienated* political culture:

> The picture of Italian political culture that has emerged from our data is one of relatively unrelieved political alienation and distrust. The Italians are particularly low in national pride, in moderate and open partisanship, in the acknowledgment of the obligation to take an active part in local community affairs, in the sense of competence to join with others in situations of political stress, in their choice of social forms of leisure activity, and in their confidence in the social environment.[16]

The Civic Culture therefore emphasizes cross-national variations, even among relatively similar postindustrial societies such as Italy and Germany. This influential study did much to establish the conventional view that, during the Eisenhower era, a period of economic abundance and cold war politics, Americans held positive views about their political system.

The mid-1960s and early-1970s, however, saw mounting concern over the capacity of democratic institutions to serve as an outlet to contain public dissent in the United States and in Western Europe. The era experienced the outbreak of tumultuous protest politics, with urban riots in Philadelphia, Watts, Newark, and Detroit symbolizing a radicalization of race relations and a breakdown of social control in the United States. Mass demonstrations on the streets of London, Paris, and Bonn catalyzed similar concerns in Western Europe. These events triggered new cross-national survey research that sought to understand the causes of protest activism.[17] The gloomy prognostications that became common during these decades received their strongest endorsement from Crosier, Huntington, and Watakuki, who, in the mid-1970s, published a major influential report for the Trilateral Commission that diagnosed a "crisis" of democratic legitimacy afflicting not just the United States but many other postindustrial societies as well.[18]

This wave of concern ebbed somewhat during the early-1980s, reflecting some subsidence of radical social movements and the more quiescent mass politics characteristic of the Thatcher-Reagan era. During these years, Lipset and Schneider compare a wide range of American public opinion polls regarding government, business, and labour.[19] They conclude that mass support for many types of political institutions in the United States had indeed eroded over time but that most criticisms were levelled at the behaviour and performance of specific power-holders rather than at the underlying structure and function of American institutions. The latter, more positive, interpretation was reinforced by the Beliefs in Government project, a multi-volume comparison of broad trends in Western Europe from the early-1970s to mid- or late 1990s. A thorough and detailed collaborative study, the Beliefs in Government project dismisses talk of a "crisis of democracy" as exaggerated. In particular, the chapters in these volumes that examine institutional confidence and trust in politicians conclude that there is little evidence of a steady secular erosion of systems support in Europe during these three decades; rather, the authors arrive at relatively sanguine conclusions that emphasize the existence of persistent cross-national differences in systems support across different European member states and a pattern of trendless fluctuations over the years.[20]

The debate over the depth of any problem was far from settled, however, and during the early to mid-1990s, as already noted, a host of American scholars continued to express worries about "disenchanted democrats," "critical citizens," and growing civic disengagement. Similar concern about political mistrust, voter apathy, and democratic disaffection echo among commentators in many other postindustrial societies as well.[21] Russell Dalton provides the most comprehensive recent summary of the cross-national survey evidence from the 1960s until the late 1990s across a range of established democracies and postindustrial societies. Dalton concludes that, during these years, citizens became increasingly detached from political parties, more sceptical towards governing elites and institutions, and less confident about parliaments, although public support for democratic ideals had not flagged.[22] Scholarly research mirrors popular commentary on contemporary phenomena in Western societies that appear to underline citizen anger, exemplified during 2009 by the public reaction to the Westminster expenses scandal in Britain and, in the United States, by the simmering rage and breakdown of civility towards elected representatives expressed by "Tea Party" activists at town hall meetings debating health care reform, the federal deficit, and the stimulus package.[23]

The Interpretive Framework: What Has Declined, When, and Where?

Before plunging into analyzing the causes of democratic deficits, it is important to establish a clear picture of trends in the evidence. Analysts need to pay attention to the depth, breadth, and timing of any changes in citizens' orientations towards democratic politics and government in the United States and Western Europe. What has declined, where and when?

In terms of *what*, bearing in mind the Eastonian framework already discussed, we need to establish whether erosion of support has occurred only at the most specific level of trust in politicians, party leaders, elected officials, and public-sector workers or whether it has spread upwards to damage confidence in many core political institutions and state agencies and even, at the most diffuse level, managed to fragment common identities within multinational communities.

In terms of *where*, we need to demonstrate whether general patterns of declining trust and confidence are evident across many comparable established democracies – suggesting general causes – or whether any serious problem of eroding system support is confined to just a few nations. Most research literature on this topic concerns the United States, but the US Constitution was founded upon classical liberal principles, emphasizing mistrust of government. Lipset notes that American culture may prove exceptional in this regard, as in so much else.[24]

Finally, in terms of *when*, close attention needs to be paid to the exact timing of any fluctuations in systems support. It is insufficient to look at net changes in different societies since countries may arrive at a similar end point by divergent paths. Moreover, the starting and ending date for many series of observations is often arbitrary, even though this can clearly colour interpretations of the trends (e.g., if the series of survey measurements commences on a relatively high point or on a relatively low point). It is more rigorous to examine whether changes happen simultaneously across states or whether trends vary in their timing.

Prior attention to the "what, where, and when" helps us to select the most plausible competing theoretical hypotheses, which can then be analyzed further in subsequent chapters. For example, any evidence of a glacial erosion of political support for parties and parliaments that persists over successive decades in many similar Western societies would suggest looking for evidence of long-term causes, such as processes of social-psychological change in cultural values among individual citizens or, on the macro-level, the impact of societal modernization, human development, the penetration of the mass media, and globalization. On the other hand, if patterns of trendless fluctuations and short-term volatility are observed, with dynamic peaks and troughs that vary across relatively similar types of societies and among different branches of government, this points towards the need to investigate specific performance- and event-based explanations within each country, such as the government's success or failure in handling the economy, the outbreak of a major parliamentary scandal, the end of an unpopular war, the rise of new parties, the polarization of party politics, or an election that has thrown the governing party out of office.

The longest continuous time-series evidence is available from the American National Election Studies (ANES), and it allows us to track half a century of trends in the standard American indicators of trust in government officials. The US General Social Survey (GSS) also regularly monitored institutional confidence in public- and private-sector agencies from 1972 to 2006. To see whether similar trends are apparent in other established democracies, we can draw upon the series of biannual Eurobarometer surveys conducted since the early 1970s. The Eurobarometer survey regularly monitors confidence in national institutions, satisfaction with the performance of democracy, and feelings of national pride and identity. It should be noted, however, that cross-national European trends can often only be examined for short periods, and the results of any estimates of net change and linear trends remain sensitive to the particular years and countries under review. It remains possible that rising European disaffection occurred in the longer-term period, but the evidence is too limited to allow researchers to refute or confirm this claim.

Given the immense outpouring of scholarly research and popular commentary, is there anything new to say? Surprisingly, perhaps a lot. Many studies of the empirical evidence provide only a partial view because they select only one aspect of the underlying multidimensional concept of systems support or focus upon only a few countries or a single global region. Much of the literature lacks a clear and comprehensive conceptual framework focused on support for the political system. In studies of the empirical evidence, both attitudinal and behavioural indicators are commonly mixed together. Equally important, even half a century after Almond and Verba's original *Civic Culture* survey, items carried in the time-series survey evidence used for identifying trends are often of limited duration and cross-national breadth, making it impossible to determine with any accuracy whether general trends have indeed occurred. To update the analysis, we can start by monitoring developments in the United States and Western Europe, which possess the longest series of indicators and the largest body of previous research. This sets the context for the broader comparison of contemporary societies worldwide presented in the next chapter.

Longitudinal Trends in the United States and Western Europe

Trust in Public Officials in the US Federal Government

As discussed earlier, the standard ANES questions about political trust ask whether the "government in Washington" or "people running the government" can be trusted to "do what is right," whether they "waste taxes," whether government is run "for a few big interests," or whether public officials are "crooked." These questions seek to tap public attitudes towards the national government, including perceptions of the ethical standards, probity, and integrity of elected officials. They also occur in other American and cross-national surveys.[25] As Russell Hardin points out, however, these questions are often used in empirical studies without anyone's having reflected upon whether they actually relate to the underlying notion of political *trust*.[26] For Hardin, trustworthiness rests on both motivations and competencies: do government officials seek to act in the public interest and, if so, do they actually have the capacity to do so? For example, people may believe that elected officials are trustworthy in their motivations for public service (e.g., that the local Congressional representative from their local district is honest and hardworking or that the president is well-meaning and likeable), and yet they may also feel that these individuals often prove generally incompetent or ineffective (e.g., when managing a major economic or foreign policy crisis). Or, conversely, citizens may logically believe that politicians are usually competent and effective but also venal (in that they may be thought to line their own pockets or those of special interests). The standard ANES battery of items mostly concerns the trustworthiness of the motivations of public officials (to "do the right thing") rather than their competencies.

Reflecting a long-standing debate, the meaning of these indicators is open to alternative interpretations. Hence, for Jack Citrin, they provide signs of *specific* support for incumbent office holders, with limited consequences. In this view, the erosion of American political trust that occurred during the 1960s can best be understood as an expression of public dissatisfaction with the performance of particular incumbent political leaders and public policies, representing part of the regular cycle of normal electoral politics and real world events.[27] From this perspective, the public popularity of members of Congress and particular presidents can be expected to ebb and flow over time, without indicating that Americans are willing to support constitutional reforms. For Arthur Miller, however, the ANES indicators tap into diffuse support. Any erosion suggests that the roots of public dissatisfaction extend more deeply to indicate a crisis of legitimacy in American democracy, representing a loss of faith that US political institutions are the most appropriate ones for American society.[28] Others suggest that, because government institutions are operated by incumbents, in practice it is difficult, if not impossible, to disentangle support for agencies and actors.[29] The ambiguity and potential measurement error when operationalizing the complex concept of political trust means that relying solely upon these indicators is unwise, and it would be prudent to see whether similar trends are evident in alternative data.[30] If the dynamics of public confidence in the executive, legislative, and judicial branches of American government reflect the peaks and troughs of confidence in the federal government, this would lend greater confidence to time-series trends and would indirectly support Miller's interpretation. If, however, there are marked variations in citizens' reactions towards different institutions, then this suggests the need to search for more performance- and event-driven explanations.

The first question in the ANES battery comes closest to the notion of general trust in public-sector officials who work within the federal government, relating to Easton's notion of specific support rather than diffuse support. It also provides the longest time-series. If we compare trends over time in the proportion of the American public reporting that it trusted the federal government to do what is right "most of the time" or "just about always," as shown in Figure 1.1, the evidence suggests that American trust in government leaders plummeted steadily every election year from the mid-1960s to the late-1970s, during the period of hot-button politics and dissent over race relations, Vietnam, the war on poverty, and Watergate.[31] Yet the subsequent trend line displays considerable volatility, with dynamic peaks and troughs rather than a simple linear fall. According to this series of observations, a sharp revival of American trust in the federal government occurred during the first Reagan administration from 1980 to 1984, despite the anti-government rhetoric of this administration, the deep recession in the American economy during the early 1980s, and the growing polarization of party politics as the Grand Old Party (GOP) moved sharply towards the right on certain moral and economic issues. Citrin and Green suggest that this happened because economic indicators for employment and inflation improved markedly after 1982, and President Reagan's leadership style exuded confidence and sunny optimism.[32] Trust in the federal government revived again from 1994 to 2002, a period of sustained economic growth

FIGURE 1.1

American trust in the federal government, 1958-2008

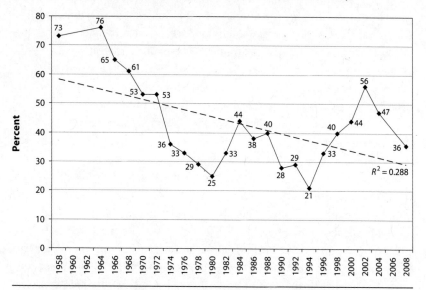

Question: "How much of the time do you think you can trust the government in Washington to do what is right – just about always, most of the time or only some of the time?"
Note: The unstandardized beta regression coefficient proved significant (> .001).
Source: The American National Election Surveys, 1958-2008.

that started under President Clinton and continued under President George W. Bush. Support peaked again after the dramatic events of 9/11, which Hetherington attributes to a "rally-around-the-flag" effect associated with any foreign policy crisis and the priority given to security issues.[33] Support then fell back during the next three national elections. Nor is this simply a product of the ANES survey measurement: similar volatility among the American public is evident when the same question is asked in a series of Gallup polls and New York Times/CBS News polls conducted since the early 1970s.[34] The overall volatility indicates that there are clearly periods during which American trust in the federal government was revitalized as well as periods during which it plummeted, and comprehensive explanations need to account for dynamic fluctuations over time.

Are similar trends evident elsewhere? Some of the ANES questions concerning trust in politicians have been asked in national election surveys conducted in some other established democracies; however, as a review by Listhaug emphasizes, comparisons of trends are limited because of considerable variations in the wording of the question and the lack of continuity of questions over successive national surveys.[35] The most thorough and comprehensive recent review of trends in sixteen established democracies using these types of questions is that by Dalton, and it concludes that they indicate a net decline in confidence in politicians in recent decades: "Regardless of recent trends in the economy, in large and small nations, in presidential and parliamentary systems, in countries with few parties and many, in federal and unitary states, the direction of change is the same."[36] Dalton's evidence that the public has become more sceptical about elected officials is certainly suggestive and important; nevertheless, some caution is needed when interpreting the results of the regression analysis used in his study since, out of forty-three separate questions, only seventeen saw a statistically significant fall in trust over time. Moreover, any erosion of support that has occurred at the most specific level of elected officials may have few important consequences; in democracies with regular multiparty elections allowing the removal of incumbents, less public trust in politicians may generate higher turnover of elected representatives without necessarily affecting more diffuse levels of public confidence in government institutions.

Institutional Confidence in the United States

The GSS monitors trends in confidence in public-sector agencies, including the three branches of the American federal government. Any sustained erosion of faith in these institutions has potentially far more serious consequences than does loss of trust in particular presidents, congressional leaders, or elected representatives. In democratic states, the popularity of elected leaders and governing parties is expected to rise and fall according to citizens' evaluation of their performance. Where opinions are overwhelmingly negative, multiparty democracies with alternating parties in government provide a safety valve for dissatisfaction through offering periodic opportunities to "throw the rascals out" via the ballot box. But institutional confidence reflects more enduring and diffuse orientations than does the popularity of specific leaders: any severe and persistent loss of legitimacy for the US Congress, the Supreme Court, or the executive branch is not easily remedied, and it has broad ramifications. The GSS also examines attitudes towards the private sector, including confidence in major companies as well as in banks and financial institutions. This helps to establish whether the American public has increasingly lost faith in many established pillars

FIGURE 1.2

American trust in the US Supreme Court and Executive, 1972-2008

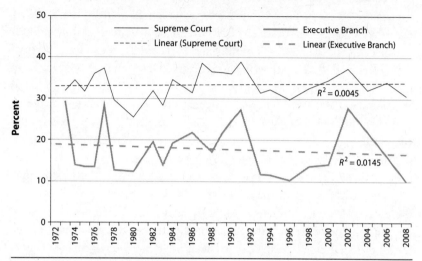

Question: "I am going to name some institutions in this country. As far as the people running these institutions are concerned, would you say you have a great deal of confidence, only some confidence, or hardly any confidence at all in them?"

Source: US General Social Survey cumulative file 1972-2008, http://publicdata.norc.org/webview/.

of authority or whether the problem is confined mainly to the image or performance of government agencies and bureaucrats working in the public sector.

The GSS, conducted by NORC, has monitored confidence in institutional leaders since the early-1970s. It begins: "I am going to name some institutions in this country. As far as the people running these institutions are concerned, would you say you have a great deal of confidence, only some confidence, or hardly any confidence at all in them?" Figure 1.2 shows the trends in American confidence in the executive branch and the Supreme Court. The dotted trend line and the R^2 coefficient summarize the overall strength and direction of any linear trends. The trend in public confidence in both the executive branch and the Supreme Court clearly demonstrates patterns of trendless fluctuation around the mean; in particular, most strikingly, *no significant overall fall in institutional confidence occurred for either of these institutions from 1972 to 2008.* The executive branch, in particular, displays considerable volatility over time, for example with the sharp peaks registered temporarily in 1977 (temporarily restoring levels of confidence under the Carter administration to the pre-Watergate era), in 1988-92 (under the presidency of George H.W. Bush), and again in 2001 (under George W. Bush, following the events of 9/11). The highs and lows are rarely sustained, however, although the White House saw lower than average confidence during Clinton's first term, before public revelations surrounding the Lewinsky affair. The trend lines for the Supreme Court and the executive branch roughly mirror each other, although the Supreme Court retains higher public confidence and more stable evaluations.

Confidence in the US Congress, illustrated in Figure 1.3, displays parallel periods of rising and falling public confidence and provides a fainter mirror of trends in the executive. Similar fluctuations can be observed in other surveys – for example, in June 2008, the Gallup poll found that just 12 percent of Americans expressed confidence in Congress, the worst rating the organization had measured for any institutions in the thirty-five-year history of

FIGURE 1.3

American trust in the US Congress, 1972-2008

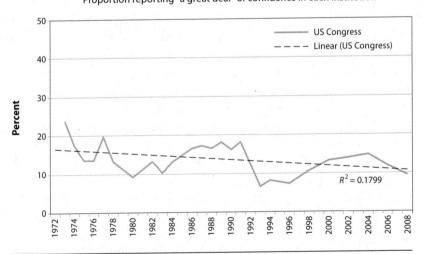

Question: "I am going to name some institutions in this country. As far as the people running these institutions are concerned, would you say you have a great deal of confidence, only some confidence, or hardly any confidence at all in them?"

Source: US General Social Survey cumulative file 1972-2008, http://publicdata.norc.org/webview/.

the question. Following the election of President Obama and the return of a Democratic-led Congress, the March 2009 Gallup poll saw Congressional approval jump to 39 percent. After an initial honeymoon period, approval fell back to 25 percent by the end of 2009.[37] Overall, however, compared with presidential approval, there is a flatter line for congressional approval in the GSS series, suggesting less pronounced volatility for the legislative branch than the executive branch. Moreover, and most important, the overall trend line since the early 1970s to 2008 shows falling net support for Congress during these decades, as many commentators have noted.[38] It appears that, in evaluations of the leadership among the core institutions of the American federal government, the public has expressed the most consistent growing doubts about the legislative branch.

But does this long-term fall in congressional approval mean a crisis of legitimacy for American *government* – suggesting the need to search for potential political explanations – or are similar trends apparent for other established institutions in the private sector as well? If there is a more generic trend affecting attitudes towards those in authority, then cultural or social reasons might provide more plausible explanations. For comparison, the bottom graph in Figure 1.4 shows parallel trends in confidence in the private sector for banks and financial institutions as well as for major companies. Most strikingly, both these private-sector institutions show overall trends of falling confidence from the start to the end of this era, with declines that are similar in strength to those experienced during the same era by Congress. It is also notable that banks and financial institutions show sharper peaks and troughs than confidence in major companies.

The GSS evidence concerning institutional trust in the United States therefore suggests several important points that challenge the conventional wisdom. First, the time-series evidence suggests that any trends in American public opinion are not simply directed towards loss of faith in all three branches of the American federal government; rather, the most consistent net loss of confidence during more than three decades focuses upon Congress. Second, the legislature is not alone in this regard, and the issue is more than simply a crisis of faith in government; other major private-sector institutions, like American banks and companies, have experienced an equivalent net loss of public confidence as well. Last, these data reinforce the point that any persuasive explanations need to account for the dynamics of public support in attitudes towards government institutions, with attention being paid to the precise timing of particular short-term fluctuations,

FIGURE 1.4

American trust in banks and major companies, 1972-2008

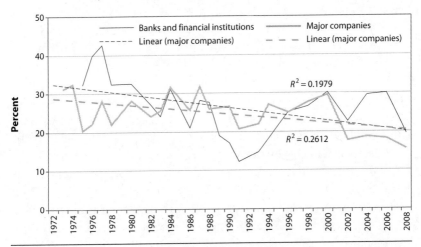

Question: "I am going to name some institutions in this country. As far as the people running these institutions are concerned, would you say you have a great deal of confidence, only some confidence, or hardly any confidence at all in them?"
Source: US General Social Survey cumulative file 1972-2008, http://publicdata.norc.org/webview/.

rather than to assume a net erosion of political trust and confidence. Often, studies have simply focused upon net percentage point change derived from the starting and end points for any time-series data, but this approach inevitably assumes certain arbitrary benchmarks: it is unclear, for example, what confidence in these institutions was like prior to the early 1970s. Analytically, it is equally important to understand the dynamic variance in the trends over time.

Institutional Trust in Western Europe

The Eurobarometer allows us to compare the United States with Western Europe. The survey monitors longitudinal trends in trust and confidence in a wide range of public- and private-sector institutions, including governments, parliaments, and parties, as well as satisfaction with the general performance of democracy and the strength of national identities. The Eurobarometer now covers public opinion in all current twenty-five EU member states. For a consistent time-series, however, the longest trend analysis from these surveys is limited to the countries that have been member states since 1973.

European Trust in Government

We can start by comparing the annual trends in institutional trust in the national government across seventeen European societies in which attitudes have been monitored during the last decade. The data illustrated in Figure 1.5 and summarized in Table 1.1 show the proportion of the public who express trust in their national government every year (allowing *comparisons* of persistent contrasts across countries, such as between Italy and Luxembourg) and the overall net change that occurred from the start to end of this decade (showing any overall *net losses or gains*). The final columns in Table 1.1 measure the strength and significance of the unstandardized OLS regression beta coefficients (which summarize the *direction* of linear trends).

Trends in European trust in national government indicate several important points. First, *during the last decade the net change in European confidence in government varied in direction and size by country*. For example, the United Kingdom, Portugal, and Ireland experienced the sharpest significant net drop in the proportion of the public trusting government during the last decade (down by twenty percentage points or more).[39] This finding would give support to the conventional assumption of steadily eroding trust but for the fact that other European societies experienced trendless fluctuations and *no* significant linear change over time, or even, in a few cases (Sweden and Belgium), a 19- to 21-point net *rise* in political trust during the same period (although this was not statistically significant as a linear trend). The assumption that trust in government has eroded consistently across established European democracies receives no support from this cross-national survey evidence. Now of course the time-series is relatively short, and it may be that trust in government eroded during earlier eras; we simply cannot determine this with the available Eurobarometer evidence, but nor can others. It is also important to emphasize that there are substantial persistent contrasts among EU member states that need to be explained. For example, just as Almond and Verba observed half a century ago, the Italian public remains deeply sceptical in its orientation towards its government.[40] By comparison, citizens in Luxembourg and Finland are generally more trusting than average. The precise reasons for the restoration of political trust in Sweden and Belgium, and the simultaneous fall in Britain and Portugal, are further scrutinized when we consider alternative explanations.

FIGURE 1.5

European trust in national government, 1998-2009

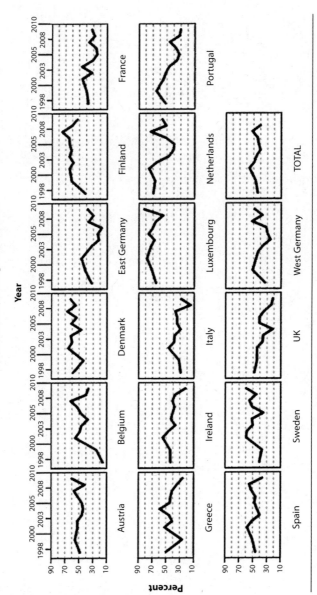

Question: "I would like to ask you a question about how much trust you have in certain institutions. For each of the following institutions, please tell me if you tend to trust it or tend not to trust it? – the national government."

Source: Eurobarometer surveys, 1998-2009.

TABLE 1.1

European trust in national government, 1997-2009

Proportion responding "tend to trust" (%)

	1997	1999	2001 spring	2001 fall	2002	2003	2004	2005	2006	2007	2008	2009	1997-2009 net change	Beta	Significance
Austria	48	56	47	52	53	46	44	46	51	57	42	60	12	.108	ns
Belgium	16	25	45	55	49	46	37	47	52	62	40	37	21	1.83	ns
Denmark	59	44	54	66	60	62	47	61	54	67	55	62	3	.458	ns
East Germany	32	41	40	47	40	32	22	24	18	37	30	38	5	-.759	ns
Finland	42	61	56	64	59	64	61	64	65	75	61	53	11	.957	ns
France	38	40	37	46	32	46	31	25	26	36	28	32	-6	-1.05	ns
Greece	50	27	39	52	41	45	59	44	43	41	34	26	-24	-.821	ns
Ireland	44	44	48	55	47	37	43	41	38	41	37	22	-21	-1.39	*
Italy	29	32	33	47	39	38	29	35	35	37	15	29	-1	-.712	ns
Luxembourg	65	71	77	78	76	72	68	76	70	66	55	82	17	-.101	ns
Netherlands	69	67	66	76	65	47	41	40	51	73	51	56	-13	-1.42	ns
Portugal	52	65	50	55	52	47	36	33	37	46	32	30	-22	-2.46	**
Spain	46	50	48	58	51	40	44	47	46	52	55	37	-9	-.327	ns
Sweden	41	37	49	59	59	50	51	35	51	55	45	60	19	.805	ns
UK	48	44	35	44	36	36	22	41	41	34	24	22	-26	-1.83	**
West Germany	34	51	47	54	43	37	25	30	31	52	37	48	15	.188	ns
Total	44	47	47	56	49	46	40	43	44	52	40	43	-1	-.346	ns

Question: "I would like to ask you a question about how much trust you have in certain institutions. For each of the following institutions, please tell me if you tend to trust it or tend not to trust it? – the national government."

Note: OLS regression analysis was used to monitor the effects of time (the survey year) on trust in the national government, generating the unstandardized beta coefficient and its significance. (* > .001 ** > .01)

Source: Eurobarometer surveys, 1997-2009, downloaded from Gesis ZACAT.

But the overall comparison suggests that performance-based explanations that affect specific government policies appear more plausible candidates than do any accounts proposing systematic shifts in cultural values towards politics and public affairs.

As Figure 1.5 illustrates, however, this does not mean that European trust in government was steady. Indeed, another important point regarding trends in European trust in national government is that *sharp fluctuations in trust in government can be observed in many countries* (e.g., the peaks and troughs occurring in Denmark, Sweden and France). A final, and equally important, point is that *two period effects register a short-term peak in trust in government occurring simultaneously across many European countries,* notably in the survey taken in October-November 2001, shortly after the events of 9/11, when average trust jumped by nine percentage points from the spring to fall, and another clear but smaller average peak in April-May 2007, which cannot be so easily attributed to any particular event or terrorist incident.

European Trust in Parliaments

As with the American data, however, we also need to establish whether there are general trends in Europe across all major branches of government. As in the United States, it may be that European publics continue to support the executive branch in their national government but that any erosion of confidence has occurred in the legislature and in political parties. Dalton suggests that public support for both institutions has fallen in a wide range of advanced industrialized democracies.[41] Evidence of eroding confidence in parliaments in his study is based on regression analysis derived from four waves of the World Values Survey as well as trends in Gallup, Harris, and related commercial polls, but, in fact, only six of the twenty-one coefficients in the Dalton study prove statistically significant and negative. Table 1.2 and Figure 1.6 show the Eurobarometer evidence when citizens were asked directly about their trust in Parliament during the last decade.

The results largely confirm the observations already made concerning government. Again, the data show that most countries have experienced trendless fluctuations in trust of parliaments, with the United Kingdom and Portugal again showing a significant growth of cynicism towards these institutions since the late-1990s (reflecting the pattern already observed for trust in government), while Denmark, Sweden, and Belgium experienced growing public trust towards their national legislatures. The overall mean trust in parties across the European Union shows no significant change. Overall, there are also marked and persistent contrasts between European societies,

FIGURE 1.6

European trust in national parliaments, 1998-2009

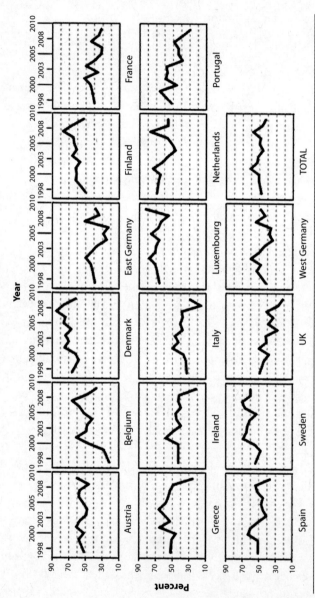

Question: "I would like to ask you a question about how much trust you have in certain institutions. For each of the following institutions, please tell me if you tend to trust it or tend not to trust it? – the national parliament."
Source: Eurobarometer surveys, 1998-2009, downloaded from Gesis ZACAT.

TABLE 1.2

European trust in parliament, 1997-2009

Proportion responding "tend to trust" (%)

	1997	1999	2000	2001 spring	2001 fall	2002	2003	2004	2005	2006	2007	2008	2009	1997-2009 net change	Beta	Significance
Austria	52	58	52	53	61	57	49	48	53	58	57	46	61	9	-0.027	ns
Belgium	22	28	46	48	61	49	48	42	52	57	66	48	43	21	1.668	ns
Denmark	66	58	62	60	75	70	74	67	76	74	85	76	78	12	0.948	ns
East Germany	39	42	44	39	50	43	36	25	29	23	51	34	38	-1	-0.724	ns
Finland	50	62	61	57	62	57	66	61	64	65	77	66	61	11	0.762	ns
France	40	43	45	41	52	36	50	39	32	31	44	35	36	-4	-0.953	ns
Greece	52	51	46	50	65	53	59	66	58	55	53	49	34	-18	-0.909	ns
Ireland	43	43	43	49	58	50	40	45	46	40	43	42	26	-17	-1.088	ns
Italy	33	34	37	38	50	43	47	38	41	38	39	16	30	-3	-0.835	ns
Luxembourg	66	69	71	75	78	71	70	66	76	67	64	55	77	11	-0.116	ns
Netherlands	69	67	65	68	74	63	56	47	51	57	77	56	58	-11	-0.978	ns
Portugal	52	66	46	58	59	57	58	39	44	44	49	39	39	-13	-1.949	*
Spain	51	51	63	52	60	51	41	45	47	45	52	54	35	-16	-0.934	ns
Sweden	54	48	55	57	69	65	64	61	53	67	70	60	68	14	0.784	ns
UK	49	44	38	36	50	41	42	28	39	33	41	27	19	-30	-1.796	*
West Germany	42	53	48	52	60	50	44	34	38	36	54	43	50	8	-0.453	ns
TOTAL	48	51	51	51	61	53	52	46	50	49	58	47	47	-1	-0.36	ns

Question: "I would like to ask you a question about how much trust you have in certain institutions. For each of the following institutions, please tell me if you tend to trust it or tend not to trust it? – the national parliament."

Note: OLS regression analysis was used to monitor the effects of time (the survey year) on trust in the national parliament, generating the unstandardized beta coefficient and its significance. (* >.01)

Source: Eurobarometer surveys, 1997-2009, downloaded from Gesis ZACAT.

with only one-fifth (19 percent) of British citizens expressing trust in their Parliament in 2009, compared with three-quarters of Danish citizens (78 percent). This strengthens the conclusion that specific cultural or institutional factors need to be explored in order to account for long-term contrasts among countries, while the dynamics of short-term fluctuations in trust over time may plausibly relate to variations in the perceived performance of governments, parliaments, and elected representatives.

Conclusion

Numerous commentators assume that support for the political system has gradually weakened in many established democracies, generating widespread public and scholarly concern about the rise of public disaffection (Torcal and Montero), mistrust of government (Dogan), or "dissatisfied democrats" (Pharr and Putnam).[42] I try to describe time-series survey evidence relating to public opinion within established democracies. My interpretation of the data challenges the over-simple view that there is an inevitable downward spiral of public disenchantment and steadily growing hostility towards government actors, institutions, and the nation-state. The evidence reinforces the conclusion that it is essential to distinguish trends in public attitudes that operate at different levels rather than to treat "political support" as though it is all of one piece. Careful attention to the precise timing and breadth of any trends is also critical for an accurate diagnosis of developments.

The most diffuse level concerns the most fundamental orientations towards the nation-state, exemplified by deep-rooted feelings of national pride and national identity. Membership in the European Union might be expected to have eroded these attachments, generating more cosmopolitan attitudes as Europeans are increasingly bound together through ties of transborder communication flows, labour force mobility, and trade.[43] Nevertheless the evidence confirms that nationalism remains strong and relatively stable, even among Western European societies that are long-standing members of the European Union.[44] Trust in political institutions such as national governments, parliaments, and parties shows systematic and persistent contrasts among established democracies in Western Europe and the United States. Overall, fluctuations over time usually prove far more common than do straightforward linear or uniform downward trends. These conclusions lend further confirmation to Levi and Stoker's observation that "despite all the verbiage decrying the decline in trust, there is little actual evidence of a long-term decline, either in the United States or in Western Europe across the board."⁴⁵ Contrasts are also evident in public attitudes towards different branches of government within each country. For example, the United States has seen a long-term significant erosion of support for the legislative branch, but this has not affected public support for the Supreme Court or the executive branch. Persistent differences in institutional trust can also be observed among relatively similar nations, such as between Italy and Spain, or Germany and France. A few European countries have experienced growing trust in state institutions, while a few have experienced the reverse. Perhaps most important, in Europe diffuse support for the nation-state remains strong and stable, and satisfaction with the performance of democracy has usually strengthened over time, not weakened.

The conventional wisdom assumes that public support for government has eroded significantly and consistently over time in Canada, as in other established democracies. If symptoms of trendless fluctuations are evident in recent decades in Western countries, however, this suggests the need to revise the standard interpretation. The complexity observed in this chapter calls for a diagnosis that can account for the dynamic fluctuations and the persistent cross-national variations in democratic deficits. This complexity indicates the need for differentiated and nuanced arguments that can account for cross-national *variance* and the *dynamics* of longitudinal flux in political support. The diagnosis suggests that it would probably be most fruitful to investigate short- and medium-term explanations of any changes in indicators of system support, abandoning over-simple claims about steadily growing public disenchantment with politics across all established democracies – or indeed across the world.⁴⁶ Hence the most promising hypotheses concern the instrumental performance of governments and public-sector institutions rather than propositions that posit glacial long-term social trends such as processes of human development and cultural evolution.

NOTES

1 Allan Tupper, "Auditing the Auditors: The Canadian Democratic Audit," *Canadian Public Administration* 50, 4 (2007): 635-53; Paul Howe, Richard Johnston, and André Blais, eds., *Strengthening Canadian Democracy: Reconsidering Provincial and Federal Debates about Democratic Reform Alternatives* (Montreal: McGill-Queen's University Press, 2005).
2 William Cross, "The Canadian Democratic Audit," paper presented at the International Political Science Association conference, Fukuoka, Japan, 2006.
3 See Russell J. Dalton, *Democratic Challenges, Democratic Choices: The Erosion of Political Support in Advanced Industrial Democracies* (Oxford: Oxford University

Press, 2004). For a counterpoint, however, see Pippa Norris, *Democratic Phoenix* (New York: Cambridge University Press, 2003).

4 Pippa Norris, *Democratic Deficits: Critical Citizens Revisited* (New York: Cambridge University Press, 2011).

5 For the debate, see Jacques Thomassen, ed., *The Legitimacy of the European Union after Enlargement* (Oxford: Oxford University Press, 2009); Andrew Moravcsik, "Reassessing Legitimacy in the European Union," *Journal of Common Market Studies* 40, 4 (2002): 603-24; Livia Door, *The Democratic Deficit Debate in the European Union* (Berlin: VDM Verlag, 2008); Peter Jancarik, *Understanding Democracy in the European Union: Democratic Deficit as a Powerful Myth?* (Berlin: VDM Verlag, 2009).

6 Victor Bekkers, Geske Dijkstra, Arthur Edwards, and Menno Fenger, eds., *Governance and the Democratic Deficit: Assessing the Democratic Legitimacy of Governance Practices* (Surrey: Ashgate Publishing, 2007).

7 Pippa Norris, ed., *Critical Citizens: Global Support for Democratic Governance* (Oxford: Oxford University Press, 1999).

8 Norris, *Democratic Deficits*.

9 Mark J. Hetherington, *Why Trust Matters: Declining Political Trust and the Demise of American Liberalism* (Princeton: Princeton University Press, 2005).

10 The "crisis" alarm warnings are most clearly exemplified by Michel Crozier, Samuel P. Huntington, and Joji Watanuki, *The Crisis of Democracy: Report on the Governability of Democracies to the Trilateral Commission* (New York: New York University Press, 1975).

11 Huge national variations, and periodic fluctuations, are also noted by others when comparing trust in national parliaments. See Bernhard Wessels, "Trust in Political Institutions," in *The Legitimacy of the European Union after Enlargement*, ed. Jacques Thomassen (Oxford: Oxford University Press, 2009).

12 See Stephen Earl Bennett, "Were the Halcyon Days Really Golden?," in *What Is It about Government that Americans Dislike?*, ed. John R. Hibbing and Elizabeth Theiss-Morse (Cambridge: Cambridge University Press, 2001).

13 Samuel P. Huntington, *The Third Wave: Democratization in the Late Twentieth Century* (Norman: University of Oklahoma Press, 1991).

14 For the intellectual history of the origins of the civic culture study, see Gerardo L. Munck and Richard Snyder, *Passion, Craft, and Method in Comparative Politics* (Maryland: Johns Hopkins University Press, 2007).

15 Gabriel A. Almond and Sidney Verba, *The Civic Culture* (Princeton: Princeton University Press, 1963), 314.

16 Ibid., 308.

17 Samuel Barnes and Max Kaase, *Political Action: Mass Participation in Five Western Democracies* (Beverly Hills: Sage, 1979).

18 Crozier, Huntington, and Watanuki, *Crisis of Democracy*; Samuel P. Huntington, *American Politics: The Promise of Disharmony* (Cambridge, MA: Harvard University Press, 1981).

19 Seymour Martin Lipset and William C. Schneider, *The Confidence Gap: Business, Labor, and Government in the Public Mind* (New York: Free Press, 1983), 6. See also

Joseph S. Nye, Philip D. Zelikow, and David C. King, eds., *Why People Don't Trust Government* (Cambridge: Harvard University Press, 1997).

20 See, in particular, Ola Listhaug, "The Dynamics of Trust in Politicians," and Ola Listhaug and Matti Wiberg, "Confidence in Political and Private Institutions," in *Citizens and the State*, ed. Hans-Dieter Klingemann and Dieter Fuchs (Oxford: Oxford University Press, 1995).

21 Susan J. Pharr and Robert D. Putnam, *Disaffected Democracies: What's Troubling the Trilateral Countries?* (Princeton: Princeton University Press, 2000); Mattei Dogan, ed., *Political Mistrust and the Discrediting of Politicians* (The Netherlands: Brill, 2005); Gerry Stoker, *Why Politics Matters: Making Democracy Work* (London: Palgrave Macmillan, 2006); Mariano Torcal and José R. Montero, eds., *Political Disaffection in Contemporary Democracies: Social Capital, Institutions, and Politics* (London: Routledge, 2006); Colin Hay, *Why We Hate Politics* (Cambridge: Polity Press, 2007).

22 Russell J. Dalton and Martin P. Wattenberg, eds., *Parties without Partisans: Political Change in Advanced Industrial Democracies* (Oxford: Oxford University Press, 2002); Dalton, *Democratic Challenges*.

23 Michael Kenny, "Taking the Temperature of the British Political Elite 3: When Grubby Is the Order of the Day," *Parliamentary Affairs* 62, 3 (2009): 503-13.

24 Seymour Martin Lipset, *American Exceptionalism: A Double-Edged Sword* (New York: W.W. Norton and Company, 1996).

25 See, for example, World Public Opinion, 2008, World Public Opinion on Governance and Democracy, Program on International Policy Attitudes, University of Maryland, http://www.worldpublicopinion.org/.

26 Russell Hardin, *Trust* (Cambridge: Polity Press, 2006).

27 Jack Citrin, "Comment: The Political Relevance of Trust in Government," *American Political Science Review* 68, 3 (1974): 973-88; Jack Citrin and Donald Philip Green, "Presidential Leadership and the Resurgence of Trust in Government," *British Journal of Political Science* 16, 4 (1986): 431-53.

28 Arthur H. Miller, "Political Issues and Trust in Government, 1964-1970," *American Political Science Review* 68, 3 (1974): 951-72; Arthur H. Miller, "Rejoinder to 'Comment' by Jack Citrin: Political Discontent or Ritualism?," *American Political Science Review* 68, 3 (1974): 989-1001; Arthur H. Miller and Stephen A. Borrelli, "Confidence in Government during the 1980s," *American Politics Research* 19, 2 (1991): 147-73.

29 Hetherington, *Why Trust Matters*, 15.

30 Paul R. Abramson and Ada W. Finifter, "On the Meaning of Political Trust: New Evidence from Items Introduced in 1978," *American Journal of Political Science* 25, 2 (1981): 297-307.

31 See the ANES Guide to Public Opinion and Electoral Behavior, http://www.electionstudies.org/.

32 Citrin and Green, "Presidential Leadership."

33 Hetherington, *Why Trust Matters*.

34 From February 1976 to February 2010, the New York Times/CBS News surveys have carried items comparable to the ANES measures for trust in the federal government.

In this series, the proportion of people in the poll expressing trust in the federal government "always" or "most of the time" was 28 percent prior to 9/11, peaked at 55 percent following the events of 9/11, and then fell to 19 percent by February 2010. See "Poll Finds Edge for Obama over GOP among the Public," 11 February 2010, http://www.nytimes.com/. For Gallup series, "Trust in Government," see http://www.gallup.com/.

35 Listhaug, "Dynamics of Trust."
36 Dalton, *Democratic Challenges*, 29-31.
37 For details, see the Gallup poll, "The Decade in Review: Four Key Trends," 23 December 2009, http://www.gallup.com/.
38 John R. Hibbing and Elizabeth Theiss-Morse, *Congress as Public Enemy* (New York: Cambridge University Press, 1995).
39 Steven Van de Walle, Steven Van Roosbroek, and Geert Bouckaert, "Trust in the Public Sector: Is There Any Evidence for a Long-Term Decline?," *International Review of Administrative Sciences* 74, 1 (2008): 47-64.
40 Almond and Verba, *Civic Culture*.
41 Dalton, *Democratic Challenges*.
42 Pharr and Putnam, *Disaffected Democracies*; Torcal and Montero, *Political Disaffection*; Dogan, *Political Mistrust*.
43 David Held, Anthony McGrew, David Goldblatt, and Jonathan Perreton, *Global Transformations: Politics, Economics, and Culture* (Palo Alto: Stanford University Press, 1999), Chap. 7.
44 See also Pippa Norris and Ronald Inglehart, *Cosmopolitan Communications* (New York: Cambridge University Press, 2009).
45 Margaret Levi and Laura Stoker, "Political Trust and Trustworthiness," *Annual Review of Political Science* 3, 1 (2000): 475-507.
46 See, for example, the claims in Stoker, *Why Politics Matters*, Chap. 2.

2
Citizen Expectations and Democratic Performance
The Sources and Consequences of Democratic Deficits from the Bottom Up

NEIL NEVITTE AND STEPHEN WHITE

Democratic deficits can be explored from a variety of vantage points, and this chapter is driven by three assumptions. First, the goal is to explore the presence of any deficit, or surplus, from "the bottom up," that is, from the vantage point of citizens. This approach may not entirely square with accounts that tackle the issue from institutional, elite, or other perspectives. But at some point any account of how far democratic practices in Canada and the United States meet or fall short of democratic ideals needs to consider citizens' evaluations. Taking a bottom-up approach also means asking a different set of questions. Rather than exploring how well legislative and executive institutions meet the democratic tests of participation, transparency, accountability, and representation, for example, the more pertinent questions from the bottom-up perspective are: To what extent are citizens satisfied with the quality of democracy in their respective countries? Do public evaluations of democracy draw citizens closer to meeting the democratic ideal of a politically engaged citizenry?

The second assumption is that a more balanced view of American-Canadian similarities and differences emerges by placing this two-country comparison within a broader perspective. Questions about the democratic deficit were initially informed by the notion that some of the difficulties facing democratic governance are somehow common to most advanced industrial states.[1] Focusing entirely on two-country comparisons, however, tends to draw attention to differences rather than to similarities. And, in the case of Canadian-American comparisons in particular, there is a strong temptation to infer that any such differences reflect American exceptionalism.[2] That may well be the case, but such a conclusion has a stronger foundation if Canadian and American variations are situated within the context of comparable evidence from publics in other advanced industrial states.

The third assumption is that, if "democracy" can mean different things to different people,[3] then it is also possible that the nature, characteristics, and consequences of a "democratic deficit" are also different. Because the focus is on citizens' perspectives, the following investigation draws on a rich body of individual-level data that come from the World Values Surveys (WVS). These surveys have a number of advantages: they use the same sampling and data collection methodologies; they have asked national random samples of publics many of the same core questions; and the questions are worded in the same way and the data are collected at roughly the same time. Although these data have been gathered in the United States, Canada, Europe, and many other countries at regular intervals between 1981 and 2006, our focus is primarily on the cross-national WVS data from the most recent round of the surveys. The reason is straightforward: the 2005-6 round of the WVS asked respondents a new, and richer, set of questions about the salience and meanings of democracy. Consequently, these particular data provide a novel opportunity to explore more precisely whether, and how, citizens' satisfaction or dissatisfaction with democracy is related to variations in their conceptions of democracy.

In five sections, we explore citizens' beliefs about democracy and the origins and significance of their evaluations of democratic performance in their respective countries. In the first section, we provide a broad aggregate picture, outlining prevailing perspectives on the central problem: confidence in government is waning, and formal political participation appears to be declining across many established democracies. In the second section, we describe citizens' democratic beliefs and their assessments of democratic performance. We consider citizens' levels of commitment to democracy and their conceptions of democracy in the United States, Canada, and other established democracies. In the third section, we explore citizen evaluations of how democratically their country is governed. It turns out that there is a considerable gap – a citizen-level "democratic deficit" – between citizens' expectations and their evaluations of democracy in most of the countries considered. In the fourth section, we compare the sources of that gap: the evidence indicates the foundations of the citizen-level democratic deficit are not the same cross-nationally. In the final analytical section, we consider some of the consequences of citizen dissatisfaction with democratic performance. In the conclusion, some of the implications of the central findings are pondered.

Discontent in Advanced Industrial Democracies

Many advanced industrial democracies have shown signs of democratic distress for several decades. Two commonly identified markers of this distress are trends in formal political participation and attitudes towards government. Both Canada and the United States have experienced a significant decline in voter turnout over the last two decades. Voter turnout in Canada in particular fell substantially between the 1988 election, when turnout was 75 percent, and the 2004 contest, when turnout slumped to only 61 percent. Citizens are turning out to vote in dwindling numbers in other political systems as well, but the size and timing of these declines varies considerably. Franklin's analysis of turnout levels for lower house elections in twenty-three countries, including Canada and the United States, found that turnout had declined by only 4.4 percent on average between 1945 and 1999.[4] The declines in Canada and the United States are steeper than the average. The trend in Canada over the period from 1945 to 2000 is a 0.14 percent annual decline in federal election turnout, or 7.5 percent over fifty-five years (Elections Canada 2008). In US congressional elections the pattern is strikingly similar, namely, an annual decline of 0.13 percent between 1945 and 2000 (Federal Election Commission 2008).

Second, observers note that citizen confidence in their political institutions has also declined over much of the same period. Figure 2.1 summarizes the proportion of citizens who express "a great deal" or "quite a lot" of confidence in legislatures between 1981 and 2006. The general trend is a decline in confidence over that twenty-five-year period, but the data suggest a distinction between two groups of advanced industrial publics: among some publics confidence in legislatures has declined modestly, while in others it has declined sharply. Canada ranks among the first grouping, while the United States falls into the second. The percentage of Canadians who express "a great deal" or "quite a lot" of confidence in Parliament has fluctuated around 40 percent during the period between 1981 and 2006, with a slight trend downward over those twenty-five years. In the United States, by contrast, the proportion of respondents who express "a great deal" or "quite a lot" of confidence dropped from 53 percent in 1981 to only 21 percent in 2006. But the United States is by no means exceptional in this regard. In France, for example, the percentage of people who express confidence

FIGURE 2.1

Confidence in legislatures, 1981-2006

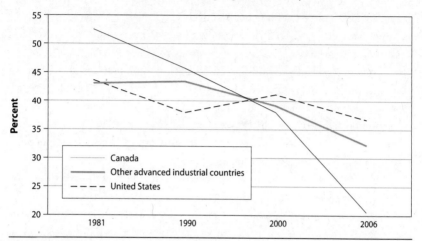

Question: "I am going to name a number of organizations. For each one, could you tell me how much confidence you have in them: is it a great deal of confidence, quite a lot of confidence, not very much confidence or none at all? – Parliament."
Source: World Values Surveys, 1981-2007.

in Parliament has also declined steadily from 56 percent in 1981 to 35 percent in 2006. And in the Netherlands and Germany, although the erosion in confidence has been more uneven it has, nonetheless, been substantial.

It is possible, of course, that these variations in public confidence in legislatures are just symptomatic of a broader decline in confidence in all institutions. But that claim is hard to sustain. Table 2.1 summarizes the cross-time evidence concerning public confidence in a variety of different kinds of institutions in multiple national settings. Certainly, there seems to be something of a North American trend when it comes to the media and business. Canadian and American confidence in those institutions has eroded since 1981, but there is no such pattern in other established democracies. Nor has there been any secular decline in public confidence in the courts, in unions, or, for the most part, in the civil service. Not surprisingly, there is an occasional spike or trough in public confidence in some settings and in some institutions. But the most consistent finding, clearly, is the erosion in public confidence in legislatures.

TABLE 2.1

Confidence in institutions, 1981-2007

	Parliament/ Congress	Courts	Civil service	Unions	Major companies	The Press
Canada						
1981-83	44	65	52	33	57	45
1989-93	38	54	50	35	51	46
1994-98	–	–	–	–	–	–
1999-2001	41	–	50	36	56	35
2005-07	37	66	56	32	37	33
Trend	None	None	None	None	Declining	Declining
United States						
1981-83	53	53	57	38	50	49
1989-93	46	58	59	33	51	56
1994-98	30	36	52	34	54	27
1999-2001	38	–	55	38	54	27
2005-07	21	57	41	30	27	24
Trend	Declining	None	Declining	None	Declining	Declining
Other established democracies						
1981-83	44	61	41	35	38	35
1989-93	42	53	39	36	48	38
1994-98	33	60	43	40	44	42
1999-2001	41	49	40	37	40	42
2005-07	35	59	42	38	37	36
Trend	Declining	None	None	None	None	None

Sources: World Values Surveys, 1981-83, 1989-93, 1994-98, 1999-2001, 2005-7.

Diminished confidence in political institutions and waning political participation are troublesome in their own right: the former threatens to undermine the legitimacy of political institutions, and the latter threatens to undermine the quality of democracy, particularly if certain segments of polities are systematically underrepresented in politics. For some analysts of democratic politics, these two trends suggest a growing democratic deficit, a widening gap between how these democracies should ideally work and how they function in practice. But these aggregate trends also raise a slightly different set of questions: Are there significant levels of disaffection among different publics with the democratic performance of their respective countries? And are these trends of declining political confidence and participation symptomatic of a democratic deficit that is systematically related to people's evaluations of democratic performance? Citizens' own perceptions of democratic performance are certainly critically important to the democratic health of any country in the long run. Eroding confidence in political institutions and declining political participation might signify diminishing support for particular political actors, such as unpopular incumbents, and specific institutions of democratic regimes. But negative perceptions of democratic performance of regimes are arguably more serious: they have the potential to undermine support for democracy itself.[5]

Democratic Beliefs

Before exploring the roots of dissatisfaction with democracy, it is important to consider two preliminary questions about people's basic orientations to democracy to: To what extent do citizens think that a democratic system is a good or a bad way of governing? And what core characteristics do people associate with the idea of democracy?[6] If democracy means different things to different people, then what needs to be established is the extent to which there is either consensus or disagreement when it comes to people's conceptions of democracy.

The WVS has asked people what they believe to be "essential characteristics" of a democracy. Respondents were presented with ten statements capturing different regime characteristics, and they were then asked to assign a score (between 1 and 10) to each characteristic, indicating whether it was "not at all an essential characteristic of democracy" (=1) or "an essential characteristic of democracy" (=10), or somewhere in between. There is no particular reason to expect complete consensus regarding the essential characteristics of democracy, but there is good reason to suspect that each different conception about democracy will tend to cluster systematically around some common essential characteristics. That possibility is probed with exploratory factor analysis. And the central empirical finding of that analysis is that people's beliefs about democracy in these countries are organized along three different dimensions.

The first and most powerful dimension clusters around what might be called the *procedural* characteristics of democracy: these include support for free elections, equal rights, and civil liberties as well as the rejection of the idea that the state should be controlled by military or religious authorities.[7] These attributes correspond to conceptions of democracy discussed elsewhere.[8] The second dimension is organized around evaluations of the *economic and legal order*, namely, that "the economy is prospering" and "criminals are severely punished." The third cluster groups views that emphasize governments' roles in *economic redistribution*, the idea that, in a democracy, "governments tax the rich and subsidize the poor" and that "people receive government assistance for unemployment."[9]

How each of these visions of democracy applies to citizens in Canada, the United States, and other countries is summarized in Figure 2.2. The top graph reports the mean scores of citizens on additive indices for each dimension; it reflects where publics stand on each of the three dimensions of beliefs.[10] Clearly, most respondents in Canada, the United States, and the other established democracies believe that procedural elements are "essential characteristics" of democracy. But they are somewhat less inclined to think that redistribution and legal and economic order are essential elements of democracy. On these dimensions, Canadian respondents resemble their European counterparts. Respondents in the United States are the least inclined to think that redistributive elements are essential characteristics of democracy.

The data in the bottom graph in Figure 2.2 capture the diversity of opinion across each of these visions of democracy; they indicate how much public consensus or division there is on these visions (measured in standard deviations). Notice that there is a relatively strong consensus about the importance of the procedural characteristics as core elements of democracy but that there is far less agreement when it comes to the other two clusters of beliefs.

Regardless of the extent to which publics share the same conceptions of democracy, the fundamental point is that Americans, Canadians, and citizens in other established democracies do express a strong commitment to democracy. The data in Figure 2.3 show the proportion of respondents in Canada, the United States, and nine other advanced industrial democracies who believe that "having a democratic political system" is a "very good" or "fairly good" way of governing their country as opposed to "fairly bad" or "very bad." In each of these eleven countries there is a near consensus that democracy is desirable: more than 80 percent of respondents in all of these countries indicate that having a democratic system is a "very good" or "fairly good" way of governing their country. Neither the United States nor Canada stands out as "exceptional." Ninety-one percent of Canadians and 86 percent of Americans think that democracy is a good thing.[11]

Taken altogether, the evidence concerning conceptions of democracy and commitment to democracy suggest that, when placed in the context

FIGURE 2.2

Conceptions of democracy

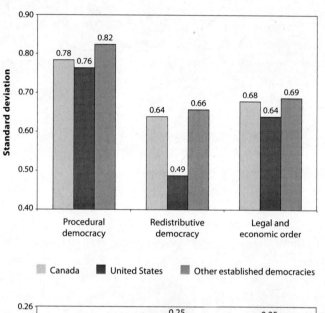

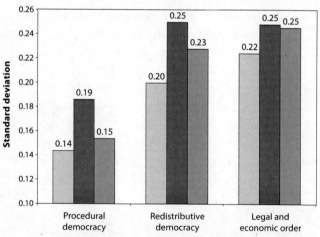

Source: World Values Surveys, 2005-6.

FIGURE 2.3

Commitment to democracy, 2005-6

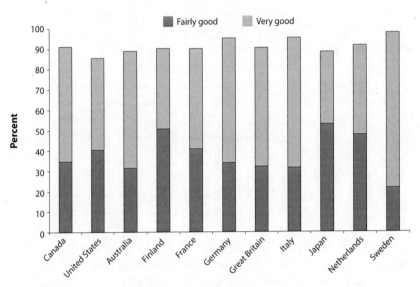

Question: "I'm going to describe various types of political systems and ask what you think about each as a way of governing this country. For each one, would you say it is a very good, fairly good, fairly bad or very bad way of governing this country? (Read out and code one answer for each): – Having a democratic political system."
Source: World Values Surveys, 2005-6.

of other established democracies, there are few outstanding differences between publics in the United States and Canada. Certainly, there are cross-national variations, but it is the similarities that are more striking. Americans are outliers when it comes to beliefs about whether economic redistribution is a core element of democracy. But when thinking about the core characteristics of democracy, although citizens across these countries discriminate between different clusters of elements, most people accept procedural elements as an "essential" characteristic of democracy. And, regardless of national setting, citizens generally express a strong commitment to democracy.

If public conceptions of, and commitment to, democracy are broadly similar, the next question to ask is: are citizens' evaluations of the democratic performance of their respective countries also similar? One approach to answering this question is to consider citizens' evaluations of democratic performance in relation to what they expect from democracy. Does democracy live up to citizens' personal expectations? Or is there what might be called a citizen-level democratic deficit? Answering this question requires us to ask first about salience: how important is it to people that they live in a democratic country? And then: do people think their country is being governed democratically? The personal salience of democracy, we suggest, is consequential when assessing people's satisfaction with that form of government. The intuition behind this proxy for an individual-level measure of the democratic deficit is straightforward: citizens who personally think democracy is very important will be more likely than those who think it is not all that important to express disappointment with their country's democratic performance if, in their view, it falls short of being governed completely democratically.

The top graph in Figure 2.4 reports the mean responses of citizens in eleven established democracies to the question about the personal salience of democracy: "How important is it for you to live in a country that is governed democratically?" (1 = "not at all important" and 10 = "very important"). Most respondents in all countries indicated that living in a democratically governed country was personally important to them. Roughly one point on the 1-to-10 scale separates the country with the lowest mean score, France (8.52), from the country with the highest mean score, Sweden (9.56). And, once again, the American (8.57) and Canadian (8.95) publics are unexceptional when compared to these other publics.

But there is one truly intriguing finding to emerge from these data: notice the striking difference between how much importance people personally attach to democracy and their evaluations of how democratically they think their own country is being governed, shown in the bottom graph in Figure 2.4. Respondents were asked: "how democratically is this country being governed today?" (1 = "not at all democratic" and 10 = "completely democratic"). Respondents were more inclined to locate themselves at the "completely democratic" end of the scale. But their evaluations of the democratic performance of their own countries were considerably less enthusiastic than were their estimations of how personally important it was to live in a democratic country. Swedes and Finns express the most positive evaluations of the democratic performance of their respective countries (7.53 and 7.42, respectively). Respondents in the United States turn out to be among the least enthusiastic about the quality of democracy in their country (6.34),

FIGURE 2.4

The salience of democracy and evaluations of democratic performance, mean scores

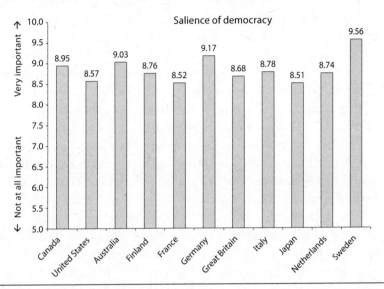

Question: "How important is it for you to live in a country that is governed democratically? On this scale where 1 means it is 'not at all important' and 10 means 'absolutely important' what position would you choose?"

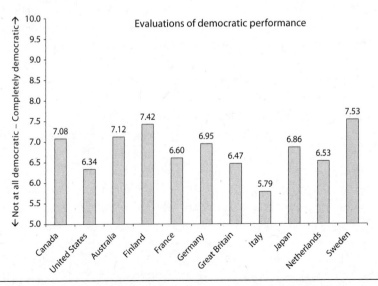

Question: "How democratically is this country being governed today? Again using a scale from 1 to 10, where 1 means that it is 'not at all democratic' and 10 means that it is 'completely democratic?'"

ranking ahead of only the Italian public (5.79). The Canadian public (7.08), by these cross-national standards, occupies the middle ground.

Significantly, there are also substantial differences when it comes to how much agreement or disagreement there is in these publics' evaluations of democratic performance. The top graph in Figure 2.5 illustrates the extent to which the samples in each country are spread across the scale measuring evaluations of democratic performance. As an interpretive benchmark for comparison, the bottom graph shows the spread of opinion about the personal importance of democracy in the same set of countries. In every country but one (Finland), evaluations of democratic performance are more divergent than are expressions about the personal importance of democracy. The most intriguing finding here is that, of all the countries considered, it is American respondents who are clearly the most divided when it comes to citizens' views about how democratically the country is being governed.

It turns out, then, that there are significant subsections of publics in all eleven established democracies who do not think their country is being governed all that democratically. More often than not, evaluations of how democratically their country is being governed fall short of estimations of how personally important it is to live in a democracy. Once again, it is the cross-national similarities, rather than differences, that are most striking. The presence of cross-national similarities in attitudes towards democracy does not necessarily mean that the sources and consequences of the individual-level democratic deficit, the gap between expectations and evaluations of democratic performance, will be the same across different political settings. To what extent, then, are there similarities or differences when it comes to the sources or consequences of these democratic deficits?

Sources of Dissatisfaction with Democratic Performance: Hypotheses

Citizens might be dissatisfied with the democratic performance of their country for any number of reasons. One possibility is that a citizen-level democratic deficit is a consequence of systematic political underrepresentation of specific groups. Where people sit in the social structure may influence their evaluations of how democratically their country is being governed. Thus, marginalized people – women, minorities, youth, and people with low levels of income and education – may well be more likely to express greater dissatisfaction with democracy than those who sit in the mainstream.[12]

A second possibility is that people's evaluations of democracy are shaped by perceptions of whether the political system matches their personal conceptions of democracy. Although it is plausible to suppose that people's

FIGURE 2.5

The salience of democracy and evaluations of democratic performance, standard deviations

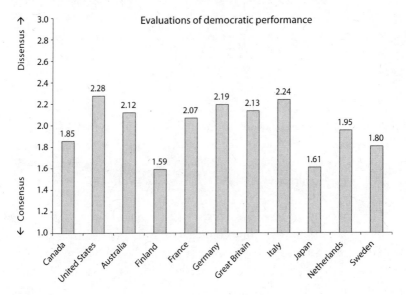

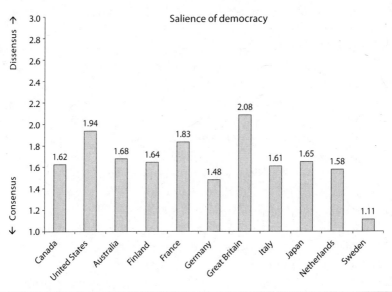

mental images of democracy itself influence their assessments of how democratic their respective political systems are, the precise expectation in this case is not entirely clear. On the one hand, it is possible that a clear understanding of the rules of the game might induce *greater* satisfaction with democratic performance simply because those who understand the rules of democracy are more likely to accept political outcomes. As Fuchs puts it:

> A liberal democracy lives from permanent disputation about the goals that are to be attained through political processes. Its life-blood is therefore disagreement, dissensus, not consensus. However, regulation of this dissensus requires rules of procedure. These rules must be accepted by those involved if they are to fulfill their regulatory function.[13]

If recognition and acceptance of democratic rules of procedure are crucial preconditions for accepting political outcomes in a democratic system, then the expectation is that citizens with a strong belief that procedural elements are the core characteristics of democracy are less likely to be dissatisfied with the democratic performance of their respective political systems. On the other hand, it is also possible that idealists, people with clear mental models of what democracy *should* resemble, may be more inclined to be disappointed by perceived discrepancies between that democratic ideal and how they evaluate democratic practice. Indeed, that expectation might be particularly relevant when it comes to those citizens who view economic redistribution or legal and economic order as "essential elements of democracy." Recall the earlier findings indicating that citizens are more divided about whether or not these dimensions qualify as "essential" characteristics of democratic systems.

Yet another possibility to consider is informed by earlier theories concerning the "crisis" of politics in advanced industrial democracies, and it focuses on citizens' political beliefs and preferences. There was no consensus among these observers about what exactly was in crisis. For some, the "crisis" of advanced industrialism concerned governability,[14] others emphasized the legitimacy of the state,[15] and yet others suggested it was the democratic system itself that was in crisis.[16] Furthermore, each perspective carries different diagnoses concerning the root causes of crisis. What many of these different strands of theorizing have in common is the view that modern governments are unable to cope with the proliferation of citizen-driven demands.

Modern democracies are finding it increasingly difficult to juggle competing interests.[17] According to Kaase and Newton, the growth of public demands on the state "makes it difficult to pick a safe political pathway through different interests and problems, and exceedingly difficult to define the national interest."[18] Governments cannot be all things to all people, thus the growing fragmentation of political preferences, not just among publics as a whole but also within individuals,[19] makes it more difficult for governments to satisfy the demands of any people. The worst-case scenario is that, consequently, the legitimacy of the state is weakened.

These different perspectives generate a variety of expectations about how citizens' values and preferences might shape levels of dissatisfaction with democracy. First, there is the prospect that citizens who hold some political beliefs will express greater dissatisfaction with the democratic performance of their political system than will citizens who hold opposing beliefs. "Values" in this particular context refers to fundamental social and political orientations rather than to opinions related to short-term political matters. Preferences about social and political issues of the day, arguably, influence people's attitudes towards specific political actors, the incumbent government, and political institutions. But if demands are to produce dissatisfaction with the core principles of democratic regimes, they are more likely to be related to something deeper than opinions on short-term issues. We consider the impact of three orientations: outlooks towards morality, views about welfare and economic competition, and ideological self-identifications. There is no reason a priori to speculate about which particular values induce greater dissatisfaction; rather, the expectation is that the *direction* of people's values – whether people are more permissive or more restrictive when it comes to individual morality, whether they are more or less supportive of free enterprise, and whether they identify themselves as being on "the left" or on "the right" politically – will systematically affect their levels of dissatisfaction with the democratic performance of their political system.

Quite aside from the direction of values, there is also the possibility that *intensity* of values matters. More specifically, it is plausible to suppose that citizens who hold more extreme social and political values, for example, might express greater dissatisfaction with the workings of democracy than would citizens who hold more ambivalent positions. The argument here is that the claims on the state made by those holding more extreme values are less likely to find a voice in modern democratic systems that face a welter of conflicting demands. That possibility seems particularly pertinent to publics

FIGURE 2.6
Predictors of the citizen-level democratic deficit

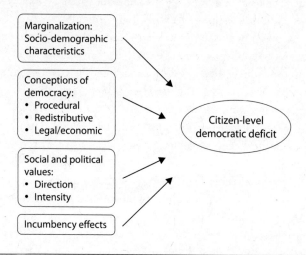

in the United States and, to a lesser extent, in Canada, where there is evidence indicating a growing divide in social and political values between those on "the left" and those on "the right."[20]

The final expectation to consider concerns the possibility that being on the losing side in elections matters. Quite aside from the social backgrounds, conceptions of democracy, and core social and political values of citizens, it is entirely possible that citizens' satisfaction with democracy is shaped by incumbency effects. People tend to be more satisfied with the way things are working when their own political party holds office. The "outs," similarly, are always more disgruntled.[21] These expectations are graphically summarized in Figure 2.6.

To empirically evaluate the citizen-level democratic deficit, we take into account whether the perceived "democraticness" of a system meets, surpasses, or falls short of citizens' expectations. We do this by taking respondents' scores on the item gauging how democratically they think their own country is being governed and subtracting them from their scores on the item measuring the personal salience of living in a democratic country. In short:

citizen-level deficit = salience of democracy − evaluations of performance

This measure of citizens' own democratic deficit is rescaled to an intuitive −1 to 1 metric, where −1 signifies respondents who indicate that living in a democratic country is not at all important and that the political system is completely democratic, and 1 signifies those who indicate that living in a democratic country is very important and that the political system is not at all democratic. Respondents who choose the same score on both separate measures score 0.

Ordinary Least Squares (OLS) multiple regression is employed because it is important to isolate the independent impact of each theoretically relevant factor on the citizen-level democratic deficit in Canada, the United States, and the four other established democracies for which we have complete data: Australia, Finland, Japan, and Sweden. We use a multi-stage explanatory model to analyze predictors of the individual-level democratic deficit in Canada and the United States. The assumption is that some of the sources are more proximate to dissatisfaction than others. Furthermore, it is entirely possible that these factors may have direct effects on citizen dissatisfaction as well as indirect effects through their influence on other more proximate sources of dissatisfaction. First, we take into account the effects of marginalization by entering socio-demographic variables in the regression model. At the second and third stages, we introduce measures of people's conceptualizations of democracy and then their social and political values. Finally, potential incumbency effects are taken into account in the last stage of the model. What core findings emerge from these analyses?[22]

Sources of Dissatisfaction with Democratic Performance: Findings

United States

Consider, first, the case of the United States. Which factors drive American respondents' levels of dissatisfaction with the democratic performance of the United States? Socio-demographic factors certainly matter, but not in entirely expecetd ways. The effects of income conform to expectations: those with the highest incomes score 0.16 lower on the democratic deficit scale than do those with the lowest incomes. Age and education, however, have unanticipated effects. It turns out that older and more educated Americans express greater dissatisfaction with that country's democratic performance than do their younger, less well-educated counterparts.

What about conceptions of democracy? How do they matter? Recall that there are two conflicting possibilities to consider. First, a clear understanding of the rules of the game might induce *greater* satisfaction with democratic performance. Second, there is also the possibility that idealism might encourage dissatisfaction with democratic performance. It turns out that the evidence is consistent with the latter expectation. The more citizens are inclined to think that procedural elements are essential characteristics of democracy, the more dissatisfied they are with the democratic performance of the American political system. Americans whose conception of democracy includes redistributive elements as essential characteristics are also more dissatisfied than others. The impact of that factor, however, is modest when compared to the impact of procedural notions of democracy.[23]

Both the direction and the intensity of social and political values turn out to have a significant impact on levels of dissatisfaction. Citizens who hold opposing social and political beliefs express different levels of dissatisfaction with the democratic performance of the United States: Americans who support free enterprise are considerably more satisfied than are people who are less enthusiastic about free enterprise and who are more supportive of government intervention in the economy. Those who think of themselves as being on "the right" politically are also more satisfied than are those who think of themselves as being on "the left." And citizens who are more permissive in their moral outlooks are more likely to express dissatisfaction than are people with more restrictive views concerning morality. Significantly, and quite aside from the specific direction of their values, however, those Americans who hold more intense social and political views are more inclined to express greater dissatisfaction with the country's democratic performance. Individuals holding more intense beliefs about free enterprise (regardless of whether they support or oppose it) and individuals who place themselves further to either "the left" or "the right" turn out to be less satisfied with the workings of democracy than do those with more moderate beliefs.

The full specification of the model includes all of the previous groups of variables but also takes into account the effects of incumbent support. It turns out that those who support the Republicans (incumbents) are considerably less dissatisfied than are others. There is also evidence that social and political beliefs affect levels of dissatisfaction indirectly, through support for the Republicans. The effects of both ideological self-placement and moral outlooks diminish when incumbent support is taken into account. The clear implication is that individuals who consider themselves to be "on the left" and who share more permissive moral outlooks are dissatisfied with the democratic performance of the American political system, in part, because they are "outs": they do not support the Republican Party.

Canada versus the United States

If these are the basic findings from the American public then the next question to consider is: to what extent are Canadians' evaluations of democratic performance structured in ways that are similar to or different from those in the United States? The empirical strategy replicates the analytic approach used to unpack the American data, and the Canadian evidence resembles the American results in some ways.[24] Procedural conceptions of democracy matter most for both publics: those with more procedural visions of democracy are most likely to exhibit a democratic deficit. Distributive and legal/economic visions have no discernable impact for either public. The most striking differences between American and Canadian findings, perhaps, concern the relatively modest effects of social background factors, social and political beliefs, and partisan preferences on dissatisfaction in Canada. Once again, citizens who think procedural elements are essential characteristics of democracy are considerably more dissatisfied with the democratic performance of the political system than are others. This relationship is more modest in Canada, but older Canadians are also more dissatisfied with their country's democratic performance than are younger Canadians. Unlike their American counterparts, however, Canadians' social and political orientations have little effect on people's levels of dissatisfaction. The only belief dimension with any discernable impact is ideological self-placement. The intensity with which social and political values are held has weak and statistically insignificant effects. Moreover, there are also Canadian-American differences when it comes to incumbency effects. Unlike their American counterparts, Canadians who supported the incumbent federal government were neither more nor less likely to express dissatisfaction with democratic performance.

Canada and the United States versus Other Countries

Are Americans exceptional or is it Canadians who stand out? To explore these questions we turn to evidence from publics in Australia, Finland, Japan, and Sweden. These data are subjected to exactly the same tests, and the basic results suggest that *both* North American publics stand out in some respects.[25] The only social background variable that has a significant effect on evaluations of democratic performance in these four other countries is age, and once again older citizens express greater dissatisfaction than do their youthful counterparts. However, the most powerful determinant of dissatisfaction in these cases is linked to people's conceptions of democracy. Citizens who think procedural elements are essential characteristics of democracy are more dissatisfied with the democratic performance of the political system than are others. And the average impact of this effect across publics in these four established democracies is essentially the same as it is in Canada and the United States.

But this is the point at which the commonalities between citizens in these four countries and their North American counterpart publics end. Australians, Finns, Japanese, and Swedes combined are more similar to Americans than Canadians when it comes to the impact of the direction of social and political values. Generally, those who support free enterprise are much less dissatisfied than are people who oppose free enterprise. Canadians are the only exception in this regard: for them, attitudes towards free enterprise have no discernible impact on levels of dissatisfaction in Canada. By contrast, the United States public stands out when it comes to the greater impact of the intensity of social and political beliefs, and partisan preferences, on levels of dissatisfaction.

Consequences of Dissatisfaction with Democratic Performance

What are the consequences of people's dissatisfaction with the democratic performance of their political systems? And are the consequences consistently the same everywhere? To explore these questions entails returning to the question with which we began, namely, the relationship between dissatisfaction with democratic performance and the two conventional markers of the democratic deficit – political engagement and institutional confidence. The pessimistic expectation is that citizens who are dissatisfied with democracy are not only politically "turned off" but also "tuned out": they express less support for their country's political institutions and are psychologically and behaviourally disengaged from politics. The more optimistic possibility is that people who are dissatisfied with the democratic performance of their political systems are inclined to be "critical citizens." In that case, the expectation here is that these critical citizens will express disapproval about how their political institutions function at present but that they are nonetheless actively engaged in politics.[29]

As it happens, the evidence supports the "critical citizens" perspective. The relevant relationship revealing that interpretation concerns the link between dissatisfaction with democratic performance and five dependent variables: confidence in government institutions, psychological engagement with politics, attention to politics, willingness to participate in "system-correcting" political acts (petitioning, boycotting, and demonstrating), and voting. In Canada, the United States, and the other established democracies, the evidence is that the citizen-level democratic deficit is associated with less confidence in government institutions.[27] But, in most cases, there is also evidence indicating that dissatisfaction with democratic performance, the individual-level democratic deficit, is *positively* associated with political engagement: dissatisfied citizens are typically more politically active. The effects of dissatisfaction are more pronounced in the United States than elsewhere. The greater the individual-level democratic deficit among Americans, the deeper are the levels of psychological engagement with politics, the greater is the willingness to engage in system-correcting political acts, and the greater is the likelihood of turning out to vote. Indeed, the probability of voting is about 25 percent higher among the most dissatisfied than among the most satisfied.[28] The evidence from other established democracies tells a similar story. Citizens' dissatisfaction with their respective countries' democratic performance does not elicit disengagement; rather, it is associated with both a deeper psychological engagement with politics and a greater willingness to engage in system-correcting political acts. Significantly, and unlike the case of the American public, however, dissatisfied citizens in these other established democracies are *not* more likely than others to vote. The case of Canada introduces yet another twist: Canadians who are dissatisfied with how democratically their country is being governed express a greater willingness than others to engage in system-correcting political acts, but they are not more inclined to participate in other forms of political engagement. Discontent prompts different sorts of political engagement in other democracies, particularly the United States, but the scope of its impact on Canadian political engagement seems more limited.

Conclusion

There are good reasons to be concerned about the apparent rising discontent with political actors and institutions and the parallel decline in formal political participation among publics across advanced industrial democracies during the last several decades. American and Canadian publics have experienced the same parallel trends. The goal of the preceding analysis has been to determine whether these trends indicate a deeper malaise with democratic systems. More particularly, the goal was to explore whether the sources and consequences of citizens' dissatisfaction with their countries' democratic performance – the citizen-level democratic deficit – are similar or different in the United States and Canada.

The core findings are:

- Citizens across advanced industrial states, including Canada and the United States, have clear ideas about what democracy is; they also express an abiding commitment to democracy.
- A significant segment of these publics is not satisfied that the respective countries are being governed completely democratically.
- The roots of this discontent vary cross-nationally. In the United States, in particular, people's discontent over how democratically the country is being governed appears to stem partly from disagreements rooted in social and political values. The same cannot be said, at least not to the same degree, in Canada or in the other countries examined.
- The evidence also suggests that citizens in Canada, the United States, and other democracies who are dissatisfied are just as likely, or even more likely, than others to be politically engaged. Once again, the data from the United States are particularly striking in this respect: dissatisfied Americans express significantly higher levels of psychological engagement with politics, and they exhibit a greater willingness to vote and to participate in system-correcting actions.

What, then, can be concluded about the democratic health of Canada and the United States? Some findings provide reasons for optimism. Despite the erosion in political confidence and formal participation over the last several decades, Canadians and Americans express a strong commitment to democracy. Then there are the consequences of democratic discontent. As Klingemann and Fuchs note, "a challenge to the institutional structure of a given democracy is conceivable only if its citizens are dissatisfied and behave accordingly. This is also true if the final cause of such change lies with the state and its actors."[29] According to the WVS evidence presented here, dissatisfied citizens in Canada, the United States, and other democracies are politically engaged. If Klingemann and Fuchs are right this is good news: it signals the potential for considerable political change, especially in the United States.

There are also reasons to temper that optimism with some caution. In an ideal world, support for democratic regimes should be able to withstand political disagreements. And, thus far, that seems to be the case. But the evidence also suggests that the polarization of citizen on some key social and political values may have the potential to generate substantial democratic discontent among the American public. And, in that particular respect, the American public appears to be rather exceptional.

The cross-national evidence also prompts reflection about the significance of declining voter turnout and waning confidence in political institutions and the relationship between the two. The growing unhappiness with political institutions is clearly associated with a deeper dissatisfaction with democratic performance across all countries. The decline in formal political participation, however, may not be symptomatic of anything more profound. Contrary to some conventional wisdom, low participation, according to our analysis, is not a consequence of the individual-level democratic deficit.

NOTES

1 Jürgen Habermas, *Legitimation Crisis* (Boston: Beacon Press, 1975); S. Brittan, "The Economic Contradictions of Democracy," *British Journal of Political Science* 5 (1975): 129-59; Anthony King, "Overload: Problems of Governing in the 1970s," *Political Studies* 23 (1975): 284-96; Michel Crozier, Samuel P. Huntington, and Joji Watanuki, *The Crisis of Democracy: Report on the Governability of Democracies to the Trilateral Commission* (New York: New York University Press, 1975).
2 Seymour Martin Lipset, *Continental Divide: The Values and Institutions of the United States and Canada* (New York: Routledge, 1990); Seymour Martin Lipset, *Agrarian Socialism: The Cooperative Commonwealth Federation in Saskatchewan* (Berkeley: University of California Press, 1950); Seymour Martin Lipset, *Political Man* (Garden City, NY: Doubleday, 1963).
3 Jacques Thomassen, "Support for Democratic Values," in *Citizens and the State*, ed. Hans-Dieter Klingemann and Dieter Fuchs (New York: Oxford University Press, 1995); Arthur H. Miller, Vicki L. Hesli, and William M. Reisinger, "Conceptions of Democracy among Mass and Elite in Post-Soviet Societies," *British Journal of Political Science* 27, 2 (1997): 157-90.
4 Mark N. Franklin, "The Dynamics of Electoral Participation," in *Comparing Democracies 2: New Challenges in the Study of Elections and Voting*, ed. Laurence LeDuc, Richard G. Niemi, and Pippa Norris (London: Sage, 2002).
5 David Easton, *A Framework for Political Analysis* (Englewood Cliffs, NJ: Prentice-Hall, 1965); David Easton, "A Reassessment of the Concept of Political Support," *British Journal of Political Science* 5 (1975): 435-57.
6 Thomassen, "Support for Democratic Values."
7 The full results of the principal components factor analysis of publics in Canada, the United States, and other established democracies are available at http://www.nevitte.org/.
8 David Beetham, ed., *Defining and Measuring Democracy: Institutional versus Socio-economic Factors* (New York: Sage Publications, 1994).

9   The same basic factors emerge when Canadian and American samples are analyzed separately.
10 These indices range from 0 to 1, where 0 indicates that all of the characteristics of democracy comprising the cluster are considered not at all essential, and 1 indicates that all of the characteristics are considered essential.
11 If this point seems too obvious to belabour, note that the proportion of publics in Guatemala and Nicaragua believing that democracy is a "good thing" is 57 percent and 48 percent, respectively. See Christopher Cochrane, Neil Nevitte, and Stephen White, "Value Change in Europe and North America: Convergence or Something Else?," in *Growing Apart? Europe and North America*, ed. Jeffrey Kopstein and Sven Steinmo (New York: Cambridge University Press, 2008).
12 Norman H. Nie, Jane Junn, and Kenneth Stehlik-Barry, *Education and Democratic Citizenship in America* (Chicago: Chicago University Press, 1996); Sidney Verba, Kay Lehman Schlozman, and Henry E. Brady, *Voice and Equality: Civic Volunteerism in American Politics* (Cambridge: Harvard University Press, 1995).
13 Dieter Fuchs, "The Democratic Culture of Unified Germany," in *Critical Citizens: Global Support for Democratic Governance*, ed. Pippa Norris (New York: Oxford University Press, 1999), 142.
14 Anthony King, "Overload: Problems of Governing in the 1970s," *Political Studies* 23 (1975): 284-96; R. Rose and G. Peters, *Can Government Go Bankrupt?* (New York: Basic Books, 1978); Anthony Birch, "Overload, Ungovernability and Delegitimation: The Theories and the British Case," *British Journal of Political Science* 14, 2 (1984): 135-60.
15 Habermas, *Legitimation Crisis*; Claus Offe, *Contradictions of the Welfare State*, ed. J. Keane (London: Hutchinson, 1984).
16 Brittan, "Economic Contradictions"; Crozier, Huntington, and Watanuki, *Crisis of Democracy*; Samuel P. Huntington, "The Democratic Distemper," in *The American Commonwealth*, ed. Nathan Glazer and Irving Kristol (New York: Basic Books, 1976).
17 Dieter Fuchs and Hans-Dieter Klingemann, "Citizens and the State: A Changing Relationship?," in *Citizens and the State*, ed. Hans-Dieter Klingemann and Dieter Fuchs (New York: Oxford University Press, 1995).
18 Max Kaase and Kenneth Newton, *Beliefs in Government* (New York: Oxford University Press, 1995), 24.
19 Russell J. Dalton, *Democratic Challenges, Democratic Choices: The Erosion of Political Support in Advanced Industrial Democracies* (Oxford: Oxford University Press, 2004).
20 Alan I. Abramowitz and Walter J. Stone, "The Bush Effect: Polarization, Turnout, and Activism in the 2004 Presidential Election," *Presidential Studies Quarterly* 36, 2 (2006): 141-54; Annenberg Democracy Project, *A Republic Divided* (New York: Oxford University Press, 2007); David W. Brady and Pietro S. Nivola, eds., *Red and Blue Nation?* Vol. 1: *Characteristics and Causes of America's Polarized Politics* (Washington, DC: Brookings Institution Press and Hoover Institution, 2006); Cochrane et al., "Value Change."

21 Christopher J. Anderson and Christine A. Guillory, "Political Institutions and Satisfaction with Democracy: A Cross-National Analysis of Consensus and Majoritarian Systems," *American Political Science Review* 91, 1 (1997): 66-81.
22 Detailed regression tables, as well as information on the wording of questions and construction of independent variables, are available at http://www.nevitte.org/.
23 In effect, conceptions of democracy also help to explain why higher levels of education generate greater dissatisfaction with democratic performance. Higher levels of education are associated with clearer notions of democracy, and these, in turn, produce dissatisfaction.
24 The full results are available at www.nevitte.org/.
25 Ibid.
26 Russell J. Dalton, "Political Support in Advanced Industrialized Democracies," in *Critical Citizens: Global Support for Democratic Governance*, ed. Pippa Norris (New York: Oxford University Press, 1999).
27 The full results are available at www.nevitte.org/.
28 The results suggest that dissatisfied Americans are neither more nor less politically attentive than others, but it is worth noting that our measure of political attentiveness may not provide the most effective means for tapping citizens' attentiveness to politics specifically as it asks about people's use of "different sources to learn what is going on in their country and the world."
29 Fuchs and Klingemann, "Citizens and the State," 10.

3

Defining and Identifying a Democratic Deficit

DAVID BEETHAM

The concept of a "democratic deficit" is said to have originated in relation to the European Union, though in that context it remains highly contested, not least because of major disagreements about what sort of political system the European Union is and what, therefore, are the appropriate criteria against which it should be assessed. As the author of one recent survey concludes: "The literature on the democratic deficit in the European Union is remarkable for its heterogeneity ... The question of what a democratic deficit is reflects the specific model of democracy one considers appropriate for the EU."[1] In the context of nation-states, however, despite obvious differences between them, it is possible to reach a greater measure of agreement on the criteria for assessing their democratic quality. I am not convinced that differences of priority over the ordering of democratic values, whether among academics or wider publics, need prevent us from achieving this agreement.

In the democracy assessment framework developed for the International Institute for Democracy and Electoral Assistance (IDEA) we seek to identify international standards of good practice for each aspect of a country's democracy to be chosen for assessment.[2] Naturally, some of these standards are more well established than others (e.g., in the field of civil and political rights), but we should not underestimate the work that has been taking place in different international agencies over the past two decades to develop standards for many aspects of democratic life.[3] As with international human rights standards, these make a distinction between a good quality of attainment and the particular institutional mechanisms used to reach it, which may well differ from one jurisdiction to the next. The fact that, as argued elsewhere in this collection, we are often confronted with the need for "trade-offs," and that all democratic goods cannot be maximized simultaneously, does not prevent us from identifying what counts as a "good" in the first place.

Now it may happen that some of the established democracies are deeply reluctant to allow themselves to be assessed against any external standard. Yet this posture is increasingly difficult to maintain in an era when the international development departments of the same countries have established sophisticated criteria for "good governance," against which countries seeking development aid or democracy assistance are externally assessed.[4] We could also mention the European Union, which established quite stringent thresholds for democracy and human rights attainment (alongside those in property and financial law) to be met by candidate countries as a condition of membership. Although the quip "if the EU itself were to seek admission it would be refused entry" may be contested in view of the disputed character of EU institutions,[5] there is no reason to regard these same standards as inappropriate for its existing member countries. It is precisely the process of institution building in the new and restored democracies that has led to the articulation of clearer standards of democratic attainment internationally.

So I would define a democratic deficit in the first instance as a substantial and systematic failing in relation to international standards of good practice in some important feature of a country's democratic life. "Substantial" means what it says – not a trivial or minor failing. "Systematic" implies a repeated failing that can be traced to some identifiable underlying deficiency. And "some important feature" signals that democracy is a multifaceted complex of many elements and that some will reach international standards of good practice more fully than others. A feature of most democracy assessments conducted using the IDEA framework is the identification of the different strengths and weaknesses of a country's democracy and the publication of a summary of the key deficits that merit public attention and concern. A draft assessment is typically subjected to wide-ranging scrutiny at a national conference, at which different experts and members of different political tendencies are present, to give greater authority to the findings.

By way of example, here is a summary of the key deficits found by the Netherlands assessment of 2006.[6] Eight of what were termed "untamed problems" were identified:

- Fragile social cohesion, especially affecting new citizens of non-Western origin, few of whom felt themselves to be Dutch.
- An increase in the number and seriousness of incidents in which freedom of expression had been suppressed due to violence.
- The larger political parties were less rooted in society and losing popular support for their candidate and policy selection procedures.
- Political arenas were being displaced from representative and accountable departments of government to new administrative bodies and quangos.
- Overlapping administrative competencies were producing unnecessary complexity for citizens.
- The vulnerability to constant media exposure had developed a political culture of risk avoidance.
- The internal procedures for overseeing EU policy and legislation were inadequate.
- Poll findings showed decreasing public confidence in politicians and government.

It is one thing, however, for assessors to identify a democratic deficit, as in the list compiled above; it is another thing for a deficit to become *politically significant* or *salient*, such as to generate pressure for reform. This typically requires a combination of two things. One is a key event or example that exposes the deficit unavoidably to public view. A second is that this should arouse widespread public concern, maybe intensified through media exposure and interest group advocacy. The assassination of the party leader Pim Fortyn is an obvious example from the Netherlands, since it shockingly demonstrated a systemic threat to freedom of expression in that country (see the second item above). Another is the US presidential election of 2000, in which the narrowness of the result and contestation over the ballots highlighted long-standing deficiencies in the registration and election procedures that broke almost every international standard of "free and fair elections." Indeed, in many countries, it is only the narrowness of an election result that makes chronic deficits in electoral procedures politically salient.

From the United Kingdom we could take as an example the Stephen Lawrence case, in which the failure of the police to investigate the murder of a black teenager with due speed or care exposed the force as "institutionally racist," to cite the conclusion of a judge-led inquiry into the affair.[7] Here it was only the determined campaigning of the teenager's parents and an active support group that kept the issue in the public view and gave it political salience. In a similarly regrettable manner, the failure of the Metropolitan Police to apprehend two serial rapists, despite the repeated availability of evidence, exposed the systemically low priority the force gave to these crimes compared to what it gave to car theft or burglary.[8] What was at issue in both types of cases was a serious and systematic deviation from standards of equal citizenship that are central to any democracy.

So a democratic deficit may require a key event or example to expose it unavoidably to public view and the arousal of substantial public concern to give it political salience. And we could conclude that what is most important for the overall health of a democracy is not so much the existence or even exposure of deficits as the capacity and willingness to make effective reforms once a deficit has become politically salient. By the same token, nothing is more guaranteed to create apathy and disaffection among a population than the failure to rectify a deficit that has become politically salient in the manner outlined above. Above all, democracies are characterized by the capacity for self-renewal without violence; and the demonstrable lack of this capacity is arguably more damaging to the quality of a country's public life than are the number of specific deficits that can be identified through a systematic assessment process.

To be sure, democratic deficits do not always need to acquire what I call "political salience" to be the subject of reform. The assessment carried out in the Netherlands using the IDEA framework was unusual in that it was organized by a democracy unit within the government's interior ministry. And it was explicitly linked to a government-initiated reform program involving wide public consultation.[9] However, even here, one would expect that the priority in such a reform program would be given to those issues that most aroused deep and widespread public concern. And where the assessment is civil-society based, as is more usually the case, it may require persistent campaigning by advocacy groups to get any of the key deficits identified to the point at which they arouse wider public concern and are able to achieve the necessary political salience to prompt reform.

At this point it is worth drawing attention to possible divergences between elite and mass publics, which may mean that even long-standing deficits that become exposed by some key event may not achieve sufficient political salience. These could be called "dogs that don't bark," and we could take as an example the UK general election of 2005. It is quite widely agreed among the politically informed that a key deficit in the United Kingdom's democracy is the plurality election system, which has produced increasingly disproportional outcomes, reduced effective electoral choice, and allowed campaigning to be concentrated on "swing voters" in a small number of marginal constituencies. The defects of the system in a multi-party context are such that it was never seriously entertained as the electoral method for the newly established parliament and assemblies in Scotland, Wales, and Northern Ireland. The result of the 2005 election exposed the perverse consequences to public view in the clearest possible manner: in the second lowest voter turnout since the First World War (61 percent) the Labour Party won 55 percent of the parliamentary seats with a mere 35 percent of the popular vote, or just over 20 percent of the total electorate. Although the result was viewed with astonishment by many abroad, it caused hardly a ripple at home, where the new government quickly proceeded to business as usual.

No doubt part of the explanation lay in the refusal of the main Opposition party to make an issue of the affair since it expected in due course to reap the fruits of single-party rule for itself, an outcome denied by the indecisive election result of 2010. Yet it must also be said that the wider public was not moved by the issue, despite two decades of active campaigning for electoral reform by a range of advocacy groups. So there is a potential divergence between the views of elite and mass publics, and between the democratic deficits that are identified in a systematic assessment and those that arouse wider public concern sufficient to prompt reform. I explore this divergence in the next section by analyzing the results of three country assessments from the developed world in which the International IDEA methodology was used.

Dogs That Don't Bark and Those That Don't Stop

The three country assessments described here, conducted at different time points between 2000 and 2007, offer three contrasting scenarios. One is a country in which assessors identified significant deficits, but these were not reflected in the popular assessment of the democracy, which was unusually positive. Second is a country in which assessors had difficulty in identifying serious deficiencies but in which public opinion remained stubbornly dissatisfied with the democratic process and citizens' ability to influence it. The third is a country that has carried out a far-reaching program of democratic reform to deal with acknowledged deficiencies, but public trust in politics and politicians has declined *pari passu* as the reforms have been implemented. These countries are Ireland, New Zealand, and the United Kingdom, respectively. Together they compel caution in moving too readily from the assessment of political analysts to the state of public satisfaction or dissatisfaction with the workings of democracy. They also throw doubt on over-generalized explanations as opposed to those that are country- or issue-specific.

The Irish Republic

The executive summary of the Irish democracy assessment of 2007 was divided into three categories: "what we are doing well; what we are doing badly; where we are in flux."[10] Some of the deficits identified were common to many European democracies: declining levels of party activism and voter turnout, poor representation of women in public life, weak parliamentary oversight of the executive and independent public bodies. Others were more specific to Ireland: high levels of poverty and inequality; limited scope and independence for local government; high level of church influence in public life, especially education; poor delivery of front-line services; over-utilization of imprisonment in the criminal justice system. Under the "in flux" category came a number of high-profile issues regarding the quality of policing and corruption in public life (reaching to the highest levels), which had been the subject of extensive legislative reform (albeit too recent to assess its impact in practice).

Although some of the deficits identified could be said to be typical preoccupations of the "political cognoscenti" – poor parliamentary oversight of the executive, limited independence for local government – others had a much wider public salience. Yet the existing survey data and polls conducted for the assessment showed levels of citizen confidence in public institutions and the workings of Irish democracy to be markedly and consistently higher than what is the case in most other European countries, as the authors emphasized:

> The evidence suggests that the Irish public retains a high degree of confidence in the system of government and the way in which democracy works. The overall level of confidence in a range of public institutions in Ireland is among the highest in Europe, and over two-thirds of people express satisfaction with the way democracy is developing, compared to less than half in the rest of Europe. Indeed, one commentator states that "the attitudes towards the political system [in Ireland] could be considered almost enthusiastic." Almost two-thirds of respondents believed that when ordinary citizens make an effort to influence political decisions they can really make a difference.[11]

In light of the democratic deficits identified in the assessment, how can this comparatively positive judgment of Irish public opinion be explained? In a national conference convened to review the draft findings of the assessment, a number of specific explanations were advanced in relation to particular issues and to one much more general one. As regards issues affecting the socially excluded, marginalized, or disadvantaged, so it was argued, these involved a minority of the population only and would not affect majority opinion. As regards high-profile cases of corruption or abuse of power, the extensive legislation to clean up politics seemed to have quietened the original public concerns, even though its effect in practice was still unclear. And the accessibility and constituency activity of elected parliamentarians encouraged by the single transferable vote (STV) voting system was seen to offset any corresponding deficit in their national parliamentary role of holding public officials to account.

At a more general level, it was agreed that the economic performance of the "Celtic Tiger" was primarily responsible for the generally positive assessment of Irish democracy despite the deficits identified. This explanation was supported by the polling evidence, which showed that Irish public opinion started diverging in a positive direction from the European average early in the 1990s and continued thereafter.[12] It was also confirmed by the rapid drop in confidence in government following the financial crisis and austerity program of 2008-9, with a poll showing 40 percent blaming the government more than the bankers for the collapse as well as for the harsh budget that followed.[13] In the general election of February 2011, the Fianna Faill Party, which had governed continuously for nearly twenty years, suffered its worst ever polling defeat, plummeting from seventy-seven to a mere twenty seats in the Dail on an increased voter turnout.[14] What remains unclear is whether the economic collapse will reduce citizens' confidence in the democratic system itself or only in the party that presided over it. One of the key advantages of a democracy is the capacity of citizens to remove a failed government through the electoral process and bring about a sense of renewal even where the structures themselves remain unchanged. Although the jury of Irish public opinion on the fallout from the credit crunch on their democracy is still out, their consistently positive verdict over a period of two decades, despite the deficits identified by expert analysts, remains remarkable.

New Zealand
In sharp contrast to Ireland is New Zealand, a country of similarly small size, where the assessors were hard put to find any serious "deficits," yet the

population showed high levels of dissatisfaction with the functioning of their democracy.[15] Among the positive features identified was the way New Zealand had modified its Westminster parliamentary system with a strong bill of rights monitored by an independent human rights commission and a mixed-member proportional (MMP) election system, delivering a politically and socially diverse parliament. Women were strongly represented in Parliament, government, and the public service, and at the highest levels, much more so than in comparator countries. Rights of the Maori population were constitutionally guaranteed, and they were represented in Parliament in proportion to their numbers in the population, albeit with evidence of some backlash from sections of the majority community. In most other respects New Zealand performed strongly against international standards of democratic performance. Here is how the authors summarize their findings:

> In many respects New Zealand enjoys a level of democracy which people in other countries would envy. Basic rights are guaranteed, public life is largely corruption-free, government is accountable to both Parliament and the electorate, representatives are readily available to their electors, and the opportunities for public consultation on legislation through the parliamentary committee system are unusually well developed. In addition, there are relatively high levels of citizen participation both in elections (85 per cent turnout) and in civic associations. Yet surveys of public opinion show that large majorities of people, while believing in the value of a democratic system, also feel themselves disempowered in relation to government. Thus some 85.4 per cent believe that the public has little control over what politicians do in office, 61.6 per cent believe that the average person will not get anywhere by talking to central government officials, and 67.4 per cent think that government is generally unresponsive to public opinion ... The discrepancy between most of the indicators of democratic performance in New Zealand, and the level of popular dissatisfaction with it, presents something of a paradox which merits further investigation.[16]

At a seminar to explore this paradox, which I took part in at the University of Canterbury in 2000, two different explanations found the most support. One explanation was generic, to the effect that popular expectations of government had risen in a context in which politicians were more exposed than before to media investigation and criticism – in effect, that dissatisfaction with government and politicians was now a normal part of the democratic condition. This explanation accords with the view put forward by Pippa Norris in Chapter 1 (this volume) and elsewhere. On its own, however, it is hardly sufficient to explain the large and specific discrepancy between a democratic system in which channels of decision making and legislation are unusually open to public input, on the one hand, and the popular sense of powerlessness about citizens' capacity to influence them, on the other.

A second explanation addresses this specific discrepancy and focuses on long-surviving memories of the Labour government under David Lange in the mid-1980s, which had introduced a raft of neoliberal economic policies without any prior consultation. These had not figured in any election manifesto, and they proved widely unpopular, whatever the economic logic supporting them may have been in terms of New Zealand's international economic position. On this view, the historical decision to reshape New Zealand's political economy and society unilaterally – by a Labour, not a Conservative or Liberal, party – may have influenced people's attitude towards the representative process for a generation.

This explanation is largely hypothetical and not open to definitive proof. Yet it serves to draw attention to a feature that is often missing from democracy assessments. This is the existence of key historical moments, events, or decisions that may shape public attitudes towards government for a generation but that will not show up in a snapshot assessment of the condition of democracy at a single moment in time. An institutional analysis may find admirable mechanisms for public consultation on policy and legislation, such as exist in New Zealand, but miss a major issue in which a government has defied public opinion even while it is consulting it obsessively on lesser ones. This must also count as a contributory factor to public disaffection with the representative process in the third country example considered here.

The United Kingdom

In the United Kingdom we have been conducting systematic audits on the condition of democracy for over fifteen years, starting under the Conservative government of 1992-97.[17] In 1997, the incoming Labour government initiated the most far-reaching program of constitutional reform that had been undertaken for a century and a half. It was said that it was the kind of reform program that normally only occurs in the aftermath of revolution or defeat in war. It included the devolution of power to Scotland, Wales, and Northern Ireland; the establishment of the Greater London Authority; the incorporation of the European Convention on Human Rights into UK law through the Human Rights Act; the introduction of the Freedom of Information Act; the abolition of the hereditary element in the House of Lords; the establishment of an electoral commission; and much more.

Admittedly, these reforms were carried out under the rubric of "modernization" rather than "democratization," a word that was never mentioned in the government literature. Yet these reforms were designed precisely to address some of the main democratic deficits that had been identified by commentators and that had been campaigned upon by civic groups for a decade or more. So when we came to undertake a major democratic audit of the first Blair administration in 2001, we were able to show systematic advance across a range of indicators towards standards of international best practice.[18] However, at the same time as the objective indicators of democratic performance were improving, public confidence in the representative process, and in Parliament and parliamentarians, was declining. Voter turnout in the 2001 election was the lowest since the First World War, party memberships were falling fast, and levels of trust in politicians had declined even further than before – processes that continued during the rest of Labour's period of office. It was as if the public either had not noticed the democratic reforms that Labour had been responsible for or had not regarded them as of any significance.

When Gordon Brown took over from Tony Blair as prime minister in the summer of 2007, one of his first acts was to publish a "green paper" entitled *The Governance of Britain*, which took as its starting point the declining public trust in the democratic process. "Action is now needed across the breadth of the political system," the paper argued, "to promote and restore trust in politics and our political institutions." There followed a new list of proposed reforms, involving the strengthening of Parliament, making the executive more accountable, offering a limited introduction of direct democracy, and expanding citizenship education to instruct the young in "the importance of the democratic process and the need for active citizenship." What was never asked was why the first set of constitutional reforms, important and necessary as they indeed were, should have had no positive effect on public confidence, or why we should expect another phase of similar reforms to be any different.[19]

So here we have another sharp divergence between the objective indicators, which showed a clear improvement following significant democratic reform, and public perceptions of, and confidence in, the representative process. Again, it seems to me too simple to fall back on the kind of general explanations that attribute declining public trust in politics to increased expectations or more educated electorates. There are a number of perfectly intelligible causes specific to the United Kingdom, or at least particularly salient under the Blair administrations, that can help account for the low levels of confidence in elected representatives and in the representative process more widely. I identify three:

- Although Blair came into office promising to eliminate Tory "sleaze" from public life, high-profile examples of the distortions of money in politics continued throughout Labour's period in office, such as peerages for those contributing to party funds, cash for parliamentary questions, gross misuse of parliamentary expenses, and so on. British public life is not particularly corrupt by international standards, but the public impression is different, not least because the issue was made so much of by Labour before it came to power in 1997.
- Labour governments created a "spin" culture, in which a host of sharp practices were employed to manipulate public opinion and marginalize independent voices in party and government, with the result that public confidence in the credibility of politicians as a class was further eroded.[20]
- Blair's project of constructing "New Labour" as a right-of-centre party, together with the workings of the electoral system, effectively disenfranchised large numbers of voters and produced successive parliaments that were seriously unrepresentative of political opinion in the country.

The gap, in other words, was not only between some of the objective democratic indicators, which had clearly improved, and public perceptions of the democratic process. It was also between what the government itself believed would restore public confidence and what might be required to do so. A typical example of this is the government's attempt to encourage more people to vote through making it easier to do so (though also more open to abuse), while not acknowledging the underlying reasons why electors might not think it *worth* voting. And the fallout from the historical decision in 2002-3 to go to war in Iraq, which demonstrated the last two failings itemized above in extreme form, remain with us. A generation of young people who participated actively in demonstrations against the war could only conclude that their voices did not count, whatever "citizenship education" might teach to the contrary.[21] The creation of a coalition government after the elections of May 2010, with further proposals for constitutional reform, has certainly changed the contours of UK politics; but there is little evidence that it has improved trust in politicians or confidence in the democratic system.

Conclusion: From Generality to Specificity in Democracy Assessment

The striking feature of all three assessments discussed is the discrepancy between the condition of democracy as judged by expert assessors and the condition of democracy as judged in opinion surveys of popular levels of satisfaction with the democratic process. In the case of the Irish Republic, popular assessment was much more positive than the deficits identified by assessors would have led one to expect. In New Zealand, the level of popular dissatisfaction and sense of disempowerment was at odds with all the objective indicators of democratic performance. In the United Kingdom, the implementation of a far-reaching program of constitutional reform to remedy long-standing deficits coincided with a continuing decline in public confidence in politicians and the representative process.

Most explanations in the literature assume that the discrepancy is all in one direction and that, while the established democracies are *comparatively* sound, levels of popular disaffection remain stubbornly high.[22] Two explanations are then usually advanced for this discrepancy: (1) on the input side, that popular expectations of government have risen with increased education and rising standards of consumer provision in the private sector and (2) on the output side, that the competence of governments has been eroded by the process of globalization (as the credit crisis, for example, has only too clearly demonstrated). Yet the Irish example shows that the discrepancy between expert assessment and popular estimation can work the other way. It also shows that the configuration of international economic conditions can be used to a country's advantage, as happened during the years of the Celtic Tiger. Whatever popular expectations and external constraints may be, politicians cannot be assumed to be impotent in face of them, as a deterministic reading of the condition of national democracies might suggest.

What we should concentrate on, therefore, is the discrepancy between elite, or expert, assessments and the judgment of wider publics in whatever direction this goes. There may be some common factors at work here. One possibility is a difference in emphasis in people's understanding of democracy. Experts are more likely to concentrate on institutional arrangements and the *process* aspects of democracy, while publics are more likely to concentrate on *outcomes*, whether in terms of personal security and economic well-being or standards of conduct of elected representatives. Of course, there is a relation between process and outcome, but this may not always be apparent. In a democracy assessment conducted across the countries of South Asia, when people were asked what components of democracy they valued most highly, the "rule of law" came at the bottom whereas "access to justice" came near the top.[23]

Another way of putting this is that people's *experiences* of democracy will differ. The politically informed, who have access to international standards of good practice, may conclude, as they did in the Irish case, that parliamentarians are relatively ineffective in their role of holding the executive to account. Yet their ready availability to constituents could be what matters and is most visible from the standpoint of the ordinary citizen. Of course a democracy assessment should be able to capture both types of experience, as the IDEA framework tries to do. So, for example, the second section of the framework is entitled "The Rule of Law and Access to Justice," with the search questions that follow divided equally between the two components. Yet more could clearly be done to capture a fuller range of what might be called the "experiential" aspects of democracy.

In order to capture these, the South Asian assessments combined the qualitative evaluations of experts with surveys of lay opinion, dialogues with activists, and case studies to tease out the "puzzles of democracy," such as divergences between different findings. In particular, the assessors found a tension between the views of the politically aware and those of other citizens – between "elite commonsense" and "people's commonsense." "When we have a dialogue with the activists," they reported, "or when we had a dialogue with the enlightened people, the trust in political parties and parliament was so low, but when we went to the people with the same questions, trust in parties and Parliament exceeded 50 per cent on average ... Teams need to think about these tensions in their reports."[24]

In light of such discrepancies, the lesson to be drawn from the three case studies described here is that we should be wary of any simple generalizations. The deeper one's analysis of an individual country, the more it is the specific features of that country's institutions, political culture, and historical evolution that assume importance in assessing its democratic condition and explaining differences in people's views about it. This does not mean that we do not need a standard framework and set of methodologies of assessment that can be applied anywhere. But they have to be used with sensitivity to the specificities of each country and each dimension of its democratic life. It is these specificities that the democracy assessments of Ireland, New Zealand, and the United Kingdom all bring out. And they are surely just as likely to be apparent in the two countries that are the main subject of *Imperfect Democracies*.

NOTES

1 Thomas Jensen, "The Democratic Deficit of the European Union," *Living Reviews in Democracy* 1, 1 (2009): 1-8.
2 David Beetham, Edzia Carvalho, Todd Landman, and Stuart Weir, eds., *Assessing the Quality of Democracy: A Practical Guide* (Stockholm: International Institute for Democracy and Electoral Assistance, 2008), 79-249. See also David Beetham, "Towards a Universal Framework for Democracy Assessment," *Democratization* 11, 2 (2004): 1-17.
3 See, for example, the work done by the Inter-Parliamentary Union on standards for "free and fair" elections: Guy S. Goodwin-Gill, *Free and Fair Elections: International Law and Practice* (Geneva: Inter-Parliamentary Union, 1994); Guy S. Goodwin-Gill, *Codes of Conduct for Elections* (Geneva: Inter-Parliamentary Union, 1998); Michael D. Boda, ed. *Revisiting Free and Fair Elections* (Geneva: Inter-Parliamentary Union, 2004).
4 Thomas Carothers, *Aiding Democracy Abroad* (Washington, DC: Carnegie Endowment for International Peace, 2006); Gordon Crawford, *Foreign Aid and Political Reform* (Basignstoke: Palgrave Macmillan, 2001).
5 See note 1 above and the literature reviewed there.
6 Netherlands Ministry of the Interior and Kingdom Relations press release 11 December 2006, "The State of Our Democracy: Towards a Policy Agenda for Democracy in the Netherlands." For the full report translated into English (5 October 2006), see http://www.onzedemocratie.nl/.
7 Sir William Macpherson, *The Stephen Lawrence Inquiry* (London: Home Office, CM4261-1, 1999).
8 See reports in *The Guardian*, 27 March 2009, and the article by Assistant Commissioner John Yates acknowledging the police deficiencies, p. 38.
9 The only other government-initiated assessment to date using the International IDEA methodology has been in Mongolia. See United Nations Development Programme, *Democratic Governance Indicators: Assessing the State of Governance in Mongolia* (Ulanbaatar: UNDP Mongolia, 2006).
10 For the full assessment, see Ian Hughes, Paula Clancy, Clodagh Harris, and David Beetham, *Power to the People? Assessing Democracy in Ireland* (Dublin: TASC at New Island, 2007). The executive summary of the same title was published simultaneously at http://www.tascnet.ie/.
11 Ibid., 492.
12 Ibid., 492-93.
13 Reported in *The Independent*, 7 April 2009, 38.
14 See http://www.ElectionsIreland.org.
15 John Henderson and Paul Bellamy, *Democracy in New Zealand* (Christchurch and Stockholm: Macmillan Brown Centre for Pacific Studies and International IDEA, 2002).

16 This summary is from David Beetham, Sarah Bracking, Iain Kearton, Nalani Vittal, and Stuart Weir, eds., *The State of Democracy: Democracy Assessments in Eight Nations Around the World* (The Hague: Kluwer Law International, 2002), 55-56.
17 Francesca Klug, Keir Starmer, and Stuart Weir, *The Three Pillars of Liberty* (London: Routledge, 1996); Stuart Weir and David Beetham, *Political Power and Democratic Control in Britain* (London: Routledge, 1999); David Beetham, "Key Principles and Indices for a Democratic Audit," in *Defining and Measuring Democracy*, ed. David Beetham (London: Sage, 1994).
18 David Beetham, Iain Byrne, Pauline Ngan, and Stuart Weir, *Democracy under Blair* (London: Politico's, 2002). We illustrated these advances with a bull's-eye chart in a pamphlet summarizing our findings. See David Beetham and Stuart Weir, *Democratic Audit of the United Kingdom, Executive Democracy in Britain* (Colchester: Essex University Human Rights Centre, 2002), 5.
19 London, Ministry of Justice, CM 7170, July 2007.
20 Peter Oborne, *The Rise of Political Lying* (London: The Free Press, 2005); George Pitcher, *The Death of Spin* (Chichester: John Wiley, 2003).
21 See my article on the Iraq war demonstrations: David Beetham, "Political Participation, Mass Protest and Representative Democracy," *Parliamentary Affairs* 56, 4 (2003): 597-609.
22 So, for example, in Pharr and Putnam, *Disaffected Democracies*.
23 Beetham et al., *Assessing the Quality of Democracy*. 261.
24 Ibid., 255.

Democracy in American Elections

MICHAEL McDONALD

A reoccurring question in American politics is: "Is voting a right or a privilege?" As Keyssar recounts, the Founding Fathers (such as Benjamin Franklin, Thomas Paine and George Mason) argued that voting was a right to be enjoyed by all American citizens – or at least all free men – since the country was founded on the principle of self-governance, and they worried that those who could not participate would feel no loyalty to the nascent country.[1] Those who argued that voting was a privilege (e.g., John Adams and James Madison) were concerned that the masses were incapable of governing themselves; at best, those of weak minds would allow their votes to be bought, and, at worst, the country would literally descend into class warfare. These positions persist, have become ideological in nature, and are perceived to have political consequences that affect the ability of citizens to participate in elections and, ultimately, influence public policy. Liberals generally believe that voting is a right, that non-voters predominantly support their policy positions, and that implementing various electoral mechanisms to encourage low-propensity voters to participate will produce an electorate favourable to their policy positions. Conservatives generally believe that voting is a privilege and that restricting the franchise directly or indirectly will favour high-propensity voters who tend to support their policy positions.

Whether or not voting is a right or a privilege, without compulsory voting American voters choose to participate. Only a little more than 60 percent of eligible citizens voted in recent presidential elections, and even fewer participated in congressional, state, and local elections. In that the quality of citizens' representation is affected by the fact that elected officials pay most attention to those who voted them into office,[2] the bias in the electorate has inspired many to consider why these disparate turnout rates exist and what can be done to rectify them[3] – questions that have also consumed policy makers. The purpose of this chapter is to explore these policy options as they have been implemented in American elections.

Administration of American Elections

The United States of America's highly decentralized electoral system is deeply rooted in the country's origins. Before there was a national government, the thirteen colonies administered their elections, each with its own rules. When the Founding Fathers convened to write a new constitution, they deliberated adopting a uniform electoral system but were unable to resolve how to reconcile state laws. The devised solution in article IV, section 4 of the Constitution allows states to administer their elections, with authority granted to the federal government to supersede state laws. In an era of jealously guarded states' rights, this arrangement ensured states could administer their elections with little or no federal oversight.

As a result, the United States has perhaps the most decentralized electoral system in the world. Even the election of the one national figure, the president, is not truly a national election. The elected candidate is the winner of the Electoral College, whose membership is determined by individual contests for Electoral College votes among the fifty states and the District of Columbia. Likewise, the electoral rules, administration of elections, and candidates' campaigns take place within localities, not nationally. Recently, the federal government began to flex its authority to regulate elections. However, aside from constitutional amendments that have set national voting qualifications and the protections for minority voters embodied in the Voting Rights Act (VRA), these forays have been limited and received considerable resistance from state and local election administrators. Perhaps this is best exemplified by the United States Electoral Assistance Commission (EAC), established by the Help America Vote Act (HAVA) of 2002 in the wake of the election administration troubles revealed by Florida's 2000 presidential election. The EAC is a shadow of other nations' electoral commissions: it has been mired in politics and, due to a lack of enforcement mechanisms, must cajole states to work it. The National Association of

Secretaries of State, which represents an important group of election administrators, has issued a resolution calling for the disbanding of the EAC.[4]

The United States' highly decentralized electoral system has allowed the best and the worst local election practices to flourish and to wither, political circumstances permitting. Epic political wars have been waged to extend voting rights to all citizens (especially minorities), to root out political corruption, and to make voting more convenient. Policy victories have often resulted in consequences – either designed or unintended – that have opened new battle fronts. On balance, the adopted policies have mostly moved in a direction favouring the position that voting is a right, although occasionally those who believe that voting is a privilege win the day. These policy victories often arise in the name of a group that defended the country, whether it be in the form of extending voting rights to militiamen following the Revolutionary War, extending voting rights to young people during the Vietnam War, or streamlining absentee voting for military personnel serving in Afghanistan and Iraq.

The American Electorate

Voting is a two-step process in the United States: before an eligible person can vote they must first be registered.[5] In many other countries, most eligible persons either find themselves automatically registered by government election administrators or their citizenship identification serves as proof of their voting eligibility.[6] To understand the American electorate, one must thus also understand who is registered to vote. Perhaps the best source for determining voting and registration rates by demographic groups is the Census Bureau's monthly Current Population Survey (CPS). This is a large-scale survey of tens of thousands of households, and it is designed primarily to measure employment rates. In November of an election year, a limited number of supplemental voting and registration questions are added to the survey questionnaire. The large number of respondents and intensive efforts to ensure participation in the survey make it the best source from which to construct voting and registration rates for relatively small populations.

The voting and registration rates among citizens of voting age for selected demographic groups are presented in Table 4.1. Rates are presented by age, gender, race, and ethnicity;[7] education; and length of time living at current residence. Additionally, I report the turnout rate for those eligible to vote.[8] These statistics are reported for the 2006 mid-term and 2008 presidential

TABLE 4.1

Selected citizen voting-age population voter turnout and registration rates, 2008 and 2006

		2008		2006	
		Voted (%)	Registered (%)	Voted (%)	Registered (%)
Overall turnout, eligible voters		62		40	
Age	18-29	51	61	25	51
	30-44	62	69	43	66
	45-59	68	74	56	73
	60+	71	77	63	78
Gender	Men	61	69	47	66
	Women	66	73	49	69
Race/Ethnicity	Non-Hispanic white	66	74	52	71
	African-American	65	70	41	61
	Hispanic	50	59	32	54
	Other	49	58	33	52
Education	Less than high school	39	50	27	48
	High school grad	55	64	41	62
	Some college/college grad	71	78	54	74
	Post-graduate	83	86	70	82
Tenure at Current residence	Less than 1 year	57	69	29	55
	More than 1 year	75	83	57	78

Sources: Turnout rates for eligible voters are from Michael P. McDonald, "United States Elections Project," http://elections.gmu.edu/. Turnout rates for citizens of voting age among various demographic categories are drawn from the 2006 and 2008 Current Population Survey Voting and Registration supplements, http://www.census.gov/.

elections. Despite that these were two favourable elections for the Democratic Party, which may have mobilized constituencies favourable to that political party, the patterns presented in Table 4.1 are largely consistent with previous CPS surveys extending back to 1964.

The statistics in Table 4.1 reveal several stylized facts about the American electorate. First, that over the past century a little more than half of eligible voters tend to participate in modern presidential elections, and a little less than half participate in mid-term elections.[9] Second, that turnout rates are uneven among demographic groups. Turnout rates tend to be higher among eligible persons who are older, white, female, educated, and have lived at their current residence for a longer period of time. These participation disparities tend to be slightly greater in mid-term than in presidential elections. There are similar patterns present for voter registration. However, since only people who have moved to a new jurisdiction or who have not voted in a recent election may be required to re-register, voter registration rates tend to fluctuate less from election to election.

These patterns in Table 4.1 illuminate the fact that voter registration may be a barrier to participation, particularly in presidential elections in which registration and turnout rates are nearly even. However, registration cannot entirely explain varying levels of participation among the electorate, particularly in mid-term elections, in which a significant percentage of citizens report being registered but being uninterested in voting. In a cost-benefit rational choice framework,[10] some of the explanation for disparate turnout rates is due to the costs of voting manifested in registration and other inconveniences, and some is due to the perceived benefits of voting manifested in candidate choices or, perhaps more to the point, in the lack of compelling choices.

Voter Registration

Massachusetts was the first state to adopt voter registration in 1801, but adoption of voter registration primarily occurred between the Civil War and the First World War.[11] Today, all states except North Dakota require voter registration. Requiring voters to register to vote was ostensibly intended to reduce vote fraud perpetrated by political machines of the nineteenth century, but, in some states, the registration burden was targeted at urbanites or minorities. The procedure could be quite burdensome. Persons were sometimes required to register months before each election in which they wished to vote, to be a resident of the jurisdiction for months prior to the election, and to provide required identification or to produce a person to vouchsafe that they were indeed eligible to vote. When accompanied with literacy tests or other devices such as poll taxes, or when registrars selectively opened their doors, voter registration was a powerful discriminatory tool to deny African Americans voting rights in the South following the end of the post-Civil War Reconstruction period:[12] "To no one's surprise, these reforms depressed voter turnout."[13]

The idea that eligible persons must register themselves before they may vote is consistent with the philosophy that voting is a privilege, and it is now deeply rooted in American politics. Those who believe voting is a right have enacted various reforms to ease the registration burden. A significant wave of reform was enacted during the 1960s primarily to address discriminatory practices in the South, but it had far-reaching effects in other states. The Twenty-Fourth Amendment, adopted in 1964, outlawed poll taxes. The 1965 VRA and subsequent amendments forbid the use of discriminatory literacy tests and other devises, then employed by twenty-one states.[14] It empowered the federal government to exert oversight of states and local jurisdictions with a past history of discrimination and even authorized the deployment of federal voter registrars.

Little known is the fact that the VRA reduced the residency and registration deadlines to no more than thirty days. While these laws may be targeted to address discriminatory practices, they broadly benefit people who move: young, less affluent, renters. The VRA also prohibited any state from denying the vote for president to a person who had moved after a registration deadline. In response, some states enacted policies to provide special "presidential ballots" to recent movers, even those registering at their jurisdiction of new residence on Election Day, while others allowed persons who establish residency in another state after that state's registration deadline to vote an absentee ballot in their state of former residence.

Presidential ballots may be considered a special case of a policy innovation known as election-day registration or – in the case when it is coupled with early voting – same-day registration. Same-day registration allows eligible persons to register and to vote an entire ballot, not just for president, in one stop either at their new polling place or at a local election administration office. Minnesota was the first state to adopt election-day registration in 1973, and a number of other states followed. Other states intentionally or inadvertently implemented same-day registration when their voter registration deadline and absentee ballot request deadline overlapped. During this window, eligible persons can register and request an absentee ballot at their local election administration office. North Carolina specifically permits same-day registration (but not election-day registration) for early voters by providing for it at special early voting polling locations.

Studies of election-day registration find that this policy is related to a substantial increase in voter participation.[15] One reason this is true is that unregistered persons tend to register closer to the election,[16] which is why shorter registration deadlines are correlated with higher turnout.[17] Tying together registration and the act of voting aligns the intent to vote expressed through registration with the act of voting. Another likely reason is that, as Squire, Wolfinger, and Glass assert, "The requirement that citizens must register anew after each change in residence constitutes the key stumbling block in the trip to the polls."[18] Same-day registration reduces the re-registration burden for recent movers. A step short of same-day registration is portable registration.[19] The 1993 National Voter Registration Act (NVRA) requires local jurisdictions to allow registrants who are recent movers within their jurisdiction to re-register their new address and to vote at one of three locations: their old polling place, their new polling place, or a central election administration office. A handful of states has broadened the scope of this policy, enabling portable registration for registrants who move anywhere within the state.[20] These policies do increase turnout rates among recent movers. However, the act of moving depresses the likelihood that individuals will vote beyond the structural impediments posed by registration, even when controlling for the lower socio-economic status of movers, perhaps because they do not feel a strong attachment to their new community.

Local election officials are tasked with the difficult responsibility of managing the voter registration rolls for persons who move or otherwise become ineligible. Persons who remain on voter registration rolls are known as deadwood, and local election officials attempt to remove these individuals through a process known as purging. The federal government has become increasingly involved in attempting to improve registration practices by setting minimum guidelines for purging through the NVRA and requiring states to create statewide registration rolls through HAVA. Still, errors remain that can prevent an individual from voting when he or she is incorrectly purged or her/his information is incorrectly entered into a registration database. A policy innovation from HAVA involves provisional balloting, which requires poll workers to provide anyone who has a voter registration problem a special ballot that can be set aside and counted later if the registration issue can be resolved upon further investigation. Of the 2.1 million provisional ballots cast in 2008, the EAC reported that 1.7 million were counted.[21] To put it another way, 1.3 percent of the voters who participated in the 2008 election were able to have their vote counted through provisional balloting.[22]

States must follow minimal NVRA guidelines when purging their voters. However, some states have adopted database matching procedures that have the potential to deny prospective registrants placement on the voter registration rolls when the information they provide on their voter registration form does not match with another database, such as a driver's licence database.[23] Likewise, persons who are unfortunate enough to have the same name and birthdate as a person in a felon database may find themselves automatically purged. Some groups have used the statistical curiosity that name and birthdate matches occur with surprising frequency when a large number of people are matched against one another in order to argue in favor of photo identification laws to prevent alleged instances of double voting, which are almost always statistical coincidences.[24] Indiana and Georgia have enacted strict photo identification laws, and Arizona has enacted a proof of citizenship as a condition of registration. These laws have sparked an intense debate reminiscent of the positions taken by those who believe voting is a right (who oppose these laws) and those who believe voting is a privilege (who support them).[25] To date, because the affected populations are small, the scholarly research is mixed as to the effects of these laws.[26]

Another approach to reducing the burden of voter registration involves providing more opportunities to register. The NVRA is better known as "Motor Voter" because it requires states to provide voter registration forms at Department of Motor Vehicles and state welfare assistance offices, thereby targeting low-propensity voters with a voter registration opportunity. Wolfinger and Rosenstone championed Motor Voter as a means of dramatically increasing the country's turnout rate by enabling registration for all persons.[27] However, that vision has not been realized. The NVRA is related only to minor, if any, appreciable turnout rate increases,[28] although some charge that states have not faithfully enacted Motor Voter.[29] Another policy innovation that has recently gained momentum among the states involves providing registration to high school students as young as age sixteen through what is known as "preregistration."[30] This policy allows registration to be coupled with high school civics education and is found to be associated with modest turnout rate increases among traditionally hard-to-reach young people who may not attend college.

While there may be some questions concerning their implementation, these policies to expand registration opportunities have realized only modest turnout rate increases. Even the most potent policy, election-day registration, only realizes somewhere between five to seven percentage points of increased turnout.[31] These scholarly findings thus support the conclusion drawn from Table 4.1. While voter registration is a barrier, there remains something that keeps many potential voters on the sidelines.

Convenience Voting
Apparent from Table 4.1, some eligible persons are registered but choose not to vote, even in a high-stimulus presidential election such as that of 2008. Another approach seeking to increase voter participation involves

making the act of voting more convenient. Primary among such attempts is a proliferation of alternative methods of casting ballots in advance of an election, either by mail or in-person at special polling locations. Another administration practice that has attracted some attention is better placement of polling places in high traffic locations.

The American experience with mail balloting dates back at least to the Civil War. Soldiers were permitted by some states to vote by mailing a marked ballot to their friends or family to be delivered to their home polling place on election day.[32] Some Civil War soldiers were permitted to vote on election day at a special polling place within their units. At the turn of the twentieth century, many states adopted a similar method of remote election day absentee voting for military personnel and for civilians who were living away from their homes.[33] In 1913, North Dakota became the first state to allow mail balloting for travelling citizens, often at a county courthouse within the citizen's home state. Wisconsin soon followed, adding provisions for sick and disabled voters.[34]

Today, there are essentially three types of mail balloting.[35] The first involves a *traditional absentee ballot* that requires a voter to provide a valid reason for receiving a mail ballot, and the second involves a *no-excuse absentee ballot* that, as the name implies, is available to all eligible voters. Depending on state law, eligible voters may obtain their mail ballots by requesting an absentee ballot or they may be allowed to sign up to permanently receive a mail ballot. The third type of mail balloting involves an *all-mail ballot election* in which all voters are required to cast their ballots by mail. In 1977, Monterey County, California, held the first jurisdiction-wide all-mail ballot election.[36] In 1998, by voter initiative, Oregon adopted statewide all-mail ballot elections. Other jurisdictions may run all-mail ballot elections for all their voters, for certain voters in precincts for which it is difficult to provide a polling place, or for only certain types of elections.

Recently, mail balloting has become intertwined with a related method of casting ballots known as *early voting*. Interestingly, early voting's historical roots extend back to the nation's founding, when voters sometimes had to travel long distances over treacherous terrain. Virginia representative Samuel Chilton, arguing in opposition of establishing a single uniform day on which to hold federal elections, stated: "frequently ... all the votes were not polled in one day [because Virginia is] mountainous and interconnected by large streams of water" that, in times of inclement weather, impede travel.[37] The modern version of early voting likely evolved from an election administration practice that allows eligible voters who are seeking to cast an absentee ballot to request and cast that ballot in-person at their central election office. Increasingly, jurisdictions have operated additional special polling places to accommodate these voters. Early voting is most commonly associated with no-excuse absentee voting at designated polling places. However, some jurisdictions that require an absentee excuse have begun providing additional polling places, muddying the definition of what constitutes an early vote.

In-person early voting is predominantly favoured in the eastern states, and mail balloting is predominantly favoured in the western states. However, it is difficult to distinguish mail ballots and early votes in statistics reported by election officials and in the minds of voters. The available statistics indicate a clear increase in their use by American voters. Historical studies in 1936 and 1960 found that absentee ballots increased from 2 to 5 percent, respectively, for all ballots counted in these elections.[38] Recent aggregate statistics indicate that absentee and early voting increased from at least 8 percent in 1992, 8 percent in 1994, 11 percent in 1996, 12 percent in 1998, 16 percent in 2000, 16 percent in 2002, and 23 percent in 2004 to 31 percent, or at least 40.6 million voters, in 2008.[39]

Providing early voting may logically appear to increase turnout rates. Early voting may lower voting costs by providing a means for a person who is unable to vote on election day to vote and by providing voters with an opportunity to carefully review information about the candidates on a ballot. Further, voter mobilization studies find that a reminder to vote increases voting propensities:[40] What greater reminder is there than having a ballot in hand? However, a method such as mail balloting may impose additional costs and reduce other benefits. A voter may be required to vote in two stages: first to request a mail ballot and second to return a received ballot. There may be benefits realized by voting in-person on election day, such as sense of belonging to a community or receiving an "I Voted" sticker. Theoretically, then, the voting calculus may not be straightforward. A new choice may have greater net costs than existing choices and, thus, may not change an individual's behaviour.

To date, a number of scholarly studies have investigated whether early voting does indeed increase voter turnout. The authors of perhaps the most comprehensive and recent of these studies find that no-excuse absentee balloting increases long-run turnout rates by an average of three percentage points and that no-excuse in-person early voting also increases long-run turnout rates by an average of three percentage points.[41] Other scholars find that early voting has a modest positive effect on turnout in state and local elections.[42] Some find that turnout is stimulated only if the political parties mobilize their supporters to take advantage of early voting.[43] On the other hand, some scholars find that positive turnout effects in presidential elections are either short-lived[44] or non-existent.[45]

A related question concerns who would be stimulated to vote. A fairly consistent finding among these studies is that early voters are different from in-person election-day voters. The 2008 CPS shows that early voters were markedly older: 36 percent of early voters were over age sixty compared with 24 percent of election-day voters. However, on other demographic profiles, such as race and education, the CPS shows that election-day voters and early voters are virtually identical.[46] This coincides with some scholarly findings.[47] In contrast, others find that voting early narrowly benefits certain groups likely to take advantage of the alternative voting methods.[48] They also find that it mobilizes persons already predisposed to vote but does not mobilize disadvantaged persons.[49]

Voting-by-mail has implementation issues that prevent some ballots from being counted as votes. The 2008 Election Day Survey reports that 3.0 million domestic mail ballots were "lost" when ballots sent to voters were unreturned.[50] These unreturned mail ballots occur predominantly among the six states that provide most of the permanent mail ballot transmissions (e.g., California alone had over 1 million unreturned mail ballots). These unreturned domestic mail ballots may be related to the challenges of maintaining accurate voter registration addresses caused by voters who are uninterested in participating in an election and fail to return their ballots. The ballot return rates are lower for overseas citizens, with about 300,000 unreturned ballots.[51] The 2008 Election Day Survey also offers various reasons why approximately 400,000 domestic mail ballots were rejected (e.g., ballots were returned after a deadline, voters failed to properly follow procedures in signing or sealing the ballot return envelopes). California attempts to mitigate these problems by allowing voters to drop their mail ballots at polling places where poll workers can verify that procedures were properly followed; in 2008, slightly more than 1 million Californians returned their mail ballots in this manner.[52]

Another way to make voting more convenient involves making polling places more accessible. In Federalist Number 61,[53] Alexander Hamilton sought to allay fears that the new government would favour mercantile interests by holding elections in large cities that were an "inconvenient distance" from agrarian interests. Section 5 of the Voting Rights Act prohibits some localities from changing polling place locations without first establishing that the new location will not have a discriminatory effect. Recently, scholars have indeed found that inconvenient polling place location can slightly depress turnout,[54] and this extends to the location of in-person early voting polling locations.[55] A related policy innovation recently implemented in some western states involves vote centers – that is, polling places situated in high-traffic areas such as shopping centers, where anyone can vote on election day. When properly located, vote centers are associated with modest positive turnout effects.[56]

The sum of the scholarly work on convenience voting generally finds that making voting more accessible modestly increases turnout rates, although there is some disagreement about the magnitude of this increase and about who benefits from mail ballot and early voting. However, it is clear that, even if the maximal increases were realized by improving access, overall turnout rates would only increase by a few percentage points. For most Americans, the source of the impediment to participation must lie elsewhere.

The Electoral System

A distinctive feature of American elections is that there is no national election for any office. Elections to the House of Representatives occur within 435 single-member districts apportioned among the fifty states, and elections to each state's two US Senate seats are similarly held within the fifty states. Even the president is not directly elected by popular vote; rather, the voters cast their vote for electors to the Electoral College, who then vote for the president. Each state receives a number of electors equal to its representation in Congress: the number of seats they have in the House of Representatives plus their two senators. All but two states award all their electors to the presidential candidate who wins the most votes in their state.

A consequence of these decentralized elections is that few voters experience high levels of electoral competition either in House elections[57] or in presidential elections for their states' electors.[58] Only approximately 10 percent of House districts are considered competitive by election handicappers, and only a few states are considered so-called presidential "battlegrounds." In numerous studies, electoral competition has been found to be consistently correlated with higher voter turnout.[59] As an example of the effect of competition on turnout, consider that North Carolina became a battleground state in 2008, whereas in 2004 it was not. The state's turnout rate increased from 58 percent (in 2004) to 66 percent (in 2008) among those eligible to vote.[60] If voters are not presented with meaningful choices, there is little reason to expect them to vote.

Changing the method of electing the president might require amending the US Constitution, which describes the Electoral College process. Amending the US Constitution is difficult because amendments require super-majority approval in Congress and state legislatures. However, a loophole exists that could bring competition to states that are not considered battlegrounds. The US Constitution is silent on how states select their electors. For example, in the early days of the country some states did not hold direct elections; instead, state governments chose who would be their electors. This loophole has inspired what is known as the National Popular Vote Plan. Under this plan, states would enter a compact whereby they would award their Electoral College electors to the presidential candidate who won the national popular vote. If the prerequisite number of states entered into this compact, such that they constituted a majority of the Electoral College, then these states would effectively elect the president based on the national popular vote. As of 2010, six states have formally entered into the compact. However, all are Democratic-leaning states. The perception exists that the compact would favour Democrats since, in 2000, Al Gore won the national popular vote but George W. Bush won the Electoral College. Such counter-majoritarian outcomes are possible in district-based systems, of which the Electoral College is an example.[61] Without strong support from Republicans, the likelihood is low that the National Popular Vote Plan will be implemented any time soon.

Congressional elections are more of a Rube Goldberg device than are presidential elections. Presidential, and often US Senate and governor, elections most often pit two highly qualified and equally funded candidates against one another. Candidates for House and state legislative offices often do not have equal resources and play on an uneven field. Sometimes there is effectively no electoral competition whatsoever because only one major-party candidate is running in a district that is highly favourable to her/his party, a situation that occurs more frequently in state legislative elections. A number of reform proposals have been proffered in various guises to increase electoral competition in House and state legislative elections, including campaign finance reform, public financing of elections, redistricting reform, and term limits.[62]

Improvements in participation do not necessarily need to arise through changing the electoral system directly or through altering the administration of elections. The campaigns have rediscovered face-to-face voter mobilization efforts, which were one of the hallmarks of the nineteenth-century political machines. In place of ward bosses we now have volunteers recruited through the internet, and in place of the ward bosses' intimate knowledge of their neighbourhoods we now have elaborate voter registration databases that enable the "micro-targeting" of messages to specific types of voters, from hockey moms to Volvo drivers.[63] These voter mobilization contacts are known to stimulate participation by upwards of nine or more percentage points.[64] A caveat is that the contact rate between volunteers and persuadable voters can be low, so these efforts require substantial resources in order to have measurable overall turnout rate boosts. These resources are typically only deployed by the political parties in competitive races, which means that people in competitive areas are maximally stimulated while those elsewhere are left to their own devices.

Conclusion

The United States has a unique, highly decentralized electoral system whose lack of uniformity may prevent the adoption of best practices to increase voter turnout. However, the flexibility in the system allows states and local jurisdictions the freedom to experiment. Much of what we know works best to stimulate voter participation, we know from the variety of practices deployed across units of analysis that have a relatively similar overarching political culture and an electoral framework. However, the downside is that, since there are perceived political consequences to changing electoral laws, the decentralized American electoral system sometimes prevents the widespread adoption of best practices. At those infrequent times when a coalition at the national level can reach consensus, the federal government will take action – as it has done with the VRA, the NVRA, HAVA, and the Military and Overseas Voter Empowerment Act.

If I were to recommend best practices to improve voter participation, I would suggest the following. First, place the responsibility for registering voters with the state and local governments, and allow same-day registration in instances in which database management errors would otherwise prevent an eligible person from voting. This would likely increase overall national turnout rates by about five percentage points. Second, move to a national popular vote for president and make other changes to encourage more completion in lower ballot races. This may be worth about another five percentage points in turnout. Third, improve the convenience of voting by further experimenting with early voting methods and other administrative changes, like smart placement of polling places in high-traffic areas and exploring the use of internet voting. This may be worth another couple of percentage points in turnout. Fourth, promote more civic education in high schools as this may be worth a percentage point.

The sum of these changes may be less than their parts as we do not truly know how these policies interact with one another. Working within the current system to enact these changes might boost participation to the low to mid-70 percent range, well short of the high watermark of turnout experienced in the heyday of American political machines during the nineteenth century, when turnout rates routinely exceeded 80 percent of those eligible to vote.[65] It may be that this is the best that Americans can do. The United States has grown too large to have political parties effectively organize its social fabric, as they did when turnout rates routinely exceeded 80 percent. Compulsory voting is not an option within the nation's current political culture, which emphasizes limited government and individual freedom. Restructuring the electoral system to experiment with some form of proportional representation has had limited success at the local level, and it is unlikely to be implemented by state or national governments since the political parties and the public are notoriously risk averse and changing the electoral system would entail major changes (assuming, given recent participation declines experienced among countries employing proportional representation without compulsory voting, that it would result in higher turnout).[66] Even my recommended best practices will likely only be adopted piecemeal among the states. The recent good news is that innovation and incremental policy steps continue to move inexorably towards the goal of making voting a right for all American citizens, thereby reducing this facet of the nation's democracy deficit. It may just take a while for that goal to be realized.

NOTES

1 Alexander Keyssar, *The Right to Vote: The Contested History of Democracy in the United States* (New York: Basic Books, 2001).
2 For example, James DeNardo, "Turnout and the Vote: The Joke's on the Democrats," *American Political Science Review* 74, 2 (1980): 406-80; Benjamin Highton and Raymond E. Wolfinger, "The Political Implications of Higher Turnout," *British Journal of Political Science* 31, 1 (2001): 179-92; Jack Citrin, Eric Schickler, and John Sides, "What if Everyone Voted? Simulating the Impact of Increased Turnout in Senate Elections," *American Journal of Political Science* 47, 1 (2003): 75-90.
3 For example, Thomas Patterson, *The Vanishing Voter: Public Involvement in an Age of Uncertainty* (New York: Alfred A. Knopf Publishers, 2002); Ruy Teixeira, *The Disappearing American Voter* (Washington, DC: Brookings Institution Press, 1992);

Raymond. E. Wolfinger and Stephen Rosenstone, *Who Votes?* (New Haven: Yale University Press, 1980).
4 See http://www.nass.org/.
5 Robert S. Erikson, "Why Do People Vote? Because They are Registered," *American Politics Quarterly* 9 (1981): 259-76; Richard J. Timpone, "Structure, Behavior, and Voter Turnout in the United States," *American Political Science Review* 92, 1 (1998): 145-58.
6 Mark N. Franklin, *Voter Turnout and the Dynamics of Electoral Competition in Established Democracies since 1945* (Cambridge: Cambridge University Press, 2004).
7 The Census Bureau asks two questions that are used here to construct turnout rates by race and ethnicity. Respondents are asked their race, with the permitted response categories being White, Black, American-Indian/Alaskan Native, Asian, Hawaiian/Pacific Islander, and all combinations of these categories. Respondents are separately asked if they are or are not of Hispanic ethnicity. Table 4.1 reports voting and registration rates for whites not of Hispanic ethnicity, all blacks in one or more combinations not of Hispanic ethnicity, and all who identified themselves as Hispanic ethnicity regardless of their race. The residual categories are not reported.
8 Michael P. McDonald and Thomas Schaller, "Voter Mobilization in the 2008 Presidential Election," in *The Change Election: Money, Mobilization and Persuasion in the 2008 Federal Elections*, ed. David Magleby (Philadelphia: Temple University Press, 2011).
9 Michael P. McDonald, "Voter Turnout in the 2010 Midterm Election," *The Forum* 8, 4 (2010): Article 8.
10 William H. Riker and Peter C. Ordeshook, "A Theory of the Calculus of Voting," *American Political Science Review* 62, 1 (1968): 25-42.
11 Keyssar, *Right to Vote*, 151-52.
12 J. Morgan Kousser, *Colorblind Injustice: Minority Voting Rights and the Undoing of the Second Reconstruction* (Chapel Hill: University of North Carolina Press, 1999).
13 Keyssar, *Right to Vote*, 153. See also Walter Dean Burnham, "Theory and Voting Research: Some Reflections on Converse's Change in the American Electorate," *American Political Science Review* 68, 3 (1974): 1002-23.
14 Michael P. McDonald and John Samples, eds., *The Marketplace of Democracy: Electoral Competition and American Politics* (Washington, DC: Brookings Institution Press, 2006).
15 For example, Glenn E. Mitchell and Christopher Wlezien, "The Impact of Legal Constraints on Voter Registration, Turnout, and the Composition of the American Electorate," *Political Behavior* 17, 2 (1995): 179-202; Staci L. Rhine, "An Analysis of the Impact of Registration Factors on Turnout in 1992," *Political Behavior* 18, 2 (1996): 171-85.
16 James G. Gimpel, Joshua Dyck, and Daron Shaw, "Election-Year Stimuli and the Timing of Voter Registration," *Party Politics* 13, 3 (2007): 351-74.
17 For example, Wolfinger and Rosenstone, *Who Votes?*
18 Peverill Squire, Raymond E. Wolfinger, and David P. Glass, "Residential Mobility and Voter Turnout," *American Political Science Review* 81, 1 (1987): 45-65.

19 Michael P. McDonald, "Portable Voter Registration," *Political Behavior* 30, 4 (2008): 491-501.
20 Ibid.
21 See http://archives.eac.gov/.
22 This is likely an overstatement for the turnout benefit since a few states use provisional ballots for other purposes. For example, Ohio uses provisional ballots to implement its statewide portable voter registration.
23 Justin Levitt, Wendy R. Weiser, and A. Ana Muñoz, *Making the List: Database Matching and Verification Processes for Voter Registration* (New York: Brennan Center for Justice at NYU School of Law, 2006).
24 Michael P. McDonald and Justin Levitt, "Seeing Double Voting: An Extension of the Birthday Problem," *Election Law Journal* 7, 2 (2008): 111-22.
25 Stephen Ansolabehere and Nathanial Persily, "Vote Fraud in the Eye of the Beholder: The Role of Public Opinion in the Challenge to Voter Identification Requirements," *Harvard Law Review* 121 (2007): 1737-74.
26 For example, see Michael Alvarez, Thad E. Hall, and Susan D. Hyde, eds., *Election Fraud: Detecting and Deterring Electoral Manipulation* (Washington, DC: Brookings Institution Press, 2008).
27 Wolfinger and Rosenstone, *Who Votes?*
28 S. Knack, "Does 'Motor Voter' Work? Evidence from State-Level Data," *Journal of Politics* 57, 3 (1995): 796-811.
29 Douglas Hess and Scott Novakowski, "Neglecting the National Voter Registration Act: 1995-2007: Project Vote and Demos Report," http://www.projectvote.org/.
30 Michael P. McDonald and Matthew Thornburg, "Registering the Youth through Voter Preregistration," *New York University Journal of Legislation and Public Policy* 13 (2010): 551-72.
31 For example, see Benjamin Highton, "Easy Registration and Voter Turnout," *Journal of Politics* 59, 2 (1997): 565-75; McDonald, "Portable Voter Registration," 2008; Mitchell and Wlezien, "Impact of Legal Constraints"; Rhine, "Analysis."
32 Duncan C. Lee, "Absent Voting," *Journal of the Society of Comparative Legislation* 16, 2 (1916): 333-45.
33 P. Orman Ray, "Military Absent-Voting Laws," *American Political Science Review* 12, 3 (1918): 461-69; P. Orman Ray, "Absent-Voting Laws, 1917," *American Political Science Review* 12, 2 (1918): 251-61.
34 Ray, "Military Absent-Voting Laws."
35 Nathan Camenska, Jan E. Leighley, Jonathan Nagler, and Daniel P. Tokaji, "Report on the 1972-2008 Early and Absentee Voting Dataset," in *Pew Charitable Trusts Make Voting Work Report* (Washington, DC: Pew Center for the States, 2009); Paul Gronke, "The Early Voting Information Center," http://www.earlyvoting.net/.
36 David B. Magleby, "Participation in Mail Ballot Elections," *Western Political Quarterly* 40, 1 (1987): 79-91.
37 *Congressional Globe* 14, 1 (1844): 15.
38 See Paul G. Steinbicker, "Absentee Voting in the United States," *American Political Science Review* 32, 5 (1938): 898-907; William G. Andrews, "American Voting

Participation," *Western Political Quarterly* 19, 4 (1966): 639-52. These estimates likely overstate absentee voting. They are constructed by extrapolating absentee statistics in a few states that maintained records of absentee voting, which were likely those states most interested in providing access to early voting to the entire country.

39 I consult, for Mitofsky International and Edison Media Research, the media's exit polling firms. To accurately project election results on election day, exit pollsters need to estimate turnout and the proportion of votes that may be cast early. Towards this end, the exit polling firms have worked with the Associated Press to collect aggregate statistics on early voting from states' election administrators. Since 2004, I have collected these early voting data from state election administrators. I work with the Associated Press Election Research and Quality Control Unit to cross-check and verify the statistics we each collect independently.

40 For example, Alan S. Gerber and Donald P. Green, "The Effects of Canvassing, Telephone Calls, and Direct Mail on Voter Turnout: A Field Experiment," *American Political Science Review* 94, 3 (2000): 653-63.

41 Jan E. Leighley and Jonathan Nagler, "The Turnout Effects of Non-Precinct Place Voting Reforms: Pew Charitable Trusts Make Voting Work Report," http://www.pewcenteronthestates.org/.

42 Adam J. Berinsky, Nancy Burns, and Michael W. Traugott, "Who Votes by Mail? A Dynamic Model of the Individual-Level Consequences of Voting-by-Mail Systems," *Public Opinion Quarterly* 65, 2 (2001): 178-97; Peter L. Francia and Paul S. Herrnson, "The Synergistic Effect of Campaign Effort and Election Reform on Voter Turnout in State Legislative Elections," *State Politics and Policy Quarterly* 4, 1 (2004): 74-93; J.A. Karp and S.A. Banducci, "Going Postal: How All-Mail Elections Influence Turnout," *Political Behavior* 22, 3 (2000): 223-39; Magleby, "Participation in Mail Ballot Elections"; Priscilla L. Southwell and Justin I. Burchett, "The Effect of All-Mail Elections on Voter Turnout," *American Politics Research* 28, 1 (2000): 72-79.

43 Eric Oliver, "The Effects of Eligibility Restrictions and Party Activity on Absentee Voting and Overall Turnout," *American Journal of Political Science* 40, 2 (1996): 498-513.

44 Joseph D. Giammo and Brian J. Brox, "Reducing the Costs of Participation," *Political Research Quarterly* 63, 2 (2010): 295-303.

45 Mary Fitzgerald, "Greater Convenience but Not Greater Turnout," *American Politics Research* 33, 6 (2005): 842-67; Paul Gronke, Eva Galanes-Rosenbaum, and Peter A. Miller, "Early Voting and Turnout," *PS: Political Science and Politics* 40, 4 (2007): 639-45.

46 In 2004, 82 percent of early voters were non-Hispanic white compared with 79 percent of election-day voters. President Obama's candidacy had an apparent mobilizing effect for minorities. In 2008, 76 percent of early voters were non-Hispanic white compared with 77 percent of election-day voters. In 2008, 60 percent of early voters had at least some college education compared with 54 percent for election-day voters. I compiled these statistics using the sources cited in Table 4.1.

47 Matt A. Barreto, Matthew J. Streb, Mara Marks, and Fernando Guerra, "Do Absentee Voters Differ from Polling Place Voters?," *Public Opinion Quarterly* 70, 2 (2006):

224-34; J.A. Karp and S.A. Banducci, "Absentee Voting, Mobilization, and Participation," *American Politics Research* 29, 2 (2001): 183-95; Leighley and Nagler, "Turnout Effects"; Pricilla L. Southwell and Justin Burchett, *Does Changing the Rules Change the Players? The Effect of All-Mail Elections on the Composition of the Electorate*, vol. 81 (Hoboken, NJ: Wiley, 2000).

48 Karp and Banducci, "Absentee Voting"; William Lyons and John M. Scheb, "Early Voting and the Timing of the Vote: Unanticipated Consequences of Electoral Reform," *State and Local Government Review* 31, 2 (1999): 147-52.

49 Magleby, "Participation in Mail Ballot Elections"; Berinsky et al., "Who Votes by Mail?"; Karp and Banducci, "Absentee Voting"; Oliver, "Effects of Eligibility Restrictions"; Robert M. Stein, "Early Voting," *Public Opinion Quarterly* 62, 1 (1998): 57-69.

50 http://archives.eac.gov/. These statistics exclude Oregon and Washington State because of the inconsistent manner in which these states report statistics for their all-mail ballot elections.

51 Ibid.

52 Personal correspondence with Joe Holland, Santa Barbara Clerk and County Reporter, 24 December 2008.

53 Alexander Hamilton, "Federalist Number 61," in *The Federalist: A Commentary on the Constitution of the United States*, ed. Alexander Hamilton, John Jay, and James Madison (New York: Random House, 1982).

54 Moshe Haspel and H. Gibbs Knotts, "Location, Location, Location: Precinct Placement and the Costs of Voting," *Journal of Politics* 67, 2 (2005): 560-73; Joshua J. Dyck and James Gimpel, "Distance, Turnout, and the Convenience of Voting," *Social Science Quarterly* 86, 3 (2005): 531-48.

55 James G. Gimpel, Joshua J. Dyck, and Daron R. Shaw, "Location, Knowledge and Time Pressures in the Spatial Structure of Convenience Voting," *Electoral Studies* 25, 1 (2006): 35-58.

56 Robert M. Stein and Greg Vonnahme, "Engaging the Unengaged Voter: Vote Centers and Voter Turnout," *Journal of Politics* 70, 2 (2008): 487-97.

57 For example, McDonald and Samples, *Marketplace of Democracy*; Gary Jacobson, *The Politics of Congressional Elections*, 7th ed. (New York: Longman, 2008); Schickler et al., "What if Everyone Voted?"

58 Thomas M. Holbrook and Scott D. McClurg, "The Mobilization of Core Supporters: Campaigns, Turnout, and Electoral Composition in United States Presidential Elections," *American Journal of Political Science* 49, 4 (2005): 689-703; Daron Shaw, *The Race to 270: The Electoral College and the Campaign Strategies of 2000 and 2004* (Chicago: University of Chicago Press, 2006).

59 For a meta-analysis of thirty-two studies, see Andrew Blais, *To Vote or Not to Vote?: The Merits and Limits of Rational Choice Theory* (Pittsburgh: University of Pittsburgh Press, 2000).

60 McDonald, "Voter Turnout in the 2010 Midterm Election."

61 Arend Lijphart, *Patterns of Democracy: Government Forms and Performance in Thirty-Six Countries* (New Haven: Yale University Press, 1999).

62 For a review of these proposals, see McDonald and Samples, *Marketplace of Democracy*.

63 Sunshine D. Hillygus and Todd G. Shields, *The Persuadable Voter: Wedge Issues in Presidential Campaigns* (Princeton: Princeton University Press, 2009); McDonald and Schaller, "Voter Mobilization."
64 For example, Gerber and Green, "Effects of Canvassing."
65 Michael P. McDonald, "American Voter Turnout in Historical Perspective," in *Oxford Handbook of American Elections and Political Behavior*, ed. Jan Leighley (Oxford: Oxford University Press, 2010).
66 Franklin, *Voter Turnout*.

5 Can Canada's Past Electoral Reforms Help Us to Understand the Debate over Its Method of Election?

JOHN C. COURTNEY

> *It's not the voting that's democracy, it's the counting.*
> – Tom Stoppard, Jumpers *(Act One)*

This chapter offers a two-part answer to the question posed in its title. The first recalls the electoral reforms of the past, the reasons they were adopted, and the set of "unwritten rules of electoral reform" they collectively introduced at the federal level in Canada. The second part examines the differences between the previous electoral reforms and the issue of replacing the current method of election with some form of proportional representation. It explains how the convergence of three events in the late twentieth and early twenty-first centuries (democratic deficit discussions, front-burner elections, and provincial initiatives on electoral change) brought the issue of replacing plurality voting to the fore. It also describes the many obstacles that changing the method of election would face, including the complexity of the issue, the absence of a single agreed-upon alternative to plurality voting, the divisions within elite and public opinions over the desirability of change, and disagreement about the purpose of elections that characterizes electoral system debates, which combine to give the issue a "stand-alone" quality.

The essential building blocks of Canadian elections described briefly in the first section of this chapter – the franchise, electoral administration, redistricting, financing of elections, and the electoral registry – have transformed the country's electoral administration from what it was at the time of Confederation into one of the fairest, most transparent and inclusive electoral democracies in the world. That is most evident to Canadians when they compare their electoral regime with that of the United States, in which many of the basic elements of electoral management – finance, redistricting, voters lists, and electoral administration – remain unresolved, contentious, and stridently partisan, as Michael McDonald reports (Chapter 4, this volume).

The second section of the chapter highlights the debate over Canada's method of election. This is a far from recent debate, having had a markedly cyclical history, with roots that can be traced back to the late nineteenth century. The theoretical context within which the periodic debates over plurality voting are positioned employs what I label a contrasting "front-burner and back-burner" explanation of elections. As well, it draws on path dependency to help explain why the sequencing of events and processes has, with time, introduced such potentially high costs for the principal political actors that changing the rules of the electoral game is not a favoured option for those closest to power. No such equivalent costs were present at the time that the earlier reforms were put in place in Canada.

In keeping with the theme of *Imperfect Democracies*, I conclude by noting that conflicting democratic theories come into play when debate focuses on replacing plurality voting with a more proportional method of translating votes into seats. This, too, was not the case with earlier electoral reforms. As would almost certainly be true of established democracies in general, the differences of opinion over the purpose that elections serve, and the relationship between elections and democracy, weigh heavily in explaining whether or not there is sufficient consensus in favour of making changes to the electoral regime.

Five Principal Electoral Reforms since Confederation

There have been five major adjustments to Canada's electoral regime since Confederation: (1) the comprehensive enlargement of the franchise; (2) the establishment of an independent office for the administration of elections; (3) the regular redesign of parliamentary constituencies by nonpartisan commissions; (4) the adoption of strict election financing legislation together with a substantial measure of state funding of parties and candidates; and (5) the introduction of a system for regularly updating an electronic database of electors. A brief description of these reforms follows.

Franchise, 1867-2002

All Canadian citizens eighteen years of age and over may vote in federal and provincial elections. That has not always been the case. Changing social values led, at the end of the First World War, to female enfranchisement and, at the end of the Second World War, to accommodations with an increasingly diverse population. Since 1945, the right to vote has been extended to groups previously denied it, such as Indians, Inuit, Chinese, and Japanese Canadians. Court rulings based on the Canadian Charter of Rights and Freedoms (adopted in 1982) explain a further widening of the franchise. In the past decade and a half, the Supreme Court of Canada and the Federal Court of Canada have struck down a number of statutory restrictions to the franchise. Citing the "right to vote" section of the Charter (section 3), the courts have extended the vote to mentally handicapped persons, judges, and prisoners. (Compare this to the ongoing debate in the United States, as Michael McDonald [Chapter 4, this volume] documents, with respect to whether voting is a privilege or a right.) There are now no groups (or, for that matter, individuals, apart from the chief electoral officer of Canada [for reasons of impartiality]) prohibited from voting federally. The expansion of Canada's electorate since Confederation has been dramatic. At the time of Canada's first federal election in 1867, 15 percent of the total population was eligible to vote. Today the figure is in the order of 70 percent.[1]

Office of Chief Electoral Officer, 1920

The first elections in post-Confederation Canada were often corrupt affairs. The electoral process, though established under statute, was skewed in the governing party's favour. Supporters of those in office were rewarded with election-day jobs, and corrupt practices by election officials and voters alike (though technically a violation of the law) were widespread. Even the counting of ballots was suspect, and reports of election fraud of various sorts were not uncommon.

Canadians have had impartial officials run their elections at the federal level for close to a century. More recently, this has been true of the provinces as well. To put an end to partisanship in electoral administration, to establish uniform operating standards and rules for the conduct of elections, and to avoid a repeat of the partisan manipulation of federal election laws that Canada had witnessed in the wartime election of 1917, Parliament in 1920 created an institution that operates independently of the provinces, parties, candidates, and governments.

The Office of the Chief Electoral Officer (as the positions are known federally and in every province) has established itself as a model of its kind. It is charged with ensuring that elections are conducted fairly and without bias or advantage for any party, candidate, or partisan interest. The chief electoral officer is chosen by the House of Commons (not the government of the day) and reports directly to Parliament (again, not the government of the day). He or she is charged with several responsibilities, including making certain that all voters have unimpeded access to the ballot box; enforcing election legislation, which includes election financing laws; maintaining the register of electors; recruiting and training election officials; overseeing the vote and certifying the count; monitoring election spending by candidates and parties; and ensuring that the broadcasting regulations of the law are respected.

Electoral Redistributions, 1964

For one hundred years after Confederation (1867), federal and provincial redistributions (electoral redistricting) were carried out by elected politicians. To be more precise, redistributions were handled by the governments of the day. The results were predictably partisan and self-serving affairs aimed at maximizing the chances of returning incumbents and of defeating political opponents. The most gerrymandered seats in Canada were often markedly smaller in population than a province's average per-district population.

Partisan gerrymanders are now in the past in Canada. Starting in the 1950s and followed soon by other provinces and the federal Parliament, Manitoba adopted a fundamental reform designed to remove partisanship from the construction of electoral districts. The model of an independent electoral boundary commission was copied from Australia and New Zealand. For federal redistributions the commissions (one for each province following each decennial census) are composed of three members. The chair, by law, must be a judge; the remaining two are typically academics and retired public servants with no overt partisan affiliations.

The commissions (with which Canada has now had five decades of experience) have brought legitimacy to a process long tarnished by its political gamesmanship. They have also reduced the population disparities among the districts to the point at which the overwhelming majority of federal and provincial districts have been constructed with populations within +/−10 percent of that jurisdiction's average population. This is the case even though the commissions have the authority, under the Electoral Boundaries

Readjustment Act, to design seats within +/−25 percent of the province's mean population and, in extraordinary circumstances, to exceed those limits in districts that deserve special attention because of their geography or particular social characteristics. The great majority of Canadians now live in provinces in which their federal vote is more or less on par with that of their fellow provincial citizens. That was rarely the case before the adoption of independent electoral boundary legislation.

That the various commissions should have, if not explicitly at least implicitly, accepted a Canadian (and, admittedly, when compared to the United States, looser) variation of the "one person-one vote" doctrine, is clear from the record. But that fact disguises a different reality with regard to Canada's redistributions. There are wide disparities among the provinces in the population per riding. These derive from the constitutional and statutory provisions governing the allocation of House of Commons seats to the provinces.[2] Comparing, on the basis of the 2001 census, the four federal electoral districts allotted to Prince Edward Island with the 106 allotted to Ontario, we find a per-seat population of 33,824 in Prince Edward Island and 107,642 in Ontario. This translates into a "vote value" that, according to critics of the current method of distributing federal seats among the provinces, gives residents of Canada's smallest province a vote that is "worth" 3.18 times that of its largest province. By contrast, the American formula for allocating House of Representatives districts among the states every ten years, together with a far tighter application of the one person-one vote principle, gives rise to a much smaller difference between the "value of the vote" in the smallest and largest states. Following the decennial American census of 2000, it was "worth" only 1.29 "more" in Wyoming than in California, a difference that is 2.5 times less than that found in the Canadian example. Legislation to add more seats in Ontario, Alberta, and British Columbia, a move proposed by the Harper government, will help – but only marginally so – to reduce the discrepancies in per-vote value.

Election Financing, 1874-

Corruption, illegal transfers of money to candidates and parties, solicitation by politicians (or their bagmen) of sizeable donations for party coffers, and other practices defined the financing of Canadian elections for decades. Consider a financial transaction, and what prompted it, during Canada's second federal election (1872). The prime minister at the time, Sir John A. Macdonald, telegraphed a Montreal rail magnate who had recently been awarded the contract to build the Canadian Pacific Railway: "Immediate and private. I must have another ten thousand – will be the last time of calling. Do not fail me; answer today."[3] When, inevitably, the contents of that telegram were leaked, the government resigned and Alexander Mackenzie and his Liberals came to power. The ensuing election (1874) left Macdonald's Conservatives on the Opposition benches for another four years. Canada's first laws requiring the reporting of election expenses resulted from that "Pacific Scandal."

Since then the laws governing party finance have been augmented and refined many times. This has not always prevented corrupt and illegal practices; however, for the most part, the level of probity in the financing of politics in Canada has been high. The details of Canada's election finance regime are explained by Lisa Young (Chapter 6, this volume). Suffice it to say that, at the federal level (as well as in many of the provinces), the basic elements of the current law are public disclosure; tight spending controls; modest limits on contribution by individuals (corporations and unions are prohibited from contributing to parties and candidates); generous tax credits for political contributions; tight spending controls on independent advocacy groups; and a substantial measure of public funding through reimbursement of candidates and parties. The per-voter subsidy to parties based on their share of the popular vote in the preceding election (introduced in January 2004) was opposed from the outset by the Conservatives. Given their majority win in 2011, the Harper government will undoubtedly bring that program to an end.

What electoral financing in Canada demonstrates, particularly in contrast to the system in place in the United States, is that a substantial role for the state is an accepted part of the electoral equation. Public funding of parties and candidates figures prominently in the current regime, and the state wields immense power in determining the pertinent rules and guidelines of election finance. Again in contrast to political financing in the United States, and as a consequence of several constitutional challenges to the validity of election expense legislation, the courts in Canada have accepted the existing finance regime as a legitimate expression of the country's democratic values.

Voter Registration, 1997
Canadians had long been accustomed at both the federal and provincial levels to door-to-door enumerations that compiled voters lists in advance of an election. From the early twentieth century enumerators were hired at the outset of a campaign for a few days' work in each of the thousands of polling divisions in the country. Their job was to assemble the lists of eligible voters for each electoral district. The system had three great advantages: currency,

completeness, and cost-effectiveness. It is estimated that between 95 and 97.5 percent of the eligible voting-age population was enumerated federally in the elections following the Second World War. As lists were compiled only when needed, costs were kept to a minimum.

A little more than a decade ago, Parliament approved government-sponsored legislation that replaced door-to-door enumerations with a regularly updated electronic register of voters. The principal reasons given for the change were that advances in technology made such a register feasible; that enumerators in large, ethnically diverse urban districts had faced increasing difficulties in constructing lists at election time; and that, to the relief of both politicians and the general public, electoral campaigns would become shorter in the absence of the need to set aside several days for enumeration and revision of lists at the outset of an election. The so-called "permanent" electoral roll has not always lived up to its advance billing; however, based on experience to date, it is within the 93 to 95 percent accuracy range – only marginally less complete than enumerated lists had been.[4]

Differences and Commonalities

The five reforms to Canada's electoral building blocks fundamentally transformed the country's electoral system. They differed, of course, from one another in several respects. Two deserve mention: (1) length of time to accomplish and (2) principal motivation. Some were carried out promptly – notably, the adoption of legislation mandating commission-designed electoral redistributions and the replacement of enumerations with an electoral registry. Others, most obviously the increasingly more inclusive franchise, took well over a century to reach their present state. With respect to motivating causes, at least two reforms (legislation creating the Office of the Chief Electoral Officer and guaranteeing periodic redistributions by arm's-length commissions) were driven primarily by a public backlash against partisan manipulation of electoral institutions. Granting the vote to women is best explained as having been driven by powerfully mobilized social movements dedicated to seeking inclusion and representation for one-half of the population. In more general terms, the extension of the franchise to women, Asians, First Nations peoples, judges, or prisoners can be interpreted as acceptance of the need to instantiate certain democratic values in the electoral regime, in some cases through court interpretations of the Charter's guarantee of the right to vote.

Together, the reforms collectively established a set of accepted norms for changing the electoral system. They collectively ensured centralized operational and regulatory control of federal elections. For a country often described as one of the most decentralized federal systems in the world, Canada has put in place an administrative and legal framework for its federal elections that stands as the obvious exception to the general rule. Uniform rules govern the conduct of federal elections in all the essential elements: franchise, financing, administration, and broadcasting. Nowhere is the electoral contrast to the United States clearer than in this respect.

In the first years following Confederation, the franchise, the voters lists, and election administration of federal elections remained in the hands of the provinces. That has not been the case now for many decades. Parliament asserted its authority (without challenges from the provinces) to define these and other elements of the electoral system. But more important is the fact that, with rare exceptions, the legal and regulatory regimes governing the conduct of federal elections were adopted with the unanimous support of all the parties in Parliament at the time. Interparty agreement became, in effect, the sine qua non of electoral system reform in Canada. The explanation for that draws on the language used to describe the adoption of election finance regulations: parliamentary unanimity on changes to the electoral building blocks provides compelling evidence of a "cartel-like collusion among parties in Parliament" to adopt rules and regulations that worked to their mutual interests or, expressed differently, to no party's disadvantage.[5]

Why Is This Issue Different?

The picture painted so far is one of an electoral regime that has transformed its fundamental building blocks since the first federal election was held in 1867. The franchise, electoral administration, constituency redistribution, election finance, and voter registration now collectively guarantee Canadians that their elections meet all reasonable criteria of fairness, transparency, responsiveness, and inclusiveness. By any international standards of democratic elections they have been success stories.[6]

But why is it that the sixth electoral building block has so far met a different fate from the earlier five? The current method of voting, whether called single-member plurality (SMP) or first past the post (FPTP), has been a fixture of Canadian elections since the pre-Confederation period. Regardless of the number of candidates contesting an election in a constituency, the winner has always been the one gaining the largest number of votes – whether a majority or a plurality of the votes cast. As the possibility (and increasingly, given the number of parties now contesting federal elections, the reality) of electing a large number of "minority" winners at the constituency level runs counter to the principle of majoritarian democracy, it might be thought that the issue of replacing the plurality vote with some variant of proportional representation would be relatively straightforward. This has not proven to be the case.

The arguments for and against proportional representation (PR) and the plurality vote are detailed elsewhere.[7] Suffice it to say for my purposes that critics of plurality voting base their case principally on grounds of proportionality (of how accurately a party's share of votes is reflected in its share of parliamentary seats) and representation. Supporters of FPTP, on the other hand, base their case on the need to ensure stability and accountability in government and to favour the election of broadly based catch-all parties over sectional parties whose support bases are limited and whose policy agendas are narrow. It is clear from these differences that the debate between the two sides is often carried out at cross-purposes for there is little agreement among the proponents and opponents of FPTP regarding the purpose of elections. More will be said of that last point near the conclusion of this chapter.

To the supporters of PR, a case can be made for electoral change given the number of parties competing in Canadian federal elections. The party winning a majority of the seats more often than not gains office with less than a majority of the votes. Most famously that happened in 1997, when the Chrétien Liberals were returned to office with slightly more than one-half of the House's seats even though they had won barely 38 percent of the national vote. Another twist on the proportionality argument comes from the fact that it is possible, under plurality voting, for the winning party to gain more seats but fewer votes than its principal opponent. This is how the Diefenbaker Conservatives came to power in 1957 and how the Clark Conservatives came to power in 1979. Proponents of PR also argue that, when compared with FPTP, voter turnout levels will rise, the number of women and visible minorities in Parliament will increase, and the probability of electing socially progressive minority or coalition governments will improve.

For their part, those who want to continue the plurality vote say it offers the only chance for a government to win an outright majority of seats in the House of Commons. They see majority governments as the best way to ensure political and economic stability and electoral accountability. They also find a virtue in plurality voting's past encouragement of broadly based accommodative and centrist parties. These are known as "catch-all" parties and are said to be better suited to a country such as Canada, with its pronounced regional, linguistic, and (at least in the past) religious cleavages, than are single-issue, regionally centred parties with relatively narrow bases of support.

Why is it that the call for some form of proportional representation in preference to FPTP has not been accepted? What is different about this issue from the earlier ones that led to fundamental changes in the electoral system? The explanation begins with a brief account of why the issue of changing the electoral system has surfaced in recent years, and it concludes with a description of the principle factors that, in combination, have resulted in the method of voting remaining unchanged to this day.

Three events converged more or less simultaneously to prompt the decade-long debate (from the mid-1990s on) over SMP elections. No previous electoral reform had been preceded by a similar confluence of events.

Democratic Deficit Debate

The "democratic deficit" burst onto the political landscape in Canada and abroad in the 1990s. The term has since gained wide coinage and has a certain obvious utility as a rhetorical device. But it is a term that was by no means applied only to the method of election. As if to underscore its definitional imprecision, the term "democratic deficit" lends itself to multiple uses. A variety of institutional, electoral, and managerial issues and practices have been faulted for contributing to Canada's democratic deficit. Principal among these are:

- an unequal and unelected Senate;
- excessive control by the Prime Minister's Office of cabinet ministers, the legislative agenda, and government operations generally;
- an overly stringent parliamentary whip;
- a demonstrated failure of House committees to act independently of party leadership;
- a general decline of citizen confidence in government, public officials, and the electoral process; and
- an electoral system faulted for its contribution to the plunging levels of voter turnout (see appendix at end of chapter), the underrepresentation of women and minorities in elected office, and the facilitation of "non-majoritarian" election outcomes (i.e., governments elected with a

majority of the seats but not a majority of the votes and/or parties winning more seats but fewer votes than other parties).

In one light, the criticisms of modern democracy encapsulated by the term "democratic deficit" can be seen as support for the "postmaterialist" explanation of contemporary democracy. A decline in the levels of trust in political institutions, of citizen deference to public authority, and of voter participation in parties and elections has characterized late twentieth- and early twenty-first century democracies. Canada has been no exception, although, paradoxically, Canadians have exhibited greater interest in politics than has been the case in most other Western democracies; however, in keeping with citizens of other countries, Canadians have voted in declining numbers in the recent past.[8] In this apparently conflicted context (greater interest in politics but dropping voter participation), it could be expected that proponents of change in the electoral system would have had a perceptible and profound impact on public opinion and have given rise to the replacement of FPTP. This has not proven to be the case.[9]

It is possible, of course, that the source of the problems that contribute to Canada's democratic deficit regarding the method of election has been too narrowly focused on plurality voting. The decline in voter turnout rates, the failure to elect women and minorities "in proportion" to their share of the general population, and the heightened levels of popular discontent with government and politics may be the result of cultural, social, and economic factors as well as the plurality vote. George Perlin identifies four contributors to what he labels the "malaise of Canadian democracy," and the method of election is not among them. They are: (1) the changing post-Second World War economic conditions prompted by the introduction of new technologies and the opening of domestic markets to international competition; (2) a substantial decline in individual participation in networks of social groups, a phenomenon forcefully described in Robert Putnam's "bowling alone" thesis; (3) the effect of television in portraying politics and election campaigns in a largely negative and image-focused style; and (4) the increasingly ineffective and inconsequential role that political parties play in connecting citizens to government.[10]

A Decade of Front-Burner Elections, 1993-2004

The issue of electoral system reform has simmered on the fringes of Canadian politics for over one hundred years.[11] Occasionally, though only sporadically, it has moved from the back to the front burner, where it goes from

TABLE 5.1

Federal election results of 1917 and 1921 / 1988 and 1993

		Seats		Votes (%)
Canada's first back-burner election to be followed by a front-burner election:				
1917	Unionist	153	(65.1%)	57.0
	Laurier Liberal	82	(35.9%)	40.1
	Other/Independent	–		2.9
	Total	235		
1921	Liberal	116	(49.4%)	40.7
	Progressive	65	(27.7%)	23.1
	Conservative	50	(21.3%)	30.3
	Other/Independent	4	(1.7%)	5.9
	Total	235		
The 1988 back-burner election followed by a front-burner election:				
1988	Progressive Conservative	169	(57.3%)	43.0
	Liberal	83	(28.1%)	31.9
	NDP	43	(14.6%)	20.4
	Other	–		4.7
	Total	295		
1993	Liberal	177	(60%)	41.2
	BQ	54	(18.3%)	13.5
	Reform	52	(17.6%)	18.7
	NDP	9	(3.0%)	6.9
	Progressive Conservative	2	(0.6%)	16.0
	Independent	1		–
	Total	295		

Sources: Howard A. Scarrow, *Canada Votes: A Handbook of Federal and Provincial Election Data* (New Orleans: Hauser Press, 1962); Chief Electoral Officer of Canada, *Official Reports on the 1988 and 1993 Federal Elections* (Ottawa, 1998 and 1993).

a simmer to something approaching a boil. I define back-burner elections as those in which a majority government is elected with a sizeable share (possibly, though rarely, a clear majority) of the votes cast and a comfortable majority of seats. The Opposition benches are occupied by one or two parties. The number of parties in Parliament (two, three, or, occasionally, four) is on the small side or at least is not totally out of line with the historic pattern to that point. The elections of 1917 and 1988 fall into that category (see Table 5.1).

Front-burner elections, by contrast, are typically found at the cusp of major shifts in the party system in terms of either or both the numbers of parties elected and/or their respective support base. The elections of 1921 and (taken as a bundle) 1993, 1997, and 2000 exhibit classic front-burner characteristics. Compared with back-burner elections, the number of parties elected to the House of Commons increases, the winning party's share of votes is more radically disproportionate to its share of seats, and the remaining parties' respective vote share may bear an even odder relationship to their share of seats than would otherwise have been expected (see Table 5.1).

One way to test the front- versus back-burner elections is to determine the number of times the issue of replacing the plurality vote with some form of PR has been the subject of parliamentary questions, debates, and votes in the House of Commons. It is reasonable to assume that the relative "hotness" of the issue would be reflected in the frequency that the issue of electoral system change was discussed in the House of Commons. One would expect that the question would surface more frequently in a House of Commons with more parties than in the preceding Parliament and/or with a more marked imbalance in the strict conversion of a party's share of the votes into its share of the seats than had previously been the case.

That has been the case, as can be seen from a session-by-session count of the number of instances in the life of a single Parliament that the electoral system was the subject of questions, debates, motions, resolutions, bills, and votes as well as from a count of the number of MPs who took part in debating the subject in the House. Two periods of Canadian electoral history illustrate the "ebb-and-flow" nature of the issue of replacing FPTP with some form of PR.

The First World War coalition of Conservatives and Liberals (Unionist Party) began to crumble at the end of the 1917-21 Parliament principally as a result of farmers' discontent in Ontario and western Canada with federal tariff policies. In 1920, T.A. Crerar of Manitoba, who had resigned his cabinet post the previous year, together with ten other western MPs formed the National Progressive Party – the first "third party" of any size in the House. One of their objects was to press for replacement of the plurality vote. Accordingly, the short fifth and final session of the 13th Parliament anticipated the electoral system debate that would take place in the following Parliament. The 1921 election saw the Progressives win the second largest number of seats in the House (sixty-five) with 23 percent of the vote and relegated the Conservatives, who won seven percentage points more of the vote than the Progressives, to third place with fifty seats. For the first time in Canadian history, the party winning the election (Liberals) failed to gain a majority of the seats in the House of Commons. The conditions were right for the considerable debate on methods of election that marked that Parliament as different from any that had gone before.

As was the case in 1921, the 1993 election also brought about a fundamental transformation of the party system with the collapse of the Progressive Conservative vote. Five parties were elected to Parliament; the Liberals won a comfortable majority of the seats with little more than 41 percent of the vote; the Bloc Québécois, a party that had not existed at the previous election, formed the Official Opposition with sixty seats; the Reform Party elected no members in the 1988 general election but in 1993 turned 18.3 percent of the vote into victory in fifty-two seats; and the governing Progressive Conservatives, with barely fewer votes than Reform (16 percent), were reduced to two seats. The conditions seemed right for a heated debate over FPTP elections.

Yet that debate did not get under way during the 35th Parliament, which is easily explained. When it came to discussing electoral issues between 1993 and 1997, MPs were fixated as never before on the federal electoral boundary redistribution then under way. Electoral debates were almost entirely devoted to halting the electoral boundary readjustments begun in 1992, recrafting the redistribution legislation, and restarting the process.[12] Accordingly, only two items on method of election and two MPs were discussed in the House over the four years of the 35th Parliament. Consideration of changes to the method of election awaited the following Parliament (36th), when the Liberals won a bare majority of the seats with 38.5 percent of the popular vote – the lowest share of popular vote gained by a party winning a majority of the seats. For their part, the Reform Party and the Progressive Conservatives won roughly the same share of the vote (19.4 percent and 18.8 percent, respectively), but a strikingly different number of seats, sixty and twenty, respectively. With electoral districting out of the way, the conditions were now right for the heated debates over the electoral system in the 1997-2000 Parliament.

The contrast between front- and back-burner elections can be seen in both tabular and graphic form. Table 5.2 and Figures 5.1 and 5.2 show the number of times electoral change was discussed in the House, the number of individual MPs who spoke on the issue, and the total number of speakers (counting individuals who spoke more than once) from the beginning of the

1st session of the 1917-21 Parliament to the conclusion of the 1st session of the 1926-30 Parliament, and from the start of the 34th Parliament to the end of the 37th (1993-2004). It is clear that parliamentary interest in the subject peaked and eventually ebbed either as a consequence of the return of something approximating the previous dominant party system (1926 and 1930 elections) or the establishment, beginning in 2004, of a "new reality" of Canadian electoral politics: minority parliaments and a four-party House of Commons.

Activity at the Provincial Level

Between 2002 and 2004, five provinces (British Columbia, Ontario, Quebec, New Brunswick, and Prince Edward Island) established inquiries to look into the desirability of replacing their FPTP systems. In every case, if a change was recommended an alternative method of voting was to be proposed. The three principal reasons for the establishment of these investigations were:

- Lopsided provincial election results prompted critics of plurality voting to call for proportional representation. In the New Brunswick provincial election of 1987, for example, the Liberals won every seat in the legislature (fifty-eight) with 60 percent of the vote, and in the British Columbia provincial election of 2001 the Liberals won all but two of the seventy-nine seats with 58 percent of the vote.
- Electoral reformers found additional reason to criticize FPTP when occasionally, as in British Columbia in 1996 and Saskatchewan in 1986 and 1999, the governing party was returned to office with more seats but a smaller share of the popular vote than the principal Opposition party.
- There was a new-found and sudden appeal for several populist institutional changes. The appeal was largely part of the package of reforms advanced by the Opposition Liberals in British Columbia. Once elected to office in 2001, they put a number of them in place. The package, parts of which have been introduced in other Canadian jurisdictions as well, included fixed election dates, open cabinet meetings, legislative recall, referendums, and replacement of the plurality vote with some form of proportional representation.

The confluence of the democratic deficit discussions, the front-burner elections, and the provincial initiatives on electoral change brought the issue of replacing plurality voting to the fore in an unprecedented fashion.

TABLE 5.2

Election system debates in House of Commons,* selected years

Years	Parliament/ Session	Number of times discussed†	Number of MPs speaking on issue	Total number of speakers on issue‡
1917-21	13th/1st	–	–	–
	13th/2nd	3	2	3
	13th/3rd	1	1	1
	13th/4th	2	2	2
	13th/5th	1	18	18
1921-25	14th/1st	2	10	11
	14th/2nd	3	26	27
	14th/3rd	19	10	19
	14th/4th	11	8	11
1926	15th/1st	6	7	7
1927	16th/1st	1	1	1
1988-93	34th/1st	–	–	–
	34th/2nd	1	1	1
1993-97	35th/1st	–	–	–
	35th/2nd	2	2	2
1997-2000	36th/1st	7	4	8
	36th/2nd	13	16	35
2001-04	37th/1st	22	41	66
	37th/2nd	18	33	47
	37th/3rd	5	6	6

* Motions, resolutions, questions, debates of bills.
† Items or terms included: electoral system(s); electoral reform; proportional representation (PR); alternative vote (AV); single transferable vote (STV); plurality vote; majority vote; list system(s); winner-take-all; first-past-the-post (FPTP); run-off elections; second ballot; mixed member proportional (MMP).
‡ Includes MPs who spoke more than once.

Yet no initiatives aimed at changing the method of election were successful. Several reasons can be suggested for this.

Issue Complexity
Extending the vote to women and racially defined groups, or establishing a central elections office with administrative and oversight responsibilities, or

FIGURE 5.1

Debates on the electoral system in the House of Commons, 13th to 16th Parliaments

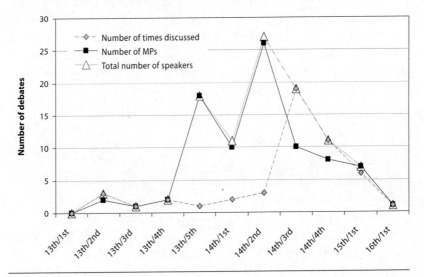

FIGURE 5.2

Debates on the electoral system in the House of Commons, 34th to 37th Parliaments

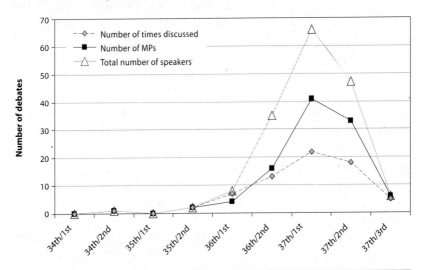

regulating the election finance regime were single-dimension issues. They were resolved by invoking doctrines or concepts of "rights," "transparency," "fairness and equity," and "impartiality." Even though much of the same language is employed in the debate over electoral systems, the issue has a complexity that previous electoral reforms did not. Earlier reforms were about making Canada a more democratic country or making Canadian democracy more efficient, or fair, or transparent, with widespread agreement about what democracy meant and about what constituted its tools or building-blocks. Electoral system debate, however, is about a more general understanding of electoral democracy (proportionality and representation or stability and accountability?) and the method of election that best fits that democracy.

Deliberations on methods of election invariably lead to discussions about different concepts of representation (mirror, delegate, trustee) or about the relative merits of multi-party coalition governments versus single-party governments.[13] These are themselves complex issues not given to a single right/wrong answer, which adds to the difficulty of reaching a widely shared consensus about the correct course of action. The British Columbia Citizens' Assembly demonstrated that, with time, expert advice, and careful study and deliberation, a group of 160 individuals could reach agreement on a preferred method of voting after a full year (in its case, STV). But even with the time, effort, public education drive, and publicity that went into that project, 43 percent of British Columbians voted against the STV proposal in a provincewide referendum on the assembly's recommendation. A citizens' assembly followed by a referendum may prove to be an inappropriate (or at least a highly problematic) institutional arrangement for bringing a population as diverse and complex as Canada's to overwhelming agreement on an alternative method of election when the issue is layered with complexities (see Lang and Warren, Chapter 13, this volume).

Fractured Elites
Media commentators, academic experts, political actors, and opinion leaders in Canada have not spoken with one voice about electoral systems. This has been true since the 1920s. The debate about the method of election is unlike those about, for example, independent commissions replacing elected politicians as the agents responsible for electoral redistributions or the chief electoral officer reporting directly to all members of Parliament rather than to the government of the day. In the earlier electoral reforms, elite opinion almost invariably pointed in one direction. Debates about the electoral

system, on the other hand, have been marked by a diversity of opinions about elections and electoral systems. This is especially obvious at the level of the political elites for there the debates about electoral system preferences are conducted by competing, often entrenched, partisan interests and actors both within parties and regions and across them.

Absence of a Single Alternative to FPTP

No single universally agreed-upon alternative to FPTP has yet emerged, as was evidenced in the proposals advanced by the five provincial inquiries. The STV was the preferred option of British Columbia's citizens' assembly; the commissions in the four other provinces favoured different variations of mixed-member proportional (MMP) system. Many informed commentators and politicians speak loosely about "proportional representation," or "PR," without specifying which model, if any, they have in mind. There is, as yet, no clear convergence of opinion on a single alternative to plurality voting.

Divided Public Opinion

The fate of each of the five provincial initiatives has varied. In two provinces (Quebec and New Brunswick) the governments have shown no sign of proceeding with either a legislative initiative or a referendum to implement their respective inquiry's proposal. In the remaining three, where provincewide referendums were held between 2005 and 2007, the public was divided. In Ontario and Prince Edward Island, proposals to adopt MMP were rejected by 63 percent of those voting. In British Columbia, proposals calling for the adoption of STV were defeated in two province-wide referendums. The upshot of the differences among the provinces and the variable fates of the proposals advanced by the five provincial inquiries is that there is no successfully implemented model of a proportional system from which the "demonstration effect" of federalism could be adopted at the federal level.

Number of Players

The 1993 election brought five parties into the House of Commons. Apart from a short period in the 1960s, this was a first in Canada's 140-year history. The 1993 election marked the beginning of a fundamental transformation of the Canadian party system.[14] From two or three (or occasionally four) parties in Parliament, as had been the case previously, the number for the past decade and a half has been consistently four and sometimes five.

The growth in party number has been matched by an increasing regionalization in their respective support bases. In contrast to the two major parties of the past that attempted (not always successfully) to build broadly based coalitions across the country as a whole, those of the 1990s and early twenty-first century became increasingly dependent upon particular (as opposed to general) support bases. The Liberals became largely a party of Ontario (and, most recently, urban Ontario); the Conservatives (Reform/ Alliance) of the west (and, in 2006 and 2008, rural and small-city Ontario); the Bloc Québécois exclusively of Quebec; and the NDP of pockets of urban and rural support across Canada.

The post-1993 situation at the federal level (the transformation of the party system combined with the increased regionalization of party support and three successive minority parliaments) might be seen as presenting an ideal opportunity for electoral reform coalition-building between or among the parties. However, that has not proven to be the case. Why not? Explanations are no doubt numerous. One helpful line of reasoning draws on path dependency theory,[15] in which sequencing of events and processes are critical to political actors and "cost reversals are very high."[16] One hundred and forty years of federal elections fought under the rules of plurality voting have contributed massively to the shaping of attitudes towards, and the institutional arrangements around, elections, parliamentary representation, and party structures. These are deeply embedded and are not easily changed.

Electoral Rules Create Electoral Incentives
What is sauce for the political goose is not necessarily sauce for the political gander. Those who stand to benefit from a particular set of election rules have an understandable predisposition to keep them.[17] By contrast, those disadvantaged by rules understandably have cause to want to change them. The difficulty for advocates of electoral system change stems from the fact that the levers of power are controlled by those least likely to want to change the system. This has been demonstrated in recorded votes in the House of Commons on resolutions calling for FPTP to be replaced by a proportional electoral system and in one survey of Canadian MPs and candidates. Government parties (regardless of political stripe) favour maintaining the status quo; NDP MPs and candidates are most likely to favour change to a proportional system; and the principal Opposition party is more cautionary about electoral change if it senses electoral victory is in the offing under FPTP.[18]

It is worth noting that the circularity here contributes to the stalemate with regard to changing the method of election. Canada's regionalized party system contributes to the "fracturing" of voter support and, more tellingly for representation in Parliament, the provinces and regions from which each party's MPs are elected. Even if a more proportional electoral system did not cost any parliamentary party any seats in aggregate (which is unlikely in the extreme), it would almost certainly cost each party seats in the provinces in which it is strong. But the very people who would have to vote "aye" in Parliament to get the process under way to reform the electoral system include the ones sitting in the seats that (in some cases at least) would be lost by the party under a different method of voting. This is a clear disincentive for officeholders to agree to change. Indeed, at another level, the incentives to change the electoral system of those already in Parliament may not be aligned with those unelected office-seekers outside Parliament. This expectation was confirmed in one study of the 2004 election that found that support for plurality voting was nearly twice as high among elected Conservatives, Liberals, and NDP as it was among defeated candidates from those three parties (51 percent versus 28 percent).[19]

Level of Citizen "Affectedness"
There is a sense in which the instruments and institutions of electoral administration make little more than a peripheral imprint on a citizen. This is not to say that electoral machinery is immaterial to an election's legitimacy. Quite the reverse, in fact. But when the nuts and bolts of an election are in place and are known to provide ground rules that are widely accepted as valid and fair (as has become the case in Canada), citizens have no reason to try to understand them or to delve into institutional alternatives.

Arguably, the most contentious post-Confederation electoral reform has to have been the franchise. Understandably, the question of who should be entitled to vote generated prolonged and heated debates whenever it surfaced in Canadian history. But in the final instance, the issue was resolved either by legislative changes or court rulings based on the reasonable presumption that, in a democracy, the franchise should be inclusive, not exclusive, and subject only to minimum age and citizenship requirements.

Save for the issue of the franchise (which has now been settled in Canada, although there are still voices of dissent with regard to prisoners' having been given the vote), voter registration, electoral districting, election financing, and electoral administration are, at best, distant and probably largely unknown facets of elections to the great majority of citizens. In other words, citizens are not explicitly or consciously aware of how directly "affected" they are by these institutional arrangements. All that really matters is that the arrangements made by the state for the casting of a ballot are accepted as fair and legitimate and that they work.

But the question of changing the ballot, or changing the way in which votes are distributed among parties or lists of candidates, or changing the representative relationship between citizens and elected MPs brings to the fore issues that directly affect how the voter sees and understands the very purpose of elections. Accordingly, views of what elections are about differ among the electorate in ways that contrast starkly to how the five earlier electoral reforms were seen.

Referendums

None of the electoral reforms of the past had to pass through a referendum hoop. They were simply debated by the parties in Parliament and voted upon, often following all-party behind-the-scenes negotiations to ensure unanimous approval. Based on the experience of the three provinces (Ontario, British Columbia, and Prince Edward Island), where the question of replacing FPTP with an alternative electoral system was put to voters via a referendum, the referendum process is not problem-free. Voter complaints of not "knowing" enough about the issue or the options, or of not being "well enough informed" of what was at stake were common, particularly in Ontario. This suggests that the referendum device (for which the precedent has now been firmly established on electoral system change – a precedent that would be difficult for any future government to ignore) may create a situation within which a significant number of individuals, being called upon to make a choice, will opt for what they know rather than for what they don't know. Paradoxically, one of the institutional reforms credited with helping to reduce Canada's democratic deficit (the referendum) may, in turn, have created an unintended hurdle to bringing about change to another institution that has also been faulted for its contribution to the democratic deficit – FPTP.[20]

Absence of a Powerful Social Movement or Advocacy Group

To date, the debate over Canada's method of election has been overwhelmingly "elite-driven." It has been confined principally to the editorial, op-ed, and letters-to-the-editor sections of newspapers; to political science literature, classes, and seminars; and to federal and provincial legislative chambers. With the possible exception of British Columbia, where consideration of STV generated widespread interest prior to the 2005 and 2009 referendums, the debate over alternative electoral systems has failed to engage the

Canadian public in any large-scale way. In spite of the efforts of a few citizens groups (such as Fair Vote Canada, formed in 2000) to promote proportional representation, electoral reform has yet to emerge as a topic of conversation and of heated exchange among the vast majority of Canadians.

As a consequence, an ingredient is missing from this issue – an ingredient that was most noticeably present a century ago in the lead-up to female enfranchisement: there has been no groundswell of mass opinion calling for voting system changes that is at all similar to that of the early twentieth century, when, as a consequence of powerfully mobilized social movements dedicated to seeking representation for one-half of the population, women were granted the vote. Nor has there been a powerful advocacy group pushing for changes to a method of election that has generated widespread and growing support among Canadians from all regions and parties.

Electoral System Debate Is Marked by Fundamental Disagreements over the Very Purpose of Elections

Changing an electoral system does not lend itself to an "either/or" or a "yes/no" zero-sum solution. Parties, leaders, candidates, and voters see elections differently. To some, elections in a democracy are about one thing and one thing only – producing a government and ensuring a means whereby the electorate, at a subsequent election, can, if deemed necessary, withdraw acceptance of that government. To supporters of FPTP, elections are about governing, responsibility, and accountability. Their predisposition is overwhelmingly to the plurality vote.[21]

To those more favourably disposed to PR, elections are about producing policies that are not necessarily based on the will of a majority but, rather, on the "will of the people" (as expressed through elections) and on ensuring that the share of popular vote is translated more or less equitably into the share of legislative seats.

To yet others, elections are about "mirroring" identified components of the larger society – such as women, visible minorities, and Aboriginals. To those predisposed to mirror representation, support for some variant of PR is overwhelming. PR supporters also include those who see non-plurality elections as a structural answer to the problem of declining voter turnout (by contrast, this is a problem that others identify as more an issue of political culture and civic society than electoral systems).

The three principal theories of legislative legitimacy that co-exist as part of politics and governance in Canada are nowhere more evident than in discussions about FPTP: parliamentary democracy, constitutional democracy, and electoral democracy.[22] Clearly, the way in which individuals or groups understand or define the relationship between elections and democracy influences their preference with regard to electoral systems. This, in turn, makes agreement on a single most-preferred alternative highly problematic.

Conclusion

Since the early 1990s, the federal political scene has been marked by several developments that bring into question the appropriateness of the electoral reform "model" of the past to the current debate about replacing FPTP with some variant of PR. The provincial "demonstration effect" is so far absent, which may in itself (based especially on the Ontario experience with its MMP referendum) offer a possible clue about the complexity of electoral system reform compared with past reforms. There is at present no widespread agreement at the elite or mass public levels about the need to abandon FPTP or, indeed, about a clearly preferred alternative to plurality voting. Superior courts, so far at least, have not been called upon to pass judgment under a section 3 ("right to vote") Charter challenge on the fairness of FPTP to individual voters and (we're speaking of Canada, after all) groups.

Reforms of the past (expanding the franchise, ensuring non-partisan electoral administration and independent boundary commissions, establishing strict election financing rules, and replacing door-to-door enumerations with a continuously updated registry of electors) naturally called for strategic moves on the part of parties and leaders as they negotiated with one another over the specifics of an acceptable reform package. But the compromises were made on a series of specific single issues, not complex issues that form the core of elections, representation, and governance. And, once reached, compromise agreements were typically adopted with the approval of all parties in Parliament at the time. A shift from FPTP to PR has so far failed the "unanimity" test given the competing strategic interests of the various players in Parliament: government versus Opposition, major versus smaller parties, and national (or at least putative national) versus regional parties.

The post-1993 change in the party system (and, coincidentally, the democratic deficit debate for which it was partly responsible) introduced some of the conditions that could be expected to lead to replacing FPTP with a proportional voting system. Principal among these are an increase in the number of parties in Parliament, a more manifestly regionalized party system, three consecutive minority parliaments, and an inequitable conversion of votes into seats. But, ironically, it also created a context within which it has so far proven impossible to achieve the support necessary to proceed with electoral system change. The electoral reforms of Canada's past, how they were achieved, and the lessons they collectively offered about the way(s) in which electoral change can be accomplished have proven to be poor predictors of change in the method of election.

APPENDIX

Voter turnout in Canadian federal elections, 1958-2008

Election date	Population	Electors on list	Ballots cast	Turnout (%)
31 March 1958	16,073,970	9,131,200	7,357,139	79.4
18 June 1962	18,238,247	9,700,325	7,772,656	79.0
8 April 1963	18,238,247	9,910,757	7,958,636	79.2
8 November 1965	18,238,247	10,274,904	7,796,728	74.8
25 June 1968	20,014,880	10,860,888	8,217,916	75.7
30 October 1972	21,568,311	13,000,778	9,974,661	76.7
8 July 1974	21,568,311	13,620,353	9,671,002	71.0
22 May 1979	22,992,604	15,233,653	11,541,000	75.7
18 February 1980	22,992,604	15,890,416	11,015,514	69.3
4 September 1984	24,343,181	16,774,941	12,638,424	75.3
21 November 1988	25,309,331	17,639,001	13,281,191	75.3
25 October 1993	27,296,859	19,906,796	13,863,135	69.6
2 June 1997	27,296,859	19,663,478	13,174,698	67.0
27 November 2000	28,846,761	21,243,473	12,997,185	61.2
28 June 2004	30,007,094	22,466,621	13,683,570	60.9
23 January 2006	30,007,094	23,054,615	14,908,703	64.7
14 October 2008	31,612,897	23,677,639	13,929,093	58.8

Source: Elections Canada, "Voter Turnout at Federal Elections and Referendums, 1867-2008," http://www.elections.ca/.

NOTES

I am grateful for the helpful comments on an earlier draft of this chapter provided by Joey Fishkin, Richard Katz, and David Smith as well as for the research assistance provided by Jade Buchanan, Daniel Macfarlane, and Kelsey Topola. The editors of this volume also offered several valuable suggestions for expanding the initial version of this chapter.

1. A more comprehensive account of the changes is given in John C. Courtney, *Commissioned Ridings: Designing Canada's Electoral Districts* (Montreal and Kingston: McGill-Queen's University Press, 2000); John C. Courtney, *Elections* (Vancouver: UBC Press, 2004).
2. Courtney, *Commissioned Ridings*, Chap. 2.
3. Donald G. Creighton, *The Old Chieftain* (Toronto: Macmillan of Canada, 1952), 163.
4. Jerome H. Black, *The National Register of Electors: Raising Questions about the New Approach to Voter Registration in Canada* (Montreal: Institute for Research on Public Policy, 2000); Jerome H. Black, "The Permanent Voters List vs. Voter Enumeration," paper delivered to a conference on "Transparency, Disclosure, and Democracy" (sponsored by the Insitute for Research in Public Policy), Ottawa, 27 February 2002; Jerome H. Black, "From Enumeration to the National Register of Electors: An Account and an Evaluation," *Choices* 9, 7 (2003), http://www.irpp.org/choices/.
5. Lisa Young, "Party, State and Political Competition in Canada: The Cartel Model Reconsidered," *Canadian Journal of Political Science* 31, 2 (1998): 339-58; Richard S. Katz and Peter Mair, "Changing Models of Party Organization and Party Democracy: The Emergence of the Cartel Party," *Party Politics* 1, 1 (1995): 5-28.
6. A worrying wrinkle was introduced in 2007 when Parliament amended the Canada Elections Act to require all voters to prove their identity by providing one piece of government-issued photo identification that shows both name and residential address. The changes amount to a retrograde move and are out of keeping with the country's earlier history of gradually instituting more expansive and generous electoral institutions and practices. (For more on difficulties this presented to voters in the 2008 election, see John C. Courtney, "Elections," in *Auditing Canadian Democracy*, ed. William Cross [Vancouver: UBC Press, 2010].)
7. They are summarized in Chapters 6 and 7 of Courtney, *Elections*.
8. Neil Nevitte, *The Decline of Deference: Canadian Value Change in Cross-National Perspective* (Peterborough, ON: Broadview Press, 1996). See, especially, Chapters 3 and 4.
9. Law Commission of Canada, "Renewing Democracy: Debating Electoral Reform in Canada. A Discussion Paper" (Ottawa: Law Commission of Canada, 2002). See also Fair Vote Canada at http://www.fairvote.ca/.
10. George Perlin, "The Malaise of Canadian Democracy: What Is It? How Is It to Be Explained? What Can We Do about It?," in *Political Leadership and Representation in Canada: Essays in Honour of John C. Courtney*, ed. Hans J. Michelmann, Donald C. Story, and Jeffrey S. Steeves (Toronto: University of Toronto Press, 2007); Robert Putnam, *Bowling Alone: The Collapse and Revival of American Community* (New York: Simon and Schuster, 2000).

11 Duff Spafford has traced the debate over Canada's method of election back to 1889, when Stanford Fleming, in a paper to the Royal Society of Canada and drawing on reasons familiar to John Stuart Mill, proposed a "scientific" electoral system based on elections by lot. See Duff Spafford, "Sandford Fleming as Electoral Reformer," paper presented at the Department Of Political Studies, University of Saskatchewan, 24 February 2004.
12 Courtney, *Commissioned Ridings*.
13 Hannah Fenichel Pitkin, *The Concept of Representation* (Berkeley: University of California Press, 1967); Jane Mansbridge, "Political Representation," *Stanford Encyclopedia of Philosophy*, http://plato.stanford.edu/; Law Commission of Canada, "Renewing Democracy."
14 Kenneth R. Carty, William Cross, and Lisa Young, *Rebuilding Canadian Party Politics* (Vancouver: UBC Press, 2000).
15 See, among others, Paul Pierson, "Increasing Returns, Path Dependence, and the Study of Politics," *American Political Science Review* 94, 2 (2000): 251-67.
16 Margaret Levi, "A Model, a Method, and a Map: Rational Choice in Comparative and Historical Analysis," in *Comparative Politics: Rationality, Culture, and Structure*, ed. Mark I. Lichbach and Alan S. Zukerman (Cambridge: Cambridge University Press, 1997), 28.
17 Elinor Ostrom, *Governing the Commons: The Evolution of Institutions for Collective Action* (Cambridge: Cambridge University Press, 1990).
18 John C. Courtney and Drew Wilby, "Staying the Course or Changing? Perceptions of Electoral Reform of Parliamentary Candidates in the 2004 Federal Election in Canada," paper delivered at American Political Science Association Annual Meeting, Chicago, 2005.
19 Ibid.
20 A referendum was no bar to electoral change in New Zealand in 1993, when 53.4 percent voted to replace FPTP with MMP; however, had the BC and Ontario requirement of 60 percent approval been in place in New Zealand, the change would not have been made. The 60 percent referendum rule in Canada, combined with the mechanism of the citizens' assembly, suggests as a possibility a blocking strategy on the part of governing elites. In other words, elites appear to do something to reform an institution while, at the same time, creating a "democratic" framework that makes the reform's adoption far from certain.
21 Joseph Schumpeter, *Capitalism, Socialism, and Democracy* (New York: Harper Perennial, 1962).
22 David E. Smith, *The People's House of Commons: Theories of Democracy in Contention* (Toronto: University of Toronto Press, 2007).

Regulating Political Finance in Canada
Contributions to Democracy?

LISA YOUNG

In December of 2008, a dispute over party financing almost resulted in the defeat of the Canadian government led by Prime Minister Stephen Harper. At the heart of the dispute was not an allegation of corruption or financial impropriety; rather, the three Opposition parties were prepared to defeat the government in order to maintain their steady source of public funding. This incident served as a reminder that, in Canada, as in many established democracies, the regulation of political finance has evolved significantly over time. While early reforms were focused on reducing the likelihood of corruption, more recent measures have been motivated, at least in part, by efforts to improve the quality of democratic competition by "levelling the playing field" for competitors, or, in other words, trying to avoid inequities in the economic marketplace from replicating themselves in the political arena. To the extent that rules governing money in politics have ceased to be designed solely to discourage corruption in favour of encouraging a broader range of democratic values, questions arise regarding the effectiveness of these measures in enhancing democratic competition.

This chapter evaluates a significant set of reforms, enacted in 2004, to party and election finance legislation in Canada. Structuring the discussion are the values of participation, inclusiveness, and responsiveness. These were the core values employed in the Canadian Democratic Audit, and they offer a useful framework for structuring a discussion of election finance laws as potential enhancers of democracy.[1] This approach requires that we consider party and election finance laws as being integral to the construction of democracy rather than simply as frameworks designed to prevent monied interests from corrupting elected officials. This alternative conceptualization is consistent with the shifting focus of the literature examining party and election finance legislation, and it offers an opportunity to evaluate Canada's reformed regulatory regime with democratic criteria in mind.

Federal elections and political parties in Canada first became subject to meaningful regulation in the 1970s. Even under these less extensive regulations, it can be argued that the rules governing election finance affected the extent and quality of participation, inclusiveness, and responsiveness. Since the 1974 reforms, a series of legal challenges and legislative changes has made party and election finance in Canada subject to much more extensive regulation and state support. Moreover, the reach of the regulatory regime has been extended to encompass the finances not only of registered political parties and their candidates but also of individuals running for party nominations and leaderships as well as groups and individuals seeking to intervene in elections as "third-party" advertisers. Given the increased scope of the legislation, there is now no question that the regulation of political finance is an important underpinning of democratic activity in federal politics in Canada.

This chapter examines Canada's new regulatory regime selectively, guided by the comparative parties and elections literature that identifies areas in which election finance is the most likely to affect participation, inclusiveness, and responsiveness. It concludes that there is only modest evidence to support the idea that the new regime is beneficial to the quality of Canadian democracy but little to support the idea that its impact is negative. To conclude that the new rules are benign is not insignificant as rules governing election finance (or their absence) can potentially be corrosive to democracy.

The Regulatory Regime

The foundation for the Canadian regulatory regime governing party and election finance was laid in 1974, when Parliament passed a series of amendments to the Canada Elections Act. These reforms established spending limits for both political parties and candidates, requirements that parties and candidates disclose the source of all donations over $100 as well as total amounts spent during campaigns, reimbursement of a portion of election expenditures to parties and candidates who met certain qualifications, and establishment of a political contribution tax credit that provided a significant tax credit for small donations from individuals.[2] The 1974 reforms also included the first effort to limit the role of "third parties" – individuals and organizations other than registered political parties – advertising during election campaigns.

Over the subsequent three decades, this initial regulatory framework remained largely intact, with minor changes to thresholds and formulae for reimbursement, thresholds for disclosure, and the value of the political contribution tax credit. In 1982, the Charter of Rights and Freedoms was entrenched in the Canadian Constitution. The Charter's guarantees of fundamental freedoms and democratic rights opened the door for tests of the constitutionality of several provisions of the Canada Elections Act. As a result of this, the courts became a significant source of change in electoral law over this period. The two most notable instances of this are the *Figueroa* decision, which struck down the requirement that a party run candidates in fifty electoral districts in order to qualify for registered party status, and the series of decisions regarding third-party advertising.

In 2003, the Liberal government introduced Bill C-24, which effectively implemented a new regulatory regime governing party and election finance in Canada. Unlike the 1974 legislation, which had support from the three major parties in Parliament at the time, this bill was introduced without prior consultation with the Opposition. The governing Liberal Party used its majority in the House of Commons to pass the legislation without the support of the two right-of-centre Opposition parties. Canada's Parliamentary system allows governments (or at least majority governments) to pass legislation governing election finance unilaterally. On the one hand, this avoids the kinds of deadlocks that for years prevented campaign finance reform in the United States; on the other hand, if governments do not feel constrained by conventions of multi-party support, they may be tempted to alter these laws with a view to enhancing their own electoral prospects. In breaking with the practice of requiring all-party support for measures relating to election finance, the Liberals in 2003 arguably opened the door to future reforms designed to enhance the competitive position of the governing party. Notably, the Conservatives in 2006 implemented legislation that created a disadvantage for the Liberals (reducing the maximum contribution limit) and tried unsuccessfully to do away with state subsidies, again to the considerable disadvantage of their main rivals. In 2011, the Conservatives passed legislation phasing out per-vote public subsidies by 2015-16, again to the considerable disadvantage of their rivals.

The 2003 legislation moved Canada from a regulatory regime that relied heavily on spending limits and offered moderate levels of state support to parties and candidates to a more comprehensive regime that combined spending limits with limits on the size and source of contributions, allowing entities other than individuals to make contributions only at the local level, and to a maximum amount of $1,000 per annum. Individuals could contribute a maximum of $5,000 per annum to each registered party, its local associations, or candidates. The legislation also instituted significant state funding for parties, to be delivered quarterly based on the number of votes the party received in the most recent election. Extending the regulatory regime into matters previously considered the private affairs of political parties, the new rules instituted limits on contributions to and spending by candidates running for a party's nomination in an electoral district and limits on contributions to candidates running for a party leadership. These changes came into effect in 2004. Only two years later, the newly elected minority Conservative government introduced and passed its Accountability Act, which banned all contributions except those from individuals and further reduced the maximum amount an individual could contribute to a registered political party in one year to $1,000. The regulatory regime in place from 2006 to 2011 is summarized in Table 6.1.[3] When the Conservative Party formed a majority government in 2011, it moved quickly to put an end to one element of this regime: the per-vote public subsidies. These subsidies are to be phased out to zero by the 2015-16 fiscal year.

The extent of state funding in place between 2004 and 2011 placed Canada firmly among the European democracies that emphasize the role of political parties in structuring democracy and provide extensive state funding to support those organizations in their democratic functions. In its new emphasis on limiting the size and source of contributions, however, the Canadian legislation has a great deal in common with the American approach detailed by Robert Boatright (Chapter 7, this volume).

Participation

In most normative accounts of democracy, citizen participation is highly valued as the means by which citizens affect the selection of public officials and the direction of public policy. High voter turnout, strong rates of party membership and activism, and other measures of engaged citizenship are

TABLE 6.1
Summary of regulation of party and election finance in Canada

Transparency

- Reporting names of all contributors over $200, including contributions to nomination and leadership contestants
- Reporting party, candidate, nomination candidate, and leadership candidate election expenses
- Reporting contributions to registered "third parties"
- Reporting expenditures by registered "third parties"
- Reporting assets held by electoral district associations

Spending limits

- Candidates' election expenses (based on number of electors in district)
- Registered political parties election expenses (based on number of candidates running for party)
- Registered "third party" election expenses ($3,666 in an electoral district; $183,300 nationally)
- Candidate nomination expenses (20% of election spending limit for electoral district)

Public funding

- Political Contribution Tax Credit (75% credit on contributions up to $400, sliding scale on larger contributions)
- Election expense reimbursements:
  – 60% for candidates winning at least 10% of popular vote
  – 50% for registered parties (winning 2% of national popular vote or 5% of vote in districts where the party ran candidates)
- Per vote quarterly allowance to registered political parties winning 2% of national popular vote or 5% of vote in districts where the party ran candidates (to be phased out by 2015/16)

Contribution limits

- Only Canadian citizens/permanent residents can make political contributions, in the following amounts:
- Maximum $1,100/annum to each registered party
- Maximum $1,100/annum in total to various entities of each party (registered association, nomination contestants, candidates)
- Maximum $1,100/annum to each independent candidate in a particular election
- Maximum $1,100 in total to leadership contestants in a particular leadership contest

generally associated with healthy democracies, and their absence is seen as a sign of democratic malaise.[4] While much of the focus is on the quantity of participation, its quality is also of considerable significance for democratic life; arguably, political systems that foster the participation of informed citizens in political organizations, encouraging them to take part in face-to-face discussions of political issues, are more desirable than those that encourage only the "thin" participation involved in casting an occasional ballot and making monetary contributions.[5] When considering potential connections between electoral finance and participation, we must cast the net broadly. "Participation" in this context encompasses citizens' participation as voters, as party supporters, as candidates, and as interveners in elections. I discuss each in turn.

Voter Participation
Voter turnout in Canada has declined gradually since the Second World War, and precipitously since 1993, with turnout in the five most recent federal elections ranging from 59 to 65 percent of registered voters.[6] Most accounts of the source of this decline focus on generational change,[7] the effects of the particular constellation of party competition during this period,[8] and the move to a permanent voter's registry.[9] Not surprisingly, electoral finance does not figure prominently in any of these accounts. Nonetheless, there is reason to give some consideration to the link, in part because some empirical analyses have found positive correlations between campaign expenditures and voter turnout,[10] and in part because the new legislation creates specific incentives to encourage parties to increase voter turnout.

Studies examining the impact of election spending on voter turnout suggest that spending on advertising provides greater information to voters and draws attention to the race, thereby increasing turnout. While it goes beyond the scope of this chapter to model any effect of spending on turnout, Figure 6.1 suggests that the increased election advertising expenditures that resulted from the new regime did not drive voters to the polls in greater numbers. In fact, during the five elections held since the law came into effect, turnout has declined while parties' advertising expenditures rose noticeably.

If increased spending can boost turnout, then the reverse can also be true. Election campaigns in which all parties, or all but one party, lack the funds to mount competitive advertising campaigns may lower voter turnout. This appeared to have been the case in the first Manitoba provincial

FIGURE 6.1

Election advertising expenses and turnout, 1997-2011

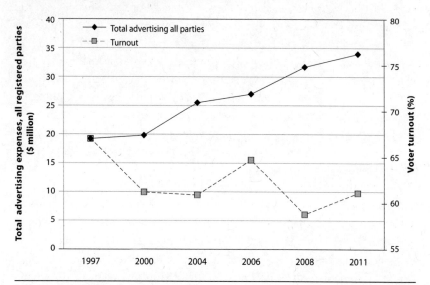

Source: Adapted from Elections Canada data.

election after the NDP government implemented a ban on corporate and union contributions but did not replace those revenues with public funds. The turnout rate in that election dropped below 60 percent for the first time.[11] The 2003 federal reforms avoided this potential pitfall by ensuring that revenues lost by banning corporate and union contributions would be replaced by public funding.

Beyond the more general relationship between election spending and turnout, there is reason to believe that the new election finance regime might have a positive impact on turnout. The formula for allocating the new quarterly allowance to political parties, from 2004, multiplied the number of votes cast for a party by a dollar amount. For each additional vote a party won in an election, it could expect to receive $1.75/vote (indexed to inflation) for each of the subsequent years. This created a clear incentive for parties to invest in "get-out-the-vote" efforts, even in constituencies where they were not competitive, in order to maximize their annual allowance. There is ample evidence that various groups and individuals used the $1.75 incentive to encourage voters to cast a ballot,[12] but there is no compelling statistical evidence that this had an impact. Loewen and Blais devised four statistical tests to evaluate the proposition that the new legislation had a positive impact on turnout in 2004, but they found no supporting evidence.[13] They note, however, that public knowledge of the provisions was very low and that parties may not have responded to the incentive structure in the first election after the new rules were adopted. While it is difficult, based on this evidence, to suggest that the electoral/party finance regulatory regime has had a positive effect on voter participation, there is certainly no evidence that it has had a negative effect.

Partisan Support
The act of contributing relatively small amounts of money to a political party or candidate is generally seen as a positive act of individual political participation in a democratic system. In its most limited form – direct mail-, internet-, or telephone-solicited contributions – financial donations to a political party engage a citizen in a political act of similar magnitude to participating in a boycott or signing a petition. It may also attach the citizen psychologically to that party and thus strengthen his/her engagement in the political system. In fairness, it must be noted that direct mail and telephone appeals to potential donors tend to try to motivate donors by exposing opponents' weaknesses and exploiting what are in some instances more extreme political views. Parties also solicit donations by selling tickets to fundraising dinners or events. In this instance, the donor attends a social event during which he or she has face-to-face interaction with party office holders and supporters. In short, for an individual to contribute a modest amount to a political party or candidate is, in democratic terms, at worst a benign and at best a meaningful participatory act.[14]

The political contribution tax credit (PCTC) first introduced in the 1974 reforms was intended to encourage small contributions from individuals and has in fact had this effect.[15] The 2003 reforms enriched the tax credit so that it is worth $300 for a $400 contribution, and $833 for a $1,000 contribution. This is an extraordinarily generous tax credit and one that the parties employ to help them solicit contributions from individuals. I argue elsewhere that the PCTC is a democratically desirable form of public funding for political parties because it encourages them to solicit small contributions from individuals.[16] Even accepting this argument, it is important to note that contributors tend to come from higher-income brackets, with the result that the participation that the PCTC encourages is not neutral in socio-economic terms.

FIGURE 6.2

Total number of individual contributors to major parties, 2002-10

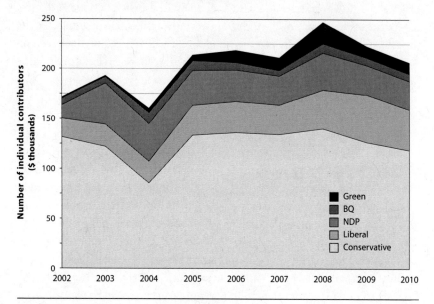

Source: Adapted from Elections Canada data.

Beyond the fundraising tool offered by the PCTC, the new regulatory regime has put a premium on individual contributions for the major parties. Beyond state funding, contributions from individuals are now the only legal source of funding for parties and candidates. When they introduced the legislation in 2003, the governing Liberals apparently believed that contributions from individuals would be a relatively minor source of income for parties under the new regime. In his speech to the House of Commons in support of the legislation, then prime minister Jean Chrétien estimated that Canadian parties would be about 80 percent publicly funded. This estimate demonstrates the Liberal Party's devastating miscalculation of their opponents' response to the new regime. Party officials did not anticipate the merger of the Canadian Alliance Party and the Progressive Conservative Party, which occurred shortly thereafter. This merger not only united the two parties but also brought together the direct-mail fundraising prowess of the Progressive Conservatives with the extensive grassroots donor database of the Reform Party and the Canadian Alliance Party. The result has been the creation of a fundraising juggernaut that has contributed to the financial devastation of the Liberal Party, which had been heavily reliant on corporate contributions prior to the legislative changes. Since 2004, the Conservative Party has raised more money than the four other major parties combined (see Figure 6.2). For a party that was not able to garner enough votes to win a majority government until 2011, this is a remarkable accomplishment.

Although the Conservatives have presented a challenge to the other parties to raise more money from individual donors, the Progressive Conservative Party appears not to have significantly expanded its pool of individual donors. In 2002 and 2003, the Canadian Alliance Party and the Progressive Conservative Party together received in the neighbourhood of 100,000 contributions from individuals. (It is, of course, possible that some individuals contributed to both parties, thereby artificially increasing this figure.) In 2008, just over 112,000 individuals contributed to the Conservative Party, a figure that declined in 2009 and 2010. The Conservatives account for just over 10 percent of the total increase in the number of individual donors between 2002 and 2008. The New Democrats, in contrast to this, accounted for 31 percent of the increase, the Liberals for 26 percent, and the Green Party for 31 percent.

Overall, between 2002 and 2008, the number of individuals who made contributions to registered political parties increased by 60,441. Even taking into account the considerable incentive for donors to split donations among spouses or within families (both to remain within the contribution limits and to maximize their tax credit), this 44 percent increase in the pool of contributors is noteworthy. This figure should grow substantially over the next decade as opposition parties work to increase their donor pools. As public subsidies are phased out, the Opposition parties will have to increase their donor pools markedly in order to compete in future elections. In this respect, the new regulatory regime has had, and is likely to continue to have, a modest positive impact on rates of participation as political donors.

Election Campaigns
Elections represent unique moments in which the public is more focused than usual on politics. Groups or individuals seeking to influence public policy outcomes understandably perceive an election campaign as an opportunity to mobilize support around their issue, to influence voters' decisions, and possibly to affect their party's stance on this issue. This is arguably part of the public discussion that is desirable in a democracy. Even when the messages take the form of less salutary attacks on politicians or parties, they are, within a democracy, afforded some protection as free speech. These

benefits, and the free speech that underpins them, must be balanced against the integrity of the regulatory regime, notably spending limits governing parties and candidates during elections and now the contribution limits that prevent corporations, unions, and other organizations from donating to parties.[17]

In the Canadian lexicon, individuals other than candidates and organizations other than registered political parties are referred to as "third parties." The 1974 reforms to election finance included a virtual ban on third-party advertising, largely in an effort to protect the integrity of the spending limits for candidates and parties. This provision and a subsequent effort to strictly limit third-party expenditures were both struck down by courts in Alberta as unconstitutional infringements of freedom of expression. The federal government did not appeal the lower court rulings in either of these instances; however, in 2000, Parliament again adopted legislation governing third-party election expenditures. This legislation, which the Supreme Court upheld as constitutional in its ruling in *Harper v. Canada (Attorney General)*, requires third parties that spend more than $500 to register, to disclose their donors and expenditures, and to limit their spending to $3,666 in an electoral district or $183,300 nationally (2008/09 limits, adjusted for inflation). Third-party election expenditures are defined as those "intended to influence how an elector might vote, by promoting or opposing a registered party or the election of a candidate, including a message that takes a position on an issue with which a registered party or candidate is associated."

While these rules strike a balance between the competing imperatives at play, they are arguably somewhat more restrictive than is desirable. A group spending its limit would have only the most modest impact on an election campaign. The legislated limits allow a third party advertising in an electoral district to spend only 4 percent of the amount a candidate can spend (on average), and they allow a third party advertising nationally to spend less than 1 percent of the amount a party running in all 308 constituencies could spend. With only eighty third parties registered to advertise during the 2006 federal election, there appears little danger that third parties will drown out registered political parties and their candidates. This stands in contrast to the experience in the United States (see Boatright, Chapter 7, this volume). Organized interests in Canada have not mobilized anything that even approaches the kinds of interventions their American counterparts have mobilized, not even during elections during which Canadian third-party interventions were effectively unregulated. This speaks to fundamental differences in the political systems of the two neighbouring countries.

Inclusiveness

While the interplay between election finance and participation was located predominantly at the mass level, the interaction between election finance and inclusiveness focuses more on elite and collective actors. In particular, this examination considers the impact, if any, of the election finance regime on the inclusiveness of the candidate selection process as well as on the inclusiveness of the party system.

Candidate Selection

Although it is a representative institution, the Canadian House of Commons is anything but inclusive of the diversity of the Canadian population. The relative underrepresentation of women and ethnic minorities in the House has been the source of considerable public and academic attention for several decades.[18] Less frequently noted, but also relevant, is the occupational and/or class composition of the House, which continues to overrepresent university-educated professionals.[19]

Of these various underrepresented groups, women have attracted the most public and academic attention and so are the focus of this analysis. In many of these accounts, by both women involved in the political system and academics, political finance has been identified as one of the barriers to the election of more women. More specifically, there is a belief that women, who earn less on average than men, and whose networks of support might disproportionately include other under-resourced women, have difficulty raising the funds necessary to mount a competitive nomination campaign. In 1991, this perception led the Royal Commission on Electoral Reform and Party Financing to recommend legislation imposing spending limits on nomination contests and extending the use of the PCTC to nomination candidates in order to help them raise funds.[20] When the government introduced its package of election finance reforms in 2003, the Liberal Party's women's caucus lobbied successfully to have the imposition of spending limits on nomination campaigns included in the bill. The extension of the tax credit was not included. The legislation did, however, impose limits on the size and source of contributions to candidates running for a party's nomination. With no individual able to contribute more than $1,100, the playing field has been levelled at least somewhat.

If inability to raise funds for nomination contests is a significant barrier to the entry of more women into the House of Commons, then the imposition of contribution and spending limits should have a positive effect on the inclusiveness of the candidate pool. The assumption that money poses a barrier is, however, difficult to support when the evidence is examined. An analysis of reported spending by nomination candidates in 2004 found no gender differences in the ability to raise money for nomination contests.[21] These findings were confirmed by a survey of individuals who were running for party nominations in 2004, which found no statistically significant gender differences in the amount of money spent in pursuit of the nomination.[22] Moreover, there is little evidence, at least in the first election after the limits were imposed, that regulation affected women's willingness to run for a party nomination.[23]

The proportion of women in the House of Commons has increased from 21 percent to 25 percent between 2004 and 2011. Much of this increase can be attributed to the number of women elected as NDP MPs from the Province of Quebec in the unexpected NDP sweep of the province. It is difficult to construct a plausible argument linking this to the regulation of election finance. That said, affluent individuals are no longer able to self-finance a run for a party nomination, at least once the formal nomination contest has started. Each individual running for a party nomination can now contribute only $1,100 to their own nomination or election campaign, thereby effectively eliminating self-financed campaigns. This stands in contrast to the American experience, in which self-finance remains a viable means of funding a bid for office.

Party System
Electoral finance reform also has the potential to affect the inclusiveness of the party system because it determines what entities are eligible for formal status as registered parties and because rules and practices governing electoral finance may erect barriers to the entry of new parties into the system. With respect to the eligibility of political parties for formal legal recognition, the current Canadian regime can only be described as highly inclusive. The Canada Elections Act had initially required that a party run candidates in fifty ridings in order to qualify as a registered party, largely as an effort to prevent the formation of "regionally" based political parties (assuming that neither Quebec nor Ontario were regions). Registered party status carries with it several advantages for a political group, most notably the ability to issue tax receipts to donors and to place the party's name on the ballot beside that of its candidates. The fifty-candidate provision was successfully challenged as an infringement of the section 3 Charter right to vote and run for office. In its 2003 ruling in *Figueroa v. Canada (Attorney General)*, the Supreme Court of Canada held that:

the ability of a party to make a valuable contribution is not dependent upon its capacity to offer the electorate a genuine "government option." Political parties have a much greater capacity than any one citizen to participate in debate and they act as a vehicle for the participation of individual citizens in the political life of the country ... The 50-candidate threshold thus infringes s. 3 of the *Charter* by decreasing the capacity of the members and supporters of the disadvantaged parties to introduce ideas and opinions into the open dialogue and debate that the electoral process engenders.[24]

Parliament responded to this ruling by (1) reducing the number of candidates a party must run to only one and (2) legislating the definition of a political party as "an organization one of whose fundamental purposes is to participate in public affairs by endorsing one or more of its members as candidates and supporting their election." At present, sixteen parties enjoy registered status.

The question of the impact of the electoral finance regime on the ability of new parties to become "major" parties is more complex. Rules governing party and election finance are clearly not the key determinants of a party's electoral success. For example, the SMP electoral system constitutes a much more significant barrier to a new party without a regionally concentrated base of support seeking to elect its candidates to the House of Commons. Even so, some critics of state funding of political parties argue that public funding serves to ossify the party system. In essence, this argument holds that established parties collude to use the resources of the state to support themselves and, in so doing, erect barriers that prevent new parties from entering the effective party system.[25] When subjected to empirical scrutiny, this proposition does not hold up. Examinations of several west European cases indicate that state funding does not freeze out new competitors and that it may, in some instances, facilitate the entry of new parties into the system.[26] Scarrow argues that this tends to be the case when thresholds for qualifying for funding are relatively low.[27]

The Canadian experience with public funding since 2004 bears considerable similarity to these findings. Arguably, the Green Party of Canada owes much of its recent growth and burgeoning electoral support to the new public financing regime. The party recognized the opportunity that public funding afforded and, in 2004, opted to run candidates in every riding across the country, with the objective of increasing its share of the popular vote from under 1 percent in 2000 to 2 percent nationally, the threshold for qualifying for funding. The Greens were successful in this effort, winning over 4 percent of the popular vote nationally and, thereby, distinguishing themselves from all the other registered political parties without parliamentary representation. Since the 2004 election, the Greens have taken in over $1 million annually in public funds. The party has used these funds to institutionalize its organization and to improve its electoral showing, increasing its share of the popular vote to 6.8 percent in the 2008 election and expanding its donor base twentyfold since 2002. In 2011, the party elected its first member of Parliament, Elizabeth May.

In the view of the other minor parties, the threshold for eligibility for the quarterly allowance is an inequitable barrier imposed on them by the established parties. Several of the minor parties launched a constitutional challenge to the threshold of 2 percent nationally or 5 percent in the electoral districts in which the party had endorsed candidates on grounds similar to those of the *Figueroa* challenge. This challenge was ultimately unsuccessful, leaving the threshold in place.[28] While at first glance the threshold for the quarterly allowance appears to be an arbitrary barrier to the electoral success of minor parties, it arguably strikes a balance between the desire to keep the party system fluid and responsive to new political impulses, on the one hand, and maintaining the fiscal integrity of the public funding program and encouraging public confidence in that program, on the other.[29]

Responsiveness

When we consider the connections between party finance and parties' responsiveness, two questions arise: First, do the rules governing political finance affect the groups to whom parties are responsive? Second, do these rules affect parties' degree of responsiveness?

The notion of popular sovereignty implies that "the choice of public officials and the nature of public policy should be determined, or at the least strongly influenced by, the people" and that "the preferences of each citizen should be weighted equally."[30] This is not an uncontested view, however, as some observers argue that responsiveness to individual citizens is less meaningful than is responsiveness to organizations (e.g., trade unions) that represent the interests of groups of citizens. Nonetheless, I use as a normative starting point for a discussion of party responsiveness the idea of popular sovereignty and its focus on citizens.

To argue that party and election finance have the potential to affect the responsiveness of parties or candidates assumes that donors individually or collectively exercise influence over party policy or politicians' decisions.

Studies trying to find connections between contributions and particular policy outcomes do not find convincing evidence to this effect.[31] A recent study concludes that there is some connection between contributions from businesses and vote choices in the US Congress but, prior to 2000, not in the Canadian House of Commons.[32] More subtly, contributions from both corporations and unions have been found to be motivated primarily by a desire to reward and protect the donor's political allies in government.[33] This can affect the ideological orientation of the legislative body and consequently expand or constrain political opportunities for certain interests as issues arise. Even so, it is important not to overstate the role that contributors play in parties' or politicians' responsiveness.

To the extent that parties and politicians are responsive to their donors, the 2004 and 2006 reforms to the Canada Elections Act should decrease parties' responsiveness to their former corporate and union contributors. In setting party policy, leaders and parliamentary caucuses no longer have to take into account any potential impact on the party's ability to raise funds from corporate or union donors. There is little reason to believe that severing the financial ties between business and the Conservatives and Liberals, or between unions and the NDP, will lead to a full severing of informal ties. Business people remain active in the two former parties and enjoy social and other ties with elected officials, while unions have maintained much of their privileged position within the NDP.[34]

Individual contributors have taken on a much greater strategic importance for parties as they are the only legal source of funding other than state subsidies. Even so, individual contributors declined in importance in relative terms between 2004 and 2011 for most of the parties as state subsidies became the most significant source of funding.

In relative terms, during the period from 2004 to 2011 parties became more reliant on the state and less reliant on individuals. Despite this, it is reasonable to argue that individual contributors increased in strategic importance, particularly to the parties that in the past relied more heavily on union or corporate contributions. The Conservative Party's ability to raise significant funds from individual contributions afforded it the ability to pay for advertising outside the writ period. Extensive Conservative advertising outside the writ period allowed the party to attack the leadership of both Stéphane Dion and Michael Ignatieff, arguably contributing to the inability of both Liberal leaders to project a positive image during the election period. The Liberals lacked the financial capacity to respond in kind. The

Conservatives' fundraising prowess challenges other parties to try to match its ability to raise money from individuals, thereby increasing the importance of individual donors, at least for the Liberals and the NDP.[35]

The end of public subsidies in 2016, coupled with the ban on corporate and union contributions, will make individual contributions the sole source of revenue for parties between elections. Ability to raise funds between elections will quite literally decide the fate of parties. If the Liberal and New Democratic parties are unable to match the Conservative Party's fundraising prowess by 2016, they will be hard pressed to mount effective campaigns in the next general election. It is difficult to imagine a more compelling set of incentives for parties to try to engage with individual donors than the ones currently facing Canadian parties.

Accepting that individual donors have become more important to all the parties and will become even more important as the public subsidies are phased out, we are left with the question of whether this increases parties' responsiveness to individuals in a democratically desirable way. Certainly, the idea of the party reliant on small individual contributions has considerable currency. British MP Matthew Taylor, for example, argues that making British parties reliant on small individual contributions would "tie political parties back to local activism ... [and] reinvigorate party politics, local party activity and turnout."[36]

In the Canadian context, there is little evidence that local party activism has been reinvigorated by the 2004 reforms. Most of the new fundraising activity has taken the form of direct mail, internet, and telephone solicitation organized by national parties, not local associations. In some parties, local associations are apparently becoming financially reliant on their national party.[37] What has emerged, arguably, is a relationship between a virtual set of donors with a relationship primarily or exclusively to the national party and whose activism is limited to making financial contributions.

Although we know relatively little about the characteristics or motivations of contributors to parties and candidates in Canada, it is safe to assume that they are not representative of the broader electorate. Analysis of use of the PCTC suggests that donors are disproportionately members of high-income groups.[38] Disproportionate participation on the part of high-income individuals may prompt greater responsiveness to their concerns.[39] Moreover, American research suggests that donors are more extreme in their political views (to both the left and the right) than are voters and that they have somewhat different issue priorities than do voters.[40] This presents a counter-balance to the centralizing tendency of voters' preferences – a counter-balance analogous to the role that more ideologically extreme party activists play in mass parties. In this respect, it is possible to think of donors as joining (or perhaps replacing) party activists as a soft constraint on party activity.

During the period from 2004 to 2011, public funding was an extremely important source of income for Canadian parties. It constituted the majority of each major party's funds in election years (when both the quarterly allowance and the election expenses reimbursement came into play) and a significant source of funding in non-election years.[41] For the Liberals, the Bloc, and the Greens, public funds comprised the majority of income even in non-election years. This raises the question of the effect of extensive public funding on parties' responsiveness to voters. The core concern in this respect is that, as parties become more financially dependent on the state, they become equally "less beholden to their voters, supporters and members, and this may erode ties of loyalty and weaken accountability."[42] Katz and Mair suggest that extensive state funding results in a particular form of party organization – the cartel party – characterized by parties' weak embeddedness in civil society.[43]

Examining the current Canadian situation in this light, Young et al. argue that "the ongoing competitiveness in the Canadian party system has created a sufficient incentive for the largest parties to engage heavily in fundraising from individuals, thereby maintaining their ties to civil society," and they note the ongoing links between party organizations and their former corporate and union donors.[44] Only the Bloc, in this analysis, has lapsed into the form of the state-dependent party, allowing its ties to former donors to fade away. The Bloc faces a very different set of strategic imperatives than do the other parties as its state funding is entirely adequate to allow it to mount competitive campaigns in Quebec, while the other parties continue to face significant pressures to fund frequent election campaigns across the country.

The mechanisms through which public funding is made available to Canadian parties arguably increases parties' responsiveness to individual donors. With the exception of election expense refunds, which are tied to the amount a party spends during a campaign period, public funding of Canadian parties is responsive to party support. The quarterly allocation is based on the number of votes the party attracts, and the PCTC is tied to the party's ability to solicit relatively small contributions from individual donors.

These mechanisms serve to give parties incentives to be responsive to the electorate and their donors and, thus, to mitigate the complacency that state funding might otherwise engender.

Conclusion

On the one hand, it is difficult to argue that reforms to Canadian political finance law have made significant positive contributions to rates of participation, degrees of inclusion, or parties' responsiveness to the electorate. There is little evidence that voter turnout has increased, and there is evidence of a only modest increase in rates of individual donation to political parties. The inclusiveness of the candidate pool has not increased noticeably, while the party system has become slightly more inclusive as the Green Party has achieved status as more than a minor party (though less than a major one). Parties' responsiveness to corporate or union interests has arguably declined, and their responsiveness to the views of their donors increased, although it is not clear to what extent.

On the other hand, there is little evidence that the reforms have been damaging to the core democratic values of participation, inclusion, and responsiveness. If we accept that the essential purpose of such reforms is designed to achieve other objectives, including decreasing the potential for political corruption, rendering the party system financially sustainable, and increasing public confidence, then an absence of unintended negative side effects is perhaps sufficient to judge the reforms a success.

Certainly, when we juxtapose the Canadian experience against that of the United States there is much to be celebrated in the Canadian model. Money poses less of an impediment to entering the political arena in Canada than in the United States and is less of a preoccupation for legislators north of the border. The heavy reliance on public funds, while controversial, limits concerns that private actors are distorting policy outcomes. The continued presence of spending limits reduces the demand for money in Canadian politics, preventing some of the corrosive impacts we have seen in the American experience. While the narrative of campaign finance reform outlined by Boatright (Chapter 7, this volume) is animated by various actors' efforts to circumvent regulations and find ways of inserting cash into the political system, the relatively restrictive rules implemented in Canada in 2004 have not had similar effects. This may change when public subsidies are fully phased out. Parties' ability to raise sufficient funds to contest elections from relatively small individual donations is doubtful. The pressure to raise money and the severe restrictions on size and source of contributions may push some parties to find ways to circumvent contribution limits, as was the case in the United States.

At the moment, however, the Canadian regime governing electoral finance serves its core purposes well. Despite the merits and comprehensiveness of the Canadian approach, there is little evidence suggesting that reforming the rules governing party and election finance has increased public trust in politicians or political parties. While significant, these rules tend to comprise the background for political competition rather than the foreground. When rules governing election finance are absent, we might well see public mistrust focused on matters surrounding election financing. But when rules are in place, public mistrust shifts its emphasis to other dimensions of the political process. For the most part, suspicion of politicians and parties in Canada and elsewhere is a diffuse phenomenon unrelated to specific events, although it may be magnified in the face of scandal. While election finance laws are important for their ability to limit corruption as well as for their ability to benefit the quality of electoral competition, they are unlikely to have such a widespread effect as to address public mistrust of political leaders.

NOTES

1. William Cross, "Canada Today: A Democratic Audit," *Canadian Parliamentary Review* 24, 4 (2001-2): 37-55.
2. For details, see Russell J. Dalton, *The Good Citizen: How a Younger Generation Is Reshaping American Politics* (Washington, DC: Congressional Quarterly Press, 2004).
3. Michael Atkinson and David Docherty, "Parliament and Political Success in Canada," in *Canadian Politics in the 21st Century*, ed. Michael Whittington and Glen Williams (Toronto: Thomson Nelson, 2008).
4. See, for example, Arend Lijphart, "Unequal Participation: Democracy's Unresolved Dilemma," *American Political Science Review* 91, 1 (1997): 1-14.
5. Robert Putnam, "Bowling Alone: America's Declining Social Capital," *Journal of Democracy* 6, 1 (1995): 71.
6. Atkinson and Docherty, "Parliament and Political Success."
7. André Blais, Elisabeth Gidengil, and Neil Nevitte, "Where Does Turnout Decline Come From?," *European Journal of Political Research* 43, 2 (2004): 221-36.
8. Richard Johnston, J. Scott Matthews, and Amanda Bittner, "Turnout and the Party System in Canada, 1988-2004," *Electoral Studies* 26, 4 (2007): 735-45.
9. Rainer Bauböck, "Towards a Political Theory of Migrant Transnationalism," *International Migration Review* 37, 3 (2003): 700-23.
10. Benny Geys, "Explaining Voter Turnout: A Review of Aggregate-Level Research," *Electoral Studies* 25, 4 (2006): 647-48.

11 Jared Wesley and David Stewart, "Electoral Financing Reform in Manitoba: Advantage Doer?," unpublished paper presented to the conference "Party and Election Finance: Consequences for Democracy Conference," Calgary, 2006.
12 C.G. Taylor, http://www.hypercube.org/; Law Commission of Canada, *Every Vote Counts: Electoral Reform in Canada* (Ottawa: Minister of Public Works and Government Services, 2004).
13 Peter J. Loewen and André Blais, "Did Bill C-24 Affect Voter Turnout? Evidence from the 2000 and 2004 Elections," *Canadian Journal of Political Science* 39, 4 (2006): 935-43.
14 It should be noted that this evaluation assumes that donations are freely given, with no quid pro quo in mind. The normative evaluation clearly changes under such circumstances. Arguably, however, by limiting donations to $1,100, the possibility of contributions resulting in undue influence over or access to decision makers is highly unlikely.
15 Lisa Young, "Party, State and Political Competition in Canada: The Cartel Model Reconsidered," *Canadian Journal of Political Science* 31, 2 (1998): 353.
16 Ibid.
17 For a discussion of the potential for corporations and unions to displace their political contributions into third-party expenditures, see Dalton, *Good Citizen*.
18 Lynda Erickson, "Women and Candidacies for the House of Commons," in *Women in Canadian Politics: Toward Equity in Representation*, ed. Kathy Megyery (Toronto: Dundurn, 1991); Michael Pal and Sujit Choudhry, "Is Every Ballot Equal? Visible Minority Vote Dilution in Canada," *IRPP Choices* 13, 1 (2007); Alain Pelletier, "Politics and Ethnicity: Representation of Ethnic and Visible-Minority Groups in the House of Commons," in *Ethno-Cultural Groups and Visible Minorities in Canadian Politics: The Question of Access*, ed. Kathy Megyery (Toronto: Dundurn, 1991); Lisa Young, "Women's Representation in the Canadian House of Commons," in *Representing Women in Parliament: A Comparative Study*, ed. Marian Sawer, Manon Tremblay and Linda Trimble (New York: Routledge, 2006); Manon Tremblay, "Women/Men Parity in Politics: A Driving Force behind the Reform of Federal Political Institutions in Canada," *Journal of Canadian Studies* 35, 4 (2001): 40-59.
19 Donley T. Studlar, Dianne L. Alexander, Joanna E. Cohen, Mary Jane Ashley, Roberta G. Ferrence, and John S. Pollard, "A Social and Political Profile of Canadian Legislators, 1996," *Journal of Legislative Studies* 6, 2 (2000): 93-103.
20 Royal Commission on Electoral Reform and Party Financing, "Reforming Electoral Democracy," ed. Royal Commission on Electoral Reform and Party Financing (Ottawa: Minister of Supply and Services Canada, 1991), 115-17.
21 Monroe Eagles and Harold Jansen, "Financing Federal Nomination Contests: An Overview of the 2004 Experience," paper delivered at Canadian Political Science Association Annual Meeting, University of Western Ontario, London, 2005.
22 A. Hauk and Lisa Young, "Gendered Pathways into Politics," unpublished manuscript.
23 Ibid.
24 Karen S. Cook and Robin M. Cooper, "Experimental Studies of Cooperation, Trust and Social Exchange," in *Trust and Reciprocity*, ed. Elinor Ostrom and James Walker (New York: Russell Sage Foundation, 2003).

25 Richard S. Katz and Peter Mair, "Changing Models of Party Organization and Party Democracy: The Emergence of the Cartel Party," *Party Politics* 1, 1 (1995): 5-28.
26 Jon Pierre, Lars Svasand, and Anders Widfeldt, "State Subsidies to Political Parties: Confronting Rhetoric with Reality," *West European Politics* 23, 3 (2000): 1-24; Susan E. Scarrow, "Party Subsidies and the Freezing of Party Competition: Do Cartel Mechanisms Work?," *West European Politics* 29, 4 (2006): 619-39.
27 Scarrow, "Party Subsidies," 624-25.
28 In April 2008, the Supreme Court declined to hear an appeal to the Ontario Court of Appeal ruling.
29 Ayaan Hirsi Ali, "Islam's Silent Moderates," *New York Times*, 7 December 2007.
30 Dahl, cited in Jonathan Hopkin, "The Problem with Party Finance: Theoretical Perspectives on the Funding of Party Politics," *Party Politics* 10, 6 (2004): 627-51.
31 For a review of the literature, see Thomas Stratmann, "Some Talk: Money in Politics: A (Partial) Review of the Literature," *Public Choice* 124, 1 (2005): 135-56.
32 Clayton D. Peoples and Michael Gortari, "The Impact of Campaign Contributions on Policymaking in the US and Canada: Theoretical and Public Policy Implications," *Research in Political Sociology* 17 (2008): 208.
33 William P. Welch, "Campaign Contributions and Legislative Voting: Milk Money and Dairy Price Supports," *Western Political Quarterly* 35 (1982): 478-95; Richard Fleisher, "PAC Contributions and Congressional Voting on National Defense," *Legislative Studies Quarterly* 18, 3 (1993): 391-409.
34 Harold Jansen and Lisa Young, "Solidarity Forever? The NDP, Organized Labour, and the Changing Face of Party Finance in Canada," *Canadian Journal of Political Science* 42, 3 (2009): 657-78.
35 The Bloc is in a rather different situation as its election expenditure limit is much lower than that for parties running nationally. Its public funds are more than adequate to meeting its electoral and other needs, and it has demonstrated little interest in fundraising from individuals post-2004.
36 Matthew Taylor, "Can Funding Reform Stir the Party Animal?" *Parliamentary Affairs* 58, 3 (2005): 621.
37 David Coletto, Harold Jansen, and Lisa Young, "Election Finance Law and Party Centralization in Canada," paper delivered at the Canadian Political Science Association Annual Meeting, Ottawa, 2009.
38 Dalton, *Good Citizen*, 452.
39 Sidney Verba, Kay Lehman Schlozman, and Henry E. Brady, *Voice and Equality: Civic Volunteerism in American Politics* (Cambridge: Harvard University Press, 1995).
40 Costas Panagopoulos and Daniel Bergan, "Contributions and Contributors in the 2004 Presidential Election Cycle," *Presidential Studies Quarterly* 36, 2 (2006): 155-71.
41 These figures underestimate the extent of public funding because they do not include the value of the political contribution tax credit, which underwrites much of the cost to individuals of their political contributions.
42 Robert Williams, "Aspects of Party Finance and Political Corruption," in *Party Finance and Political Corruption*, ed. Robert Williams (Houndsmills: Macmillan, 2000), 7.

43 Katz and Mair, "Changing Models."
44 Lisa Young, Anthony Sayers, and Harold Jansen, "Altering the Political Landscape: State Funding and Party Finance," in *Canadian Parties in Transition,* 3rd ed, ed. Alain Gagnon and A. Brian Tanguay (Peterborough: Broadview Press, 2007), 349.

7
Campaign Finance Reform in the United States

ROBERT G. BOATRIGHT

A favourite argument of American campaign finance reform opponents has been that reform will have little effect on public opinion about government. As John Samples argues, citizens may say they want reform, but they will not notice it when it happens, they will not change their views about government, and they do not rank campaign finance reform as a particularly pressing priority.[1] This is a somewhat cynical argument in so far as the values inherent in the campaign finance reform debate – values such as public participation, transparency, competition, and decreasing corruption – are worthy of consideration on their own, regardless of public sentiment. Yet Samples's argument poses a dilemma for those who would consider campaign finance reform in light of the democratic deficit argument. To wit, what is the purpose of reform? And how can we evaluate it if it has little measurable effect on the public?

In this chapter I argue that the goals of reformers are sufficiently varied that we should not necessarily assume that, just because the public continuously clamours for reform, we should view all reform proposals as means of satisfying public demands. The Bipartisan Campaign Reform Act (BCRA) of 2002, the United States's most recent comprehensive campaign finance reform, was surrounded by rhetoric regarding public dissatisfaction with politicians, but its goals were decidedly modest – the authors did not aspire to make dramatic changes in the conduct of elections, largely because the Supreme Court's interpretation of permissible reforms has made it difficult to enact the sort of legislation that would be consequential for the average citizen. There are proposals on the post-BCRA agenda that might hold greater promise for increasing citizens' trust in politicians or involvement in the political process, but it is not clear that politicians have the appetite to take this challenge on, in part because of the deregulatory stance taken by the Supreme Court in the *Citizens United v. FEC* decision and elsewhere, and in part because developments in campaign finance over the past three election cycles have made many long-held assumptions about the system suspect.

Many who have studied the United States in comparative perspective have claimed that Americans, like citizens of other Western democracies, have over the past forty years exhibited a greater desire for political participation, a growing distrust of politicians, and a growing sense that organized interests wield too much power – at the same time as they are turning to groups in order to press their demands upon government and are demanding more of their politicians.[2] In general terms, this trend has been characterized as an increase in the "democratic deficit" – a growing gap between citizens' expectations of government and the performance of government. Nevitte and Dalton argue that increasing education and income levels in these countries correspond to an increasing cynicism among citizens about what government can do, at the same time as citizens have become more confident in their own ability to understand political decisions.[3]

Campaign finance reform would seem like an appropriate response to this problem on the part of government. Citizens tend to blame interest groups or "big money" for many of these problems. Hibbing and Theiss-Morse found that 59 percent of the respondents in their 1998 survey contended that interest groups had too much power, and, in surveys conducted between 1970 and 2000, between 48 and 76 percent of American National Election Study respondents agreed that "government [was] pretty much run by a few big interests looking out for themselves."[4] Limiting the role of interest groups and large donors in campaigns would thus be an obvious response, even given Samples's claims about the lack of long-term consequences with regard to public opinion. If reform might be seen as an obvious response, however, it is not one that fits neatly into politicians' own goals. That is, it seems more likely than not to threaten legislators' electoral prospects, their prospects for advancement, or their ability to pursue larger policy goals.[5] To the cynic, toothless campaign finance reforms may be popular among politicians, but serious, comprehensive reforms will be rare and are likely only to be precipitated by crises.

We should not, then, expect too much from campaign finance reform, in part because its technical nature tends to obscure the important values from public inspection and in part because the types of radical reforms that might prompt a public response do not square with the goals of politicians. If we are to talk about the results of and future prospects for campaign finance reform, then we wind up making subjective claims. Is the American system getting better or worse? In the absence of agreed-upon guidelines, we fall back on values. We can use empirical trends to justify value-based claims, but we are necessarily looking at small changes, changes that could well be influenced by myriad factors other than the regulatory regime. In this chapter I summarize developments in American campaign finance law over the past decade and the consequences of these reforms for parties, politicians, organized interests, and citizens. I then survey the values that have been offered in the campaign finance debate and discuss how the consequences of BCRA, as well as the purported consequences of other proposed reforms, have squared with these values.

A Brief History of American Campaign Finance Reform

For most of the twentieth century, the United States had no effective system for regulating election spending. The few laws that did exist either were not consistently enforced or were easily circumvented by candidates.[6] It was not until the 1970s that congressional Democrats, responding to the real and perceived campaign finance abuses of the Nixon administration, passed comprehensive reform laws that could actually be enforced. The Revenue Act, 1971, created a system in which presidential candidates could voluntarily accept spending limits in the primaries in exchange for public funding, and general election candidates could voluntarily forego fundraising entirely in exchange for a flat grant from the federal government. The Federal Election Campaign Act (FECA), 1972, went still further, establishing limits on candidate spending and on the amount of money candidates could contribute to their own campaigns. And, for each election cycle, the 1974 FECA Amendments established caps on contributions by individuals to candidates ($1,000), to political parties ($20,000), to political action committees (PACs) ($5,000), and in sum ($25,000). There was also a $5,000 limit on PAC contributions to candidates or parties.[7] FECA's candidate spending limits were subsequently overruled by the Supreme Court in the *Buckley v. Valeo* decision (424 US 1 1976), which established candidate spending as a freedom-of-speech issue; the United States was left again with a sort of patchwork of the components of FECA that the court had allowed to stand.

According to most analyses, the reforms associated with FECA did contain political spending during the late 1970s and early 1980s.[8] The growth in candidate and party spending roughly tracked with inflation through this period. FECA had, however, implicitly encouraged an increase in interest group spending because it set PAC limits so much higher than individual limits and because it did not establish overall limits on what PACs could raise and spend. FECA has been held responsible by many for the growth in the number of PACs during the 1970s. By 1980, the number of PACs had grown to 2,551, up from 608 in 1974.[9] Despite the fact that no individual donor could plausibly claim credit for ensuring the election or re-election of a member of Congress on the basis of direct contributions, many critics argued that officeholders were now beholden to corporate donors in general.[10]

Many observers within Congress and without worried in the late 1970s that FECA had weakened political parties at the expense of candidates and interest groups. Accordingly, Congress amended FECA again in 1979, allowing parties to solicit unlimited "soft money" contributions from individuals, labour unions, or corporations. These funds could not be contributed to candidates or used to directly advocate for a candidate, but they could be used for voter registration, get-out-the-vote efforts, or to air so-called "issue advocacy" advertisements that discussed issues of concern to the party but did not endorse candidates.[11] Although the parties were slow to exploit this new source of funds, by 1996 the six party campaign committees were raising and spending over $250 million in soft money, and this amount nearly doubled by 2000, with the parties raising and spending a total of $495 million in soft money.[12] Not to be outdone, organized interests also began to conduct their own issue advocacy campaigns. The AFL-CIO spent an estimated $35 million in treasury (as opposed to PAC) funds on issue advocacy during the 1996 election, airing as much as $1 million worth of television advertisements in the districts of some Republican House members.[13] Although these advertisements stopped short of telling voters to vote for or against a candidate, they tended to discuss the candidate's record in sufficiently positive or negative terms that few voters could have been in doubt about the preferences of the AFL-CIO. Other organizations, most notably groups with ties to the pharmaceutical and insurance industries, ran their own issue advocacy campaigns during the 1998 and 2000 election cycles.[14] Overall spending on elections thus began to outstrip inflation and, at the presidential level, to outstrip the inflation indexing of the spending caps. All of the major presidential candidates had abided by the Revenue Act's voluntary spending limits during the 1980s and the early 1990s, but by 1996 they found themselves at a disadvantage relative to parties and organized interests. Those candidates who could fund their own campaigns were tempted to do so, and candidates who could substantially exceed the spending limits also now had more reason to do so.

Senators John McCain and Russell Feingold introduced a raft of campaign finance reforms in 1997; although these reforms originally included free television time for candidates, a system of voluntary caps on congressional candidates' spending, and restrictions on PAC spending, by 2002 the McCain-Feingold reforms, by then known as the BCRA, were pared down to address the soft money spending of parties and the issue advocacy advertisements of non-party groups. The BCRA prohibited soft money contributions entirely, and it prohibited groups that accept corporate or labour funds (a category that applies to almost all advocacy groups) from airing radio or television advertisements that name a candidate for election in the area the ads are run during the thirty days preceding a primary election or the sixty days preceding the general election. In a bid to secure Republican support, the BCRA also doubled individual contribution limits and indexed them to inflation. It left PAC limits unchanged. The BCRA was explicitly tailored to the Supreme Court's *Buckley* argument about preventing quid-pro-quo corruption; rather than serving as a panacea to those who favoured public funding or a radical reshaping of the campaign finance regime, it sought to return campaigns to the footing they had before the 1979 FECA amendments.

Although the Supreme Court upheld almost all of the BCRA in its five to four *McConnell v. FEC* (540 US 93, 2003) decision, the Court has steadily chipped away at the law since Sandra Day O'Connor stepped down from the Court in 2006. In *FEC v. Wisconsin Right to Life* (551 US 449, 2007), the Court expanded the scope of permissible group advertising within the sixty/thirty-day window, and in *Davis v. FEC* (554 US 724, 2008) the Court struck down the so-called "millionaire's amendment" to the BCRA, which increased contribution limits for candidates running against opponents who self-funded their campaigns. Finally, in 2010, the Court struck down the BCRA's electioneering provisions entirely, as well as the older prohibition against direct advocacy by corporations, in its *Citizens United v. FEC* (558 US 08-205, 2010) ruling.

Apart from the court's trajectory, however, the major development in campaign finance since the BCRA has been in presidential fundraising. By 2008, the presidential public financing system was all but obsolete – few of the major primary candidates accepted federal matching funds in their primary campaigns, and Barack Obama declined federal funding for his general election campaign as well. In announcing his decision to decline public funds, Obama argued that "the public financing of presidential elections as it exists today is broken, and we face opponents who've become masters at gaming this broken system."[15] He went on to argue that, if he accepted public funds, he would be at a disadvantage since Republicans would benefit from independent spending on their behalf, and he reiterated an argument he had been making since April, which held that his small donor base constituted a "parallel public financing system."[16] Obama ultimately raised $765 million in his campaign, shattering all previous records. As his comments indicate, however, many viewed this as a triumph for small donors. Through August of 2008, Obama raised $153 million from donors of under $200, indicating that a candidate could raise large sums of money without over-reliance on large donors (although he clearly also benefitted from the BCRA's increase in hard money contribution limits for individuals).[17] Although there had been a movement afoot, within Congress and within various Washington think tanks, to reform the presidential public financing system, it is not at all clear that the system will be changed in the near future.

American Campaign Finance Reform: Immediate Effects

The BCRA's expected consequences quickly proved to be more important to many political elites than were its actual consequences. In the early days of the 2004 presidential campaign, Democratic elites assumed that their nominee would not be able to forego matching funds, but they did expect that President Bush would decline matching funds, as he had done in 2000. According to this line of reasoning, Bush, with no primary opponent, would have the luxury of using his campaign funds to define the Democrats' de facto nominee, while the Democratic nominee would be unable to respond and the Democratic Party, lacking the soft money resources it had had in 1996 and 2000, would also be unable to compete with Bush.[18] Labour unions and liberal advocacy groups would also be prohibited from criticizing Bush during that same time period. This did not come to pass, in part because the Democratic Party exceeded expectations in its hard money fundraising and in part because Howard Dean, and then John Kerry, declined matching funds.

Political Parties

Fundraising figures from the 2004 election make it difficult to argue that either party was harmed by the BCRA in the short run. Table 7.1 shows

TABLE 7.1

Party campaign committee fundraising, 2000-10 (millions of dollars)

Party/Committee	2000	2002	2004	2006	2008	2010
Democratic						
Democratic Congressional Campaign Committee	105.1 (56.7)	102.9 (56.4)	92.9	139.9	176.2	163.9
Democratic Senatorial Campaign Committee	104.2 (63.7)	143.4 (95.0)	88.7	121.4	162.8	129.5
Democratic National Committee	260.6 (136.6)	162.0 (94.6)	311.5	130.8	260.1	224.5
Republican						
National Republican Congressional Committee	144.6 (47.3)	210.8 (69.7)	185.7	179.6	118.3	133.8
National Republican Senatorial Committee	96.1 (44.7)	125.6 (66.4)	79.0	88.8	94.4	84.5
Republican National Committee	379.0 (166.2)	284.0 (113.9)	392.4	243.0	427.6	196.3

Note: "Soft money" totals for 2000 and 2002 are in parentheses.
Source: Center for Responsive Politics.

fundraising by all six party campaign committees over the period from 2000 to 2010. At the presidential level, hard money fundraising by both parties surpassed their hard and soft money fundraising levels of 2000.[19] Fundraising by the congressional party committees was down slightly from 2002, but neither party had a clear advantage compared to fundraising numbers of 2000 and 2002. By 2008, most party campaign committee fundraising totals were well above what they had been in 2000 and 2004, and those that were not were likely affected more by factors unrelated to the BCRA than by the soft money restrictions.[20]

The surprising fundraising numbers at the presidential level no doubt bear some relation to the close, and highly contentious, 2004 election, but they also show the resilience of the parties, and they bear testament in particular to the increased emphasis on grassroots fundraising by the Democratic National Committee. Fundraising at the congressional level also may be influenced by context: because it was evident throughout the year that the presidential election would be close and costly, the presidential campaign committees may have absorbed money that might otherwise have gone to the congressional committees. In addition, few political elites believed that it was likely that the Democratic Party could gain a majority in either the House or the Senate, so there may have been less of an incentive for donors to give to the parties than there had been in 2000 or 2002. In 2006, with Republican majorities looking more tenuous in both chambers, Democratic committee receipts increased almost 50 percent while Republican receipts remained constant, and party campaign committee receipts remained near 2006 levels in 2008 – although on the Democratic side, they might have been higher had the Obama campaign not declined public funding.

One consequence of the widespread expectation that Democrats would be hurt, however, was the formation of new "527" organizations, so named because of the section of the US tax code under which they were organized. On the Democratic side, these organizations were established with the aim of offsetting Bush's anticipated fundraising advantage. The two largest 527 groups, America Coming Together and the Media Fund, raised and spent a combined $139 million in 2004. These groups benefited from several large individual contributions – most notably, those of financier George Soros and insurance company owner Peter Lewis – and they received much of their start-up money from labour unions. Labour contributed a total of $92.0 million to 527 groups as compared to $54.8 million in 2002.[21] Corporations also increased their contributions to 527 groups, giving $69.1 million in 2004 as compared to $16.3 million in 2002. This increase did not, however, come close to replacing the soft money that unions and corporations had previously given to the parties.

For all the talk of the 527 "loophole," 527s did not replace soft money, nor did parties need a replacement for soft money in order to remain financially competitive with each other. In addition, despite complaints to the Federal Election Commission (FEC) and more recent attempts to rein in 527 organizations, there was no prima facie evidence that the BCRA merely directed political money in a new, and potentially less transparent, direction. The primary focus of 527 groups was the presidential election, and FEC decisions after the election made it clear that many of their activities were illegal. Their activities were premised, in part, on the accurate assessment that FEC would not act quickly enough to shut these groups down. FEC did act against these groups in 2006, and 527s (particularly those not connected to PACs or 501(c) groups) were not as much of a factor in 2006 or 2008.

Organized Interests

Just as the most dire predictions about the future of the parties were not realized in the years immediately following the BCRA, so the forecasts about a declining role for labour and business were also not realized. In the years preceding the passage of the BCRA, views within the AFL-CIO about soft money and about television advertising had evolved significantly. In part, unions had become dissatisfied with soft money contributions because these contributions had not necessarily helped give them more power within the Democratic Party. Furthermore, internal polls indicated that the AFL-CIO had little success in mobilizing non-union members to vote for pro-labour candidates in 1996 or 1998, but the organization's member contacting program did appear to have swayed union members to vote for Democrats.[22] Advertisements and contributions appeared to have mattered less than did voter mobilization, an activity untouched by the BCRA. Accordingly, the AFL-CIO began to invest in repeated member contacts, using paid and volunteer organizers to discuss politics with members.[23]

In 2002, in fact, the AFL-CIO had ceased all of its political advertising by early September (when the sixty-day window would have taken effect had the BCRA been law). In 2004 it aired only one-third the number of ads it had run in 2000, and it sought instead to emphasize member communication. The political strategy of America Coming Together (ACT), which received ample union funding, was basically the AFL-CIO strategy applied to non-union members. ACT volunteers canvassed neighbourhoods deemed sympathetic to Democratic causes, carrying palm pilots and noting issues of concern to residents. Despite the reelection of President Bush, ACT leaders insisted after the election that they had hit their targets for registration and turnout in all of the major battleground states.[24] ACT suspended operations in early 2005, but the ACT database was used by other groups in 2006 and 2008, and ACT leaders undertook similar endeavours in both of those elections. The turn to mobilization appears to have been a response to the BCRA, but it is not something that was directly addressed by the law.

Similarly, many business groups opposed the BCRA but were not necessarily harmed by it. Business groups have, like unions, been among the major purchasers of issue advocacy advertisements, often under deliberately vague names. The Coalition: Americans Working for Real Change, a group established by many large businesses and peak business associations, ran advertisements responding to the AFL-CIO's electioneering activities in 1996. Citizens for Better Medicare (ostensibly formed by several large pharmaceutical companies), the United Seniors Association (also allegedly formed by pharmaceutical companies), and Americans for Job Security (allegedly funded by the insurance industry) also engaged in late issue advocacy activity in the pre-BCRA elections.[25]

Businesses, and business executives, have also been among the largest soft money contributors. Not all businesses were enthusiastic contributors, however. As of early 2001, many major companies had adopted policies against giving soft money,[26] while others had announced their support for a soft money ban but continued to make soft money donations. Many expected that corporations would respond to the BCRA by dramatically increasing their PAC receipts, but the increase in total PAC spending in 2004, 2006, and 2008 did not dramatically outstrip the secular increase in PAC fundraising that had been going on for decades, nor does the increase seem surprising given the heightened public interest in these elections.

Just as unions responded to the BCRA by increasing their efforts to communicate with members, so business groups redoubled their efforts to communicate with employees. Led by the Business-Industry PAC, the Chamber of Commerce, and the National Federation of Independent Businesses (NFIB), peak business associations have sought to use the internet to provide customized candidate information to businesses. Although businesses are limited in the amount and nature of the political information they can provide to employees, these associations have trained business owners as to how they can encourage workers to vote as well as provide them with information without expressly advocating for any candidate.

The diminished role of industry-sponsored front groups following the passage of the BCRA no doubt hurt some major industries. For the most part, however, business groups' strategies likely would have been little different (albeit more costly to individual companies) had the BCRA not been in place in 2004. As is the case for organized labour, the BCRA at most pushed business groups in a direction that they either would have or should have (in the view of trade association leaders) taken anyway.

Summary

Many recent analyses of the BCRA have claimed that it has had little influence on campaign fundraising, and the large sums spent in the 2008 presidential and congressional races provide some evidence of this. Now that the Supreme Court has struck down the electioneering restrictions of the BCRA, we will likely never know what the long-term consequences of the law would have been. In the three elections following its enactment, however, the BCRA did change the priorities of groups, parties, and candidates.

The BCRA had three major consequences. First, the soft money prohibitions do not appear to have harmed the ability of either party to raise money, but they did arguably force the parties to be more aggressive in their fundraising, particularly in their efforts to procure small contributions. Because the Republican Party has traditionally raised more hard money than the Democratic Party, and because of the demonstrated skill of President Bush at raising hard money, it had been expected that the Democratic Party might be at a disadvantage. This was not the case, however, in 2004, 2006, 2008, or 2010. The Democrats outperformed expectations in 2004 in part because of antipathy towards President Bush among their supporters, in part because of the small-donor databases they had built in 2002, and in part because their eventual nominee chose not to accept matching funds. The increase occurred primarily in contributions from individuals – particularly small donations – not in PAC contributions. However, anticipation on the part of party elites that the Democratic Party would have fundraising difficulties led to the formation of several "quasi-party" organizations in 2004. These organizations were not built to last, however, and they played only a minor role in 2006 and 2008. The *Citizens United* decision has removed one premise for these groups to exist – they clearly are not needed to advertise any more – but, as conflict in 2010 over Republican National Committee fundraising and the development of American Crossroads showed, these groups can still fill a temporary role as quasi-party organizations.[27]

Second, there was no overall decline in issue advocacy, despite the restrictions.[28] The established, issue-oriented groups dominant in the elections of the late 1990s aired far fewer advertisements, while new 527 groups, which often had names unfamiliar to the public, took their place. Issue advocacy had, by 2008, become the domain of ephemeral groups formed expressly for the purpose of airing ads. The issue advocacy restrictions also contained several limitations that might have gradually rendered the restrictions obsolete even absent the Supreme Court's *Citizens United* ruling. Most notably, they applied only to television and radio advertising; internet-based communications are harder to regulate.

Third, there was a marked increase since 2004 in the use of "ground war" tactics – voter registration drives, get-out-the-vote efforts, and various forms of personal contacting. For business groups, this often took the form of internet-based workplace communication. For labour unions and liberal advocacy groups, this took the form of door-to-door campaigning and extensive volunteer work in swing states. Some of this likely would have happened without the BCRA, but the BCRA did encourage this development.

There was little persuasion that could be conducted in 2004, and thus unions chose to focus their efforts on working class or minority voters in swing-state cities such as Cleveland and Philadelphia while conservative groups sought to mobilize voters in more conservative areas of these same states. This type of strategy may be useful in future elections as well, but a less polarized United States could severely diminish the value of such tactics. The expanded playing field of the 2008 election was, in part, the result of a dramatic increase in spending on mobilization, but the economic downturn shortly before the election likely rendered such mobilization efforts less pivotal to the outcome of the campaign than had been the case in 2004.

Beyond the BCRA: The Changing Campaign Finance Landscape and the Changing Reform Movement

As of 2012, proposals for change in American campaign finance laws have a strikingly different complexion than they had in the early 2000s. The *Citizens United* decision has clearly set back the reform movement; instead of pushing for further reform, proponents of regulation must now develop disclosure-based remedies to the Court's decision merely as a means of resuscitating the advocacy restrictions of the BCRA. Because the Court has not yet taken a stance against disclosure, the leading congressional response to *Citizens United* (the so-called DISCLOSE Act) has sought to expand the amount of required disclosure of corporate contributions to advocacy campaigns and to expand the amount of information provided in these advertisements' "stand-by-your-ad" disclaimers. The DISCLOSE Act contains a variety of other reform ideas of long standing, such as a guarantee of preferential pricing for candidate ads; however, at its heart it is an attempt to limit the damage *Citizens United* has done to the BCRA.

Even before *Citizens United*, however, rhetoric regarding political corruption was largely gone from reform proposals, and there was little discussion of the role of the BCRA in either encouraging or restraining spending. Instead, the dominant topic was the presidential public financing system. Many proposals for reforming the primary matching-fund system have consisted of some combination of increases in the aggregate spending limit, an abandonment of the state-by-state spending limits, or an increase in the match for small contributions. The leading proposal of this sort during 2007 was the Presidential Funding Act, sponsored by Senator Russell Feingold. While this act and other (earlier proposed) reforms might have been effective in restraining spending or levelling the playing field in 2000 or 2004, it is not clear that they would have made a difference in 2008. Even a substantial increase in what candidates could spend would have fallen far short of what Barack Obama and Hillary Clinton raised. Any future proposals about presidential public financing will also have to reckon with the emergence of Super PACs (organizations sanctioned by the *Citizens United* decision that can raise money in unlimited amounts for independent expenditures) in the primaries; while a case could be made that at least some of the 2012 Republican candidates might have been better off receiving matching funds, the majority of election-related spending in many of the primary states came not from the candidates themselves but from the independent expenditure-only PACs backing their campaigns.

Because the increase in fundraising in 2008 came exclusively from individual, hard money contributions, it is not at all evident that it represents the same type of problem reformers saw in the years preceding the BCRA. There is still a potential argument for subsidizing campaigns; but, ironically, it may now be strongest with regard to Congress, where public financing has never been available. Strong presidential candidates are able to raise money from many donors without trying – that is, citizens are drawn to the campaign even without being solicited by the campaign. The public knows about these campaigns. This is generally not the case for congressional candidates. Few congressional candidates have been able to use the internet as effectively as did Howard Dean or Barack Obama, and, as a result, many promising non-incumbents struggle to raise money during the crucial early months of their campaigns. Congress has shown little appetite for providing public funds for candidates, but some proposals have sought to creatively lower the costs of campaigning in other ways. One current reform proposal, introduced in the past three sessions of Congress by senators McCain, Feingold, and Durbin, would mandate defined amounts of television coverage of candidates and campaigns and provide candidates with vouchers to use for television advertising.[29] Giving candidates and parties more access to television provides a threshold for poorer candidates and serves to multiply the value of their initial contributions, much as does the presidential system.

Another proposal that has circulated for several years takes as its premise the notion that political contributions are an important form of public engagement in politics. The argument is that even a token contribution to a candidate can heighten citizens' interest in campaigns – in the same way that anyone who places a small bet on a horse race will pay closer attention to the horses, and the race, than will someone who has not. One means of gaining this kind of public engagement involves providing incentives to citizens to make small political contributions. As Lisa Young discusses in

Chapter 6 (this volume), the Canadian campaign finance system currently provides a tax credit for political contributions. This credit is structured so that citizens can claim credit for a larger percentage of small contributions than they can for larger contributions. The United States had a small individual tax credit from 1971 to 1985, and six states currently have small tax credits.[30] Tax credits have the potential not only to encourage citizens to give but also to encourage candidates to seek out small donors. Ackerman and Ayres present a more ambitious proposal, in which citizens would be given "patriot dollars," federal funds that they could designate for their candidate of choice in an election. Under their proposal, anyone who wishes to support a candidate can do so without even the short-term loss inherent in the tax credit provision.[31]

Lessons of the BCRA

It would be a mistake to argue that, just because some of the concerns of reformers receded from public view between 2004 and 2010, the United States had taken a step towards a normatively better system before *Citizens United* (or after, for that matter). This is so, in part, because the campaign finance system is not necessarily *about* the values reformers have posited: it has something to do with them, but changes in campaign finance law intersect with the decisions of candidates, parties, and groups in such a way that any change in campaign finance law cannot necessarily go very far in changing our normative assessment of what takes place during elections. These values are all interrelated, but they vary in the degree to which they are actually related to politicians' actions. To illustrate this, let us consider some of the most frequently posited values in play in the campaign finance reform debate.

Transparency, Corruption, and the Appearance of Corruption

Transparency and corruption are in many ways the same issue. To wit, if the public is able to observe that there is a relationship between large campaign contributions and policy making, the incentive for politicians or parties to accept suspect contributions is reduced. The BCRA did not seek to directly address issues of transparency, but the abolition of unrestricted contributions to the parties ensures that, in a system in which contributions are a matter of public record, one cannot draw a line between hard money contributions and politicians' actions. There were already few compelling arguments that contributions from individuals or groups actually lead to corruption on a large scale; however, because the public often makes this link, the removal of suspect categories of fundraising may increase citizens' confidence in the system.

Many of the avenues for unrestricted spending that remain in the American system are among the least transparent areas of spending – expenditures, for instance, by 501(c) 4, 5, and 6 organizations – but they are also sufficiently removed from politicians' own campaigns that they do not necessarily corrupt. Take, for instance, the expenditures of the Chamber of Commerce and the AFL-CIO during the 2008 election. Much of this spending was directed towards congressional campaigns, and it was clearly driven by these groups' concerns about the Employee Free Choice Act. On the one hand, these expenditures were not scrutinized very extensively by a public concerned with the presidential election and the issues at stake there. It was not until several months after the election that relatively precise spending totals for these groups were made available. This issue, however, is hardly a matter of corruption, in that neither side would deem it corrupt for a candidate to take a position for or against the issue: it is simply too large an issue, with no obvious particularized benefits. The donors receive no immediate benefits that can be tied to the contribution, in the manner that some feared that individual soft money donors to the parties might have done during the 1990s. Removing the link between candidates and high-spending groups, then, can remove smaller issues from the agenda and ensure that the issues brought up will be those whose benefits are dispersed, not concentrated. It remains to be seen whether the sort of direct corporate advocacy now permissible following the *Citizens United* decision and the establishment of so-called "Super PACs" will establish such a link.

Mobilization and Engagement

A common theme for all types of interest groups over the past decade has been the turn towards voter mobilization. This trend could well have happened without the passage of reform laws, but the BCRA clearly encouraged group mobilization. It allows groups greater control over their message than do contributions, and it is generally more effective than persuasion, the major goal of electioneering advertisements. One might contend that mobilization is a value in its own right, at least in so far as greater citizen participation (whether in the form of group-sponsored direct contact or, as Young [Chapter 6, this volume] discusses, in the form of solicitation) is generally held to be a good thing. Yet the turn towards mobilization did not come without costs. The increase in voter turnout in the American elections of 2004 and 2008 reversed a trend several decades in the making. Yet mobilization is both a cause and a consequence of the polarization of the American electorate. The increase in small donations has been, in part, a consequence of the scramble by parties to raise money in small amounts.

Mobilization efforts can be viewed through two lenses. First, face-to-face communications are generally held to be a "nicer" version of democracy, at least in so far as the most effective face-to-face fundraising efforts and turnout efforts have depended upon citizens who are, in some sense, "like" the targets of mobilization. The fellow union member or employee, or, for advocacy groups, an activist who shares social traits with those whom he or she seeks to engage, has greater credibility than does someone who is unknown to the voter. A turn towards mobilization thus can strengthen social ties; but mobilization, and the micro-targeting that goes with it, means that citizens lose any sort of shared information source or ability to use the political information they have gathered in conversation with those who do not already share their views. Second, mobilization efforts, especially face-to-face fundraising efforts, have been compared to wagering at a horse race. If a voter has made a small commitment to a candidate – making a small contribution, signing a petition, taking some small step to voice his or her support for a candidate or party – she may make an increased effort in the campaign because she now feels she has a stake in it.

Viewed through both these lenses, any reform that increases citizen engagement is a good thing. Again, it is not clear that campaign finance reform on its own had a substantial effect on the propensity of parties and candidates to do this, and different groups have different abilities to engage in this sort of activity. Mobilization may, then, be felt unequally among citizens. It is one thing to claim that mobilization of the public is a good thing; it is another to argue that mobilization of, for instance, union members is a good thing for those who are not sympathetic to unions' political goals.

Competition and Campaign Discourse

Few American observers saw the BCRA as a measure designed to increase competition in elections. There is little evidence that it influenced competition at the presidential level, in large part because the ongoing breakdown of the presidential public financing system overshadowed any effects that it might have had. At the congressional level, many argued that both of its major provisions would reduce competition: the removal of soft money and the increased restrictions on electioneering would ensure that candidate fundraising was more important than ever before, and incumbents would have an easier time raising money than would challengers.[32] The 2006 and 2008 elections do not necessarily support this claim: in many of the most competitive congressional races, the party campaign committees made up for candidate fundraising differences, and interest group spending in several races also remained a major equalizing factor. Shifting the funding sources has implications for discourse. In other words, it is unlikely that lopsided elections will feature issue-related discourse among the candidates or will educate the voters. Competitive elections may feature more discourse, but here the issue of the quality of discourse becomes a factor. That is, simply because candidates are forced to talk about an issue, or voters are forced to think about an issue, does not mean that this is an issue that *should* be an important factor in the election. However, the predictions about the BCRA's effects on competition and discourse pose a dilemma. On the one hand, an election in which the lion's share of the spending is done by the candidates may result in an advantage for the incumbents and may result in diminished discourse on issues; on the other hand, party electioneering in 2006 and 2008 suggests that the party campaign committees are more likely to air attack ads and less likely to discuss issues than are candidates. Parties can be a nationalizing force, and they can present a set of overarching issues, but there is little reason to suspect that they will do this, with or without soft money. The same can be said about the super PAC and 501(c) groups active in 2010 and 2012.

The most persuasive claims about the consequences of reform for discourse have been made by groups, not parties. Steve Rosenthal, former political director of the AFL-CIO (2002) notes that groups can most effectively raise issues while campaigns are being waged. It is important to note, however, that the American restrictions (as they stood before the *Wisconsin Right to Life* and *Citizens United* decisions) explicitly limited electioneering only where candidates' names are mentioned. This can result merely in coded messages about the candidates, as was the case in the Service Employees International Union (SEIU) advertisements in 2006 that proclaimed that it was "time for a change," but it may also result in more purely issue-oriented advertising during elections. The advertisements run regarding health care by the "Divided We Fail" coalition, which included the American Association of Retired Persons (AARP), the Business Roundtable, the SEIU, and the NFIB, are one example of this. These advertisements ran during the summer of 2008, and they discussed issues and made note of the unusual coalition behind them, but they did not single out candidates. More advertisements of this nature may well be a good thing, but they also comprised a small percentage of the post-reform ads and may well have been unique to the circumstances of the 2008 election.

In addition, any claims regarding discourse founder on the subject of what constitutes legitimate issues.[33] The 2004 Swift Boat Veterans for Truth ads or the 2008 ads linking Barack Obama and former Weatherman Bill Ayers were about issues, albeit issues that were inseparable from one of the candidates. Drawing the line between legitimate and illegitimate issues is difficult, and one can argue that the Divided We Fail ads were the product of a particularly deep-pocketed set of organizations. Groups that have fewer resources but wish to promote their issues may grab the most attention only when their advertisements make strong claims about candidates. Ultimately, the quality of discourse may well have far more to do with the candidates and the nature of the election than with changes in electioneering regulations.

It is easy, then, to connect reforms to the values discussed within the American campaign finance reform movement, but it is hard to draw strong conclusions, in part because so many of these values are affected by so many factors other than the campaign finance system. Limiting the potential for corruption or fixing documented abuses are in themselves legitimate goals for any set of reform proposals, but such fixes are unlikely to influence public sentiment about elections. The BCRA effected the most sweeping change to American campaign finance laws in the past three decades, and it poses the potential that their passage may have exhausted reformers while providing little in the way of measurable results. The reforms that are still on the table in the United States – for instance, pressuring the television networks to provide free air time for candidates, adjusting the public financing system for presidential candidates, or changing tax laws governing political contributions – are in themselves worthy goals, but they are more modest in scope.

NOTES

1 John Samples, *The Fallacy of Campaign Finance Reform* (Chicago: University of Chicago Press, 2006).
2 Russell J. Dalton, *Democratic Challenges, Democratic Choices: The Erosion of Political Support in Advanced Industrial Democracies* (Oxford: Oxford University Press, 2004).
3 Neil Nevitte, "Introduction: Value Change and Reorientation in Citizen-State Relations," in *Value Change and Governance in Canada*, ed. Neil Nevitte (Toronto: University of Toronto Press, 2002); Dalton, *Democratic Challenges*.
4 John R. Hibbing and Elizabeth Theiss-Morse, *Stealth Democracy: Americans' Beliefs about How Government Should Work* (Cambridge/New York, UK/NY: Cambridge University Press, 2002), 99.

5 This typology loosely follows David Mayhew's (1975) typology of the goals of members of Congress. See David Mayhew, *Congress: The Electoral Connection* (New Haven: Yale University Press, 1975).
6 Anthony Corrado, "Money and Politics: A History of Federal Campaign Finance Law," in *Campaign Finance Reform: A Sourcebook*, ed. Anthony Corrado, Thomas E. Mann, Daniel R. Ortiz, and Trevor Potter (Washington, DC: Brookings Institution, 1997), 30-31.
7 For a summary of FECA, see Trevor Potter, "Where Are We Now: The Current State of Campaign Finance Law," in *Campaign Finance Reform: A Sourcebook*, ed. Anthony Corrado, Thomas E. Mann, Daniel R. Ortiz, and Trevor Potter (Washington, DC: Brookings Institution, 1997). For comparisons of FECA and BCRA, see Marian Currinder, "Campaign Finance: Funding the Presidential and Congressional Elections," in *The Elections of 2004*, ed. Michael Nelson (Washington, DC: Congressional Quarterly, 2005); Michael J. Malbin, "Assessing the Bipartisan Campaign Reform Act," in *The Election after Reform: Money, Politics, and the Bipartisan Campaign Reform Act*, ed. Michael J. Malbin (Lanham: Rowman and Littlefield, 2006).
8 Frank J. Sorauf, *Inside Campaign Finance: Myths and Realities* (New Haven: Yale University Press, 1994), 230-35.
9 Norman J. Ornstein, Thomas E. Mann, and Michael J. Malbin, *Vital Statistics on Congress* (Washington, DC: American Enterprise Institute, 2002), 106.
10 See, for example, Frank J. Sorauf, "Political Action Committees," in *Campaign Finance Reform: A Sourcebook*, ed. Anthony Corrado, Thomas E. Mann, Daniel R. Ortiz, and Trevor Potter (Washington, DC: Brookings Institution, 1997), 125.
11 Michael J. Malbin, "Thinking about Reform," in *Life after Reform: When the Bipartisan Campaign Reform Act Meets Politics*, ed. Michael J. Malbin (Lanham: Rowman and Littlefield, 2003), 5-6. Soft money as a category had existed since 1980, as detailed in Corrado, "Money and Politics," 171-73, but the aggregated amount of soft money raised and spent never exceeded $100 million before 1996.
12 Malbin, "Thinking about Reform," 5-6.
13 Taylor E. Dark, *The Unions and the Democrats: An Enduring Alliance* (Ithaca: Cornell University Press, 1999), 184-86.
14 Anna Nibley Baker and David B. Magleby, "Interest Groups in the 2000 Congressional Elections," in *The Other Campaign: Soft Money and Issue Advocacy in the 2000 Elections*, ed. David B. Magleby (Lanham: Rowman and Littlefield, 2002); David B. Magleby and Jonathan W. Tanner, "Interest Group Electioneering in the 2002 Congressional Elections," in *The Last Hurrah? Soft Money and Issue Advocacy in the 2002 Congressional Elections*, ed. David B. Magleby and J. Quin Monson (Washington, DC: Brookings Institution, 2004).
15 Shaleigh Murray and Perry Bacon, "Obama to Reject Public Funds," *Washington Post*, 20 June 2008.
16 Jake Tapper, "Obama Prepares Argument to Discard Public Financing Principle," *ABC News Blog*, 8 April 2008.
17 This amount is calculated from data by Campaign Finance Institute, "CFI Analysis of Presidential Candidates' Financial Activity through August 31," press release, 26 September 2008.

18 According to many accounts, Bill Clinton was able to do this to Robert Dole in 1996. During that election, however, Clinton did accept matching funds and both parties were able to spend soft money.
19 Anthony Corrado, "Party Finance in the Wake of BCRA: An Overview," in *The Election after Reform: Money, Politics, and the Bipartisan Campaign Reform Act*, ed. Michael J. Malbin (Lanham: Rowman and Littlefield, 2006).
20 In the case of the NRCC and the NRSC, the decline likely reflects the party's loss of seats in Congress; in the case of the Democratic National Committee, the decrease in funds from 2004 to 2008 is a function of Barack Obama's decision to continue to raise money during the general election.
21 Robert G. Boatright, Michael J. Malbin, Mark Rozell, and Clyde Wilcox, "Interest Groups and Advocacy Organizations after BCRA," in *The Election after Reform: Money, Politics, and the Bipartisan Campaign Reform Act*, ed. Michael J. Malbin (Lanham: Rowman and Littlefield, 2006).
22 These comments, as well as information below on union and corporate strategy, are drawn from interviews conducted for Boatright et al., "Interest Groups and Advocacy Organizations after BCRA."
23 Steven Rosenthal, "Response to Malbin et al.," *Election Law Journal* 1, 4 (2002): 552.
24 Steven Rosenthal, "Okay, We Lost Ohio. The Question Is, Why?," *Washington Post*, 5 December 2004.
25 Anna Nibley Baker and David B. Magleby, "Interest Groups in the 2000 Congressional Elections," in *The Other Campaign: Soft Money and Issue Advocacy in the 2000 Elections*, ed. David B. Magleby (Lanham: Rowman and Littlefield, 2003); Magleby and Tanner, "Interest Group Electioneering."
26 Brody Mullins and Charlie Mitchell, "Saying "No" to Soft Money," *National Journal*, 24 March 2001, 870-75.
27 Chris Cillizza, "Republicans Plan $50 Million Independent Effort in 2010," *Washington Post*, 5 April 2010.
28 Boatright et al., "Interest Groups"; Michael M. Franz, Joel Rivlin, and Kenneth Goldstein, "Much More of the Same: Television Advertising Pre- and Post-BCRA," in *The Election after Reform: Money, Politics, and the Bipartisan Campaign Reform Act*, ed. Michael Malbin (Lanham: Rowman and Littlefield, 2006).
29 Paul Taylor, *The Case for Free Air Time* (Washington: Alliance for Better Campaigns, 2002); Robert G. Boatright, *Political Advertising Vouchers for Candidates: What Difference Could They Make?* (Washington, DC: Campaign Finance Institute, 2005).
30 David Rosenberg, *Broadening the Base: The Case for a New Federal Tax Credit for Political Contributions* (Washington, DC: American Enterprise Institute, 2002); Robert G. Boatright and Michael J. Malbin, "Political Contribution Tax Credits and Citizen Participation," *American Politics Research* 33, 6 (2005): 787-818.
31 Bruce Ackerman and Ian Ayres, *Voting with Dollars* (New Haven: Yale University Press, 2002).
32 James E. Campbell, "The Stagnation of Congressional Elections," in *Life after Reform: When the Bipartisan Campaign Reform Act Meets Politics*, ed. Michael Malbin (Lanham: Rowman and Littlefield, 2003).
33 Larry M. Bartels and Lynn Vavreck, eds., *Campaign Reform: Insights and Evidence* (Ann Arbor: University of Michigan Press, 2000).

# 8 Imperfect Legislatures

DAVID C. DOCHERTY

Legislatures are the heart of a democratic society. This is where the laws of the land are debated, altered, approved, or rejected. The US Congress and the Canadian Parliament are two models of liberal democratic legislatures, each of which poses its own challenges with respect to the democratic deficit and the quality of democracy in the two countries. Like all institutions of government, legislatures are far from perfect. Some assemblies may have strengths in some elements of representation (such as powerful individual members) but major weaknesses in others (such as an inability to achieve consensus on large policy issues). Some assemblies might have too much authority vested in too few hands but have more freedom to quickly respond to a crisis; others may disperse power widely but be unable to act effectively or quickly.

The Canadian Parliament (and its provincial assemblies) are highly centralized and executive centred. Characterized by high levels of party discipline and a lack of a meaningful independent role for individual members, Canadian assemblies are often criticized for not properly performing the scrutiny and oversight for which they were originally designed, much less the role of legislative initiator often ascribed to the US Congress. Even by Westminster standards, Canada has a weak legislature. The ability of private members, either as individuals or as Opposition parties, to hold the feet of the executive to the fire of public scrutiny and accountability is limited.

By contrast, the US Congress is among the strongest legislative bodies in the world. Despite the continual complaints of American political observers that Congress is characterized by excessive self-interest, parochialism, and partisanship, there is one overriding task that Congress regularly performs that makes the Canadian Parliament pale by comparison. Simply put, Congress is a tremendously effective check on presidential power, to the point that even presidents with strong popular mandates face severe obstacles in accomplishing their electoral goals.

It might be expected that the most visible and powerful political institutions, like Congress, would command greater public confidence than weaker institutions. As in other Western democracies, political institutions in both Canada and the United States, including legislatures, have lost public confidence. But the US Congress has declined much more dramatically in public esteem than has the Canadian Parliament. In 2010, Congress ranked last in public confidence among sixteen public and private institutions. Only 11 percent of Americans had a great deal or quite a lot of confidence in Congress, dramatically down from levels in the 1970s and 1980s. Half of Americans voiced "little or no" confidence in Congress.[1] According to the 2005-6 World Values Survey discussed in Stephen White and Neil Nevitte's chapter,[2] the US Congress enjoyed less public confidence than legislatures in sixteen other advanced countries.

By contrast, almost 40 percent of Canadians voiced confidence in Parliament – almost twice the American level. Canada ranked sixth out of the sixteen nations. The Canadian numbers were slightly lower than they had been in the 1980s, but not greatly so. This is surprising, given the widespread belief that Parliament is powerless in the face of executive dominance and the extensive criticism of excessive partisanship. In its "Report Card" on "Confidence in Parliament" the Conference Board of Canada noted "slight improvement" and gave a rating of C, in contrast to Congress, which rated a D.[3] In both cases, however, the legislature ranked considerably lower than the esteem accorded to some other institutions. There is more support for the judicial system and the courts than there is for elected members of the national legislature.

The low regard for both bodies suggests that the problem does not lie in the powers each assembly deploys, these being so different; rather, the democratic deficit seems to lie elsewhere. If this is true, then what is its cause? And does this suggest that the so-called democratic deficit in Canada is different than that faced in the United States? Indeed, this seems to be the case. Parliamentary reform proposals in Canada focus on strengthening

Parliament, its committees, and its members against an overweening executive. American reformers tend to call for more coherence, discipline, and less partisanship and dependence on "special interests, gerrymandered districts and an unregulated system of financing elections." Each has its distinct reform agenda.[4] The common criticism of both institutions is focused on perceived excesses in partisanship. Put another way, much of the democratic deficit lies with the performance of legislatures and not with their design. The rules *permit* high levels of party discipline in Canada and high levels of partisanship in the United States, but they do not *require* such behaviour.

In order to properly assess the work of each institution we must understand their underlying logic. Legislatures and other institutions must be assessed on the performance of the roles they were meant to perform, not on roles that they are neither equipped nor designed to perform. The fundamental institutional difference is between (1) Westminster style parliamentary, cabinet, or "responsible government" (characterized by a close link between legislature and executive) and concentrated authority in Canada and (2) separation of powers, checks and balances, and dispersal of authority in the United States. This chapter argues that these imperfect assemblies do indeed have room for improvement. But this does not require wholesale reformation of the Westminster (or the Congressional) system itself; rather, it requires allowing Canadian legislators some of the freedoms and resources provided to American lawmakers while avoiding a system that favours legislative gridlock over consensus and deliberation, the bane of the American congressional system.

The Democratic Role of Legislatures

Representation
The three principle functions of assemblies are to represent, to legislate, and to keep the administration accountable. The legislature is the key link between citizens and the state. There are other important roles for assemblies to perform as well. They help to recruit potential new leaders and act as a training ground for future leadership. In addition, assemblies should serve as debating forums whose purpose is to provide the public with alternative public policies and leadership.

There are many ways to measure equality of representation. The most obvious in a constituency-based system, as exists in Canada and the United States, is to determine whether constituencies are equal in size. Here the

TABLE 8.1
Population of districts in the Canadian House of Commons

Jurisdiction	Number of seats in Commons	Population	Citizens per district
British Columbia	36	4,460,300	123,897
Alberta	28	3,670,700	101,964
Saskatchewan	14	1,029,100	73,507
Manitoba	14	1,219,600	87,114
Ontario	106	13,064,900	123,254
Quebec	75	7,828,400	104,379
New Brunswick	10	749,300	74,930
Nova Scotia	11	939,100	85,373
Prince Edward Island	4	141,100	35,275
Newfoundland and Labrador	7	508,100	72,586
Nunavut	1	32,200	32,200
Northwest Territories	1	43,700	43,700
Yukon	1	33,700	33,700

Note: Population figures are based on Statistics Canada 2009 population survey. Seat numbers are based on the 2008 federal election.

United States is far closer to equality than is Canada. Redistribution in Canada is based on the fundamental principle that no province will lose seats in the House of Commons as a result of population growth or population shifts.[5] Thus, the size of the House of Commons increases with each decennial census. Combined with seat protection for smaller provinces and Quebec, this has created huge gaps in the population of ridings across the country. As Table 8.1 indicates, the largest disparity exists between the high-growth provinces of British Columbia, Alberta, and Ontario and Prince Edward Island (the smallest province). Within US states, by contrast, one person, one vote is the rule.

The US House of Representatives operates with a fixed number of members. Based on population changes various states may gain or lose seats in the House of Representatives. Further, the disparity in Canada works in favour of less populous provinces; the opposite is true in the United States. North Dakota does not have the population to warrant two districts in the lower house, and thus its nearly 1 million residents must share one representative. By contrast, seat protection in Canada ensures that Prince Edward

Island will always have a minimum of four seats, no matter what its population. The same population in Ontario and BC suburbs would only have one member.

The disparity in federal riding sizes has caused concern among political observers, who suggest that it might be contrary to the equality of vote provision required by the Charter of Rights and Freedoms.[6] In their analysis of minority representation in the Canadian system, Choudhry and Pal show that the combined effect of Canadian practices results in serious lack of inclusion for minorities and recent immigrants, the great majority of whom live in a few metropolitan areas.[7]

Neither legislature comes close to representing women and men equally. In 2011, according to the Interparliamentary Union, Canada ranked thirty-eighth in the world, with women comprising just 24.7 percent of members in the House of Commons and 35.9 percent in the Senate. The United States ranks seventieth, with 17 percent of members in both houses being women.[8] Both countries use the single-member district electoral system.

On the other hand, justification for some deviancy in constituency size is justified in terms of the massive distances involved in remote Canadian (and American) districts. In northern ridings many communities are not accessible by road, and a member could spend several days in a single sweep of her or his district. In these latter cases, the linkage between the citizen and the state via a member of Parliament is particularly crucial as it may be the only form of contact between the two.

Equality of population is not a factor in either upper national chamber. California has the same number of senators as does North Dakota – two. The seat distribution of the Canadian Senate is set out in the original and amended BNA acts and is based on regional distribution. It provides twenty-four seats to each of the West, Ontario, Quebec, and the East. Newfoundland and Labrador were given seven seats when it entered Confederation in 1949, and the three territories each have one senate seat.[9]

An important difference between members of the two houses involves the extent to which they hold office by virtue of their own initiative and the extent to which their success depends on their personal characteristics. Interestingly, there is little evidence that much personal voting occurs in Canada. Most studies indicate that incumbency rarely accounts for more than 5 percent of a local vote total;[10] instead, party and leader are the largest determinants of electoral outcomes. By contrast, American legislators enjoy substantial personal and incumbency benefits, despite much larger districts. At first blush the lack of a personal vote suggests that Canadian legislators have been unable to connect with voters, a possible sign that Canadians are disenchanted with their parliamentarians. However, a closer examination suggests that this may not be all bad news. First, the lack of a personal vote is not a recent phenomenon in Canadian politics. It goes back well over forty years,[11] and thus it is not directly tied to more recent questions about the democratic deficit. Second, Canadians are not averse to "throwing the bums out." Despite occasional talk of term limits and recall in Canada, there is no obvious need to legislatively control how long members can stay in office.[12] Finally, repeated electoral studies have demonstrated that a small but critical mass of Canadians do vote based on the merits of local candidates. However, this number pales in comparison to Canadians whose vote choice is dictated by party or leader. Turnover in Canadian parliamentary elections is far greater than it is in American elections. This may be due, in part, to the lack of influence of Canadian MPs, making the position far less attractive than that of an American senator or representative.[13]

Perhaps discouragingly, but not surprisingly, the appointed Senate has done a much better job at representing the demographic profile of Canada than have the elected chambers. Over one-third of senators are women, compared to just over 22 percent of members of the lower house (2010 figures). Aboriginal Canadians are also better represented in the Senate than in the House of Commons. The percentage of women in the US Senate is approximately that found in the House of Representatives (but it is far lower than what is found in the Canadian upper chamber). African Americans are vastly underrepresented in both bodies. Presently, no African American sits in the US Senate, and only forty-four of the 435 members of the House of Representatives are African American.[14]

If the priority of legislatures is to closely mirror the population, then elected assemblies are not necessarily "better" at better representing citizens. Of course, the power of the appointed Senate, while constitutionally strong, has less legitimacy in the eyes of the public than does the power of the House of Commons, thus substantive representation in the Senate is difficult to achieve.

Legislation
Aside from representation, assemblies play an important law-making role in democratic states. Here there is a stark difference between Canada and the United States. The US Congress is a powerful legislative body by any measure. Not only does it accept, reject, and amend legislative initiatives

proposed by the administration, but it also initiates much legislation. Similarly, it not only accepts or rejects the administration's budget proposals but also initiates taxing and spending proposals.

All legislatures face the charge that they are little more than arenas of partisan confrontation rather than arenas of consensus building and deliberation. Those concerned with fixing the democratic deficit have argued that a more civil and deliberative assembly focused on problem solving would have greater public legitimacy than would one filled with acrimony and vitriol. Whether true or not, such an assessment ignores the larger benefits provided by the confrontational nature of both Westminster and congressional democracies. They both provide choices about governments and potential alternative governments, and they both allow policies to be thoroughly debated, weighed, judged, and scrutinized.

In Canada, only the executive can introduce legislation that calls for the introduction of taxes, thus effectively preventing private members from engaging in broader public policy initiation. Private members have more leeway when it comes to the introduction of legislation that would not require the spending of public monies, but they do not have nearly as much freedom as do cabinet ministers.[15] It is much harder for a private member, belonging either to the government or to the Opposition, to successfully shepherd her/his bills through the legislative process. Members of the US Congress are much more likely than are members of Parliament to act as legislative entrepreneurs.

The fusion of the executive and legislature in Canada is perhaps most obvious in the government's control over legislation. The executive enjoys a near monopoly on bills that would cause a spending of public funds and effectively controls the legislative timetable (though the government House leader does work with Opposition House leaders to try to coordinate the timing of hearings so as to allow Opposition critics the ability to participate in debates). The most obvious sign of the strength of cabinet is the fact that the House as a collectivity does not initiate legislation; rather, it passes, defeats, and fine-tunes bills originating in cabinet.

Minority government has increasingly become the norm in Canada. In one sense, this increases the role of Parliament because the governing party must bargain with Opposition parties for support on legislation, thus providing them some policy leverage. This, however, does not mean any weakening of party discipline or more autonomy for individual members. Legislation emanates from the government, not from individual members and certainly not from bipartisan-sponsored legislation. This is one of the most dramatic differences between the Westminster and congressional forms of government.[16]

MPs do have a say on government bills after they have been introduced in the House of Commons. Participation in the legislative process typically occurs in debates during second and third reading and in the amending of bills in House committees. With the passage of second reading, a bill is agreed to in principle. This does not mean that it cannot be amended, and most legislation does change at least in detail in committee – often at the government's behest. However, the passage of the bill does, in principle, commit political parties to a particular view on the bill and thus can tie the hands of party members who may wish to break ranks with their colleagues.

Attempts have been made to have more legislation sent to committee earlier in the process, which may result in more bipartisan amendments made to legislation, more constructive use of witnesses (both expert and interested individuals and groups), and less confrontational hearings.[17] However, use of this legislative practice remains rare in Canada; it is more common in Great Britain, where party discipline is less entrenched than it is in Canada.

The fact that Canada traditionally places such strong emphasis on party discipline discourages all attempts at minimizing adversarial governance. Canadian prime ministers have typically treated even minor matters as questions of confidence, requiring their members to vote as a block. Opposition parties do the same, and thus the outcome of most votes is known well in advance. This strong commitment to strict party discipline has been practised by both Liberal and Conservative prime ministers. Its virtue is that it can allow parties to demonstrate a united front on an issue and provide citizens with clear choices between political parties. Its danger is that it can paint leaders as intransigent and MPs as mere followers who may have to ignore the views of constituents on critical issues, thus making a mockery of the democratic process.

Perhaps the most damning example of the latter occurred during the last days of the Chrétien regime in 2003. Chrétien introduced substantial changes to public funding of elections, which dramatically increased public funding of political parties and just as dramatically decreased the amount that corporations and unions could donate to parties. For individual MPs, the most difficult piece of the proposed legislation involved changes that would have made it more difficult to raise and spend money locally, thereby further increasing the hold that the central party had on them.[18] Thus, one arguably democratic reform – namely, reducing the influence of business and labour in politics – had an arguably undemocratic consequence: namely, further strengthening party discipline and executive dominance.

Prime Minister Chrétien took considerable heat from his own caucus over this legislation, in part due to the fact that his retirement was forthcoming and he seemed to be creating legislation that his successor would have to live with but he would not. Instead of altering his own legislation, Chrétien threatened his own members by treating it as a matter of confidence and vowing to call an election if the bill was defeated. Effectively, he would have then been in a position of travelling the country asking Canadians to vote for Liberal candidates to pass a bill that many had just voted against.[19] The absurdity of this aside, the larger point remains. Prime ministers use party discipline not just to work against the Opposition but also to keep their own MPs on a very short leash.

By contrast, the McCain-Feingold Bill in the United States dramatically altered finance laws and attempted to decrease the use of "soft money" spent prior to and during election campaigns.[20] The bill was co-sponsored by Republican senator John McCain and Democratic senator Russell Feingold. Bills in the US Congress are often co-sponsored, though those that find support and sponsorship that cross party lines are thought to have better chances at success.

Party unity and control of members by the party leadership has increased in the Congress in recent decades as politics has become more polarized. But this leadership and discipline comes from within congressional ranks, not, as in Canada, from the executive; and individual members are still left with more freedom of action than are Canadian MPs.

The separation of executive and legislative branches in the congressional system renders questions of confidence moot. Congress cannot unseat the president, except through impeachment. The president does not technically control the legislative agenda but, more often, reacts to it, either by signing or vetoing legislation that originates in Congress. The executive can send legislation (such as the budget) to Congress, and presidents spend a great deal of time trying to convince members of both parties to support presidential measures; however, the only power he/she has at his/her disposal is the power of persuasion. Further, whipped votes can mean little in the United States, where the president's party might not control the House or Senate. Since 1992, the party of the president has controlled the House only 55 percent of the time and has controlled the Senate only 45 percent of the time. Even before questions of party discipline arise, the president starts at a huge disadvantage compared to the prime minister. "Divided government" cannot exist in the Canadian system. Put another way, during times of majority government in the Canadian House of Commons, the cabinet rules. In the United States, rule is conducted through shifting coalitions of minorities.

The legislative role of Congress starts from a different premise than does the legislative role of Westminster assemblies like Canada's. As Mayhew points out in his seminal piece on Congress, the actions of all legislators are geared towards their re-election.[21] Sponsoring, co-sponsoring, and actively engaging in the legislative process is a part of the re-electoral process that is virtually non-existent in Canadian assemblies. Private member's bills in Canada have far less importance or chance of success than do bills either individually sponsored or co-sponsored in Congress. Further, the need to placate voters at home encourages the type of pork-barrelling legislation that has come to haunt the American system, something also absent from legislation in the Canadian system (largely because legislation in Canada is not directly connected to electoral success).

Accountability

Differences in the oversight function also exist between the two assemblies. The notion of scrutiny, or accountability, is at the core of responsible government. Cabinet ministers are responsible for the actions and decisions of their respective departments, and all members of the House of Commons, including government private members, are responsible for holding cabinet to account for spending and the administration of public policies and legislation. There are a number of ways to accomplish this, many of them institutionalized in the rules and roles of House procedure. Unlike in the congressional system, in the parliamentarian system the fusing of the executive and the legislature promotes an adversarial relationship not just between political parties but also, and particularly, between Opposition parties and the executive. The focus then is not between competing legislators but, rather, between the prime minister and his or her cabinet and the Opposition, with its leader and shadow cabinet. And, in stark contrast to what occurs in the United States, this adversarial relationship is played out face to face every day the legislature meets.

The most successful form of accountability in the Canadian setting takes place during the daily Question Period. It has been noted that Question Period is a bloodier battlefront than World Wrestling Entertainment and that the words and antics displayed are not fit for children, or adults, to witness. While this is a caricature, there is enough acting out and childish behaviour present to allow such comparisons to be made. Recent parliaments in Canada have become more acrimonious, and the anger and tension felt between the major political parties is palpable. The same is true in the United States.

Question Period allows the Opposition to place unscripted questions directly to the executive.[22] A skilled Opposition can sometimes use this opportunity to effectively seize the government's agenda. A cabinet minister who is not well briefed can look like the proverbial deer in the headlights, and this can have a lasting impact on his/her career. If a cabinet minister becomes part of the casualties of this war, all the better for the Opposition.[23]

And it is precisely because these stakes are so high that Question Period is not only the most watched part of the legislative calendar but also the least attractive. This is the Catch-22 of Question Period. When accountability works best, it looks worst. If a cabinet minister has not lived up to executive responsibility or has transgressed rules of ethical behaviour, then it is typically during Question Period that these matters come to the floor. Opposition members, smelling victory over the government, are loathe to let up, while cabinet ministers fighting for their political lives will not back down unless told to do so by the prime minister. Yet even if the drama is unpleasant to watch, and the conduct of MPs often irresponsible, we cannot hide the simple fact that Question Period does produce the results it was designed for – namely, ensuring government accountability in a very public forum. An adversarial process can have positive results for effective scrutiny.

There are other forms of scrutiny in Canada, including set-piece debates on the Speech from the Throne (which opens Parliament and is somewhat equivalent to the president's State of the Union address in the United States) and on the budget, which provide opportunities for broad criticism of the government and possible votes of confidence that could bring the government down. Parliamentary committees provide opportunities to question ministers and officials, but in most cases their work is dominated by the governing majority MPs.

Accountability operates very differently in the United States. Most simply put, the US Congress has vastly more resources and political autonomy to exercise accountability than do MPs or Parliament as an entity. For example, the Congressional Budget Office is a long-established and legitimate body that advises Congress on budgetary matter. In 2010, it had a budget of $46.8 million and a staff of 250. Canada established a somewhat similar body in 2008, the Parliamentary Budget Office. In 2010, it had a budget of

$2.8 million and a staff of fourteen. Given the complexity of the American system, a large Congressional Budget Office (CBO) is understandable, though perhaps not at nearly twenty times the budget and staff of its Canadian counterpart. Moreover, the CBO is an authoritative alternative source of fiscal information and advice; in Canada, the government has given the parliamentary officer little weight.[24]

By contrast, there is no daily face-to-face interaction between members of Congress and the executive in the congressional system. As a result, whether or not the president's party controls either of the chambers, the accountability mechanisms are such that cabinet does not answer directly to members within either the Senate or House. While the checks and balances on a president's authority are strong, they do not include having to face a daily grilling such as Canada's Question Period. They do not effectively hold the government as a whole responsible. As a result, a president can be more successful in avoiding the type of scrutiny that could be the downfall of a prime minister. For example, whether or not the impeachment proceedings for Bill Clinton would have succeeded, it is difficult to imagine any president surviving a daily onslaught of questions that crossed both personal and professional lines. Lying at the heart of the charges against Clinton were ideological and political goals. The lines between Congress and the Presidency afforded some opportunity for the president to distance himself from the hearings. Whereas loyalty to the leader becomes the starting point for most legislative careers in Canada, in the United States the Congress is a common starting point for a presidential campaign and most American legislators are individual actors.

The lack of party discipline in the United States compared to what we find in Canada is perhaps the largest contrast between the two nations. Party leaders in the United States have fewer carrots or sticks with which to tempt or threaten caucus members. That is not to suggest that party discipline is not present in the United States, merely that it is lacking compared to the overwhelming concern with party voting in Canada. Party whips do exercise authority over their members, particularly when the vote outcome is in doubt and when there is not a huge divide within the party.[25] Further, when Newt Gingrich flexed his muscles with new (and veteran) Republican House members with his Contract with America in the 1994 mid-term vote, it was less a contract with the people and more a contract with the soon-to-be House Speaker. Party discipline again came to the fore in the deeply divided Congress during the Obama presidency.

For members of the US House of Representatives, party loyalty is important but not as critical as understanding and playing by the informal rules that govern the assembly. Seniority is just as critical as is heeding the party whip. With little prospect (or even desire) to leave a secure House seat for a cabinet spot, members are more content to build policy expertise through the committee system. In this light American members hold much more in common with British MPs than with Canadian MPs. UK members understand that the opportunities for cabinet service are slim and thus build legislative careers that include long-term service to one or two committees.

The difference between US House of Representative committees and Canadian House of Commons committees is striking. At the heart of the difference lie two factors: resources and expertise. In terms of resources, committees in the Canadian House of Commons have made significant advances over the past two decades. Committees are active, having full-time clerks and staff resources for research. The Parliamentary Library provides non-partisan research services for MPs. However, even these resources (not to mention caucus and individual MP's staff support) are not sufficient to provide a level of professionalism that matches the American committee structure.

Members in the Canadian House of Commons are too often stretched thin on committees. This is as much a result of the reality of the multi-party system in Canada since 1993 as it is a structural design of committees. Since the success of the sovereigntist Bloc Québécois in the post-Meech Lake period, the House of Commons has had either four or five active political parties, each of which has been eligible to sit and vote on committees since 1997.[22] The number of committees, the size of committees, and the number of smaller parties meant that many MPs were on two or three committees, while some government MPs had the luxury of sitting on only one committee. Thus government MPs, who often ignored their scrutiny function in defence of the cabinet, were at a distinct advantage when it came to displaying knowledge of matters in front of a committee.

Table 8.2 delineates some comparisons between American and Canadian legislative committees. The US House of Representatives is almost defined by the work of its committees. With over one hundred more members than its Canadian counterpart and the same number of committees, its members understand that their careers are in many ways defined by their role on committees and subcommittees. While the hard and fast seniority rule that governed promotion through the committee ranks is no longer followed, it is

TABLE 8.2
Committee sizes in selected lower chambers

Jurisdiction	Size of Assembly (House in US case)	Number of committees	Size of committees	Number of subcommittees (per committee)
House of Commons	308	26	11-12	0-2
House of Representatives	435	25	30-58	5-7
Prince Edward Island	27	7	8	typically none
North Dakota	94	19	8-14	typically few
Ontario	107	9	9	ad hoc
New York	150	37	12-31	0-1

Note: Committees for both House of Representatives and House of Commons include joint House and Senate committees. Note also the nineteen North Dakota committees include procedural committees that can do the work of subcommittees.

understood that committee chairs are still reserved for the more senior members of the House. Likewise, positioning on the right subcommittee and committee is still regarded as essential to a successful legislative career.

By contrast, committees in the Canadian House are less highly regarded, even by members themselves. It is true that most members still see committee work as less partisan and more constructive than work conducted on the floor of the House, but few members are under the illusion that there are electoral rewards for efforts put into work on committees. Further, the control that the executive exerts on party discipline can also be felt in determining the leadership of committees.

While committees formally elect their own chair in the Canadian House, the process is stage managed by the prime minister's and government house leader's office.[26] Thus, promotion to committee chair is not seen as providing peer recognition of either seniority or policy expertise but, rather, as reinforcing loyalty to the party leader. This effectively undermines much of the effectiveness of committees in undertaking their scrutiny function.

By contrast, American committees are effective participants in the oversight function as their independence from the executive and the bureaucracy is institutionally enshrined. Committees can effectively scrutinize the operations of government to a much greater degree than can Canadian committees. At the same time, the independence that congressional committees enjoy from the executive facilitates incremental and seemingly irreversible increases in government spending, often aimed at members' districts. This so-called pork barrel politics has been pegged as the culprit for ever-increasing government debt and a lack of any ability to make long-term and strategic policy decisions.

The fusion of executive and legislature has an impact on committees even beyond questions of party discipline and leader control. This is seen more readily at the subnational level. Even in less populous states (such as North Dakota), committees are more numerous and have more members than in larger Canadian provinces (such as Ontario). In the case of the Canadian provinces, the problem is largely one of numbers, with the size of the assembly an often misleading figure. Although there are 107 members in the Ontario Legislative Assembly, only roughly eighty of them are eligible to serve on committees. Cabinet is typically about twenty-five members: the speaker and the two Opposition Party leaders do not serve on committees. In Prince Edward Island, lopsided elections in that two-party province have often left the Opposition with fewer than half a dozen members. Larger numbers of committees and larger membership on committees is an ineffective vehicle for accountability.

The Challenges of an Upper Chamber

The fact that Canada appoints and the United States elects members to the Upper House underlines the many differences in power and legitimacy between the two bodies. On 27 August 2009, Prime Minister Stephen Harper made nine appointments to the Canadian Senate, colloquially referred to as the Red Chamber. Of the nine appointees, five had direct ties to the ruling Conservative Party and two others were Conservative supporters. There is nothing surprising about these appointments. The power to select senators rests with the prime minister.[27] The prerequisites for office set out in the Constitution are straightforward: a minimum age of thirty and an outdated property requirement of four thousand dollars. Senate appointments last until the incumbent reaches seventy-five, thus avoiding the distraction of upcoming elections looming in the background.

In making these appointments, Harper was violating commitments to Senate reform that had been a major part of his own election platform. Among other things, proponents of Senate reform have campaigned to have senators elected, to change the regional balance of the Senate, and to limit the time that senators can sit in the Red Chamber. In its current form, the

Senate has little political legitimacy and little political influence. Yet it is not clear that changing the way senators are selected would solve its legitimacy problems. In fact, such reforms may well create new problems for Parliament.

If one looks at the powers of each assembly as outlined in their respective constitutions, one might be surprised to find more similarities than differences. Both are supposed to be chambers of intra-state federalism, both must approve legislation prior to its becoming law, both are seen to represent higher national and regional interests than the lower assembly, both are seen as independent of the executive (though this feature is shared by the American lower House as well), and both were originally conceived as elite checks on more populist elected bodies. Yet the US Senate has evolved into the preeminent democratic chamber in the country, while the Canadian Senate struggles to maintain any form of public support.

Indeed, the US Senate, as the "senior" chamber, enjoys a level of legitimacy that allows it to openly challenge the executive. The Canadian Senate does this at its own peril, often drawing attention to its own democratic shortfalls. The US Senate is not above filibustering bills or executive appointments. The Canadian Senate treads very rarely and very carefully into these waters, though members of the Senate often threaten the government with such tactics. Sadly for Canadian senators, they can talk loudly but they carry a very small stick.

It is unfortunate that the considerable good work of Canadian senators is lost in the minds of a public that questions the very legitimacy of the body in which they serve. Among other attributes of the Senate is its ability to limit the level of partisanship that dominates the House of Commons. This is particularly true with regard to major pieces of government policy when legislation goes to Senate committees. In some instances these committees will hear from more witnesses and allow them greater freedom to present their views than is granted those who appear before House committees.[28] Senators are freer to shed their partisan clothes precisely because they are appointed and not beholden to either party leaders or voters to continue their political careers. In this sense, the Canadian Senate has a more collegial "club"-like manner, similar to that which historically defined the US Senate (though much less so recently), at least in comparison to the two "junior" houses." A life term, with no need for re-election, lends itself to bipartisanship even more so than does a six-year term with high re-election rates.

As Franks notes, senators tend to be far more informed on committee matters than MPs, if only due to the time they have to spend on committee work. With fewer competing demands on their time, senators are more likely to become well versed in the issues in front of their committee.[29]

Senators are also freer than are members of the House of Commons to become policy entrepreneurs. Senators have been able to use the freedom of their position to not only develop expertise in specific public policies but also to use the Senate as a forum for keeping policies in the public mind. Most recently, for example, Senator Colin Kenny (Liberal) developed a national reputation as an expert in national security. His profile is due in large part to his position as a senator and, thus, his ability to keep issues publicly front and centre.

Finally, it is worth noting that the Canadian Senate can serve as a chamber of sober reflection. The Senate does provide an opportunity for legislation to be fine-tuned and altered and even sent back to the House of Commons. While this type of action can allow the government to score political points regarding the unelected nature of the Senate, it does require prime ministers to be mindful of legislation that the Senate sees as problematic. The Senate's informal power in this regard is really dependent upon how many times it goes to this particular well. If the Senate were to continually send legislation back to the House, it might face criticism not only from government MPs but also from Canadians. The fact that this power is rarely used by the Senate means that a threat to use it would have to be taken seriously.

Despite a public that sees little good in the Senate, there is little prospect of major Senate reform in the foreseeable future. Attempts over the past two decades to bring major change to the Senate have failed, largely due to the over-ambitious agenda of both the reform issues themselves and the other constitutional questions to which they were tied. For example, attempts to alter the regional balance of representation have raised quite different issues than have attempts to secure the election of members or shorter terms. Even incremental attempts at Senate reform, such as limited terms and advisory elections, have made little progress, despite frequent promises by the Harper government.[30]

It is difficult to predict whether and how an elected senate would change the political dynamic of Canadian parliamentary government or address the democratic deficit. Senators more closely tied to local and provincial constituencies might, as in the United States, inject a greater measure of intra-province or legislative federalism into the Canadian system, challenging the current dominance of executive federalism. A senate elected to different terms and constituency boundaries could provide an alternative basis for representation to that offered in the House of Commons. On the other hand, alternative models could easily produce a senate that mimicked the House, replicating current party discipline. There is also fear that party discipline would rob the Senate of its present real, if limited, independence. An elected senate would challenge the legitimacy of the House of Commons and raise questions about the dynamics of "responsible government."[31]

Strengthening the Good and Opportunities for Further Reform

There is still a great deal that could be done to improve the capacity of legislatures to properly represent voters and scrutinize the government. Yet, at the same time, we should not overlook some of the many strengths of the Westminster government as practised by Canadian assemblies. Westminster systems are nothing if not versatile, and Canadian assemblies have embraced some significant changes in the past two decades.

C.E.S. Franks argues persuasively that high party discipline combined with the centralization of authority in the Canadian House of Commons has provided the necessary conditions for a more collectivist government.[32] As a result, policies such as health care, national pensions, and employment insurance have become national policies that most Canadians hold as sacred. By contrast, the more individualistic-based US Congress has faced tremendous obstacles in passing legislation aimed at providing comprehensive national health care. More than one president's plans to implement national programs have been foiled by a Congress that is more geared to local concerns than to pan-American policies.

Further, Canadian assemblies have not been stagnant in addressing some aspects of the democratic deficit. Like the United States, the federal government and all but one province now have fixed election dates. The standard notion of confidence in Westminster systems was traditionally seen as incompatible with fixed election dates. After all, governments must have the confidence of the assembly throughout their terms. Once that confidence is gone, premiers or prime ministers must either call an election or vacate their posts at the behest of the governor general (or subnational head of state) and allow an alternative government to be formed.[33] Fixed election dates fly in the face of Westminster understandings of confidence. Yet the manner in which fixed election dates have been introduced in many Canadian assemblies suggests a willingness to incorporate congressional type rules into a different setting. Nine legislatures in Canada, including the federal government, have legislated fixed terms. In each case, the legislation explicitly indicates that defeats on votes of confidence trump set election dates. Simply put, the fixed election dates are designed not to override confidence conventions but, rather, to reduce the ability of the head of government to select an election date that best suits his or her chances of victory.

Critics of fixed election dates have suggested that these new laws will open a never-ending campaign. However, the reality of non-fixed dates suggests that all parties begin campaigning a year prior to an expected election call. Removing one piece of a government leader's arsenal and creating a level playing field with Opposition parties, while bringing some certainty to the public, is a strong example of bending the rules of Westminster government without sacrificing the norms of confidence.

Reform of the committee system is also high on the agenda. Committees have the potential to consult with citizens and to build a dialogue between voters and legislators. They also provide a somewhat less partisan forum for debate. They can thus enhance both democracy and the legitimacy of the parliamentary process. Yet committees face some challenges. They have little opportunity to examine government bills that are still in a draft stage and, thus, more open to change. Seldom are broad-based bills that would benefit from public input sent to committee.[34] In the United States, legislatures have broad authority to set their own agendas and to draft legislation; in Canada, with minor exceptions, the executive controls the legislative agenda and the work of committees. This places the onus of accountability on the backs of governments, private members, and Opposition parties. For many, it is an uphill struggle.

To some critics, executive dominance in the parliamentary system renders Parliament powerless and irrelevant. That is an over-statement. Canadian governments must face Parliament in Question Period and at other times, and they must retain majority support in the House of Commons. Executive authority is rooted in parliamentary legislation, and public spending must be approved in a parliamentary budget. Where is the democratic deficit here? As this chapter shows, the bill of particulars can be long: distortions in representation; underrepresentation of women, ethnic minorities, and urban areas; powerful party discipline that hugely undermines the ability of individual MPs to act as autonomous political decision makers; and lack of human and fiscal resources for Parliament and its committees effectively to debate issues and to challenge the government. Opposition parties and government private members often have neither the tools nor the independence to properly fulfill their jobs. The rules are stacked in favour of the government. Nevertheless, while imperfect, Westminster legislatures in Canada do allow legislators to ensure significant accountability, to criticize incumbents, and to develop their own programs for the future. The hopes of some commentators for a less partisan, more consensual and deliberative assembly are frustrated by the very logic of the Westminster system.

Similarly, the US Congress operates within its own logic – that of checks and balances and the separation of powers. It is a vastly more powerful and independent body than is Parliament. Congresspeople and senators have personal independence and standing far beyond that of an MP. Small wonder that many Americans favour their local member of Congress over the institution of Congress.[35]

It is important to emphasize the dispersal of power in the United States. It is not only the separation between legislature and executive but also the dispersal of power within the legislature itself, most fundamentally between two equally influential legislative bodies, each with great flexibility in managing its own affairs and with a full array of powerful committees and staffs. Passing legislation and budgets thus involves far more participants and far more veto points in the United States than in Canada.

That two such well-established liberal democracies should have such different legislative patterns is a fascinating conundrum in itself. The obvious explanation is institutional: one is congressional and one is parliamentary. But this may not be the whole explanation. Differences in political culture identified by Seymour Martin Lipset and others may play a role as well.

In any case, to a considerable degree, the democratic deficits are mirror images of each other. In Canada, Parliament is weak and executive dominated; in the United States, Congress is strong and largely independent of the executive. Canadian reformers tend to ask: how can we empower legislators and have a more powerful legislature? For Americans, Congress's widely dispersed powers mean legislative incoherence – seen in the proliferation of "earmarks" and in the legislative mishmash of such initiatives as recent health care legislation. American reformers – dating from the early 1960s appeal of a committee of the American Political Science Association for responsible party government in Congress – have called for something closer to the Canadian model: strongly led, disciplined parties that advocate clear programs. Stronger party discipline and stronger party leadership have developed in the United States, but the pattern remains very different from that in Canada.

Three elements of a democratic deficit do appear to have more purchase in the United States than in Canada. First, the pressures on American members of Congress are highly local because of their capacity to deliver local benefits through provisions in American laws. Canadian MPs certainly love to deliver cheques to their constituents, but their capacity to write these into legislation is much less than that of their American counterparts. Second, American legislators are by necessity virtually full-time fundraisers, raising the pervasive worry that they are beholden to their financial supporters. Canadian parliamentary candidates receive public funding, and their revenue-raising activities are highly circumscribed. Third, for the simple reason that they are more influential, American members of Congress are far more subject to pressures from lobbyists than are Canadian MPs. These factors may well account for the observed difference in trust in the two institutions noted out at the outset.

NOTES

1 For data, see http://www.jdsurvey.net/.
2 Kenneth Newton and Pippa Norris, "Confidence in Public Institutions: Faith, Culture or Performance," paper presented at American Political Science Assocation, Atlanta, 1999. See http://www.hks.harvard.edu/.
3 These data are drawn from Conference Board of Canada, *Report Card: Confidence in Parliament*. See http://www.conferenceboard.ca/.
4 See for example the various platforms of the American Libertarian Party and other Conservative reform movements, such as http://www.corrupt.org/opinion/politics and http://www.liberty-northwest.org.
5 This guarantee is accomplished through a number of vehicles, including the Senatorial Floor provisions delimited in the BNA Act, 1867, for some departments, and provisions in the Redistribution Act for others.
6 John C. Courtney, *Elections* (Vancouver: UBC Press, 2005).
7 Michael Pal and Sujit Choudhry, "Is Every Ballot Equal? Visible Minority Vote Dilution in Canada," *IRPP Choices* 13, 1 (2007), http://papers.ssrn.com/.
8 See the Interparliamentary Union website at http://www.ipu.org/.
9 When it entered Confederation in 1949, the province was known only as Newfoundland.
10 See William P. Irvine, "Does the Candidate Make a Difference? The Macro-Politics and Micro-Politics of Getting Elected," *Canadian Journal of Political Science/Revue canadienne de science politique* 15, 4 (1982): 755-82; John Ferejohn and Brian Gaines, "The Personal Vote in Canada," in *Representation, Integration, and Political Parties in Canada*, ed. Herman Bakvis (Toronto: Dundurn Press, 1991); André Blais, Elisabeth Gidengil, Agnieszka Dobrzynska, Neil Nevitte, and Richard Nadeau, "Does the Local Candidate Matter? Candidate Effects in the Canadian Election of 2000," *Canadian Journal of Political Science/Revue canadienne de science politique* 36, 3 (2003): 657-64.

11 J.A.A. Lovink, "Is Canadian Politics too Competitive?," *Canadian Journal of Political Science/Revue canadienne de science politique* 6, 3 (1973): 341-79.
12 British Columbia is the only province to experiment with recall. Term limits have been suggested by the present Conservative federal government as part of its larger non-constitutional plans for Senate reform.
13 C.E.S. Franks, *The Parliament of Canada* (Toronto: University of Toronto Press, 1987).
14 Jennifer E. Manning and Colleen J. Shogan, "African-American members of the United States Congress, 1870-2011, Congressional Research Service, Library of Congress, April 2011.
15 Robert Marleau and Camille Montpetit, eds., *House of Commons Procedure and Practice* (Toronto: McGraw-Hill, 2000).
16 For a more detailed discussion on C-24 – An Act to Amend the Canada Elections Act and the Income Tax Act – see David Docherty, "The Rebels Find a Cause: House of Commons Reform in the Chrétien Era," in *The Chrétien Legacy: Politics and Public Policy in Canada*, ed. Lois Harder and Steve Patten (Montreal: McGill-Queen's University Press, 2006).
17 David Docherty, *Legislatures* (Vancouver: UBC Press, 2005).
18 Docherty, "Rebels Find a Cause."
19 Docherty, *Legislatures*.
20 See http://www.campaignfinance.org/.
21 David Mayhew, *Congress: The Electoral Connection* (New Haven: Yale University Press, 1975).
22 The actual length of time for Question Period varies by jurisdiction. All provinces save Nova Scotia have a daily period, which runs from fifteen minutes in British Columbia to an hour in a number of jurisdictions (and, on some days, ninety minutes in Nova Scotia). The Canadian federal government has a daily forty-five-minute Question Period.
23 While members of Congress can call administration officials before committees, there is no equivalent to the questioning of the prime minister and his or her cabinet in the US system.
24 See http://cbo.gov/ and http://www2.parl.gc.ca/.
25 See Erin Bradbury, Ryan A. Davidson, and C. Lawrence Evans, "The Senate Whip System: An Exploration," in *Why Not Parties? Party Effects in the United States Senate*, ed. Nathan W. Munroe, Jason M. Roberts, and David Rhode (Chicago: University of Chicago Press, 2008), 82-83.
26 In the last years of the Chrétien administration, some maverick Liberal MPs joined with the opposition parties to pass a motion requiring secret ballot election of committee chairs. Then leader of the Canadian Alliance, Stephen Harper, supported this move, which allowed committees to select their own chairs in both theory and reality. Once he became prime minister, Harper quickly reverted to the old practice and controlled the selection of committees.
27 The Crown technically makes the appointments, though in practice this means the prime minister. When the prime minister made emergency appointments to ensure

passage of a general services tax, the additional appointments were technically made by the queen, though the prime minister selected the individuals who served.
28 Docherty, *Legislatures*.
29 Franks, *Parliament of Canada*, 169.
30 Paul Thomas, "An Upper House with Snow on the Roof and Frozen in Time: The Case of the Canadian Senate," in *Restraining Elective Dictatorships: The Upper House Solution*, ed. Scott Prasser, Nicholas Aroney, and J.R. Nethercotte (Brisbane: University of Queensland Press, 2008), 138-39.
31 For an excellent examination of the differences between the Canadian and US Senate, see Roger Gibbons and Peter McCormick, "A Tale of Two Senates," in *Canada and the United States: Differences That Count*, ed. David Thomas and Barbara Boyle Torrey (Peterborough: Broadview Press, 2008).
32 Franks, *Parliament of Canada*.
33 P. Russell and L. Sossin, eds., *Parliamentary Democracy in Crisis* (Toronto: University of Toronto Press, 2009).
34 Docherty, *Legislatures*.
35 See, for example, John R. Hibbing and Elizabeth Theiss-Morse, *Stealth Democracy: Americans' Beliefs about How Government Should Work* (Cambridge/New York, UK/NY: Cambridge University Press, 2002).

9

Democracy's Wartime Deficits
The Prerogative Presidency and Liberal Democracy in the United States

DANIEL J. TICHENOR

The word "democracy" appears nowhere in the US Constitution, a reflection of the fact that its framers were devoted to a "republican form of government" (article IV) rather than to modern democratic principles.[1] These "republican" commitments were especially significant to the invention of the American presidency, an institution designed to employ "the executive power" (article II) with broad discretion, especially during times of national crisis. In this way, the American constitutional presidency ironically constructed the presidential office with John Locke's defence of "prerogative" in mind: "The Power to act according to discretion, for the publick good, without the prescription of the Law, and sometimes even against it, is that which is called Prerogative ... The power whilst imployed for the benefit of the Community, and suitably to the trust and ends of the Government, is undoubted Prerogative, and never is questioned."[2] As this chapter shows, the seeds of presidential unilateralism were thus sewn well before the rise of the popular modern executive. The origins and development of the prerogative presidency places significant limitations on democratic accountability and control. Indeed, as presidential unilateralism has become institutionalized over time, this manifestation of the democratic deficit has become more norm than exception.

The American presidency today presents important contradictions in terms of both its power and its impact on the democratic aspirations and ideals of the citizens it serves. Consider two of the most striking tensions associated with the modern American executive. The first centres upon the gap between popular expectations and presidential performance. The contemporary White House is the focal point of enormous popular yearnings for major reform that will solve the nation's most daunting problems, a development fuelled by lofty promises on the campaign trail as well as by presidential addresses, public appearances, and political travel that represent "the repertoire of modern leadership."[3] As Bruce Miroff observes, the president "not only responds to popular demands and passions but also actively reaches out to shape them."[4] Yet, as much as American presidents cultivate popular support for their policy initiatives, their domestic agendas are almost routinely frustrated. Citizens are encouraged to expect presidents to achieve sweeping innovations, yet nearly all occupants of the Oval Office confront significant veto-points and limited political resources. In their study of presidents and domestic policy making, William Lammers and Michael Genovese conclude that, "regardless of the strategies they choose," modern presidents "face a series of roadblocks, checks, and balances that inhibit behavior and make governing difficult."[5] The struggles of the Obama administration, dedicated to producing "change we can believe in," only underscores these hurdles. Executive policy leadership has grown increasingly arduous over time due to budgetary constraints, unprecedented partisan polarization, past policy commitments, and other formidable challenges. We can safely say that the democratic deficit in the United States is worsening.

The second tension springs from the liberal democratic contradictions of presidential unilateralism in foreign affairs, national defence, and warfare. The American people place special normative weight on freedom and embrace separate institutions sharing power as a bulwark for liberty. The architects of the US Constitution were unambiguous in their insistence that the protection of liberty and constitutional government demanded that declaring and waging war, in the words of James Wilson, "not be in the power of a single man."[6] James Madison echoed these views when he warned that war is "the true nurse of executive aggrandizement." War powers, he insisted, must be shared between the executive and the legislature:

> Those who are to *conduct a war* cannot in the nature of things, be proper or safe judges, whether *a war ought* to be *commenced, continued or concluded*. They are barred from the latter functions by a great principle in free government, analogous to that which separates the sword from the purse, or the power of executing from the power of enacting laws.[7]

Of course, presidents now exercise largely autonomous command over an expansive national security state. "The period after 1945 created a climate in which Presidents have regularly breached constitutional principles and democratic values," Louis Fisher notes: "Under these pressures (and invitations) Presidents have routinely exercised war powers with little or no involvement by Congress."[8] These trends have only accelerated in the shadow of the 9/11 attacks.

These contrasting realities of presidential leadership today – one of recurrent White House frustration in advancing domestic reform and another of broad executive prerogatives in the name of homeland security – are hardly surprising. For almost half a century, journalists and scholars alike have oscillated between characterizing the presidency as menacingly "imperial" or distressingly "imperiled." Richard Neustadt's classic treatment of the subject, *Presidential Power*, describes an office with limited command power, one highly dependent on the good will, shared interests, or bargained support of other political actors.[9] In the throes of the Vietnam War and the Watergate scandal, however, Arthur Schlesinger's *Imperial Presidency* chronicled the presidency's steady appropriation of powers reserved to other branches.[10] These competing models of presidential power have found repeated expression in the popular and scholarly literature on the American executive. For instance, the embattled Ford and Carter administrations led presidency scholars to question notions of executive dominance,[11] only to once again highlight the growth of presidential authority and unilateralism during the Reagan, Bush, and Clinton years amidst congressional inertia and public passivity.[12] After Bill Clinton's second-term impeachment, experts like presidential historian Michael Beschloss predicted that George W. Bush would be "the first truly post-imperial president."[13] The terrorist attacks of 9/11 and subsequent war on terror turned this logic upside down.

The Bush administration was defined by its unflinching assertion and expansion of presidential power. It most aggressively accumulated power in the field of national security and in the name of defending against future terrorist attacks. The Bush White House viewed the president's commander-in-chief powers as sweeping and unfettered, using claims of expediency and secrecy to justify what became signature national security innovations: extraordinary rendition, warrantless surveillance, the creation of a detention facility on Guantanamo Bay, and torture – or, in the administration's preferred Orwellian parlance, "enhanced interrogation techniques." The US Constitution left room for presidents to exercise broad emergency or "prerogative" powers to meet the nation's most serious threats. Against the backdrop of an Obama administration inheriting extraordinary national security authority and exercising control over much of the banking, auto, and other industries, this chapter fittingly trains a spotlight on the prerogative presidency.

Executive power has often fit uncomfortably with liberal democracy. Committed democrats like Thomas Paine have long viewed executive leadership with dread since it has a tendency to make citizens passive, dependent, and deferential – qualities decidedly ill-suited for self-government. The architects of the US Constitution, by contrast, were profoundly wary of democracy, and they breathed life into an independent presidency designed to check various problems they attributed to legislative supremacy (especially as it operated after the American Revolution). The framers also expected national security, or "self-preservation," to be the first priority of the American presidency, a responsibility fortified by the "energy" and "dispatch" sewn into the nature of their unitary executive.[14] Indeed, the particular ambiguity of presidential war powers in the Constitution and the broader elasticity of article II assured that American chief executives would command immense power during wartime. These blueprints laid the foundation for the prerogative presidency, fostering secrecy, covert action, and executive aggrandizement during national security emergencies.

This chapter examines the impact of the prerogative presidency on liberal democracy, with a view to pointing to its contribution to increasing the democratic deficit in the United States. But it also considers how dominant conceptions of executive representation – rooted in evolving ideas about constitutional processes and executive authority – have influenced wartime presidents. The exercise of prerogative powers, I argue, has assumed strikingly different forms under the nineteenth-century and modern presidencies, with profound implications for US democratic liberties. I carefully consider the prerogative presidencies of Lincoln during the Civil War, Wilson during the First World War, and Roosevelt during the Second World War and how these have influenced the Obama administration's response to the Bush-initiated post-9/11 War on Terror. More to the point, I explore two questions for each of these presidents who led the nation decisively during its most unsettling national security crises. First, to what degree have prerogative presidents forcefully addressed national security imperatives while also striving to keep unnecessary intrusions on individual and group freedoms to a minimum? Put another way, when granted the opportunity to use broad unilateral power in the midst of crises, have these major wartime presidents uniformly seized it or have they demonstrated the capacity to exercise self-control? Second, what has been the relationship between major wartime presidents exercising broad emergency powers and the American people? Have mass publics embraced or resisted extraordinary presidential actions advanced in the name of national security? To what extent have prerogative presidents shaped or followed public opinion as they respond to what are perceived as dire threats?

In the pages that follow, I find that Lincoln was virtually alone among these prerogative presidents in recognizing the value of executive restraint and demonstrating a capacity for self-control. This conclusion will no doubt vex those who perceive Lincoln as the American constitutional dictator par excellence, but I argue that the evidence shows that he was more circumspect in his exercise of emergency powers than were the major wartime presidents who succeeded him. At the heart of his careful exercise of unilateral powers was a theory of executive leadership rooted in Whig philosophy and nineteenth-century conceptions of constitutional and partisan order. Significantly, as we shall see, Lincoln took great pains to educate the American people about when and why he chose to take emergency action or to embrace inaction. By contrast, Wilson, Roosevelt, and Bush evidenced little to none of Lincoln's guardedness in exercising prerogative power that enervated democratic liberties. The marriage of immense presidential warrants to keep the nation safe and modern conceptions of independent executive leadership produced wartime commanders-in-chief who had little interest in limiting their own power. Given this trajectory, the secrecy, covert activism, and unfettered unilateralism of the Bush presidency may be the natural outgrowth of long-term developments.

Strikingly, the interaction between these "modern" prerogative presidents and mass publics only served to reinforce these trends. Wilson did not hesitate to employ his vision of the president as "interpreter-in-chief" to shape public opinion during the war, but his popular rhetorical leadership demanded 100 percent Americanism, justified emergency measures, and stoked public hysteria about alleged enemies within. Roosevelt's decisions on Japanese internment and German saboteurs were in perfect stride with the views of most ordinary citizens, and neither pressed the other to think otherwise. Bush considered it both necessary and honourable to aggressively exercise emergency power, often without public knowledge or, when his administration's covert activities were revealed, without regard to approval. In particular, my investigation of the wartime leadership of Abraham Lincoln, Woodrow Wilson, and Franklin Delano Roosevelt raises fresh questions about how we conceive idealized forms of executive leadership.

As I show, studying the historical contours of the American prerogative presidency during major wars helps us discern why the Obama administration's commitment to fight the global war on terror while adhering to the rule of law and respecting individual rights is so politically fraught.

Lincoln and the Forgotten Virtues of Restraint

Eleven weeks after he rushed into the breach when armed rebellion broke out on 12 April 1861, Abraham Lincoln was, true to form, wrestling with nettlesome questions. For the first meeting of Congress since his assumption of unprecedented emergency powers, Lincoln issued a remarkably candid message to lawmakers in which he wondered aloud whether there was "an inherent and fatal weakness" in all republics when forced to defend themselves against the gravest threats to their security. "Must a government of necessity be too *strong* for the liberties of its people," he asked, "or too *weak* to maintain its own existence?"[15] This fundamental issue of balancing security and liberty – of what must of necessity be sacrificed in the face of emergency and what should be preserved – was on Lincoln's mind when he suspended habeas corpus, addressed matters of press freedom and censorship, and refused to suspend the presidential election of 1864 whatever the outcome.[16] He was, in short, wrestling candidly with lost freedoms and injustices rent by wartime necessities.

Lincoln's circumspection was informed in no small part by Whig principles to which he openly adhered throughout his political life. As Daniel Walker Howe observes, Lincoln's loyalty to the Whig Party until its eventual demise is not a familiar part of his popular legend. Yet Whig philosophy strongly conformed with his faith in the inner-directed "self-made man," in the need for widespread education to nurture a virtuous citizenry, and in the importance of law and reason to discipline dangerous popular passions.[17] He shared the disdain of Whig leaders like Henry Clay and Daniel Webster for the "executive usurpation" of Andrew Jackson, whose leadership unleashed "a total change of the pure republican character of [the American] government" by concentrating "all power in the hands of one man." In his famous 1838 address to the Young Men's Lyceum of Springfield, Lincoln railed against the "increasing disregard for law that pervades [the] country" and warned that ambitious demagogues would exploit the "wild and furious passions" of the people to control the political system. The future of the nation, he asserted, rested upon "the capability of a people to govern themselves" both personally and as a political collective.[18] He backed William Henry Harrison, the first Whig president, who proclaimed in his inaugural address that "it is preposterous to suppose that ... the President, placed at the capital, in the center of the country could better understand the wants and wishes of the people than their own immediate representatives." In short, Congress should set policy and presidents should execute it: to do otherwise is to permit a deficit in democratic governance. As Lincoln later complained of James Polk, his "high handed and despotic use of the veto power" showed "an utter disregard of the will of the people, in refusing to give assent to measures which their representatives passed."[19]

These beliefs were in ready evidence when Lincoln ascended to the presidency. As the nation's first Republican president, Lincoln steadfastly adhered to the Whig creed that healthy republican government required firm limits on executive power. Not long after his 1860 election victory, Lincoln announced that he considered it untenable for the White House to propose bills to Congress or to veto legislation already passed. Throughout the Civil War, he reminded administration officials that the executive branch should not "expressly or impliedly seize and exercise the permanent legislative functions of the government." He added: "I have been unwilling to go beyond the pressure of necessity in the unusual exercise of power."

Of course, not everyone agreed with this assessment of Lincoln's prerogative presidency. During the heat of the Civil War, *Harper's Weekly* offered a familiar critique of the unprecedented executive power that Lincoln had accumulated and wielded. "The President of the United States has, in effect, been created Dictator," it proclaimed, "with almost supreme power over liberty, property, and life – a power nearly as extensive and as irresponsible as that which is wielded by the Emperors of Russia, France, or China."[20] Lincoln's enemies routinely castigated him as a tyrant throughout his tenure, and his contemporary critics have sounded similar refrains by offering disquieting portraits of a darker Lincoln who unflinchingly aggrandized executive power and ruled with an iron fist.[21] Characterizations of Lincoln as an unscrupulous despot are hardly surprising given the fact that he was both the original architect and builder of the United States's prerogative presidency. My aim in this section is to take seriously the most significant and frequent charges against Lincoln – namely, that he demonstrated a disregard for individual rights by suspending habeas corpus, for freedom of the press by suppressing critical publications, and for political opposition by jailing dissidents. In contrast to maudlin treatments of Lincoln, my analysis suggests that Lincoln was no saint and that he sometimes went too far in restricting basic liberties in the name of wartime imperatives. But it also shows that he was decidedly more ambivalent and restrained in his use of prerogative power than any of the major wartime presidents who followed.

Lincoln suspended habeas corpus soon after the war began, and his action led to a confrontation with the federal judiciary that culminated in his openly defying a ruling of the chief justice of the Supreme Court. At first blush, these facts offer devastating evidence of Lincoln's disregard for fundamental individual rights or the constitutional order. But Lincoln's actions are less troubling when we consider their broader context. After strong initial reservations, Lincoln suspended habeas corpus in response to active sabotage and genuine threats of rebellion in Maryland, which was a crucial territory through which troops, goods, and communications flowed from northern states into Washington, DC. The fact that prominent political officials in Maryland were supportive of the Confederate cause added to the crisis. When angry Baltimore mobs attacked federal troops in their passage to Washington and southern sympathizers cut telegraph lines, stopped mail shipments, and attempted to blow up railroad tracks, Lincoln determined that he was compelled to suspend habeas corpus so that military authorities could arrest civilians engaged in rebellious activities lest the nation's capitol be cut off from the rest of the country.[22] John Merryman, a Maryland politician detained by the army for participating in a plot to sabotage the rail lines, had his case heard by Chief Justice Taney. Significantly, Merryman was able to file a habeas petition precisely because he was permitted to remain in contact with his family, friends, and lawyers (in contrast to most Arab and Muslim detainees under Ashcroft's preventive detention program or Guantanamo detainees). Taney, acting independently of the Court, ruled that only Congress could suspend habeas corpus. Lincoln ultimately defied the ruling because he believed that rebellious agitation in Maryland endangered the very survival of the nation. His decision to suspend habeas corpus in two other border states where key portions were in rebellion, Kentucky and Missouri, rested upon similar arguments of extreme threat.

Scholars like Daniel Farber aptly observe that military arrests and trials during the Civil War were "less a matter of a strong, centralized police state than one that was weak and balkanized."[23] In contrast to the presidents during the two world wars, Lincoln had no federal law enforcement agencies like the Justice Department or the Federal Bureau of Investigation to rely upon in neutralizing enemy spies, agents, and active supporters in the north who were virtually indistinguishable from others. In terms of federal law enforcement officers, not including seventy federal judges, there were eighty-one federal attorneys, marshals, and other court officers during the Civil War. Consequently, Lincoln had little choice but to depend upon the military to deal with suspected enemies and to grant considerable discretion to subordinates. Historians estimate that nearly all military trials took place within southern or border states involving citizens of the Confederacy. Mark Neely's exhaustive work on the subject finds that Lincoln's suspension of habeas corpus led to roughly fifteen thousand civilian arrests by the military not for arbitrary offences but, rather, from draft evasion and desertion to running the federal blockade on southern ports, fraud in government contracts, and acts of spying and sabotage.[24] According to James Randall, Lincoln's "character operated to modify and soften the acts of overzealous subordinates and to lessen the effect of harsh measures upon individuals ... Though there were arbitrary arrests under Lincoln, there was no thorough-going arbitrary government."[25] If Lincoln was inclined to soften the hard edges of federal law enforcement during the Civil War, he was certainly not immune from excess. In September 1862, Lincoln suspended the writ of habeas corpus for the entire nation, extending military authority over northern states far removed from "Cases of Rebellion" like Maryland.[26]

The election of 1864 provides us with a second glimpse of Lincoln's self-restraint as a crisis president. The northern Democratic Party, which continued to operate after southern secession, elected a variety of anti-war candidates during the Civil War. In 1864, the Democrats named General George McClellan as their presidential candidate and drafted a platform that attacked their Republican rivals as the authors of "four years of failure to restore the Union by the experiment of war."[27] If elected, the Democrats vowed to end the war swiftly. In Lincoln's view, the outcome of the election would determine the survival of the Union. "The present presidential contest will almost certainly be no other than a contest between a union and a disunion candidate, disunion certainly following the success of the latter," he wrote privately. "The issue is a mighty one, for all people, and all times."[28]

During the summer of 1864, the progress of the Union forces slowed and northern fatigue with the war effort grew. With political opposition in the north mounting, Republicans made a bid to win over war Democrats by changing their name to the National Unity Party for the 1864 campaign and nominated the Democratic senator Andrew Johnson for vice-president. In August 1864, General Ulysses S. Grant noted that the Confederacy had a decided interest in seeing McClellan elected on a "peace at any price" platform.[29] That same month, Lincoln's political advisers told him his electoral fortunes were very much in doubt. Republican Party leader Thurlow Weed commented to Secretary of State William Seward: "I have told Mr. Lincoln that his re-election was an impossibility."[30]

Despite the grim prognosis, Lincoln refused to heed recommendations that he suspend the election or attempt to rig the outcome by means of sweeping partisan arrests. Lincoln's determination to hold the 1864 election even when he had good reason to anticipate defeat is a powerful illustration of his own efforts to circumscribe the prerogative presidency he created. As Herman Belz observes, by embracing the 1864 democratic contest, especially when his re-election was very much in doubt, Lincoln "accepted a risk and permitted his power threatened in a way that no dictator, constitutional or not, would have tolerated."[31] Consistent with his more famous pronouncements educating the American people on the necessities and boundaries of wartime power, Lincoln's public explanation for guarding the electoral process regardless of its national security implications is a poignant argument for democratic freedom even during perilous crises:

> The election was a necessity. We cannot have free government without elections; and if the rebellion could force us to forego or postpone a national election, it might fairly claim to have already conquered and ruined us. What has occurred in this case must ever recur in similar cases ... [T]he election has demonstrated that a people's government can sustain a national election in the midst of a great civil war. Until now, it has not been known to the world that this was a possibility.[32]

Basking in a 10 percent margin of victory, Lincoln remained painfully aware that his choices of when to assert broad emergency power and when to refrain from exercising such power might "recur in similar cases" of "great national trial." His conception of how to balance prerogative power with liberal, democratic, and constitutional principles was a product of the nineteenth-century ideas of executive (and legislative) representation that shaped his political time.

Countering Dangers, Real and Imagined: Wilson's "Stern Hand of Firm Repression"

When we look back at the First World War today, the immediate dangers posed by the conflict to the nation's safety seem modest compared to those of the Civil War, the Second World War, or 9/11 and the War on Terror. But to many Americans of the early twentieth century, the war's threats to domestic security were significant. They were especially alarmed by the prospects of espionage and sedition on the home front, fears that were heightened by presumed disloyalty among the nation's large foreign-born population. Wilson, credited by executive scholars with consolidating the popular rhetorical presidency,[33] used his "bully pulpit" in a manner that stoked these anxieties. Although Congress delegated extraordinary powers to the executive branch during the war, Wilson also led the pressure campaign to win significant delegatory statutes, implemented them with zeal, laboured to keep them intact well after the hostilities of war ceased, and undertook a variety of independent actions that further limited civil liberties. Let us focus our attention on a few telling examples of how Wilson influenced and dealt with the security-liberty balance.

Wilson's wartime rhetoric fuelled nativist and anti-German sentiment in the United States as well as both popular and official intolerance of any overt expression of anti-war beliefs. After the sinking of the *Lusitania* in July 1915, Wilson warned the public that significant portions of the country's foreign-born population, both naturalized citizens and newly arrived immigrants, imperiled national security. "The gravest threats against our national peace and safety have been uttered within our borders," he declared. "There are citizens of the United States, I blush to admit, born under other flags but welcomed by our generous naturalization laws to the full freedom and opportunity of America, who have poured the poison of disloyalty into the very arteries of our national life."[34]

On the same day that Wilson's War Resolution passed Congress (6 April 1917), Wilson issued an executive order imposing regulations for controlling non-citizens of German ancestry living in the country. The regulations included an extensive list of restrictions on the movement, employment, property, and activities of these so-called enemy aliens. These enemy aliens were required to register and to provide fingerprints to the federal government, and they were subject to summary arrests by federal officials. During the course of the war, more than sixty-three hundred non-citizens of German descent were arrested and more than twenty-three hundred were confined to internment camps.[35] Wilson issued a secret executive order the next day that empowered federal bureaucratic heads to remove any employee considered a loyalty risk "by reason of his conduct, sympathies, or utterances, or because of other reasons growing out of the war."[36] Publicly, Wilson warned German Americans and legal permanent residents that, if they demonstrated an ounce of disloyalty, "it [would] be dealt with a firm hand of stern repression."[37]

In 1917, Wilson also demanded legislation authorizing his administration to limit press and speech freedoms. According to Wilson: "From the very outset of the present war [Germany] has filled our unsuspecting communities and even our offices of government with spies and set criminal intrigues everywhere afoot against our national unity."[38] Congress responded to Wilson's urging with passage of the Espionage Act, 1917, which made it a crime for anyone to convey information that might hurt the operations or success of the American Armed Forces or promote the success of its enemies. Section 3 of the law stipulated sentences of up to twenty years in prison for those who "shall willfully cause or attempt to cause insubordination, disloyalty, mutiny, or refusal of duty in the military or naval forces of the United States, or shall willfully obstruct the recruitment or enlistment service of the United States." One year after the law was enacted, Eugene Debs, the Socialist Party presidential candidate, was arrested and sentenced to ten years in prison for making a speech that "obstructed recruiting."[39] Two thousand others were prosecuted under the Espionage Act, including roughly 150 leaders of the Industrial Workers of the World. Additional delegatory statutes gave Wilson an unprecedented hold over the nation's economic life as well as over its communication and transportation systems.

Wilson's postmaster general, Albert Burleson, was vested with vast authority to suppress critical opinion during the First World War. Under the Espionage Act, the postmaster general was empowered to declare any magazine, newspaper, circular, pamphlet, letter, or other material that violated the statute to be barred from the mails. On 12 October 1917, Wilson issued an executive order creating a board of censorship headed by Burleson to scrutinize all correspondence and communications leaving the country. The order strengthened Burleson's authority to scrutinize private letters and other materials using the postal system.[40]

Strikingly, Attorney General Thomas Gregory wrote a detailed memo to Wilson raising serious doubts as to whether the censorship powers granted to the postmaster general were constitutional. As Gregory saw it, Burleson's new authority could not be constitutionally justified because it enabled an executive official to have a "far reaching inhibitory effect upon the right of free public discussion."[41] Wilson dismissed Gregory's concerns, reaffirming Burleson's broad censorship powers "upon evidence satisfactory to him." Burleson maintained draconian control over domestic and international mails, including stringent restrictions on dozens of periodicals that either lost their mailing privileges or were compelled to print nothing about the

First World War for its duration. When prominent figures such as Herbert Croly or Upton Sinclair privately complained to Wilson about Burleson's iron rule over the mails, he staunchly defended his postmaster for using censorship powers as the president intended to curb disloyal speech.[42]

At the urging of the administration, the Sedition Act, 1918, extended the Espionage Act to make it illegal to speak out against the government. "Dangerous enemies within our confines," Wilson officials warned, exploited "the lack of laws relating to disloyal utterances."[43] The law added eight new offences to the Espionage Act, including "uttering, printing, writing, or publishing any disloyal, profane, scurrilous, or abusive language" directed toward the US government. Enforcement of the Espionage Act and the Sedition Act was shaped by district attorneys and judges scattered across the country who, almost invariably, implemented the new laws with severity. Attorney General Gregory privately worried both before and after passage of the laws about how popular anxieties and local prejudices might lead to overzealous prosecutions.[44] Oliver Wendell Holmes soberly concluded that the federal judiciary proved "hysterical" in its treatment of charges brought under the espionage and sedition acts. Likewise, the Justice Department investigators quietly noted that both judges and juries, eager to demonstrate their support for the war effort, were often too quick to convict suspects under these laws and regularly imposed overly harsh sentences.[45]

As the First World War neared a close, the editors at *The Nation* unleashed a blistering attack on Burleson for draconian and capricious enforcement of his fleeting censorship authority. Yet they reserved their fiercest criticism for Wilson, who, in their estimation, sat silently by as unconscionable abuses of power took place on his watch. As "every tenet of democracy was violated," they noted, there was "scarcely a protest from the great democrat in the White House."[46] Not only did Wilson permit abuses of power in the name of national security, but he also played a key role in nurturing the hysterical climate that made legislation such as the espionage and sedition acts possible. Perhaps most revealing of all, Wilson ordered administration officials to continue to target and prosecute hundreds of cases under these acts well after the armistice of 11 November 1918. In May 1920, Wilson vetoed a bill that would have terminated the statutes. It is a veto that speaks volumes. Wilson ultimately accumulated vast emergency powers with little if any regard for cherished freedoms or constitutional norms.

Freedom in the Good War: FDR, Japanese Internment, and German Saboteurs

In leading a stubbornly isolationist nation to recognize its international interests and obligations in the Second World War, Franklin Roosevelt proved adept both at deception and unilateral action. It is an example of prerogative leadership that is, as Erwin Hargrove poignantly illuminates, both controversial and exemplary of presidential leadership.[47] Yet when we turn to the question of balancing security and liberty, of reigning in the excessive prerogative power, Roosevelt's record is at least as flawed as Wilson's. FDR defenders may wish to quarrel with this assessment, contending that civil liberties were generally well protected during the Second World War save for Japanese internment. Moreover, Japanese internment is sometimes characterized as a regrettable but understandable overreaction by Roosevelt based on the flawed information he received. In truth, however, FDR was as unrestrained and unreflective as was Wilson in his exercise of prerogative power. His decision making on Japanese evacuation and the trial of eight German saboteurs captures these tendencies well.

Given the abundant literature on Japanese internment, a thick historical description of the official repression of Japanese Americans during the Second World War is not required here.[48] Rather, my focus is squarely on the information received by Roosevelt before he issued his infamous Executive Order 9066. After the Japanese attack on Pearl Harbor, west coast political leaders, military commanders, and mass publics viewed Japanese-American citizens and Japanese legal permanent residents (Japanese immigrants were not allowed to naturalize until after the McCarren-Walter Act, 1952) as a menacing fifth column that aided and abetted the enemy. Early on, California's governor Culbert Olson and its attorney general Earl Warren urged the president to evacuate and intern the Japanese. This recommendation was forcefully echoed by the army's commander of the Western Theater of Operations, Lieutenant General John L. DeWitt. He was convinced that the tens of thousands of Japanese Americans born in the United States and Japanese immigrants who lived on the Pacific Coast were sympathetic with the Japanese cause and that many were actively aiding the enemy. The fact that most of those he presumed to be disloyal were born in the United States made little difference, according to DeWitt, because "the racial strains were undiluted" regardless of how long one's family lived in the country.[49]

In his advocacy of Japanese removal from the west coast, DeWitt received strong backing from the top brass of the Armed Forces. Roosevelt listened to their recommendations sympathetically,[50] but his top intelligence advisers, William Donovan and John Franklin Carter, made it clear to him that the army's proof of Japanese disloyalty was spurious. This proof included unsubstantiated reports from California that ground glass had been found in seafood canned by Japanese workers and that Japanese field hands had sprayed arsenic on vegetables. Donovan and Carter informed FDR that no one had been arrested for this alleged sabotage and that there was no evidence of ground glass or arsenic in the food supply or, indeed, of other forms of rumoured sabotage.[51] When confronted with the absence of reliable evidence of Japanese sabotage, DeWitt remained adamant about the impending threat posed by the Japanese-American population. "The very fact that no sabotage has taken place to date is a disturbing and confirming indication that such action will be taken," he reasoned.[52]

At the same time as Donovan and Carter were quietly presenting Roosevelt with information and arguments that challenged the case for Japanese internment, Attorney General Francis Biddle argued openly and vehemently against the move. He was "sturdily backed" in resisting "the Army's pressure to evacuate the Japanese" by none other than FBI director J. Edgar Hoover. After reviewing the best available intelligence, Hoover put the matter frankly to FDR: "The necessity for mass evacuation is based primarily upon public and political pressure rather than on factual data. Public hysteria and, in some instances, the comments of the press and radio announcers have resulted in a tremendous amount of pressure being brought to bear on Governor Olson and Earl Warren."[53] Thanks to Donovan, Roosevelt also knew the assessment of General Ralph Van Deman, head of military intelligence during the First World War, who held that evacuation and internment of Japanese Americans was not only unnecessary but "about the craziest proposition that [he had] heard of yet."[54]

Despite these formidable challenges to the army's position, Roosevelt issued Executive Order 9066 on 19 February 1942 authorizing the army "to apprehend, restrain, secure and remove" Japanese Americans from the west coast. Roughly 114,000 men, women, and children of Japanese ancestry – more than two-thirds of whom were birthright citizens – were evacuated under armed guard to "concentration camps."

Given the strong factual challenges to DeWitt's case for internment raised by Hoover, Biddle, Deman, Donovan, and Carter, we clearly cannot characterize Roosevelt's decision as the culmination of faulty "groupthink" or inadequate information. Tellingly, when army commanders on the east coast raised the possibility of evacuating Italian and German aliens (*not* citizens of German and Italian origin), Roosevelt swiftly savaged the idea as harmful to national unity and morale. In contrast to Japanese internment, the German and Italian immigrants (a relatively modest number) who were relocated during the war were judged as dangerous on an individual basis.[55]

As FDR ordered 114,000 men, women, and children of Japanese descent to what he himself called "concentration camps," Attorney General Biddle observed no hesitation or reflection on the president's part. "I don't think he was much concerned with the gravity or implications of this step," Biddle wrote.[56] Public opinion broadly supported Japanese internment throughout the war. Only a few notable dissenting voices warned Americans of what was at stake, and this only well after the immediate crisis had subsided. As Yale law professor Eugene Rostow put it in 1945, Japanese internment established the proposition that "in time of war or emergency, the military ... can decide what political opinions require imprisonment, and which ethnic groups are infected with them." As a consequence, "men, women, and children of a given ethnic group, both American and resident aliens, can be presumed to possess the kind of dangerous ideas which require their imprisonment."[57]

Conclusion

During the election campaign of 2008, Barack Obama stated plainly that he intended to be a very different president than was George W. Bush with regard to how he exercised prerogative power to fight global terror and to protect homeland security. Rejecting the aggressive unilateralism of the Bush years, Obama told voters: "it's time to restore our Constitution and the rule of law." The important demands of national security after 9/11, he argued, did not mean that the US commander-in-chief should treat civil liberties and human rights as an afterthought:

> It's time to reject torture without equivocation. It's time to close Guantanamo and to restore habeas corpus. It's time to give our intelligence and law enforcement agencies the tools they need to track down and take out terrorists, while ensuring that their actions are subject to vigorous oversight that protects our freedom. So let me be perfectly clear: I have taught the Constitution, I understand the Constitution, and I will obey the Constitution when I am President of the United States.[58]

In an election season ripe with comparisons between the Illinois senator and Abraham Lincoln (more than a few nurtured by his campaign), Obama was channelling a conception of executive restraint that Lincoln embraced even as he employed unprecedented emergency power to hold the Union together.

As much as Obama touted his reverence for individual rights and the rule of law during the election, he also underscored that he would vigorously protect the nation from "the legitimate threats [it] face[d]." He parted company with some of his most ardent liberal supporters in the summer of 2008, when he cast his Senate vote in favour of sweeping national intelligence surveillance legislation that he thought "necessary to protect the lives ... of the American people."[59] At the same time, he tangled with his Republican opponents who may have distanced themselves from the Bush administration's economic legacies but who were also eager to reprise the 2004 strategy of casting Democratic standard-bearers as unreliable guardians of national security. In September, Republican vice-presidential nominee Sarah Palin delighted supporters by mocking Obama's constitutional propriety in the face of grave terrorist threats. Partisan crowds roared approval when she delivered one of her most successful applause lines: "Al-Qaeda terrorists still plot to inflict catastrophic harm on America and he's worried that someone won't read them their rights."[60]

In response, Obama defended the writ of habeas corpus as the "foundation of Anglo-American law." The safeguard was vital because "we don't always catch the right person," he explained. "We may think it's Mohammed the terrorist, but it might be Mohammed the cab driver. You might think it's Barack the bomb-thrower, but it might be Barack the guy running for president." As his partisan supporters cheered, Obama scolded Palin: "The reason that you have this principle is not to be soft on terrorism. It's because that's who we are. That's what we're protecting. Don't mock the Constitution. Don't make fun of it. Don't suggest that it's not American to abide by what the founding fathers set up. It's worked pretty well for over 200 years."[61] This did not mean, however, that he would not pursue terrorist threats with a vengeance. "My position has always been clear: If you've got a terrorist, take him out," he proclaimed. "Anybody who was involved in 9/11, take 'em out." Obama's straightforward message was that he would employ broad power to keep Americans safe from terrorists who targeted the United States but that he would also undo the constitutional abuses and "imperial" excesses of his predecessor. He would, in effect, reduce the democratic deficit that had grown so large during the Bush presidency.

There are at least a couple of reasons why one might have anticipated marked success for the Obama administration in redefining national security policy. First, constitutional norms and civil liberties traditionally enjoy some resurgence when the sense of urgency surrounding a national security crisis subsides. To be sure, the war on terror may be an indefinite – if not a perpetual – struggle, but the anxieties and immediate warrants for exercising prerogative power have lessened over time. A commander-in-chief who willingly imposed limits on his own executive emergency power and who sought to restore key individual rights might be expected to find broad support from other branches (especially from members of his own party controlling both houses of Congress) and from the American people.

Second, one also might logically presume that a president would enjoy smoother sailing in redefining national security policy, an area of purported executive dominance if not unilateral control, than in achieving landmark domestic policy changes as politically bruising and elusive as health care reform. Fittingly, Obama initiated revisions in national security policy "with the stroke of a pen," issuing three early executive orders consistent with his commitment to "end the false choice between our safety and our ideals." Analyzing the staying power of Bush's secret order authorizing the National Security Administration's warrantless surveillance program (in violation of the Foreign Intelligence Surveillance Act, 1978), Kenneth Mayer aptly observes that the success of his unilateral action was "anchored to core executive functions: the president's constitutional authority as commander in chief and the president's historical control over foreign intelligence gathering."[62] One might reasonably presume that a popular new president with fellow partisans in control of Congress would enjoy at least as much leeway and formal command power over national security policy as did Bush during his final months in office.

As we know now, the impassioned conflicts that Obama's constitutional propriety touched off during the election were only a hint of the profound challenges that his team confronted once it assumed power. Although it is still early, to date the administration has been embattled in its pursuit of a greater "balance between the security we demand and the civil liberties that we cherish."[63] Congressional Republicans, more preoccupied with putting Obama on the defensive than with checking the post-9/11 expansion of executive power, effectively bludgeon the White House for being "soft" on terrorists and making the country "less safe." Most Americans have found these charges persuasive, opposing closure of the Guantanamo Bay prison, civilian trials for detainees, and due process rights for terror detainees. Many Democratic lawmakers have preferred to delay action on these issues, worried about appearing weak on homeland security during a tough election and wary that they would be blamed for endangering the country if a new terrorist attack were to occur. And civil libertarians on the left have denounced the administration for failing to charge full steam ahead. Today we are far removed philosophically, structurally, and politically from the world in which Lincoln exercised emergency power with ambivalence and circumspection. Understanding the wellsprings of our present dilemmas requires us to take stock of earlier times when Americans felt most threatened and presidents seized breathtaking authority to quiet those fears.

During the first decade of the twentieth century, one of the United States's most ambitious and aggressive chief executives, Theodore Roosevelt, rued the relatively peaceful times in which he served. "A man has to take advantage of his opportunities, but the opportunities have to come," he lamented not long after leaving office: "If there is not the war, you don't get the great general; if there is not the great occasion, you don't get the great statesman; if Lincoln had lived in times of peace, no one would know his name now." Roosevelt yearned to shoulder the challenges Lincoln had during his presidential tenure, and he later expressed profound disappointment that he missed the opportunity to lead the nation through the First World War.[64] I offer a contrasting view of presidential greatness, one that elevates leadership qualities of which Theodore Roosevelt was in short supply. If, as we have seen, the formal and informal limitations on American commanders-in-chief during severe national crises are unmistakably meagre,[65] then the capacity of presidents to exercise some measure of constitutional propriety and self-restraint is critical.

The American system of checks and balances was designed to provide energy and effective leadership while also diffusing power in the interest of safeguarding democratic liberties. Yet this delicate balance has rarely been pursued amidst dire national security crises. Indeed, the willingness of most citizens and political leaders to readily sacrifice broad freedoms to neutralize security threats presents its own formidable democratic deficit.

NOTES

1 Sanford Levinson, "The Democratic Deficit in America," *Harvard Law and Policy Review*, 6 December 2006, http://hlpronline.com/.
2 John Locke, *Second Treatise on Civil Government* (London: Hackett Publishing Company, 1980), Chap. 14; and Sanford Levinson, "Constitutional Dictators," *Dissent* (Summer 2009): 102.
3 Samuel Kernell, *Going Public: New Strategies of Presidential Leadership* (Washington, DC: Congressional Quarterly Press, 1997), 106.
4 Bruce Miroff, "The Presidential Spectacle," in *The Presidency and the Political System*, ed. Michael Nelson (Washington, DC: Congressional Quarterly Press, 2010), 210.

5 Michael Lammers and Michael Genovese, *The Presidency and Domestic Policy* (Washington, DC: Congressional Quarterly Press, 2000), 3 and 356.
6 Wilson is quoted in Louis Fisher, *Presidential War Power*, 2nd ed. (Lawrence: University of Kansas Press, 2004), 9.
7 Ibid., 10-11.
8 Ibid., xi.
9 Richard Neustadt, *Presidential Power and the Modern Presidents: The Politics of Leadership from Roosevelt to Reagan* (New York: Free Press, 1991).
10 Arthur M. Schlesinger, *The Imperial Presidency* (Boston: Houghton Mifflin, 1973).
11 Thomas Cronin, "An Imperiled Presidency?," *Society* 16, 1 (1978); Vincent Davis, *The Post-Imperial Presidency* (New York: Transaction Publishers, 1980); James Sundquist, *The Decline and Resurgence of Congress* (Washington, DC: Brookings Institution Press, 1981).
12 Andrew Rudalevige, *The New Imperial Presidency: Renewing Presidential Power after Watergate* (Ann Arbor: University of Michigan Press, 2005).
13 Quoted in Jonathan Mahler, "After the Imperial Presidency," *New York Times Magazine*, 8 November 2008.
14 Alexander Hamilton, James Madison, and John Jay, *The Federalist Papers* (New York: Oxford University Press, 2008), nos. 70 and 71.
15 Abraham Lincoln, "Message to Congress in Special Session," 4 July 1861, in John G. Nicolay and John Hay, eds., *Complete Works of Abraham Lincoln* (New York: Lamb Publishing Company, 1905), vol. 10, 304.
16 See, for example, Lincoln, "Response to a Serenade," 10 November 1864, in Nicolay and Hay, *Complete Works of Abraham Lincoln*, vol. 10, 263.
17 Daniel Walker Howe, "Why Abraham Lincoln Was a Whig," *Journal of the Abraham Lincoln Association* 16, 1 (1995).
18 Roy P. Basler, Marion Dolores Pratt, and Lloyd A. Dunlap, eds., *The Collected Works of Abraham Lincoln* (New Brunswick: Rutgers University Press, 1953), vol. 1, 108-15.
19 Quoted by David Herbert Donald, *Lincoln Reconsidered: Essays on the Civil War Era*, 3rd ed. (New York: Vintage, 2001), 144.
20 *Harper's Weekly*, 14 March 1863.
21 See, for example, Thomas Dilorenzo, *The Real Lincoln* (New York: Prima Lifestyles, 2002).
22 See William H. Rehnquist, *All the Laws But One: Civil Liberties in Wartime* (New York: Alfred A. Knopf, 1998).
23 Daniel Farber, *Lincoln's Constitution* (Chicago: University Of Chicago Press, 2004).
24 Mark Neely, *The Fate of Liberty: Abraham Lincoln and Civil Liberties* (New York: Oxford University Press, 1992).
25 James G. Randall, *Constitutional Problems under Lincoln* (Urbana Champaign: University of Illinois Press, 1926), 519-20.
26 Proclamation Suspending the Writ of Habeas Corpus, 24 September 1862, in Nicolay and Hay, *Complete Works of Abraham Lincoln* (New York: Lamb Publishing Co, 1905), vol. 7, 281.
27 Edward Stanwood, *A History of Presidential Elections* (Boston: Houghton, Mifflin, and Co., 1896), 237-43.

28 Letter to Abram Wakeman (private), 25 July 1864, in Nicolay and John Hay, *Complete Works of Abraham Lincoln*, vol. 10, 171.
29 Sidney Milkis and Michael Nelson, *The American Presidency: Origins and Development, 1776-2002* (Washington, DC: Congressional Quarterly Press, 2003), 161-62.
30 Brian Dirck, *The Executive Branch of the Federal Government: People, Process, and Politics* (Santa Barbara: ABC-Clio, 2007), 164.
31 Herman Belz, *Lincoln and the Constitution: The Dictatorship Question Reconsidered* (Fort Wayne: Louis Warren Lincoln Library, 1984), 15.
32 Response to a Serenade, 10 November 1864, in Nicolay and Hay, *Complete Works of Abraham Lincoln*, vol. 10, 263-64.
33 Jeffrey Tulis, *The Rhetorical Presidency* (Princeton: Princeton University Press, 1988); Melvin Laracey, *Presidents and the People* (College Station: Texas A&M Press, 2002); Richard Ellis, ed. *Speaking to the People: The Rhetorical Presidency in Historical Perspective* (Amherst: University of Massachusetts Press, 1998).
34 Wilson's Annual Message of 7 December 1915, *Congressional Record*, 64th Congress, 1st Session, 95-100.
35 *Annual Report of the Attorney General, 1917* (Washington, DC: Government Printing Office, 1917), 57-59; and David Cole, *Enemy Aliens* (New York: The New Press, 2003).
36 Paul Van Riper, *History of the United States Civil Service* (Evanston: Greenwood Press, 1958), 266.
37 *Congressional Record*, 65th Congress, Special Session, 2 April 1917, 104.
38 Ibid.
39 See Eugene Debs, "Antiwar Speech in Canton, Ohio," *The Call*, 16 June 1918.
40 John R. Mock, *Censorship, 1917* (Princeton: Princeton University Press, 1941), 110-30.
41 Thomas Gregory to Woodrow Wilson, 14 May 1917, Woodrow Wilson Papers, Mudd Library, Princeton University.
42 Ray Stannard Baker, *Woodrow Wilson: Life and Letters* (New York: Doubleday, 1939), vol. 7, 318-19, 323.
43 Ibid., 22-23.
44 Thomas Gregory to G.W. Anderson, 16 May 1916, Thomas Watt Gregory Papers, Manuscript Division, Library of Congress, Washington, DC, box 7; Harry Scheiber, *The Wilson Administration and Civil Liberties* (Cornell, NY: Cornell University Press, 1960), 42-43.
45 Ibid., 43.
46 *The Nation*, 3 May 1919, 674.
47 Erwin Hargrove, *President as Leader: Appealing to the Better Angels of Our Nature* (Lawrence: Kansas University Press, 1998).
48 For example, Peter Irons, *Justice at War: The Story of the Japanese Internment Cases* (Berkeley: University of California Press, 2003).
49 See quote in Rehnquist, *All the Laws but One*, 123.
50 Francis Biddle to Roger Baldwin, 7 January 1952, Roger Baldwin Papers, Mudd Library, Princeton University, box 4, fol. 15.

51 Joseph Persico, *Roosevelt's Secret War: FDR and World War II Espionage* (New York: Random House, 2001).
52 Quoted in ibid., 168.
53 Christopher Andrew, *For the President's Eyes Only: Secret Intelligence and the American Presidency from Washington to Bush* (New York: Harper Collins, 1995), 127-28.
54 Bradley Smith, *The Shadow Warriors: OSS and the Origins of the CIA* (New York: Basic Books, 1983), 99.
55 See, for example, Memorandum for the President, 9 April 1942, President's Office Files 4805, Franklin D. Roosevelt Presidential Library, Hyde Park, New York; Biddle to Baldwin, 7 January 1952, Roger Baldwin Papers, Mudd Library, Princeton University, box 4, fol. 15.
56 Francis Biddle, *In Brief Authority* (Garden City: Doubleday, 1962), 328.
57 Eugene Rostow, "Japanese American Cases: A Disaster," *Yale Law Journal* 54 (1944): 532.
58 "Barack Obama on Senator Dodd's Endorsement," 26 February 2008, http://www.BarackObama.com.
59 Paul Kane, "Obama Supports FISA Legislation, Angering the Left," *Washington Post*, 20 June 2008.
60 Peter Slevin, "Obama to Palin: Don't Mock the Constitution," *Washington Post*, 8 September 2008.
61 Ibid.
62 Kenneth Mayer, "Executive Orders," in *The Constitutional Presidency*, ed. Joseph Bessette and Jeffrey Tulis (Baltimore: Johns Hopkins University Press, 2009), 158.
63 "Barack Obama on Senator Dodd's Endorsement," 26 February 2008.
64 Quoted in David Gray Adler, "Presidential Greatness as an Attribute of Warmaking," *Presidential Studies Quarterly* 33, 3 (2003): 471.
65 Interestingly, the most promising liberal defenders against executive excess in times of crisis may lie not in Madisonian safeguards of interbranch rivalry but, rather, in obscure heroes from our least trusted "fourth" branch of government: the federal bureaucracy.

10 The "Centre" of the Democratic Deficit
Power and Influence in Canadian Political Executives

GRAHAM WHITE

Concern about the democratic deficit in Canada and other advanced democracies is real and it is important. As the title of the conference that gave rise to *Imperfect Democracies* sagely notes, however, we must define and measure the democratic deficit before we set out to remedy it. The term has gained such wide currency – even prime ministers-in-waiting toss it around with abandon[1] – that it is routinely applied to any perceived flaw in modern political-governance regimes.

In analyzing Canadian political executives and the democratic deficit, issues of definition and measurement loom especially large. We all "know" that power is becoming increasingly – and dangerously – centralized in the prime minister and the courtiers surrounding him, few of whom are elected. Prominent academics and journalists have published persuasive books detailing the accretion of power to "the centre" and the eclipse of Parliament and even of cabinet, which is argued to have atrophied into little more than "a focus group for the prime minister."

But just how is it that we "know" this? Influential and extensively researched as the critiques are, they tend to be weak on the admittedly difficult questions of definition and measurement. Without necessarily disputing the overall message from these well-informed analysts, if we are to fully understand how the structure and operation of the political executive relate to the democratic deficit, we need to pay closer attention to these basics.

This chapter, accordingly, has two principal objectives. First, it works towards developing a systematic approach to defining and measuring the democratic deficit as manifested in Canadian political executives. Second, it considers possible ways of addressing this facet of the democratic deficit. This necessarily means that, like an Oreo cookie with the filling already licked out, the middle is missing: an assessment of the magnitude of the democratic deficit in the realm of political executives. It is not, of course, that such judgments are unimportant – on the contrary, they are essential – but, rather, that in the limited space available I want to emphasize elements of the topic that have received less attention in the literature: issues of definition and measurement and potential means for reducing the democratic deficit.

It may thus seem that inordinate time and energy is given to the packing of conceptual and methodological bags, and insufficient attention devoted to actually travelling towards judgments regarding the seriousness of the democratic deficit and suggestions for dealing with it. Perhaps so, but one of my central arguments is that Canadian analysts have not been sufficiently careful in setting out their criteria for defining and measuring the democratic deficit in terms of political executives, especially first ministers.

Criticisms that the executive has become too powerful, especially vis-à-vis Parliament and the provincial/territorial legislatures, and thus undemocratic are of long standing in Canada and must be taken seriously. Since Denis Smith's landmark 1969 essay, "President and Parliament," the lion's share of criticism of executive dominance in Canada has been focused on the first minister and his or her close advisors.[2] Accordingly, this chapter is primarily devoted to looking at the power of the first minister. I say "first minister" rather than "prime minister" since the analysis encompasses both the national prime minister and the premiers of the provinces and territories.[3]

Pogo Was Wrong: We Have Seen the Enemy and It Is "the Centre"

The evidence supporting the "governing-from-the-centre" thesis, or what Herman Bakvis astutely labels the "prime minister-as-autocrat" interpretation,[4] is substantial. The most notable academic proponent of this view is Donald Savoie, who has written a justly acclaimed series of books on the pathology of current-day Canadian governance. The gist of Savoie's case is set out in his *Governing from the Centre: The Concentration of Power in Canadian Politics*.[5] His more recent books, *Breaking the Bargain* and *Court Government* reiterate but do not fundamentally advance the argument in

Governing from the Centre.[6] Jeffrey Simpson, who ranks among Canada's most insightful and prominent journalists, adopts a similar line of argument in his *The Friendly Dictatorship*.[7] Newspaper reports in the same vein are commonplace. Perhaps most strikingly, a recent systematic comparison of prime ministers in twenty-two countries (including all five national Anglo-Celtic Westminster systems – Australia, Canada, Ireland, New Zealand, and the United Kingdom) rated the Canadian prime minister not only as the most powerful (overall score: 8.24 on a scale from 1 to 9) but also as the most powerful by a wide margin (the next highest score, for Malta, was 7.16; the rating of the closest Anglo-Celtic system, Australia, was 6.98).[8]

Few if any credible analysts dispute that Canadian first ministers are very powerful, though a few scholars have raised questions, both analytic and substantive, about the "governing-from-the-centre" interpretation.[9] These cavils relate both to the actual extent of the prime minister's power and to claims that the degree of centralization has increased significantly (and worryingly) in recent years and continues to increase. A recent collection of essays on cabinets and leadership in the provinces – stimulated to an important degree by a desire to determine the applicability of the Savoie thesis provincially – reports a good deal of evidence confirming that Savoie's analysis applies in the provinces, but it also supplies evidence suggesting a need for qualifications and refinements.[10]

Towards an Understanding of the Democratic Deficit and First Ministerial Autocracy

The term "democratic deficit" is an evocative one, drawing considerable force from the obvious and intentional reference to financial deficits, which, by the 1990s (in Canada at least), had ceased to be a subject open to rational discussion as to possible pros and cons: all government deficits were unrelievedly bad under all imaginable circumstances. Accepting that the term is useful and, more significantly, is likely here to stay, we might ask whether the allusion to economic circumstances might be helpful in analyzing institutions of governance. Canadian political scientists who study political-governmental institutions tend not to think that we have much to learn from the economists. I certainly have no intention of attempting to apply the arcane tools of modern mathematical economics to Canadian political executives, yet, in a broad sense, the economists' general conceptual and methodological approaches to analyzing deficits do commend themselves to the task at hand.

Conceptually, economists distinguish deficits from debt. A deficit is the amount by which revenue falls short of expenses over a specific short term (usually a year), whereas a debt is the accumulated total of all deficits (offset by any surpluses). A deficit, in other words, is a short-term phenomenon potentially subject to significant reduction or even elimination within a short time frame, albeit perhaps through drastic action. By contrast, debt is far more substantial and enduring and, as such, can only be reduced in any meaningful way over a much longer term. Rendered thus, perhaps it might be more accurate to speak of a "democratic debt," but "democratic deficit" is not about to be replaced in common parlance by a term with a decidedly less euphonious ring. Terminology aside, the debt/deficit distinction encourages us to think about which democratic shortfalls might be fixed through quick, decisive reform and which will change only very slowly no matter how drastic the short-term actions.

Economists also draw another important conceptual distinction between cyclical and structural deficits. Cyclical factors fluctuate over the short- and medium term, and, while they might have far-reaching effects, they are temporary and may be amenable to short-term remedial action. Structural factors reflect the fundamental organization and capacity of the economy and can be changed only with prolonged, sustained effort.

In terms of methodology, economists have precise standards as to what should and should not be included in determining surpluses and deficits (operations of state-owned enterprises and certain capital expenditures, for example, are excluded). Clearly, the precise measurement tools available to economists in the form of government financial accounts have no analogue in the analysis of political power and its distribution within government, but the goal of having clear definitions and standards is nonetheless a worthy one. A more readily transferable methodological tool is the explicit use of time-series analysis. Not, of course, that political scientists can develop year-by-year measurements of democratic deficits in the manner of economists plotting fiscal trend lines, but we do need to pay special attention to change over time.

This last point draws to our attention one of the many basic problems confronting analysts of the democratic deficit unknown to the economists. A balanced budget is today precisely what it was in 1900 and 1950 and at all other times: revenue matching expenditures. Not so in the political world. The notion of just what constitutes "democracy" is constantly in flux. Consider a now obscure assessment of Canadian democracy rendered some years ago.

In 1921, Lord James Bryce – the prominent British academic and MP, author of one of the pioneering books in comparative politics (*Modern*

Democracies) – wrote a short but insightful book entitled *Canada: An Actual Democracy*.[11] By no means uncritical of what he saw of Canadian politics, Bryce's overall view was that Canada indeed constituted "an actual democracy." But what was the state of Canadian democracy in 1921? Women (other than those with relations in the military) were only permitted to vote in federal elections that very year, and in Quebec would not get the vote for another generation. Aboriginal Canadians were only allowed to vote if they legally renounced their Aboriginal status; within a few years, Parliament would make it illegal for "Indians" to raise money or to hire lawyers to pursue legal cases against the Crown. Candidates and parties were free to raise and spend money in any amounts and in any ways they wished, with no public scrutiny and subject only to the legal prohibitions in the Criminal Code of Canada against bribery and corruption. Freedom of information legislation was unknown. The public and organized groups, save the well-heeled and well-connected, had few opportunities to put their views on policy issues before decision makers through mechanisms such as public hearings. The country did have far more newspapers than today and all were independently owned, but many if not most were closely tied to political parties and offered their readers highly partisan and parochial slants on the news. The Canadian Charter of Rights and Freedoms was scarcely imaginable and no human rights codes existed; factories in Toronto and elsewhere could with impunity post signs saying "Men wanted. No Irish or Jews need apply." Moreover ... well, let us not belabour the point: by current standards, many aspects of Canadian democracy were deeply flawed, making for a huge democratic deficit.

This is by no means to suggest that we should be smug about how far we have progressed beyond the democratic shortcomings of 1921 Canada: it is sobering to think of how scholars of comparative democracy in 2103 might judge present-day Canadian democracy. Rather, we should note two things: first, we have made great strides towards a more robust democracy since 1921; second, and more important for present purposes, in 1921 most Canadians and most analysts likely would have agreed with Lord Bryce that Canadian democracy was strong and healthy. Otherwise put, in assessing democratic deficits we must be clear and careful to specify the standards by which we assess whether a democracy such as Canada is in deficit – and by how much.

This is all very interesting (I hope!), but just how does it relate to the analysis of Canadian political executives and the democratic deficit? Perhaps we cannot establish anything like a precise benchmark for a "balanced democratic budget," but we should still try to be explicit. Let us begin with the recognition that, by definition, political executives take and implement decisions and, in so doing, superimpose their own values and preferences on the advice or instruction they have received, including that from elected legislatures. In short, political executives in democracies have power and they use it.

The Westminster cabinet-parliamentary system is, by its very nature, characterized by extensive concentration of power. No one "designed" the system; it simply evolved over the centuries. A key element of that evolution was a gradual transfer of scarcely constrained power from the monarch to Parliament and, subsequently, to the prime minister and the cabinet. As discussed below, Canadian first ministers and cabinets face significant constraints in the exercise of power, but it is well to appreciate that concentrated power is an inherent characteristic of Westminster-style democracies.

This concentration of power is evident both in constitutionally mandated governance practices and in everyday political realities. A telling illustration is the constitutional monopoly the cabinet enjoys in virtually all matters of public finance. Only ministers of the Crown are permitted to *introduce* into Parliament (or the provincial/territorial legislatures) measures, including bills or amendments to bills, supply motions, and the like, that would impose or increase taxes or that would directly allocate spending. Any non-cabinet MP – including those of the governing party – attempting even to introduce a "money bill" or similar measure would immediately be ruled out of order by the Speaker.[12]

Politically, premiers in the pre-Confederation United Province of Canada may truly have been "first among equals" in terms of their relations with cabinet, but from Sir John A. Macdonald forward, the prime minister of Canada has had no equal in cabinet. No better illustration of Canadian first ministers' political pre-eminence could be cited than their unquestioned authority to appoint, shuffle, and remove ministers as they see fit.

The power of Canadian first ministers derives in no small measure from the comfortable position they typically enjoy atop majority single-party governments characterized by strong party discipline. Minority governments, in which no single party holds a majority of parliamentary seats, are, if not unknown, far less common, both nationally and provincially, than majority governments. Nationally, although no party held a majority in Parliament between mid-2004 and the May 2011 election, in all but three of the previous thirty-six years majority governments held sway. Minority governments are even less common at the provincial level. The frequency of majority governments largely reflects the distorting effects of the single-member plurality ("first-past-the-post") electoral system employed nationally and in all provinces since only rarely does a Canadian political party attract 50 percent or more of the votes in an election.

Does all this imply that Canada's Westminster cabinet-parliamentary system constitutes a massive, indeed insurmountable, structural democratic deficit? Not at all. Canadian first ministers and their cabinet colleagues are very much components of an unquestionably democratic system. They achieve and retain their power through continued support – "the confidence"[13] – of a majority of the members of the legislature, who have been elected through free and fair elections. Moreover, in a system ultimately subject to the public will exercised through the ballot box, concentrated power has an important democratic benefit: strong accountability through clear lines of authority. Especially in majority government situations, voters know precisely who is responsible for government policies and actions and can reward or punish those in power come the next election.

In assessing any person's or institution's power, real-life constraints on that power must be factored into the equation. And to be sure, Canadian first ministers face substantial constraints, formal and informal. Consider their previously cited prerogative of picking and choosing – and dismissing – their ministers. In the first place, the field is a narrow one: with rare exception, prime ministers' choices are limited to the 120 to 180 MPs in their caucuses (provincial premiers, who may find themselves appointing half or more of the members of their caucuses to cabinet, enjoy even fewer options). But the constraints are far more substantial than overall numbers might suggest since a strongly entrenched political imperative requires Canadian cabinets to be "representative." Every province and every principal region in the larger provinces plus the very largest cities must have a voice at the cabinet table, as must the country's major linguistic and ethnic-cultural communities. Gender must be respected in first ministers' cabinet picks and party factions must also be accommodated. All told, substantial power hemmed in with significant constraints.

Canada is a very federal country in that its provinces rank among the most powerful subnational governments on the planet. The extensive financial and jurisdictional powers of the provinces, combined with massive policy and administrative overlaps between the national and provincial governments, represent very significant constraints on all Canadian governments and, by extension, on their leaders. So, too, a clear consequence of adopting the Canadian Charter of Rights and Freedoms in 1982 has been a restriction on governments' – and thus on ministers' and first ministers' – scope for action (accompanied by a clear shift in power away from the executive towards the judiciary). Parliament and the provincial assemblies clearly lack the capacity to control and direct first ministers and their cabinets but, nonetheless, can constitute substantial constraints on executive power. In the House of Commons and its committees, the opposition parties can make life difficult for governments via the very public accountability mechanisms available to them and also by obstruction and through mobilization of public opinion. Behind the scenes, the government caucus enjoys virtually no formal power,[14] but astute and effective first ministers and their cabinet colleagues take pains to maintain caucus support. Like executives everywhere, Canadian first ministers are constrained by international events, developments, and pressures, be they social, economic, or military. And, of course, first ministers must contend with the power of the media.

Researching the Democratic Deficit and First Ministers

Canadian first ministers unquestionably make what in everyday parlance would be called (tellingly, in my view) "executive" decisions – decisions that override or ignore those of cabinet colleagues or are made without informing or consulting them. Few would disagree, I think, that the first minister's prerogative to make such decisions on occasion is justified and acceptable. Occasional "executive decisions" are one thing, but first ministers who constantly engage in such behaviour clearly warrant being labelled autocratic. Yet how common are they? A number of provincial premiers have been described as "one-man bands" who ran their governments all but singlehandedly and often highhandedly. Joey Smallwood of Newfoundland, Ontario's Leslie Frost, and W.A.C. Bennett of British Columbia come to mind. Significantly, though, all passed from the scene decades ago. To be sure, more recent premiers such as Ontario's Mike Harris and Alberta's Ralph Klein have been accused of exercising an untoward degree of power, but not of being "one-man bands."[15] Government has grown too large and complex for any one person (and his or her minions) to decide and run everything.

How then are we to identify autocratic, highly centralized power as exercised by the first minister? We would need to address such questions as the following:

- how often does the first minister take "autocratic decisions" (defined as those which override or ignore the views of cabinet colleagues or are made without informing or consulting them)?
- should we consider as autocratic a first minister's decision that runs counter to the apparent majority of ministers but is made after extensive discussion and is supported by a significant segment of cabinet?
- how many of the first ministers' autocratic decisions relate to major policies and critically important government initiatives and how many relate to low- and medium-level issues?
- how often and how extensively do the first minister and his or her political and bureaucratic officials intervene – micromanage – in routine decisions and operations of ministers' departments?
- how extensive is the control exercised by a first minister and his or her immediate circle of advisors and aides over important institutions beyond cabinet and Parliament – the senior bureaucracy, the government party, and the media?

Good questions all, but how do we go about answering them? Research into cabinet processes, of which the role of the first minister is a special case, is fraught with difficulty. Cabinet processes are among the most secretive in government. Researchers have no access whatsoever to cabinet and cabinet committee meetings and only the most limited access to cabinet documents less than twenty or thirty years old (though federal cabinet documents released under the "thirty-year rule" have been put to good analytic use by political scientists).[16] In the absence of the ability to observe first-hand or to review the most pertinent documents, researchers must rely on information that is publicly available and on interviews with knowledgeable observers and participants.

"Publicly available" information on cabinet decision making generally means media reports. To be sure, such reports can be telling about the role of the first minister in decision making, and other cabinet processes as well, but they must be interpreted with caution. Even assuming that they are entirely accurate – it is well to consider that when inside information on cabinet/first minister decisions is leaked to the press it is almost always to further someone's political agenda – it is difficult to judge how representative they are. We already know that, from time to time, first ministers announce important government initiatives without the approval or even the knowledge of their cabinets: Prime Minister Pierre Trudeau's imposition of a sweeping austerity program on his return from the Bonn summit in 1978,

BC Premier Vander Zalm's announcement of his government's opposition to abortion, Ontario's Bill Davis's surprise purchase of an oil company are but a few illustrations. This is what Savoie refers to as "governing by bolts of electricity;"[17] but, to extend his metaphor, how often are people actually struck by lightning? In other words, are such clearly autocratic actions a first minister's normal modus operandi or are they newsworthy precisely because they are highly unusual?

I do not suggest that, in attempting to assess the democratic deficit, we ignore media reports for, indeed, they do contain much of value. However, their utility must be assessed not assumed. Consider how often one reads in the newspaper that the current prime minister or the current premier – and his courtiers – have gone further than any predecessor in centralizing power. It may well be that this is precisely the case. But could not such conclusions be a function of a constant upping of the journalistic ante in relation to reporting about first ministerial autocracy? In order to rate as newsworthy, accounts of first ministers exercising their power need to claim or demonstrate a new level of excess. Stories about a first minister who prefers more consensual decision making than his predecessors are rather less likely to make it into print than ones about unprecedented centralization of power. We need to ask, however, on what basis the judgment is made that things are indeed worse now than in the past. Most indicators of violent crime in Canada have for years been steadily declining, but the public believes that crime is on the rise and that our cities and streets are increasingly unsafe. Much of this disconnect can be traced to media emphasis on especially sensational violent crimes. Can we be sure that media accounts of unprecedented centralization of power are not subject to a similar dynamic?

Relatedly, it is well to bear in mind that public image, which of course is largely generated by media accounts, may not be a reliable guide to assessing first ministers' exercise of power. Prime Minister Trudeau was widely viewed as highly autocratic and was judged to have been the most powerful Canadian prime minister in the expert survey mentioned earlier, albeit not by a very wide margin.[18] The judgment of those who sat with him at the cabinet table belie this public image. Eugene Whelan, as plain-speaking a minister as ever was, said of Trudeau: "Contrary to what many people think, Trudeau ran his cabinet with a very loose hand ... I always laughed when people described him as a dictator."[19] Veteran minister Mitchell Sharp wrote: "I never knew him [Trudeau] to anticipate a decision [in cabinet] by giving his opinion before asking the opinions of his colleagues, except, of course, with respect to constitutional questions. He genuinely sought for consensus."[20] Not the least of the reasons why we must be careful about reading too much into first ministers' public images as autocratic are the political benefits they may reap from being perceived by voters as strong, tough, decisive leaders, even if the reality is rather more complex.

As the preceding paragraph suggests, insiders' published accounts of their times in government can be useful sources, though we need to recall that memoirs can be self-serving and selective in their recollections. In terms of insiders' accounts, the recently published perspectives of two long-serving top political operatives on the power of the prime minister and his courtiers deserve serious attention. In a wide-ranging report on parliamentary reform, Tom Axworthy, who served for nearly a decade as Prime Minister Trudeau's principal secretary, writes: "the PMO may look 'almighty' from the outside, but from inside the bunker, the impression is more akin to the Wizard of Oz, pushing levers that lead nowhere."[21] In a similar vein, in his book *The Way It Works*, Eddie Goldenberg, legendary political fixer for Prime Minister Chrétien, dismisses what he terms "the mythology about excessive centralization or inordinate concentration of power" as a misunderstanding of the crucial need for coordination in a modern complex government.[22] (How quintessentially Canadian, by the way, that two exceptionally powerful backroom politicos should be at pains to *downplay* their putative influence.) To be sure, we must be careful in accepting such assessments at face value. Still, they are consistent with lamentations that senior political officials in the Ontario premier's office have made to me (some in an actual research context, others in casual conversation) that they only wished they had anything resembling the power and control over ministers attributed to them. Significantly, these comments came from politicos from all three parties that have governed Ontario in the past two decades – the Liberal Party, the Conservative Party, and New Democratic Party.

As well, we must try to discern patterns rather than focus unduly on isolated incidents lest we give credence to the chemists' and physicists' gibe that a social scientist is someone who thinks the plural of "anecdote" is "data." Savoie and others, for example, make much of Trudeau's infamous conversion to a far-reaching austerity program on his return from the Bonn economic summit in 1978, which he announced without even consulting his finance minister, Jean Chrétien, who thought seriously of resigning. Yet Chrétien himself described this episode as uncharacteristic, commenting: "In cabinet Trudeau listened more and compromised more than most Canadians imagine ... I never subscribed to the notion that Trudeau was a dictator. Often knowing what he thought, I saw him accepting the views of his ministers despite his own wishes."[23]

Interviews must necessarily serve as our principal data source – as indeed they do in other realms of academic research into matters political, from policy studies to analyses of political party operations or interest groups. Having conducted many dozens of interviews of ministers, political staff, and senior bureaucrats about cabinets and cabinet processes at the provincial and territorial level, my view is that former ministers and politicos are far superior respondents than are those still engaged in the political process. Not only do they have much more time to offer but, being removed from the hurly-burly, they also tend to be more thoughtful about their experiences and less defensive and self-centred. As well, their comments and judgments are more likely to draw upon their entire range of experiences as opposed to the immediate issues of the day, which often preoccupy ministers and political staff still in office. (Senior bureaucrats typically have long time horizons and are by nature more analytical than are political figures about government structures and processes, so that it matters a good deal less, at least in my experience, whether they are interviewed before or after they leave office.)

Expert surveys offer an alternate approach, yet the twenty-two-nation study alluded to at the outset, which employed expert opinion to develop comparative ratings, illustrates the difficulties of measuring first ministers' powers and securing systematic data on them. To be sure, expert surveys have their uses: I contemplated conducting one in a major research project into provincial cabinet structures and processes but abandoned the idea largely because it became evident that the numbers of reliable respondents would be so small as to render the exercise all but useless. Still, their shortcomings are well known, not least with regard to the selection of experts. In the Canadian case, since relatively few scholars have published on the cabinet and the prime minister, one has to wonder to what extent the fourteen experts' rating reflected their own research and observation and how much was attributable to the influence of Savoie's *Governing from the Centre*.[24]

In attempting to establish whether first ministers act autocratically towards their cabinets, we need to distinguish the "A Team" ministers from their less formidable colleagues. According to a Conservative insider quoted by the *Toronto Star*, Prime Minister Harper's former Chief of Staff, Ian Brodie "frequently reduce[d] cabinet ministers to tears" with his tirades and his heavy-handed wielding of authority on the prime minister's behalf.[25]

Even assuming the accuracy of the insider's claim – that the tears were said to flow "frequently" strains credulity – it is well to recall that, like the denizens of Animal Farm, some ministers are more equal than others. It would seem a very safe bet that, among the ministers who were *not* reduced to tears by Ian Brodie would be the likes of heavyweights such as Jim Flaherty, Jim Prentice, John Baird, and David Emerson. Particularly since all Canadian cabinets necessarily include at least a few second-stringers in order to accommodate the "representational imperative," it would hardly be surprising if the first minister and his staff pushed some weaker ministers around in an autocratic fashion. The real test of autocracy on the first minister's part, I suggest, lies in his dealings with the tough, able ministers at the core of government. At the provincial level at least, and I suspect in Ottawa as well, the evidence suggests that, while on occasion first ministers may well override any minister's preferences, or even fail to inform them of crucial decisions, they do not – indeed cannot – consistently act autocratically towards the leading ministers.[26]

As the final bullet point on page 234 suggests, the question of first ministerial autocracy goes beyond power relations within cabinet. Significantly, Savoie's more recent book on "court government" in Canada and Britain advances the "governing-from-the-centre" argument in its allusions to the Harper government's unprecedented attempts at news management and in its analysis of the success of the Canadian (and British) prime ministers and their "courts" in rendering the senior bureaucracy more "responsive" to their political agendas.[27] Based partially on his close reading of testimony before the Gomery inquiry into the so-called "sponsorship scandal" – he was the commission's research director – Savoie's analysis of the centre's increasing control of the senior bureaucracy rings true. Clearly, though, more research on this key issue is needed, not least in the wake of evidence from a recent book focusing on Canadian secretaries to cabinet, which indicates that these critical players – at least the successful ones – perform multiple roles, requiring the confidence of the first minister, the cabinet, and the senior mandarinate, and that "hard-won confidence does not imply blind subjugation of the clerk to the prime minister."[28] Whether the Harper government's efforts at news management succeeded or backfired – no government in Canadian history experienced the same level of noxious, mutually contemptuous relations with the media as did the Harper government in its first mandate – remains to be determined. Similarly, though media reports point to extraordinary efforts on Harper's part to centralize control of the entire government apparatus in the Prime Minister's Office,[29] systematic research on the extent and success of such activities is all but entirely lacking.

A final methodological observation before turning to possible remedies for the executive democratic deficit derives from the earlier suggestion that we follow the economists' lead in taking seriously change over time. In so doing, we need to balance the accretion of power to first ministers against changes in the constraints they face. A particularly significant example relates to the widespread increase in the number, sophistication, and combativeness of first ministers' communications staff. It was only in the late 1950s that the prime minister of Canada first acquired a press officer,[30] but now hordes of media advisors and spin doctors serve first ministers of even the smallest provinces and territories. As well, "the centre" often exercises stringent oversight on departments' and ministries' dealings with the media. Surely this is a strong indication of the greatly enhanced control enjoyed by first ministers over the political agenda and over the operations of government. But is it really? The capacity is clearly much greater but so, too, is the challenge: a world of continuous and instantaneous news dissemination, spearheaded by aggressive, ambitious reporters with access to all manner of previously secret or hard-to-find information by virtue of modern communications technologies (the internet, Xerox machines, cell phones and the like). Perhaps the greater resources devoted to managing the media have only allowed first ministers to keep pace with such changes. It is fair to add that the emergence of a 24/7 news environment and reductions in press gallery complements owing to media consolidation and convergence have rendered it substantially more difficult for reporters and editors to gather and analyze information about government. The point here is not to argue that first ministers' control of the media has grown or diminished but, rather, to suggest that analyzing change of first ministers' power requires close attention to constraints as well as to enhanced sources of influence.

Power *Is* Concentrated at the Centre

Savoie is unquestionably correct that power is heavily concentrated at the centre of the Government of Canada (as indeed it is in the provinces), though without a precise benchmark it is less clear that the degree of concentration is increasing significantly, as he argues. Stéphane Dion, writing on the basis of both strong academic credentials and years of experience as a federal cabinet minister, observes:

The works of Donald Savoie and Jeffrey Simpson ... are at times captivating, but to my mind they do not prove the thesis of an increasing concentration of power as the years go by ... [H]owever, if I compare their descriptions with analysis of an earlier time, like the one penned by Jack Granatstein on the Mackenzie King era in *The Ottawa Men* (1998), it is clearly evident that power at that time was far more concentrated in a few hands than it is today ... [T]he political system then was less complex, there was less expertise, and there were far fewer checks and balances on power. Perhaps – in an age characterized by "the decline of deference" – it is less a case of increasing concentration of power than increasing sensitivity to and declining tolerance of concentrated power.[31]

Clearly, the inherent nature of the Westminster cabinet-parliamentary system, with its effective fusion of executive and legislative functions, offers strong opportunity for the concentration of power at the centre. Savoie has documented the accretion of power at the centre, focused, of course, on the prime minister, and I have argued that the potential for concentrated power is markedly stronger at the provincial level than federally: as Walter Young and Terry Morley put it, "provincial government is premier's government."[32] Although we do need to be careful to demonstrate rather than to assume that power is unduly and increasingly concentrated in the first minister and his or her courtiers, no one familiar with Canadian politics can doubt the very extensive powers exercised by our first ministers. And, as O'Malley's findings indicate, Canadian first ministers are unusually powerful even by Westminster standards. In my book, *Cabinets and First Ministers,* I look at two quantitative measures of first ministers' power: length of tenure in office (the presumption being that longer-serving, more experienced first ministers are more powerful than are their shorter-term colleagues) and likelihood of being removed from office by one's party. At the national level, Canadian prime ministers are the longest serving in the Anglo-Celtic world, and, while no sitting Canadian prime minister in living memory has been ousted by his or her party,[33] such a fate befell at least two prime ministers in each of the other Anglo-Celtic Westminster systems. Subnationally, Canadian premiers enjoy substantially longer runs in office than do their Australian counterparts.[34]

If the overall conclusion about concentration of power is not in doubt, we nonetheless need to be more attentive to the issues of definition and measurement (not least in terms of change) set out in earlier sections of this chapter. The need for greater precision does not, however, in any way diminish the importance of finding ways to reduce what is clearly a serious democratic deficit. Let us conclude by looking briefly at some possibilities.

Measures to Reduce the Democratic Deficit and the Democratic Debt

The proposals outlined below are a mixture of minor adjustments and major institutional reforms that would, to varying degrees, constrain the power of the first minister. Some are ideas to reduce the cyclical democratic deficit, while others are better thought of as addressing the structural democratic deficit.

Fixed Election Dates

Advocates of fixed election dates usually emphasize their value in establishing a "level playing field" by preventing the government from scheduling elections so as to maximize their re-election prospects. This is doubtless desirable; however, for present purposes, establishing fixed elections is more important for removing one minor yet undeniable source of first ministers' power – the capacity to get their way by threatening ministers or backbenchers with an early, unwelcome election call. The federal government and several provinces have adopted fixed election dates.

As welcome as a move to fixed elections might be, Canada's limited experience with even this limited reform illustrates just how difficult it can be to constrain first ministers' power. Despite having argued strongly for fixed elections while in Opposition, and having showcased passage of the requisite legislation as a top priority early in his mandate, Prime Minister Harper showed no hesitation whatsoever in exercising his prerogative to request the governor general to dissolve Parliament (i.e., call a federal election) in September 2008 – a year earlier than stipulated in the legislated schedule – in order to advance his political agenda.[35] A first minister heading a majority government would presumably find it more difficult to justify ignoring a legislated fixed election date than did Harper, who claimed that Parliament had become dysfunctional to the point where his minority government could not operate effectively. However, the clear lesson of this episode is that moving to fixed elections is no panacea.

Leadership Selection Processes

That Canadian first ministers enjoy longer terms than do their other Westminster counterparts and are virtually never removed from office reflects the broadly based processes by which the political parties choose their leaders. Party leaders are selected through extensive, party-wide processes

– delegated conventions or universal votes of all party members – in which thousands of party activists participate. Accordingly, while party caucuses can make life unpleasant for unpopular or unsuccessful leaders, leaders who wish to stay on can only be removed by similar, formal party-wide processes, which are slow, messy, and uncertain. And first ministers typically go to considerable lengths to retain a firm hand on their parties, rendering them all but impervious to removal processes. Thus, a powerful constraint on autocratic behaviour by the first minister available to parliamentary caucuses in other Anglo-Celtic systems (though they would not use the "caucus" terminology) is not available in Canada. Limiting first ministers' power in this way would be a useful reform. I leave it to colleagues more knowledgeable than I about political parties to devise some mechanism for involving caucuses in at least triggering, if not carrying out, leadership reviews.

Strengthening Parliament
To the extent that parliamentary power is conceived as a zero-sum game – what the executive gains, Parliament loses – any reform that significantly enhances the capacity of Parliament and the provincial/territorial legislatures to hold governments to account or to develop a modicum of genuine law-making (as opposed to law-passing) power is a worthwhile advance. It has become commonplace to bemoan the decline of Parliament as an effective governance institution. Especially problematic are the oftentimes cavalier, pernicious attitudes exhibited by governments towards Parliament. Consider, for example, the Harper government's manual for its MPs on how to stonewall troublesome parliamentary committees and, in Ontario, the McGuinty government's shifting of Question Period into the morning despite howls of outrage from the Opposition and the Press Gallery.

Without for a moment discounting the significance of such troubling developments, we should avoid falling victim to golden ageism in thinking about the role of Parliament and the provincial/territorial legislatures. I am not sure I fully accept David Smith's claim, in his wonderful, prize-winning book, *The People's House of Commons*, that, "while far from total, members [of Parliament] have greater control over their activities and more opportunity to influence legislation than at any time in the past century."[36] It is certainly true, though, that legislators in this country enjoy remarkably better support services and access to information than they did three or four decades ago. They are also better educated and more interested in and knowledgeable about policy. Potential reforms in this realm, be they essentially structural/procedural in nature or primarily rooted in attitudinal change, while obviously and closely linked to issues of executive power, are beyond the purview of this chapter – with one fundamentally important exception, as highlighted in the next paragraph (for more on mechanisms by which to strengthen Parliament, see David Docherty [Chapter 8, this volume]).

Minority Governments ... and the Way to Ensure Them

If power is overly concentrated in "the centre," two routes towards rectifying the problem suggest themselves. One entails dispersing power and influence more broadly within the executive, rebalancing the power relations between the first minister and his entourage and the full range of ministers – returning, in other words, to cabinet government from prime ministerial government. The other approach would see an overall reduction in the power of the executive. Improbable and naive as the latter appears, it is readily achievable through a steady diet of minority government. As Peter Russell's recent *Two Cheers for Minority Government* argues persuasively, minority governments are our best hope for curtailing prime ministerial government and restoring a modicum of parliamentary effectiveness.[37] Yet, as suggested by the success of the minority Conservative government elected in January 2006 in cowing the opposition, enabling Prime Minister Stephen Harper to operate almost as if he enjoyed a majority, intermittent bouts of minority government will not do the trick. What we need is minority government as a permanent condition. But that is unlikely to occur in the absence of fundamental structural reform: replacement of the current single-member plurality electoral system with a system of proportional representation or another electoral regime without the bias towards "false" majorities inherent in first-past-the-post.

Involving Government Backbenchers in Cabinet Decision Making

In my book for the Canadian Democratic Audit, *Cabinets and First Ministers*, I briefly review the experiences of several provinces that have given private members from the government party a tangible, if usually limited, role in cabinet decision making. This can take several forms, including regular attendance by caucus members (sometimes on a rotating basis) at cabinet supplemented by access to relevant documentation, genuine participation of caucus in the process of developing legislation, and replacement of conventional cabinet committees with combined cabinet-caucus committees, sometimes chaired by private members. Clearly, such innovations – none of which contravene any fundamental precept of "responsible government" – hold great promise for significantly increasing the numbers of political figures with real clout in government decision making and, thereby limiting the concentration of power at the centre. Just as clearly, though, they may be little more than hollow public relations exercises or make-work projects for restless backbenchers, having no palpable effect on the distribution of real power. Of the various potential reforms considered in this chapter and elsewhere, none are as little known and understood as are mechanisms for involving government backbenchers in cabinet decision making. They thus cry out for serious research attention.

Conclusion

This chapter does not directly challenge the conventional wisdom in Canada about the growing concentration of power "at the centre" – the first minister and his or her courtiers – but does attempt to focus attention on the way we think about the democratic deficit as it relates to the executive and the way we go about measuring it. That my principal argument is that the Canadian academic (and journalistic) community has not been sufficiently precise about identifying and measuring the democratic deficit, at least as far as the power of the first minister is concerned, does not prevent me from offering some suggestions for "fixing" this component of the democratic deficit. That we are not exactly sure how serious the problem is – and whether it is, as is frequently argued, growing – does not mean that we should not be thinking about solutions.

NOTES

1 Paul Martin, "The Democratic Deficit," *Policy Options* 24, 1 (2003).
2 Denis Smith, "President and Parliament: The Transformation of Parliamentary Government in Canada," in *Apex of Power: The Prime Minister and Political Leadership in Canada*, ed. Thomas A. Hockin (Toronto: Prentice-Hall, 1971). Smith's chapter was first presented at a Conservative Party conference in 1969.
3 Two of Canada's three territories, which are perhaps best understood as proto-provinces, follow the constitutional precepts of the Westminster cabinet-parliamentary system but operate without political parties in a distinctive "consensus government" model, which is intriguingly congruent with traditional northern Aboriginal governance. Space, unfortunately, does not permit an account of the unusual roles and circumstances of their first ministers. See Graham White, "Traditional Aboriginal Values in a Westminster Parliament: The Legislative Assembly of Nunavut," *Journal of Legislative Studies* 12, 1 (2006): 8-31.
4 Herman Bakvis, "Prime Minister and Cabinet in Canada: An Autocracy in Need of Reform," *Journal of Canadian Studies* 35, 4 (2000): 60-79.

5   Donald Savoie, *Governing from the Centre: The Concentration of Power in Canadian Politics* (Toronto: University of Toronto Press, 1999).
6   Donald Savoie, *Breaking the Bargain: Public Servants, Ministers and Parliament* (Toronto: University of Toronto Press, 2003); Donald Savoie, *Court Government and the Collapse of Accountability in Canada and the United Kingdom* (Toronto: University of Toronto Press, 2008).
7   Jeffrey Simpson, *The Friendly Dictatorship* (Toronto: McClelland and Stewart, 2001).
8   Eion O'Malley, "The Power of Prime Ministers: Results of an Expert Survey," *International Political Science Review* 28, 1 (2007): table 3.
9   Bakvis, "Prime Minister and Cabinet"; Paul Thomas, "Governing from the Centre: Reconceptualizing the Role of the PM and Cabinet," *Policy Options* 25, 1 (2003-4: 79-85); Graham White, *Cabinets and First Ministers* (Vancouver: UBC Press, 2005).
10 Luc Bernier, Keith Brownsey, and Michael Howlett, eds., *Executive Styles in Canada: Cabinet Structures and Leadership Practices in Canadian Government* (Toronto: Institute of Public Administration of Canada and University of Toronto Press, 2005).
11 Lord James Bryce, *Canada: An Actual Democracy* (Toronto: Macmillan, 1921).
12 Non-cabinet MPs are permitted to bring into Parliament measures to reduce taxes or spending, and they may, of course, vote against any cabinet-sponsored financial measure.
13 In the distinctive terminology of British parliamentarianism, "confidence of the House" has a very specific meaning: the capacity of the government – the first minister and cabinet – to win all the important votes, "important" having been established over centuries of parliamentary convention.
14 In Canada, the term "caucus" refers to a party's contingent of elected members (plus, at the national level, senators, who in Canada are unelected). The term also refers to the group's regular – usually weekly during parliamentary sessions – closed-door meetings.
15 The provincial premiers alluded to in this paragraph held office as follows: Smallwood 1949-72; Frost 1949-61; Bennett 1952-72; Harris 1995-2002; Klein 1992-2006.
16 See, for example, Christa Scholtz's analysis of the process leading up to Canada's decision to engage in a land-claims process with its Aboriginal peoples. Christa Scholtz, *Negotiating Claims: The Emergence of Indigenous Land Claim Negotiation Policies in Australia, Canada, New Zealand and the United States* (New York: Routledge, 2006), Chap. 3. H.D. Munroe, "Style within the Centre: Pierre Trudeau, the War Measures Act and the Nature of Prime Ministerial Power," *Canadian Public Administration* 54, 4 (2011): 531-49.
17 Savoie, *Governing from the Centre*, Chap. 10.
18 O'Malley, "Power of Prime Ministers," 20.
19 Eugene Whelan (with Rick Archibold), *Whelan: The Man in the Green Stetson* (Toronto: Irwin, 1986), 195.
20 Mitchell Sharp, *Which Reminds Me ... A Memoir* (Toronto: University of Toronto Press, 1994), 167.
21 Thomas S. Axworthy, *Everything Old Is New Again: Observations on Parliamentary Reform* (Kingston: Queen's University Centre for the Study of Democracy, 2008), 26.
22 Eddie Goldenberg, *The Way It Works: Inside Ottawa* (Toronto: McClelland and Stewart, 2006), 75.

23 Jean Chrétien, *Straight from the Heart* (Toronto: Key Porter Books, 1985), 75.
24 Full disclosure requires that I point out that my views were not solicited in O'Malley's research. The survey was likely conducted before publication of my book *Cabinets and First Ministers*, but I had published on Canadian cabinets in Canadian and British journals and in a prominent collection on cabinets, edited by leading scholars. See Michael Laver and Kenneth Shepsle, eds., *Cabinet Ministers and Parliamentary Government* (New York: Cambridge University Press, 1994). The observation that I might have been expected to have been consulted as an expert is offered not out of pique but to emphasize the uncertainty of the methodology.
25 Tonda MacCharles and Richard Brennan, "PM's Man in the Shadows," *Toronto Star*, 8 March 2008.
26 White, *Cabinets and First Ministers*, Chap. 3.
27 Savoie, *Court Government*, Chap. 10.
28 Jacques Bourgault, "Clerks and Secretaries to Cabinet: Anatomy of Leadership," in *Searching for Leadership: Secretaries to Cabinet in Canada*, ed. Patrice Dutil (Toronto: University of Toronto Press, 2008), 60. Their responsibilities vary, as do their titles, but cabinet secretaries/clerks of executive councils are the most senior bureaucratic officials in government, typically serving not only as deputy minister to the first minister but also as head of the public service.
29 See, for example, Linda Deibel, "Harper's Powerful 'Political Pit Bull,'" *Toronto Star*, 6 September 2008; James Travers, "The Quiet Unravelling of Canadian Democracy," *Toronto Star*, 4 April 2009; and Lawrence Martin, *Harperland: The Politics of Control* (Toronto: Viking Canada, 2010).
30 David Taras, "Prime Ministers and the Media," in *Prime Ministers and Premiers: Political Leadership and Public Policy in Canada*, ed. Leslie A. Pal and David Taras (Scarborough: Prentice Hall, 1988), 41.
31 Stéphane Dion, "Institutional Reform: The Grass Isn't Always Greener on the Other Side," in *Political Leadership and Representation in Canada: Essays in Honour of John C. Courtney*, ed. Hans J. Michelmann, Donald C. Story, and Jeffrey S. Steeves (Toronto: University of Toronto Press, 2007), 178. It is fair to point out that Dion's reservations about recent accretions of power to the centre were based on a comparison of Prime Minister Chrétien's government with those of Pierre Trudeau and Brian Mulroney, whereas Savoie and Simpson argue that the main break with the past occurred in the Trudeau era.
32 Walter D. Young and J. Terence Morley, "The Premier and the Cabinet," in *The Reins of Power: Governing British Columbia*, ed. J. Terence Morley, Norman J. Ruff, Neil A. Swainson, R. Jeremy Wilson, and Walter D. Young (Vancouver: Douglas and McIntyre, 1983), 54. For a broader discussion, see White, *Cabinets and First Ministers*, 74-77.
33 It could be argued that Prime Minister Chrétien was ousted by the Liberal Party, but he could have stayed on to fight had he so desired, and certainly his departure was not nearly formally stipulated nor as swift and brutal as were those of prime ministers in the other Anglo-Celtic countries.
34 White, *Cabinets and First Ministers*, Tables 3.1-3.3. Note that these data do not include the remarkable ouster of Australian Prime Minister Kevin Rudd in June 2010.

35 For various discussions of the governor general's powers as they relate to dissolution, see Peter H. Russell and Lorne Sossin, eds., *Parliamentary Democracy in Crisis* (Toronto: University of Toronto Press, 2009).
36 David Smith, *The People's House of Commons: Theories of Democracy in Contention* (Toronto: University of Toronto Press, 2007), 87.
37 Peter H. Russell, *Two Cheers for Minority Government* (Toronto: Emond Montgomery Publications, 2008).

11

Extending the Franchise to Non-Citizen Residents in Canada and the United States
How Bad Is the Democratic Deficit?

PATTI TAMARA LENARD AND DANIEL MUNRO

Canada and the United States are both immigrant nations and both welcome newcomers and incorporate them, as full citizens, quickly and largely effectively. It should therefore not come as a surprise that, as a political issue, the salience of extending the (mainly municipal) vote to permanent residents is low: the period during which newcomers are unable to participate, fully, in the political institutions that shape their lives is short, and the obstacles to gaining entry are manageable. Yet, as many permanent resident migrants and their advocates point out, there is nevertheless a democratic deficit. Between the time of arrival and naturalization (if naturalization ever occurs) many decisions that have tremendous effect on the lives of non-citizen residents are made without their having a formal political voice to be heard and to influence decision making. In the words of Ron Hayduk, co-director of the American Immigration Voting Project, "today, the US is home to more partial members than at any time in its past, creating a crisis in our democracy."[1] As Ruth Rubio-Marin and others have noted, the phenomenon raises a serious "democratic legitimacy concern."[2] That non-citizen immigrants pay taxes, for example, without being able to participate in choosing their representatives "challenges the very legitimacy of ... American democracy."[3] In both Canada and the United States, non-citizen – and thus non-voting – adult permanent residents make up between 4 to 5 percent of the population. This proportion is likely to increase as the foreign-born populations of the United States and Canada continue to grow.[4] The normative urgency of granting the right to vote to non-citizen residents is therefore increasing.

The purpose of this chapter is to examine the normative dimensions of the democratic deficit that emerge from the exclusion of permanent migrants from the franchise. We argue that, although there is a veritable democratic deficit in these cases, there are normatively defensible empirical reasons to focus more of our attention and political activity on other social and political deficits that afflict our political community with greater consequences.

It is worth noting, by way of introduction, that, outside of Canada and the United States, it is more and more frequently found that non-citizen residents are entitled to vote in at least local elections. In the early 1990s, the Maastricht Treaty granted all citizens of the European Union the right to vote in local elections of the country in which they reside (if they reside outside of their home country). EU citizens are also permitted to vote in European parliamentary elections from wherever they live.[5] A variety of European states, moreover, extend the right to vote to residents who hail from outside of the European Union, so long as they meet certain residency requirements. Finland requires a residency of two years, for example, and Denmark, Sweden, and Norway all require three years of residence before the right to vote in local elections is granted to residents. New Zealand permits all residents to vote in *all* levels of elections after one year of residence (although they are not permitted to stand for election until they are citizens).[6] It would therefore be in keeping with global trends to extend permanent residents the right to vote, at least in local elections, in Canada and the United States. As we note below, some municipalities in the United States have already decided to do so.

Historical Trends towards Inclusion

The history of both Canada and the United States, albeit with bumps along the road, suggests a history of general expansion of the franchise. There is, Alexander Keyssar observes, "a deeply embedded, yet virtually unspoken, notion that the history of suffrage is the history of gradual, inevitable reform and progress."[7] That there is such a story about the progress of political participation and steady expansion of the franchise, however, is not the only reason to think that we are being pressed towards extending at least some form of the right to vote to non-citizen residents.

Another reason has to do with a deep commitment to liberal principles (which reveal to us the ideal that all individuals deserve equal respect) and to democratic principles (which encourage us to give a voice to all individuals who are subject to the laws of a community). The logic of these principles suggests a need to rethink the sharp division that we have drawn with respect to insiders and "outsiders" and the unequal treatment of different groups that results.[8] Listen to Joseph Carens explain the trend in the American context, in particular:

> On the whole, the history of liberalism reflects a tendency to expand both the definition of the public sphere and the requirements of equal treatment. In the United States today, for example, in contrast to earlier times, both public agencies and private corporations may not legally exclude women simply because they are women (although private clubs still may). A white shopkeeper may no longer exclude blacks from his store (although he may exclude them from his home). I think these recent developments, like the earlier extension of the franchise, reflect something fundamental about the inner logic of liberalism. The extension of the right to immigrate reflects the same logic: equal treatment of individuals in the private sphere.[9]

Historically, nation-states have generated all kinds of distinctions – legal, political, social, economic – between citizens and non-citizens. Foreigners have, says William James Booth, "historically been the targets of 'internal' closure, that is, the denial of access to various rights accorded to members: voting, protection under the law, social welfare benefits [and so on]."[10] Yet, he continues, "the justice of this internal closure, of distinguishing sharply between members on the one hand and strangers here to stay on the other, has become, in stages and falteringly, open to dispute."[11] It is not only the expansion of immigration that suggests the need to revisit these sharp distinctions, though the rate of immigration certainly does force us to think more seriously about what justifies seemingly unequal treatment of citizens and non-citizens.

This historical trend is evidenced in relatively recent American Supreme Court rulings, which have steadily eroded the distinctions made between citizens and non-citizens in the United States. The Supreme Court of late has shown a distaste for distinguishing sharply between the treatment of citizens and non-citizens, at least along economic and social dimensions. Among other relevant decisions, the Supreme Court has ruled that the children of illegal immigrants cannot be barred from free public education; that legal aliens cannot be denied access to state benefits; that the Equal Protection Clause applies to all residents of the United States, regardless of citizenship. These rulings suggest that, for many important purposes, there is no legal basis on which to distinguish between citizens and non-citizens (and, in many cases, even when these non-citizens are illegal immigrants). Yet, as many scholars observe, these rulings have remained committed to an important distinction between economic rights and political rights. Whereas there is little cause to discriminate against non-citizens with respect to economic and social rights, the Court has remained comfortable with discriminating against them with respect to political rights: "A line seems to be drawn between social and economic inclusion on the one hand, and political inclusion on the other."[12] It is not clear, however, that this distinction can be maintained at the level of practice. As Rubio-Marin explains, it may prove impossible to separate economic and political rights, as the Supreme Court encourages: "To deny resident aliens the benefits of political cooperation is often impossible, as many such benefits (e.g. national security or public order) are non-excludable goods open to all members. But, even concerning excludable benefits, such as the exercise of political rights, it might also be manifestly unfair to the extent that it denies both the political relevance of the contribution of immigrants and the economic relevance of immigrants' political exclusion."[13]

Normative Justifications for Extending the Franchise to Non-Citizen Residents: The All-Affected Principle

A variety of arguments is advanced to justify extending the franchise to permanent residents. One argument suggests that extending the vote gives newcomers the opportunity to participate in the political system and thus ensures that they are able to become full members of their new community as quickly as possible. Another argument suggests that there is a basic element of fairness involved: permanent residents pay taxes and therefore deserve to participate in electing those who make decisions about the taxes that they are required to pay. Space does not permit an exhaustive account of the reasons advanced in favour of granting the right to vote to residents,[14] and we will therefore defend what is, in our view, the most plausible of them – namely, the all-affected principle.

In its primary role, the all-affected principle is relied upon to answer a key question in democratic political theory: even as democratic decisions are said to be taken by "the people," we must answer a prior question – namely, who are the people who are entitled to make the decision in question. The all-affected principle offers an answer: the principle that "all those people who are affected by a particular law, policy, or decision ought to have a voice in making it" is, at first glance, "the most intuitively plausible proposal with respect to the proper scope of democratic governance."[15] It seems clear enough that all those who are likely to be affected – whether we mean "significantly" or "possibly" affected – by a given political decision have the right to participate in the decision-making procedure and that the procedures ought to be crafted in such a way that this right can be met. It is certainly the all-affected principle that has, by and large, justified extending the franchise across liberal democracies in the past: "Historically, of course, the principle that those affected by decisions ought to have a say in their making has played a central role in progressive extensions of the franchise to middle-class men, working-class men, women and younger men and women, [and so on]."[16] Given this primary role, then, it is no surprise that the all-affected principle is invoked to justify extending the franchise to newcomers prior to their being granted citizenship. Permanent residents are clearly *affected* by decisions made by the polity in which they reside.

The principle is subject to a range of vagueness objections, with which its advocates are familiar. For example, if we take the principle to mean all *actually* affected interests, it quickly becomes incoherent. For one thing, who is in fact affected by a decision depends on what the decision turns out to be, and, consequently, "it is unable to tell us who is entitled to vote on a decision until after that very decision has been decided."[17] Alternatively, if we interpret the principle to mean all *possibly* affected interests, we run into a different problem, namely, that we will be forced to consider "what interests would or could be affected by any possible outcome" of a decision process, and the expansionist impact of engaging in this exercise may well be near infinite.[18] If we included all those who *might* have been affected by the outcome of the presidential race in 2008, we would have good reason to extend the vote to include Iraqis, if not most of the rest of the world.[19] Robert Dahl makes the same observation in his own discussion of the principle: "It forces us to ask whether there is not after all some wisdom in the half-serious comment of a friend in Latin America who said that his people should be allowed to participate in our elections, for what happens in the politics of the United States is bound to have profound consequences for his country."[20]

One response to this worry observes that, even if people are affected by a polity's decisions, they are by no means affected equally. We might therefore implement institutional procedures whereby those who are *most* affected have the most say, and those who are less affected have correspondingly less of a say.[21] In other words, it is only if we are *significantly* affected by the decisions that a particular decision-making body takes that justice will demand that we have a (relatively) significant say in what decision is taken. This response serves to allay one worry and raise another. It allays the worry – and this is an observation about democratic politics in general – that polities regularly make decisions that affect those who have no say in them. Among the obvious examples are immigration policies, which have a tremendous impact on outsiders who wish to enter the country but who are not permitted input.[22] We may not like to agree that merely being affected by policies is sufficient to garner the right to have a say in what they contain.

On the other hand, a commitment to an all-affected justification for granting rights to have a say in decision-making procedures also forces us to acknowledge that, in fact, not all policies affect resident aliens (indeed, not all policies affect all citizens). And, as a practical matter, it seems next to impossible to generate an environment in which aliens participate only in the policies that will have an impact on them (it would be impossible to know in advance, as we saw above, whether or not a policy would affect them). Being "affected," then, does not appear to be sufficient to ground the claim that one deserves to have input into the decision being made. One response to this worry is to offer a distinction between being "affected by" and being "governed by," which suggests that what is really at stake is the issue of being governed by a set of representatives whom one has no say in selecting. This is tantamount to tyranny – no resident or citizen in a democratic regime should be subject to rules that he or she did not participate in creating or modifying. But this response – which alters the meaning of "affected" to "governed" – goes precisely to the issue at stake without offering an answer. Is the status of permanent residents such that we would describe them as being "governed" by the rules of the state and, thereby, deserving of a say in them? Or is it such that we would describe them as merely "affected" by them in the same way as are, say, guest workers or foreign students or visitors?[23]

Whatever interpretation we give the principle, however, it appears to go at least some way to giving an account of why non-citizen residents ought to have the vote. They are affected by many, if not most, policies determined by the communities in which they live; or, if one prefers, we can say that they are in effect governed by these decision-making bodies. It may, however, prove useful to modify the all-affected principle to give it some additional strength with respect to the case of non-citizen residents. The all-affected principle can usefully be modified by an additional claim, namely, that it is especially those who are in positions of vulnerability with whom we ought to be concerned. We might even say that the way to determine who is significantly affected is to ask who is particularly vulnerable to the decisions that are made. In other words, these arguments rely on our view that aliens are ripe for exploitation at the hands of arbitrary power and that, therefore, we are morally required to extend them the means by which they can protect themselves. Let us first outline the central principles of the republican tradition that we believe serves to resolve the unanswered questions raised by the all-affected principle.

Republican political theory is typically described as centrally concerned with freedom, where freedom is defined in terms of "nondomination." For Philip Pettit, "domination is subjection to an arbitrary power of interference on the part of another – a *dominus* or master – even another who chooses not actually to exercise that power. Republican freedom, I maintained, should be defined as nondomination."[24] In Pettit's formulation, then, we are dominated under two conditions: if our action is illegitimately constrained by government action or if our actions *are at risk of* being illegitimately constrained by government action. Either we are the victims of arbitrary power or we are at constant risk of being the victims of arbitrary power, and both these conditions generate an objectionable unfreedom.[25] To be free, therefore, is to be free from *arbitrary power* exercised by another and so to remain independent in some important sense. We are free if our rights are not "precariously dependent on the government's" action or inaction.[26]

When aliens are said to deserve the vote because they are "affected" (or "governed") by the policies determined in their place of residence, and when they are said to deserve the vote because they are, or are learning to be, members of a community, what is genuinely at stake is their vulnerability to arbitrary power. Because permanent residents – without the vote – are subject to a set of policies into which they have no input, they are at risk of being victims of arbitrary power (arbitrary because they do not have a say in the outcome). They are, in republican parlance, dependent on the will of their communities and, thus, unfree. For example, in explaining the motivation for working so hard to have voting rights extended to aliens, Ron Hayduk observes that "groups can be more easily subordinated by depriving them of the vote, and conversely, can attain greater freedoms when they possess the vote."[27] Elsewhere he explains the urgency of this issue in even more compelling terms: "The problem is not merely that immigrants pay taxes and don't have the vote; the problem is that the US is undergoing another nativist period that threatens the rights and civil liberties of immigrants who have no formal voice to protect themselves."[28] Likewise, in her analysis of the efforts made in San Francisco to grant aliens the right to vote in school board elections, Tara Kini points out that aliens "lack any power to protect their interests and are subject to discriminatory acts of government, through both representative government and the process of direct democracy ... noncitizens currently lack this protection and are subject to the whims of the standing electorate."[29] And, again, Rainer Bauböck explains that, "by including the last big disenfranchised group of persons, namely foreign residents, into the electorate, the chance of winning elections on the basis of a campaign in which persons without electoral rights are used as scapegoats is reduced."[30]

All of the scholar-activists are pointing to an emerging theme in movements to grant aliens the right to vote. In the movement in Washington, DC, for example, the commission that recommended granting aliens the vote pointed first to the rampant discrimination and harassment to which Latinos – immigrants and otherwise – were subject: "The Civil Rights Commission said a variety of governmental and institutional obstacles denied Latinos equality of opportunity in criminal justice, employment, education and social services."[31] Equally, in Massachusetts, the movement to grant voting rights to aliens grew out of efforts to protect new immigrants from discrimination. The movement is spearheaded by an organization called "Eviction Free Zone," whose initial mandate was to protect affordable housing for low-income immigrants, many (if not most) of whom are Haitian immigrants.[32]

This concern to motivate support for granting rights to aliens is consistent with the motivation given by the Supreme Court to extend them economic and social rights (even while resisting extending them political rights). The reasons for doing so have to do with its concern that aliens – because they cannot vote – are especially vulnerable to exploitation of various kinds. As per the Supreme Court Ruling in *Graham v. Richardson* (1971), alien status is "suspect," and, therefore, all legislation that pertains to aliens is subject to additional scrutiny, the intention of which is to protect them from exploitative discrimination from which they cannot protect themselves. In explaining this, Rubio-Marin says, "not surprisingly, aliens' political powerlessness has been accepted as the most obvious reason to apply heightened scrutiny" to legislation that has an impact on their lives.

She maintains that being alien is "suspect because of aliens' vulnerability in the political process."[33]

It is precisely this powerlessness that modifies the all-affected principle in such a way as to provide a plausible argument for granting the right to vote in the first place. It is also worth noting that this justification serves to respond to one conventional way of objecting to granting the right to vote to aliens, namely, that they have access to other political avenues for expressing grievances. Residents can sign petitions, they can organize in support of causes and political campaigns, they can write letters to congresspeople, and so on. But these opportunities alone do not serve to protect against the vulnerability that non-voters face, not least because political actors are more likely to respond to those with the power to elect them into and out of office.

A Case Study: Toronto

In both Canada and the United States, municipal voting is permitted as a matter of subnational discretion, the demands for these rights are more likely to arise in municipalities that receive large numbers of immigrants, and the movement to secure these rights is small but growing. Here, by focusing on the discourse about non-citizen resident voting that has emerged in Toronto, we consider how the theoretical arguments that underpin the earlier section of the chapter play out in practice. The lessons learned here are, in our view, generalizable across both American and Canadian municipalities.

The City of Toronto sits in the densely populated Golden Horseshoe region of the Province of Ontario. Toronto is part of the Greater Toronto Region (GTR), which is home to over 5.5 million people, and the cities that make up the GTR each have their own municipal governments. The City of Toronto proper has a population of approximately 2.5 million, of whom approximately 1.2 million are identified as immigrants[34] and just over 380,000 are not Canadian citizens – that is, they are non-citizen residents.[35] Extrapolating from 2006 census data, an estimate of the number of non-citizen permanent residents of voting age in Toronto would be 261,000.[36] This would include both non-citizens who are eligible for citizenship but who have not yet naturalized and those recent immigrants who are not yet eligible for citizenship.[37]

The motto of the City of Toronto is "Diversity Our Strength," which is not surprising given that 47 percent of the population (1.16 million people) falls into the category of "visible minorities."[38] Katherine A.H. Graham and Susan

D. Phillips observe that, "although meant to celebrate the city's demographic, [the motto] has become more than a slogan."[39] Kristin Good, for example, "contends that this motto reflects a consensus among Toronto's municipal, voluntary and private sector leaders that the city needs to focus on the integration of immigrants," and she points to a variety of programs the city has adopted to pursue that aim.[40] Such programs include the establishment of the city Task Force on Access and Equality, the Diversity Management and Community Engagement Unit, and the Toronto Region Immigrant Employment Council, which was a joint initiative by the city and the Maytree Foundation – a Canadian charitable foundation that focuses on issues of poverty and diversity, among other things.[41] The programs and activities are "consistent with" and often motivated by the City of Toronto Immigration and Settlement Policy Framework, adopted by City Council in 2001, which aims

> to enable the City, within its mandate as municipal government and service provider, to work with all other orders of government, all sectors that make up the economic, social and cultural web of the City and immigrants to ensure that it continues to: (a) attract newcomers and (b) provide supports to enable them to develop a sense of identity and belonging and fully participate in the social, economic, cultural and political life in the City.[42]

Thus it will come as no surprise that, in the summer of 2006, a non-citizen resident of the City of Mississauga (a suburb of Toronto) made a formal request to city council to allow him and other non-citizen residents the right to participate on official municipal boards and committees – a right not currently extended to non-citizen residents. The resident in question is a German citizen who, despite having lived nearly thirty years of his life in Canada, has not obtained Canadian citizenship for reasons having to do with German inheritance laws and his economic interests in Germany.[43] The request was rejected by a majority of Mississauga city councillors, with many expressing disbelief that a non-citizen would even make such a request. One councillor went so far as to say that immigrants who have not yet obtained citizenship should stop treating Canada as if it is a "buffet table" of "rights and other good things."[44]

Mere weeks after the Mississauga controversy, the then mayor of Toronto, David Miller, took a different position than that of his suburban peers. He publicly expressed his support for a policy that would extend the municipal franchise to Toronto's roughly 261,000 non-citizen residents, arguing that people should have "a real say in the decisions that are affecting them" whether they were citizens or not. Additionally, Miller suggested that perhaps one of the reasons why neighbourhoods, "where there are often high proportions of landed immigrants, [have] deteriorate[d]" is that those landed immigrants "haven't had a vote."[45] Nevertheless, despite receiving the support of the mayor and several other city councillors, Toronto's non-citizen residents still do not have the right to vote in municipal elections. The Ontario provincial government, which has the power to amend electoral eligibility regulations for Toronto and all other municipalities in the province, has opposed the policy. Indeed, the premier of Ontario, Dalton McGuinty, said that he would not support such a change in elector eligibility for Ontario's towns and cities. Consequently, in both Mississauga and Toronto, much of the steam has been taken out of campaigns to achieve greater political rights for non-citizen residents.[46]

The path leading to the mayor's announcement was also paved by a widely distributed and influential paper written by Ryerson University professor Myer Siemiatycki for Inclusive Cities Canada.[47] It reveals that those Toronto neighbourhoods with the poorest performance on standard socio-economic measures were also more likely to be home to recent immigrants and non-citizen residents. Siemiatycki argues that the socio-economic conditions in those areas could be explained, at least in part, by the fact that immigrants and non-citizens were in some cases effectively, and in other cases formally, excluded from participating in political life. He sees an increase in political participation among the residents of these poorly performing neighbourhoods, as well as improvements in "social inclusion" more generally, as necessary if the socio-economic measures of those neighbourhoods are to improve. Siemiatycki concludes that Toronto could follow the approach of Mississauga and deny political rights to non-citizen residents or it could "recognize non-citizen residents as municipal taxpayers and as members of the civic community." He continues: "Their global experience, knowledge and networks can contribute to the municipality's success. Extending political participation rights to them will strengthen their attachment to Canada and their Canadian hometown."[48] Siemiatycki's paper was a catalyst for extensive discussion among city officials, non-profit organizations, and those in the media. Toronto's One Resident, One Vote (OROV) coalition[49] – which includes Inclusive Cities Canada and the Maytree Foundation – relied on it heavily in making its case to Mayor Miller, and it was reportedly a critical factor in his decision to support non-citizen resident voting.[50]

Invigorated by the mayor's support, OROV coalition leaders pursued their advocacy with those remaining city councillors who were not yet convinced, with immigrant communities themselves who had not yet grasped the idea, and with officials in the provincial government.[51] The coalition maintained that an extension of the municipal franchise to Toronto's non-citizen permanent residents was not only a requirement of democratic fairness – that is, that all those affected by decisions ought to have a say in those decisions – but that formal electoral inclusion of all residents had the potential to improve civic life according to a variety of measures. It would afford permanent residents (who are potential citizens) opportunities to improve their political skills by participating as equals in the municipal electoral process. Additionally, the OROV coalition held that socio-economic improvements for newcomers and ethno-cultural minorities in Toronto would be easier to achieve if permanent residents had the vote, thereby creating an incentive for elected officials to be more responsive to their needs and claims.[52]

In the end, however, despite the high-level support of the mayor, non-citizen residents of the City of Toronto still lack the right to vote. Support for the policy among other critical political actors, and even some recent immigrants, was almost non-existent. The democratic deficit faced by Toronto's non-citizen permanent residents was either not recognized or opponents did not think that it was as burdensome as proponents claimed. How could it be that what many regard as an appropriate policy for a progressive city would be ignored or opposed by actors who, in most cases, are no less committed to progressive arrangements for newcomers? Why is this democratic deficit ultimately not seen as salient?

Salience

Though one might be persuaded by the claim that non-citizen residents, in so far as they lack the vote, face a democratic deficit, a no less important issue is whether action should be taken to repair that deficit. One would expect that, once a democratic deficit has been identified, any sincere democrat would support measures that would serve to eliminate or repair it. At the same time, however, we know that simply identifying deficits is insufficient to motivate action, even among the very people who face the consequences of the deficits. In some cases, this may be a function of fear: a democratic deficit is tolerable when the perceived costs of action may be, for example, social marginalization or even deportation. There is an implicit or explicit weighing of the democratic deficit and expectations of success in eliminating that deficit against the costs that one might face in advocating for change. This suggests that it might be useful to begin thinking about the salience of a democratic deficit. Though a deficit might exist as a matter of fact, whether action *will* or *should* be taken to eliminate it depends on how important and burdensome it is perceived to be compared with alternatives.

The discussion in this section follows two paths – an explanatory path and a normative path. The aim is to offer a preliminary examination of some hypotheses that could explain why non-citizen voting arrangements are not (yet) especially pervasive. As it turns out, certain widely shared norms about citizenship and associated rights conspire against extending the franchise to non-citizen residents generally and indicate that whatever cross-national variation exists is likely explained by perceptions about the difficulty or ease of acquiring citizenship.

Alternative Means of Participation

One line of explanation for not extending the franchise to non-citizen residents points to a popular perception that these people already have sufficient ways of participating in the decision-making processes of the cities in which they live. Permanent non-citizen residents may lack the franchise, but in many cases they do have constitutional protection guaranteeing various other forms of political participation, including a right to free speech, freedom of association, and access to and standing in the legal system, among others. Arguably, these "other" rights protect modes of political participation that are more likely to influence decision makers than is voting. Meeting with a local politician may have more of an impact on that politician's views than simply voting in an election. Indeed, even for citizens, the act of voting has come to be seen as something more symbolic than effective as a means of political influence. In short, there is little motivation, and perhaps little reason, to enfranchise non-citizen residents because they already have participatory rights that allow them to voice their concerns as effectively as citizens.

However, the value of these alternative means of participation is likely discounted for non-citizen residents precisely because the views expressed through them are not backed up by the currency of a vote. From a normative perspective, if we think that non-citizen residents ought to have these other means of participating, and we recognize that the worth of these other means is diminished as a consequence of not having the vote, then we should extend the vote to those non-citizen residents in order to improve the value of their political liberties.[53] Still, there are those who would argue that non-citizen residents should not have even these political rights and, thus, would not be prepared to endorse an argument for improving their value for non-citizens. For the moment, it appears that the (mis)perception that non-citizen residents already have sufficient means for making their views known contributes to explaining why their lack of enfranchisement does not constitute an especially salient democratic deficit.[54]

Fairness and the Rewards of Citizenship
Another widespread perception that serves to undermine efforts to extend the franchise to non-citizen residents is the belief that it would be unfair to extend the rewards of citizenship – particularly, the vote – to individuals who have not "earned" them in the way that others have.[55] The vote is regarded as a good to be distributed only to those who deserve to have it. Previous immigrants, the argument goes, have already paid their dues by learning about the society in which they live and by passing a citizenship test. To give the same rewards to immigrants who have not passed the necessary hurdles diminishes the significance of the efforts of those who have passed them. In the absence of a demonstrated commitment and successful citizenship test, the rewards of citizenship – particularly the franchise – should not be granted.

Notwithstanding the comical fact that many of those who make this argument have themselves acquired citizenship through an accident of birth rather than individual effort, the pervasiveness of these norms about demonstrated commitment and earning the rewards of citizenship serves to block efforts to enfranchise non-citizen residents. To be sure, democratic stability requires that both newcomers and residents by birth become integrated into the norms and practices of the democratic societies in which they live. If integration is best achieved by denying newcomers the franchise for some suitable duration while they learn about, and develop a commitment to, their adopted homes, then a concern for democratic stability would recommend such a scenario. However, the question of whether integration is best achieved by making newcomers wait before acquiring the vote or, conversely, by allowing them to participate as equals from the moment they arrive is an empirical question. Until that question is answered, there is no reason to think that the former arrangement is any better than the latter, and thus it cannot sensibly be appealed to as a reason to exclude non-citizen residents from the franchise.[56] Nevertheless, in this case, as in others, the fact that these norms are widely held by citizens in liberal democracies helps to explain why movements to extend the franchise to non-citizen residents have such difficulty.

A variation of this objection suggests that if we grant residents the right to vote, there will be no real distinction between citizens and non-citizens. The right to vote, on this view, serves as a motivation to naturalize as quickly as possible: it is the prize granted to those who carry out the work necessary to attain citizenship in a new country. There is an additional element of concern here having to do with how citizenship rights are conceived. Citizenship confers the right to vote, among other rights, but it imposes corresponding obligations. In the United States, for example, citizens are required to participate on juries and (at least in some periods) join the military, whereas non-citizen residents are exempt from these requirements. If we granted residents the right to vote *without* requiring them to carry out these parallel duties, it would be unfair and, perhaps, unjust: residents would have all the benefits of citizenship without being required to fulfill any duties (and these duties would therefore be unfairly shouldered by citizens).[57] However, surely the relevant difference between citizens and non-citizens is not access (or lack of access) to the vote but, rather, protection against deportation. Citizens cannot be deported for any reason, whereas aliens must live with the knowledge that they can be deported at any time. And the list of "deportable offences" is only getting longer. The motivation to secure citizenship, then, remains intact: in order to protect themselves from deportation to states that are no longer viewed as home, residents will naturalize even if they are extended the vote (especially if this vote is only at the municipal level).

Residency Requirement for Citizenship Application
Although the previous two considerations help to explain why there has been resistance to the idea of extending the franchise to non-citizen residents generally, they do little to explain the cross-national variance on the matter. For example, non-citizen residents in European cities are much more likely to receive the franchise than are non-citizen residents in Canadian and American cities.[58] Much of that variation is at least partly explained by the difference in residency requirements with regard to acquiring citizenship. In Canada, a permanent resident can apply for citizenship a mere three years after arriving, whereas in European countries the residency requirement is usually more than five years and is not uncommonly ten years or more.[59] As the length of time to acquire citizenship increases, there is an associated increase in the normative salience of the democratic deficit non-citizen residents face in not having the vote. This means that we should expect more robust campaigns for non-citizen resident voting rights in those

jurisdictions where the residency requirement for citizenship is high and less robust campaigns where the residency requirement is comparatively low.[60]

This explanation dovetails with the alternative-means-of-participation explanation: that is, the salience of the democratic deficit is higher where the available means of participation are comparatively lower. In short, the deficit is more deeply felt when non-citizen residents lack other ways to make their preferences and opinions known to decision makers or where the expectation that they will be able to do so in a reasonable period of time is low.

To be sure, even in those jurisdictions, like Canada, in which the residency requirement is relatively low, there will be those non-citizen residents who will never acquire citizenship and will therefore face a more burdensome deficit. In those cases, different dynamics may come into play, both empirically and normatively. It is likely not a coincidence that the individual who made the case for extending greater participation rights to non-citizens in Mississauga is a resident who has spent thirty years in Canada without acquiring citizenship. Still, where an individual has no plans to acquire citizenship we should not assume, as many do, that this indicates a lack of commitment to the country of residence. It may simply reflect complications arising from the lack of international coordination on the rules of citizenship and the costs and benefits of relinquishing one citizenship while obtaining another.

Conclusion: Is Every Democratic Deficit an Injustice?

When there are so many other pressing injustices in a democratic society, how concerned should we be with a problem that, in many cases, will simply take care of itself in a little more than three to five years (at least in the Canadian and American contexts)? Strictly speaking, the lack of the franchise for non-citizen residents is a democratic deficit, but its temporary nature significantly diminishes its salience as a motive for action. Given the availability of alternative modes of participation, and given that the deficit will effectively disappear in the normal course of affairs, even non-citizen residents themselves tend to discount the burden of the deficit.

Even so, that is not to say that non-citizen residents should continue to be excluded from the franchise. While the burden that unenfranchised non-citizens face, at least in Canada and the United States, is not terribly heavy, neither is enfranchising them especially burdensome to society. Other cities in liberal democratic states have done so without experiencing democratic collapse. And, for what it's worth, there may be at least one significant psychological benefit to extending the franchise to these potential citizens: granting the right to vote in a political community is an act of recognition, and acts of recognition contribute to the development of mutual respect and political equality. As Charles Taylor explains, in the modern world, recognition and worth are not functions of traditional rank and status but, rather, the products of a *politics* of recognition. One develops self-respect and a sense of self-worth not simply when one has confidence in oneself and one's own projects but, crucially, when one perceives that others recognize one's worth.[61]

By recognizing non-citizens as worthy of the local franchise in the democratic system, a political community sends a signal that non-citizens are not outsiders but, rather, a group of potential citizens who should be treated with respect and as political equals. Indeed, when residents and potential citizens are included in the shared public political dialogue we can avoid the emergence of an exclusionary us-versus-them discourse or, when such a discourse already exists, take a decisive step towards eliminating that discourse. And when that exclusionary discourse is diminished or eliminated, non-citizen residents and potential citizens are on a much more secure path towards being fully integrated into the democratic political community. In this respect, we may even make some headway in avoiding the sorts of democratic deficits faced by immigrants even after they acquire citizenship.

NOTES

The authors would like to thank Ofrit Liviatan for comments on a much earlier draft of this chapter.

1 Ronald Hayduk, *Democracy for All: Restoring Immigrant Voting Rights in the United States* (New York: Taylor and Francis, 2006), 58.
2 Monica W. Varsanyi, "The Rise and Fall (and Rise?) of Noncitizen Voting: Immigration and the Shifting Scales of Citizenship and Suffrage in the United States," *Space and Polity* 9, 2 (2005): 115; Ruth Rubio-Marin, *Immigration as a Democratic Challenge: Citizenship and Inclusion in Germany and the United States* (Cambridge: Cambridge University Press, 2000), 5.
3 Elize Brozovich, "Prospects for Democratic Change: Non-Citizen Suffrage in America," *Hamline Journal of Public Law and Policy* 23 (2002): 438.
4 These numbers have been calculated using data from a range of sources. See Kelly Tran, Stan Kustec, and Tina Chui, *Becoming Canadian: Intent, Process and Outcome* (Ottawa: Statistics Canada, 2005), http://www.statcan.gc.ca/. Tran et al. note that 16 percent of eligible immigrants (i.e., those who have been in Canada for three or more years) have not yet acquired citizenship. See also Statistics Canada, *Immigrant Status (4) for the Population of Canada, Provinces and Territories, 1911 to 2006*

Censuses (Ottawa: Statistics Canada, 2011), which provides an estimate of the total immigrant population at approximately 6.2 million in 2006; and Kurtis Kitagawa, Tim Krywulak, and Douglas Watt, *Renewing Immigration: Towards a Convergence and Consolidation of Canada's Immigration Policies and Systems* (Ottawa: Conference Board of Canada, 2008), which provides data and estimates for the number of new immigrants who have arrived in Canada each year for the past few years – between 250,000 and 280,000 each year from 2008 to 2010. Thus, we estimate that there are 864,000 immigrants who are eligible for, but have not yet acquired, citizenship (i.e., 16 percent of the 5.4 million who are eligible for citizenship) and an additional 800,000 who are not yet eligible for citizenship. Of these 1.66 million, approximately 69 percent are eighteen years or older (i.e., voting age). In total, then, there are 1.15 million permanent residents who cannot vote in Canada, or just under 5 percent of the total resident voting age population. Population estimates for the United States are from CIA, *The World Factbook: United States* (Washington, DC: CIA, 2011), https://www.cia.gov/. If we include illegal immigrants to the United States, the total number of non-citizen, voting age residents would be about 17.5 million, or a little over 8 percent of the US voting age population.

5 Ofrit Liviatan objected that it is unwise to invoke comparisons to voting rights in the European Union. She observes that the *motivation* for extending this right emerges from a desire to generate a new "supra-national political space," and this motivation is absent in the Canadian and American contexts. This may be true, but it does not serve to explain the additional openness of many European states to extend the same rights to residents whose national origins are non-European.
6 The details in this paragraph, and many more, are found in Harald Waldrauch, "Electoral Rights for Foreign Nationals: A Comparative Overview," http://en.scientificcommons.org/.
7 Alexander Keyssar, *The Right to Vote: The Contested History of Democracy in the United States* (New York: Basic Books, 2001), xvii.
8 William James Booth, "Foreigners: Insiders, Outsiders and the Ethics of Membership," *Review of Politics* 59, 2 (1997): 262. Cosmopolitan political philosophers have been at the vanguard of this shift and have worked very hard to persuade us that the priority we place on state sovereignty serves, in part, to justify the differential treatment of citizens and non-citizens. Since, they say, the state in which we live is arbitrary from a moral point of view, we have no grounds for treating insiders and outsiders differently.
9 Joseph Carens, "Aliens and Citizens: The Case for Open Borders," *Review of Politics* 49, 2 (1987): 268.
10 Booth, "Foreigners," 272.
11 Ibid.
12 Rubio-Marin, *Immigration*, 43. Or, as William James Booth explains, "the Court now distinguishes between the economic and sovereign functions of government, and treats the citizen-alien divide as normally irrelevant for the former, meaning not only in the alien's access to the 'common occupations' of the community but to its public resources as well, but not at all irrelevant to the self-definition of the community in the vital dimension of its self-governance." See Booth, "Foreigners," 275.

13 Rubio-Marin, *Immigration*, 58.
14 See, instead, Ron Hayduk, "Democracy for All: Restoring Immigrant Voting Rights in the United States," *New Political Science: A Journal of Politics and Culture* 26, 4 (2004): 499-523.
15 Frederick G. Whelan, "Prologue: Democratic Theory and the Boundary Problem," in *Nomos 25: Liberal Democracy*, ed. J.R. Pennock and J.W. Chapman (New York: New York University Press, 1983), 160.
16 Michael Saward, *The Terms of Democracy* (Cambridge: Polity Press, 1998), 125.
17 Robert Goodin, "Enfranchising All Affected Interests, and Its Alternatives," *Philosophy and Public Affairs* 35, 1 (2007): 52.
18 Ibid., 54. In his article, Goodin assesses a range of distinct interpretations of the all-affected principle and concludes that it remains the best of all possible ways to determine who the people are, even if it demands some modification in practice.
19 Robert Pastor pointed this out to us.
20 Robert Dahl, *After the Revolution? Authority in a Good Society*, rev. ed. (New Haven: Yale University Press, 1990), 51.
21 Ibid., 50.
22 Arash Abizadeh does argue, however, against the right of democratic states to control their borders unilaterally. On his view, any decision to close borders demands justification that might satisfy both insiders and outsiders. See Arash Abizadeh, "Democratic Theory and Border Coercion: No Right to Unilaterally Control Your Own Borders," *Political Theory* 36, 1 (2008): 37-65.
23 For an argument that defends the all-affected principle – whatever its interpretation – as the right way to justify extending the franchise to aliens, see Ludvig Beckman, "Citizenship and Voting Rights: Should Resident Aliens Vote?," *Citizenship Studies* 10, 2 (2006): 158. He writes: "I will argue that the vagueness of the all-affected principle is no obstacle in assessing whether voting rights should be conferred on resident aliens. The reason is that the right of resident aliens to participate in the democratic process follows on any interpretation of this principle."
24 Philip Pettit, "Keeping Republican Freedom Simple: On a Difference with Quentin Skinner," *Political Theory* 30, 3 (2002): 340.
25 Philip Pettit and Quentin Skinner are jointly responsible for reframing the republican tradition – from a focus on political participation to a focus on political liberty. They both argue that this reframing serves to capture the central insights developed in the history of republican theory and to modify it in such a way that it is made plausible to contemporary ears. Yet, they differ in their respective emphases: Skinner is keen to defend a kind of liberty described as "non-interference," whereas Pettit offers a robust account of liberty as "non-domination."
26 M.M. Goldsmith, "Republican Liberty Considered," *History of Political Thought* 21, 3 (2000): 551.
27 Hayduk, "Democracy for All," 510.
28 Ibid., 66. For evidence of nativism, see, for example, Lynn Zimmerman, "The English-Only Movement," in *Language of the Land: Policy, Politics, Identity*, ed. Katherine Schuster and David Witkosky (Charlotte: Information Age Publishing, 2007).
29 Tara Kini, "Sharing the Vote: Noncitizen Voting Rights in Local School Board Elections," *California Law Review* 93, 1 (2005): 306.

30 Rainer Bauböck, "Expansive Citizenship: Voting beyond Territory and Membership," *PS: Political Science and Politics* 38 (2005): 6.
31 Hayduk, *Democracy for All*, 164.
32 Ibid., 174.
33 Rubio-Marin, *Immigration*, 146-47.
34 Immigrants are "persons who are, or have ever been, landed immigrants in Canada. A landed immigrant is a person who has been granted the right to live in Canada permanently by immigration authorities" (Statistics Canada, 2008), http://www12.statcan.ca/.
35 Michael Atkinson and David Docherty, "Parliament and Political Success in Canada," in *Canadian Politics in the 21st Century*, ed. Michael Whittington and Glen Williams (Toronto: Thomson Nelson, 2008).
36 Using 2006 Census data, if we subtract from the number of non-citizens living in the City of Toronto (i.e., 380,135) those 54,610 people who are not permanent residents (e.g., foreign students, long-term visitors), and then adjust the result (using data about age distribution for the population as a whole) to include only those who would be eighteen years of age or over (i.e., of voting age) we get a rough estimate of 261,000 non-citizen permanent residents of voting age in the City of Toronto. A similar calculation by Siemiatycki, using 2001 census data and slightly different assumptions, produced an estimate of 263,000 non-citizen permanent residents of voting age in Toronto.
37 M. Siemiatycki, "The Municipal Franchise and Social Inclusion in Toronto: Policy and Practice," Inclusive Cities Canada, http://www.inclusivecities.ca/.
38 City of Toronto, "Backgrounder: Release of the 2006 Census on Ethic Origin and Visible Minorities," http://www.toronto.ca/.
39 K. Graham and S. Phillips, "Another Fine Balance: Managing Diversity in Canadian Cities," Institute for Research on Public Policy, http://www.irpp.org/.
40 Kristin Good, "Multiculturalism in the City: A Comparative Analysis of Municipal Responsiveness to Immigration in the Greater Toronto Area (GTA) and the Greater Vancouver Regional District," paper presented at Canadian Political Science Association Annual Meeting, University of Manitoba, Winnipeg, 2004; Kristin Good, "Patterns of Politics in Canada's Immigrant-Receiving Cities and Suburbs," *Policy Studies* 26 (2005): 3-4; Graham and Phillips, "Another Fine Balance."
41 See http://www.maytree.com. See also Good, "Multiculturalism in the City"; Good, "Patterns of Politics"; Graham and Phillips, "Another Fine Balance."
42 City of Toronto, "Immigration and Settlement Policy Framework," http://www.toronto.ca/.
43 Rudy Czekalla, e-mail communication with author, 2007.
44 M. Funston, "'Canadians Only' Policy for Mississauga," *Toronto Star*, 20 April 2006; Daniel Munro, "Integration through Participation: Non-Citizen Resident Voting Rights in an Era of Globalization," *Journal of International Migration and Integration* 9, 1 (2008): 63-80.
45 Miller quoted in V. Lu, "Let Immigrants Vote: Miller," *Toronto Star*, 24 October 2006.
46 Advocates for extending the municipal franchise to Toronto's permanent residents report that, when subsequently pressed about his position behind closed doors, the

premier indicated that he would be willing to investigate the idea further and that he would be open to changing it (A. Melles, telephone interview with author, 2008). However, more recently, an official in the Ontario government's Ministry of Municipal Affairs and Housing has said that the policy was reviewed following the 2006 debate, that no change was made to the Municipal Elections Act, and that no change was forthcoming (J. Sidebottom, telephone interview with author, 2008).

47 Siemiatycki, "Municipal Franchise."
48 Ibid.
49 In late 2008, OROV was folded into a newer and larger coalition – I Vote Toronto – that pursues the same goals and that not only maintains original coalition members but also significantly extends the umbrella. See http://www.ivotetoronto.org/.
50 Melles, telephone interview with author, 2008.
51 Ibid.
52 Ibid.
53 On the worth of political liberties, see John Rawls, *Political Liberalism* (New York: Columbia University Press, 1996); John Rawls, *A Theory of Justice*, rev. ed. (Cambridge: Belknap Press of Harvard University Press, 1999).
54 Recognizing that many non-citizen residents also hold this view, campaigners in the OROV movement in Toronto report that one of their primary tasks has been to educate non-citizen residents about the democratic deficit they face and why alternative means of participation alone are not enough to ensure that their voices are heard and respected by decision makers (Melles, telephone interview with author, 2008).
55 Rubio-Marin, *Immigration*.
56 Daniel Munro, "Enfranchising Immigrants: Should Non-Citizen Residents Have the Right to Vote?," *Inroads: The Canadian Journal of Opinion* 23 (2008): 23-25.
57 We thank Ofrit Liviatan for pointing out to us this objection and the next one.
58 D.C. Earnest, "Non-Citizen Voting Rights: A Survey of an Emerging Democratic Norm," http://www.odu.edu/.
59 Joseph Carens, "Citizenship and Civil Society: What Rights for Residents?," in *Dual Nationality, Social Rights, and Federal Citizenship in the US and Germany*, ed. Randall Hansen and Patrick Weil (New York: Berghahn Books, 2002).
60 See Patrick Weil, "Access to Citizenship: A Comparison of Twenty-Five Nationality Laws," in *Citizenship Today: Global Perspectives and Practices*, ed. Alexander Aleinikoff and Douglas B. Klusmeyer (Washington: Carnegie Endowment for International Peace, 2002); Earnest, "Non-Citizen Voting Rights."
61 Charles Taylor, *Multiculturalism and the Politics of Recognition* (Princeton: Princeton University Press, 1994).

12

Citizen Representation and the American Jury

ETHAN J. LEIB AND DAVID L. PONET

In recent years, scholars and citizens around the world have witnessed a proliferation of practices and proposals rooted in theories of participatory and deliberative democracy. Many have been adopted to relieve the apparent crisis of legitimacy faced by contemporary polities. These practices and proposals seek to engage small groups of "lay" citizens in policy formation and consultation, empowered participation, and deliberation.[1] Advocates of citizen empowerment argue that engaging citizens more actively in policy making may remedy the democratic deficit with which this volume is concerned. Yet these proposed mechanisms for participation and deliberation often fail to consider adequately the problem of representation in citizen groups.[2] Resolving pragmatic issues such as participant eligibility, participant selection methods, and how citizens should act in their representative capacities may be just as important as defending the theoretical basis for assigning small groups of citizens with tasks of governance.

Self-selection, for example, vitiates many proposals' representative credibility. Advocates often rely on random sampling of one form or another to vindicate claims that participants in selected groups for focused deliberation are indeed representative of the polity. Yet random sampling does not solve the self-selection problem because it is extremely rare for these proposals to recommend *mandatory* participation on deliberative panels. Only those who wish to engage in deliberation are seated – and there may be substantial differences between those who are interested in spending time deliberating and those who are not. In short, there may be a representation problem with many participatory and deliberative experiments. This challenge must be resolved if citizen juries and other proposed democratic practices are to mitigate the democratic deficit.

However, as such proposals gain traction, the task of developing an adequate account of citizen representation is more pressing than ever. California, for example, is contemplating a "citizens' assembly" modelled on a recent experiment with a group of citizen representatives in British Columbia (as described in the last chapter). The Netherlands, Australia, Britain, and Taiwan, among others, have followed suit or will do so in the near future.[3]

This chapter contributes to a fledgling effort to build a theory of "citizen representation." We begin with a general discussion about representation in liberal democracies. Placing the theoretical debate within a unique context highlights the often under-appreciated importance of institutions and context in understanding how representation works.[4] We then focus on the institution of the American jury. To be sure, Canada also has a jury system, and Canada's jury system has the same ancestry as does the system in place in the United States, sharing many distinctive features with the American case (like the general requirement of unanimity).[5] But we explore the American context in what follows, given our expertise and experience with that system.

We argue that the American jury system contains an implicit theory of proper "citizen representation," and we identify its central desiderata. Our methodological innovation is that, unlike other theorists,[6] we do not commence with a general theory and then project or devolve that theory onto forms of citizen representation; rather, we attempt to "build up" a theory of citizen representation, using the American jury's pre-existing form to illuminate such practices more generally. Of course, the "is" does not implicate the "ought." We do not conclude that all citizen representation must mirror the practices and normative aspirations of the American jury. Indeed, the Canadian jury could evidence different aspirations for citizen representation. But there is no doubt that an entrenched practice that closely mirrors newer institutions might be especially instructive. At the very least, we think these practices offer a better starting point for further normative development than do theories not created specifically for the unique institutional context of direct and deliberative citizen decision making.

Accordingly, we analyze six elements of the American jury that are relevant to a theory of citizen representation: deliberation, impartiality, cross-sectionality, civic responsibility, legitimacy, and indirect accountability. These six elements form the core of what we take to be the American jury's implicit account of proper citizen representation. We hope to explain not only how these desiderata function in our long-standing practices of citizen representation but also why they are normatively attractive when they function properly.

We conclude by briefly explaining how this theory is ripe for application in the context of experimental efforts to bring groups of lay citizens into the tasks of governance. Ongoing debates about political representation in general are a plausible place to begin thinking about how to properly employ "citizen representatives" in deliberative democratic action. But exploration of citizen representation in the jury system reveals much more about good design tactics and best practices. More normative argumentation and institutional sensitivity will be necessary, of course, before theorists and practitioners can settle on the right mix of concepts and norms to guide these new institutions. And any application will need to be sensitive to local differences in conceptualizing the use of citizen representatives (e.g., Canada's jury system could recommend different local design based on idiosyncratic features of its own jury system). But we hope to help get the conversation off the ground – and from the ground up, too.

Representation Theory

Are Democracy and Representation Compatible?

Although we are primarily concerned with uncovering a theory of citizen representation, any discussion of the topic must begin by acknowledging that democracy and representation hardly make for an obvious fit. Precisely because many theorists interested in decision making by lay citizens aim to enhance democracy, it is worth asking whether the democratization project can really admit representative institutions in the first place.

Some argue that representation stands at complete odds with democracy since individual members of society avoid developing deeply democratic practices themselves when they delegate the work to representatives. Others instead emphasize a distinction between direct democracy and indirect democracy. In a direct democracy, all citizens assemble and participate in governing the affairs of the state. In this model, democracy entails the actual *presence* of citizens in the halls of government. Representative democracy, by contrast, is an indirect form of governance, arguably a second-best solution to the problem of feasible democratic governance in large nation-states. In an indirect, or representative, democracy, citizens appoint others to do the governing but retain the right to hire and fire their appointees. It may be that the vast majority of Americans actually live in what Beth Garrett calls a "hybrid democracy," a polity engaged in both direct and indirect forms of governance.[7]

Under any circumstances, political representation involves a delicate balancing act mediating between the few who actually participate in politics and the many who are represented, between particular interests and common goals.[8] Representatives at once represent partial or sectarian interests as well as collective interests. What perhaps distinguishes *democratic* representation is its focus on *the people* – and its attempt to ensure that representative institutions give maximal expression to the subdivisions within that collectivity. Yet *the people* are not necessarily unified. Accepting the internal heterogeneity of *the people*, what would government by *the people* really mean?

Upon examination, popular sovereignty proves a nebulous concept. In his discussion of the early United States, Edmund Morgan observes that "the people whose sovereignty was proclaimed were the people of the country or colony, far too numerous a group to deliberate or act as a body."[9] The people's sovereignty did not reside in any "particular constituency [but rather] in the people at large and reached the representatives without the people at large doing anything to confer it."[10] Morgan concludes that representation rests on a fiction – either the fiction that representatives *are* the people or that representatives do not just represent their own class or own voters but the entire population. Of course, political fictions must enjoy some basis in perceived fact lest the people's "willing suspension of disbelief" collapse.[11]

Critics of political representation argue both that representatives abscond with popular sovereignty and that subjects or citizens in representative polities abdicate power and authority. Benjamin Barber, a proponent of "strong democracy," insists that citizens are "passive constituents of representatives,"[12] merely selecting officials who "exercise every ... duty of civic importance."[13] Similarly, Rousseau maintains that citizens in representative polities are only free on election day. Subsequently, they are worse than passive: they are enslaved.[14] While tempting, such a sharp distinction between democracy and representation is misleading. The question is not as stark as democracy or representation but can be rendered in a more nuanced way: what kind of representation and in what kind of institution?[15]

In this regard, the jury system sheds light on one context in which a particular group (and a particularly small group) of citizens is generally taken to represent the whole. Our inquiry aims to isolate the conditions that make such representation plausibly democratic. Analysis of the American jury system against the backdrop of contemporary theories of representation shows that the system's underlying theory of "citizen representation" has much to teach those attempting to utilize citizen representatives in governance.

Contemporary Theories of Representation

Any account of democratic representation should be guided by an articulation of both *extrinsic normative desiderata* and *targeted institutional considerations about the context of the relevant form of representation at issue*. A brief glance at representation theory suggests that this rule of thumb is rarely heeded: abstract and prescriptive theories of representation are routinely divorced from institutional considerations of political representation.

Hannah Pitkin[16] and Bernard Manin[17] continue to be regarded as standard-bearers of representation theory. Pitkin's study helpfully provides norms from which to begin evaluating representation. For example, norms of *accountability, responsiveness, symbolic efficacy*, and *the representative's orientation to the common good* are touchstones in her survey of representation theory. But while these norms are essential for reaching an understanding of representation at some very general level, Pitkin neglects institutional considerations that could illuminate representation-as-practised. For instance, she makes little mention of electoral systems and neglects to consider the kinds of institutional designs that might incentivize desirable behaviour. Consequently, she leaves us with little sense of how her various categories of representation coalesce into actual representation that is normatively attractive, realizable, and credibly democratic.

Pitkin espouses a notion of representation in which the representative responsively "acts for" her constituency. While she qualifies the representative's independence with a call for "responsiveness," she neglects to discuss this further, hinting at standards without taking on the vagaries of a collective will or the feasibility of measuring it precisely. Absent an institutional analysis, Pitkin's study makes it difficult to envision active representation and how it ought to be operationalized in the multiplicity of sites where representation happens in modern democracies.

Manin, on the other hand, barely prescribes what a representative should do.[18] Manin proffers an insightful excursus on the logic and institution of election – including the history of certain institutions. His discussion of elections and retrospective voting as the citizen's primary tool of influence assists our understanding of representative democracy, particularly the electoral system's ability to guarantee limited accountability. But his normative treatment of representation is thin. In fact, Manin concludes that political representation is inherently undemocratic, an aristocratic phenomenon bridled by the occasional election to give some forms of representation a "mixed" status: democracy mixed with representation.

Manin's focus on the logic and institution of election underscores the aristocratic feature of political representation. The representative is defined precisely by the ways she is different from and even superior to the people. Elections serve to recognize the aristocrat and place some constraints – through periodic electoral approbation – on what she can do.

Election, however, is a highly varied practice and electoral systems can range from highly proportional to disproportional, from instant runoff to those highly filtered through primary elections. But Manin treats election in a generic form in which the people render their verdict.[19] He says little more on the matter, simply treating the people as a fixed and coherent subject. Like other theorists of representation, Manin makes intimations of a collective will without offering an adequate discussion of its problematic nature.[20] And, although Manin's account illuminates underappreciated aspects of representative government, it tells us little about what the representative actually does or what it means to represent democratically.

Indeed, to build a normative account of genuine democratic representation, Pitkin and Manin are both inadequate. Yet their respective works enjoy canonical status despite their silences and oversights. Few scholars have figured out how to position representation within a democratic perspective or within a framework that melds normative inquiry with targeted institutional analysis.[21] Consider Brian Seitz, who argues that political representation is a way to take the "unworkable multiplicity" of many voices and viewpoints and turn them into a unitary working order – or at least into something like a univocal decision.[22] Seitz argues that the unity or existence of the people is a mirage constructed by representation. With such a strongly constructivist view, however, Seitz renounces civil society's diversity and leaves us with no ability to distinguish good construction from bad.

Our objective in this chapter is to contribute to the political theory of representation by considering it in a particularly well established institutional context: American juries.[23] We seek to address certain aspects of representation too often ignored and to bridge the gulf that separates Pitkin and Manin by wedding normative desiderata to a particular institutional configuration. By analyzing the American jury, we identify one way in which representation can be compatible with and enhance democracy, even when that representation does not utilize elections or other obvious mechanisms of democratic accountability. Here we wish to make explicit the American jury system's theory of representation and, by importing it into the political context, suggest that it can provide a useful model for certain forms of citizen political representation.

To the extent the institution of the jury models a form of representation, it could be said to embody what theorists of political representation describe as "descriptive representation," given its focus on cross-sectionality. According to this view, the representative body should mirror the represented body. So, for example, the descriptive view might mandate a representative assembly's ethnic, racial, or gender composition, mirroring or reflecting the same exact distributions found in the populace at large and, thus, approximating a representative sample of sorts. But a well accepted critique of descriptive representation – shared by Manin and Pitkin – rests on the fact that people's characteristics (such as ethnicity, gender, or race) do not necessarily guide their actions, with the result that confining attention to the representative's appearance may not mirror the preferences or interests of the community. However, given our orientation towards institutional sensitivity, we think it worth considering whether some political domains can accommodate descriptive representation better than others.

In what follows, we explore jury selection techniques as one mechanism for arriving at descriptive representation. We augment this account with a theory of citizen representation that privileges more active dimensions of representation as well, accounting for the critique often levelled against descriptive representation: that it places too much premium on the appearance of the representative and too little on how the representative ought to act. Considering descriptive views in tandem with the American jury system's implicit theory of citizen representation helps to identify evaluative criteria by which to assess representative activity.[24]

The Jury: Six Elements
Participatory and deliberative democrats routinely invoke the model of the jury to bolster their proposals for inclusion of citizens in day-to-day decision making of the republic.[25] The jury enjoys widespread support,[26] and it has a great deal of power in American society. It can bankrupt multinational

conglomerates, sentence individuals to their deaths, and decide that the law is to be ignored in a particular circumstance, letting guilty persons go unpunished. Juries are routinely conceptualized as "mere" fact-finders, but they operate in thickly normative territory, where values are routinely very close to the surface.

The US Supreme Court has determined that the primary function of the jury is "to prevent oppression by the Government" with the "commonsense judgment of a group of laymen ... representative of a cross-section of the community."[27] For Akhil Amar, the jury exists primarily to give power to ordinary citizens, against the government.[28] Citing Tocqueville, Amar finds the jury to be principally a "*political*" institution, not a procedural one. It exists to promote democracy for the jurors, not efficient adjudication for the parties."[29] Tocqueville claims that "the jury is both the most effective way of establishing the people's rule and the most efficient way of teaching them how to rule."[30] He thinks that "to use a jury ... seems ... to introduce an eminently republican element into the government ... inasmuch as it puts the real control of affairs into the hands of the ruled, or some of them, rather than into those of the rulers."[31]

For these reasons, among others, participatory and deliberative democrats turn to juries for the cultivation of better citizens who keep the common good in view. We think there is also an implicit theory of citizen *representation* in the practices associated with the jury system. In the jury context, the judgments of very few stand in for the judgments of many; and many proposals for citizen participation mimic just this feature of jury adjudication. Accordingly, it may be appropriate to borrow the lessons of jury selection and representation for those interested in utilizing a small group of citizens for policy impact.

At least six central elements in the design of the jury system are relevant when focusing on the present inquiry: deliberation, impartiality, cross-sectionality, civic responsibility, legitimacy, and indirect accountability. In some ways, the criteria or desiderata we isolate cannot be neatly traced to the representative role of the jury in particular. Indeed, they may emerge from its functioning within the context of the legal system rather than in representative democracy per se. Nevertheless, we think these features can form the bedrock of a theory of citizen representation.

Deliberation
Jurors do not simply vote on matters before them; rather, they deliberate about what course of action to take individually and as a group. Although

many social science experiments testing juror behaviour utilize non-deliberating juries[32] – and a jury can avoid deliberating[33] – it is widely assumed, very likely, and generally desirable that the vast majority of actual juries engages in some degree of reasoned deliberation. Deliberation refers to discussion among relatively open-minded and equal parties who are willing to be persuaded by the strength of the best arguments rather than swayed by power relations, money, or other corrupting influences of bias or prejudice. The jury system is, it seems, structured to facilitate deliberation by providing for and enforcing juror secrecy and privacy.[34] Indeed, some argue that the unanimity rule, in effect in forty-eight state criminal court systems and the federal court system (as well as in Canada), incentivizes deliberation.[35]

There is a deep lesson here. When our political, legal, and constitutional culture furnishes a small class of lay citizens with the right and power to speak for the entire community, it insists that citizen representatives deliberate: mere voting is not enough. Bargaining and trading cannot overwhelm the process, and virtually all decisions are preceded by the authentic discussions of citizen representatives as they seek to forge consensus. Such deliberation must be ensured through several features of institutional design. Admittedly, non-unanimous verdicts are acceptable for a range of cases, but deliberation is required all the same: reaching a reasoned outcome after time for debate is essential, even when consensus is not.

Cass Sunstein[36] and Tali Mendelberg[37] have brought empirical social science to bear on a pressing question: is fruitful deliberation even possible in group settings?[38] Ultimately, Sunstein and Mendelberg proffer tentatively negative conclusions, suggesting that intrinsic group dynamics prevent deliberation and further entrench prior positions and prejudices.[39] But both Sunstein and Mendelberg similarly acknowledge that such group propensities can be averted through careful institutional design. They do not conclude that deliberation is worthless, only that it must be perfected.

In sum, the jury system is deeply committed to the virtue of deliberation as essential to lay participation and representation. Unanimity, privacy, structure, and secrecy all contribute to safeguarding the role of deliberation in the decision making of citizen representatives.[40] Pathologies of polarization may be counteracted through balanced presentations and using moderators and facilitators. These designs would be relatively easy to implement in citizen panels, even if not in juries.

Impartiality

As a background precondition for deliberation, jurors are to assume an impartial position. Indeed, the Sixth Amendment requires as much.[41] Discernible prejudice, pre-judgment, overt public refusal to follow the law, and/or a close personal stake in the matter can all be predicates for disqualification. This commitment to what are called "challenges for cause" highlights the centrality of impartiality to the jury process. Even "pre-emptory challenges" contribute to the commitment to impartiality by giving parties a chance – however imperfectly – to cleanse the pool of subtle bias. Of course, the challenging process risks reintroducing bias of a different kind.

As Abramson stresses, there are at least "two understandings of the jury's role in a democracy. The first envisions ... jurors ... as spokespersons for competing group interests."[42] The other understanding conceives of the jury as a site of communally situated rational discourse. Certainly the latter model is highly idealized, and cases of self-government, as opposed to other-government (deciding about the fates of others), will be much more likely to trigger self-interested behaviour during deliberations because deliberators may be more directly affected by a determination of policy than they would be by the guilt or innocence adjudication in one criminal case.[43] Therefore, we must carefully consider how to ensure impartiality through institutional design. And the jury suggests some ways to accomplish impartiality through selection mechanisms, charges from authority figures, and otherwise.

From one perspective, some may argue that a "doctrine of affected interests" requires that all who may be affected by a policy choice must be included (or represented) in the deliberation.[44] Alternatively, one could argue that citizen representatives may *not* participate in any dispute for which their interests are heavily vested. Granted, such a standard would need a more detailed articulation. But it suffices to say here that citizen representatives must have a commitment to impartiality when they are empanelled.

The jury enjoys a series of institutional designs aimed at ensuring impartiality with regard to fairness and good deliberation, such as fair cross-section requirements (on which more below) and limitations on how jurors may be excluded from service. Any effort to use citizen representatives in exercises of self-government will likely need to develop similar protocols to achieve some modicum of impartiality.

Cross-Sectionality
At the heart of the American jury's commitment to impartiality is a very particular manner of achieving it: the "fair cross-section" requirement. The

Sixth Amendment of the US Constitution announces that "in all criminal prosecutions, the accused shall enjoy the right to a speedy and public trial, by an impartial jury of the State and district wherein the crime shall have been committed."[45]

In a series of cases, the Supreme Court has articulated the cross-sectional ideal: the pool from which juries are drawn must be "representative" of a fair cross-section of the community.[46] This coheres with a certain conception of "descriptive representation," explained above. For example, in 1942, *Glasser v. United States* held most generally that the jury itself must be representative of the community.[47] In 1946, *Ballard v. United States* clarified that such representation may not exclude women.[48] That same year, *Thiel v. S. Pac. Co.* held that the cross-section requirement prevents intentional exclusion of wage-earners, requiring the inclusion of all socio-economic classes.[49] By 1954, in *Hernandez v. Texas*, the cross-section requirement enjoyed constitutional magnitude as the selection of jurors on any ethnic basis whatsoever was proscribed.[50]

Beyond the courts' activism in ensuring cross-sectionality, Congress has also taken action to guarantee a jury's "descriptive" representativeness in the Jury Selection and Service Act.[51] The statute requires that juries be "selected at random from a fair cross-section of the community," highlighting that *randomness* is the statutorily chosen means of jury selection and representation.[52] Even the mechanics for random selection are codified by Congress at 28 U.S.C. § 1863.

Although a random lottery system was once a credible democratic system of representation,[53] the jury system's use of the lottery and randomization technique is unique. Congress chose randomness on the theory that random selection has special properties that render it a very good way of securing a fair cross-section of the community. But note that, despite its potential merits, neither Congress nor the courts have required proportional representation in the jury context.[54] This may hint that, as a matter of institutional design, when small groups of lay citizens are called into duties of governance, descriptive representation is important but should be achieved through randomness, without applying a proportional representation principle.

Finally – and perhaps most remarkably – American legislatures have made jury service *mandatory*. Indeed, Congress has authorized penalties of fines and terms of imprisonment for citizens' failure to comply with jury summonses.[55] So committed is Congress to the need for representation that extends beyond self-selection that it abandons the otherwise deep US commitment to voluntarism and non-coercion. Although *United States v. Gometz* otherwise held that the words "selected at random" were not intended by Congress literally and that self-screening was not wholly outlawed,[56] courts cannot undo the statutory penalties associated with a juror's noncompliance.

In short, the jury system may be read to recommend a fair cross-section requirement along with random selection and mandatory service in the design of citizen representative political bodies. Although many proponents of citizen representation have embraced random selection, the jury's use of *mandatory* participation to overcome self-selection is not quite as popular among theorists.[57] More proposals ought to draw upon the provisions for compulsory service that contribute to the jury's representativeness and reflect its commitment to impartiality.[58] Without compulsory service, we cannot help but systematically exclude those who are too busy or too timid to participate.

Civic Responsibility

Distinct from mandatory service's contribution to representativeness and impartiality is its reinforcement of the jury as a civic responsibility of all citizens. For example, many courts have articulated the proposition expressed in *Taylor v. Louisiana:* trial by jury exists because "sharing in the administration of justice is a phase of civic responsibility."[59] In *United States v. Raszkiewicz*, the Seventh Circuit notes that jury service "further[s] the notion that participation in the administration of justice is a part of one's civic responsibility."[60]

The civic duty element of jury service helps explain part of the rationale for mandatory service laws. Significantly, however, the form of citizen representation expressed in the jury system is not merely designed to enforce responsibility from above; rather, the jury is intended to be a form of civic responsibility that reinforces a vision of popularly controlled political participation.[61] It is a direct democracy of sorts – but one that is not voluntary, as is participating in referendums, initiatives, or more broadly in civil society. Nor is this form of direct democracy sanguine about the obvious deliberative failures in most other exercises of direct democracy.

Certainly, people often seek to be excused from jury service, and it would be dishonest not to acknowledge that it is relatively easy to get excused or challenged if one is persistent. Nevertheless, as a society, we think of jury service as one of the few duties of citizenship. As Abramson writes, "Jury duty falls upon millions of Americans each year, making the jury system the most widespread example of participatory democracy in the United States today, despite all the loopholes that permit persons to escape service."[62]

Participatory and deliberative democrats are generally sensitive to the role of civic responsibility in the healthy functioning of a republican polity. To the extent that popular sovereignty is an ideal of participatory and deliberative democrats, achieving it in a "nonfictively attributable sense" must be part of the project of institutional redesign.[63] The jury accomplishes this by establishing in our otherwise voluntary political system an elaborate and mandatory practice of participation and deliberation. Although proposals for new compulsory programs are likely to be viewed with suspicion by the citizenry, the jury is one old institution that enjoys continued support despite its mandatory character. Even its most trenchant critics tend not to impugn its mandatory character. It is therefore surprising that so few deliberative and participatory democrats argue for mandatory regimes, although otherwise making wide use of the jury analogy. Despite the resistance, the jury system suggests its centrality to proper use of citizen representatives.

There is one more point to be made here: by reinforcing that jury service is a civic responsibility, we might contribute to the *accuracy* of the system. When people come to a full appreciation that they have a duty to discharge their responsibilities with care, they are perhaps more likely to take their role seriously and arrive at "right" (or at least reasoned) answers. Institutional designers aiming to make use of citizen representatives would be well advised to follow the model of the jury and make clear to each participant in such institutions that a serious civic responsibility rests on the shoulders of the few who adjudicate any one question.

Legitimacy

While the previous four elements of jury design we canvassed above grew increasingly specific, the fifth element operates at a more general level: it is the jury's role in a polity's quest for political and democratic legitimation. The jury system is designed to garner the voice of the people more deliberately and deliberatively than electoral politics can. Although many deliberative democrats surely favour citizen participation for its "educative" effects with regard to helping citizens better understand themselves and their polity,[64] consider also Abramson's channelling of Aristotle: "Aristotle suggested that democracy's chief virtue was the way it permitted ordinary persons drawn from different walks of life to achieve a 'collective wisdom' that none could achieve alone. At its best, the jury is the last, best refuge of this connection among democracy, deliberation, and the achievement of wisdom by ordinary persons."[65]

The jury system – although tasked to adjudicate *factual* rather than *legal* or *value* questions – cannot help but generate important general judgments about the law and values. In particular, Kalven and Zeisel trace a series of value judgments that juries regularly decide: excusing defendants for contributory fault of the victim (when it is not a legal excuse);[66] excusing defendants because the harm they caused was *de minimis* (even when the law recognizes no *de minimis* exception);[67] excusing defendants because they are being subjected to unpopular laws;[68] excusing defendants because they have already been subjected to enough punishment;[69] considering that the punishment for a conviction is too severe;[70] excusing defendants because other defendants are getting preferential treatment;[71] excusing defendants for improper conduct by the police (when such conduct is not a legal excuse);[72] and treating crime in subcultures differentially within different cultural contexts.[73] In turn, these general political and legal judgments filter through to prosecutors and law makers. In other words, citizen representatives in the jury system provide input, albeit indirectly, into how we govern ourselves. And that contributes to the *internal* legitimacy of the regime under which we all live.

In addition to enhancing a polity's internal legitimacy, the use of lay citizens endows the polity with greater *external* legitimacy in the eyes of those viewing the system from outside. This may be useful for compliance in the global order: as other countries grow to respect our commitment to democracy through the implementation of citizen representation, we may have more capital to spend in the world community as well.

In short, the prizes of internal and external legitimation are keys to designing institutions of citizen representation. Although abstract and aspirational, it remains relevant to the project of figuring out how to include citizen representatives in the enterprise of law and politics – and how to embed participation into larger schemes of governance to better approximate democratic representation all the way down.

Indirect Accountability

The final criterion in the theory of citizen representation evidenced by the jury is the jury's unique form of indirect accountability. It is commonplace for political theorists of representation to try to develop an account of accountability.[74] To wit, democratic representation demands some form of accountability from the representative to the represented. At first glance, juror representatives stand in stark contrast to legislative representatives, who are traditionally subject to electoral mechanisms or recall.[75] However, elections and recall are not the only types of democratic accountability. Modern complex liberal democracies have many state officials and judges subject to different mechanisms of accountability that do not detract from their democratic credibility as representatives.

Of course, the institution of the jury is not the only locus of indirect accountability in the American polity: many independent agencies in the American administrative state and the federal judiciary rely on accountability mechanisms that are at some remove from majoritarian electoral politics. But juries exist at quite a far extreme: the citizens doing the representing seem traceable to no moment of election and the populace has no opportunity to disaffirm or reaffirm a jury's decision. Perhaps we can ultimately trace accountability back to a fictional and tacit consent to the federal or state constitutions that bless the institution in the first place. Yet we suspect that most would find it difficult to square this degree of attenuation with the concept of accountability.

There are still other ways the juror representative strains the idea of accountability. A common conception of representative accountability is that representatives must give their constituents reasons for their decisions.[76] Yet jurors issue verdicts without providing reasons. Unlike many judicial opinions that offer an accounting, a jury verdict in the United States (and Canada) stands alone. Although jurors are prototypical deliberators in their pursuit of a verdict, they need not disclose reasons to the outside world, only to one another, a feature that insulates citizen representatives even further from accountability. Not all countries design their jury systems in this way: Spain, Denmark, and some Swiss jurisdictions, for example, do ask jurors for explanations. But most jury systems around the world do without this type of accountability.[77]

Finally, to the extent that citizen representatives are "descriptive" mirrors, their service as representatives takes place, in part, through their identities rather than through their actions. Descriptive representation focuses on immutable characteristics for which an individual cannot be held accountable in any meaningful sense.

Nevertheless there are a few indirect accountability mechanisms suggested by the jury that may be useful for citizen representation. First, there is a form of *deliberative* or *discursive* internal accountability embedded in each juror's responsibility to debate and to provide reasons to fellow decision makers. Deliberative accountability can also be found in the jury's relationship with the judge overseeing the trial (an arm of the state) and the counsel for each side (in the criminal context, one side is an arm of the state as well). Jurors participate in a deliberative practice with other institutional actors, some of whom are answerable to the state and to the persons whose interests are directly affected. This design feature could be useful in thinking about how to integrate citizen panels into governance.

Trustee accountability is also given expression through the jury. Jurors are imbued with a sense that they "stand for" and "act for" the community at large.[78] They are charged with a responsibility that purports to make them *feel* accountable. The very process of selection – during which jurors see many of their fellow panel members challenged for cause, for bias, or for other reasons – and jury instruction contribute to this sense of accountability, signalling to those actually chosen that their role is to be impartial and to serve the public good.[79]

Additionally, there are also *external* accountability mechanisms. There is indirect dialogue between jury and state as the latter receives relevant information filtered through patterns of jury decision making. This dialogue ensures that citizen representatives furnish input to the state, which is later held to account through electoral mechanisms.

Finally, the jury is embedded within a complex legal system that routinely takes decisions away from it through directed verdicts, dismissals, or appellate review. In the context of British Columbia's citizens' assembly, for example, which utilized a randomly selected group of citizen representatives to debate electoral reform, the designers of the assembly built in an indirect accountability mechanism: the province had a mass referendum on whether to adopt into law what the citizen representatives decided. As it turned out, the deliberative preferences of the few who participated in the assembly did not achieve the super-majority required to have it enacted into law.[80] This layered form of representation is typical of democracies and is well demonstrated through the indirect accountability mechanisms to which citizen representatives in the jury are subject. As Warren and Mansbridge articulate, it may be that a lack of formal or electoral accountability can actually facilitate accountability to the public good in some design schemes.[81]

Conclusion

We have identified six elements embedded in American jury practice that might prove useful in constructing a fuller account of citizen representation. These elements are not the only ones that one might consider, but they are especially important in understanding how the jury represents. They are deeply relevant to new proposals and practices of deliberative and participatory democracy that draw upon the jury analogy.

Our method of inquiry here does more than describe a particular institution and its parochial history. We are, like Pitkin, engaged in a normative project. However, unlike Pitkin, we are attempting to delineate our account of representation within a very particular and unique institutional context. Conjoining normative criteria with sensitivity to the institution of the jury is a new direction for "rethinking representation."

In addition, the normative and institutional account of citizen representation developed here provides important lessons to those proposing new mechanisms of citizen representation. We suggest to those institutional designers that they not only draw upon certain mechanics of the jury system but also upon its underlying theory of citizen representation – one that draws upon deliberation, impartiality, cross-sectional ideals, regime legitimacy, and modes of indirect accountability.

There are, of course, important differences between juries and proposals for utilizing citizen representatives in other more legislatively oriented contexts – contexts within which people will be deciding their own fates rather than the fates of others, and in which difficult value questions rather than factual questions will be at stake. Accordingly, the account of citizen representation we sketch here will need to be modified and revised to accommodate these differences. Still, we feel confident that proposals seeking to revivify citizen participation through lay representatives all have a family resemblance to the jury. And the implicit theory of citizen representation in the jury is a good place to start the conversation about how to think of citizen representatives who will be employed in our continuing commitment to self-government.

NOTES

We thank Katherine Kao for research assistance, the 1066 Foundation for financial support, and Mark Brown, Mark Warren, Mary Dietz, and Christopher Elmendorf for thoughtful comments on prior drafts. We presented a version of this chapter at a panel of the Midwestern Political Science Association in Chicago and received very helpful feedback from participants there.

1 See, for example, Ethan J. Leib, *Deliberative Democracy in America: A Proposal for a Popular Branch of Government* (University Park: Penn State Press, 2005); Robert Dahl, *After the Revolution? Authority in a Good Society*, rev. ed. (New Haven: Yale University Press, 1990); James Fishkin, *Democracy and Deliberation: New Directions for Democratic Reform* (New Haven: Yale University Press, 1991); Archon Fung, *Empowered Participation: Reinventing Urban Democracy* (Princeton: Princeton University Press, 2004).
2 But see Mark B. Brown, "Survey Article: Citizen Panels and the Concept of Representation," *Journal of Political Philosophy* 14, 2 (2006): 203-25; Mark Stephan, "Citizens as Representatives: Bridging the Democratic Theory Divides," *Politics and Policy* 32, 1 (2004): 118-35.
3 J.H. Snider ran a blog at http://www.snider.blogs.com/ devoted to tracing these developments around the world. Its focus was on the "Citizens' Assembly" model recently implemented in British Columbia, Canada. That blog stopped being updated as of 15 September 2007 but coverage continues at http://www.isolon.org/.
4 Of course, we are not the first to endorse context-sensitivity in the derivation of theories of political representation. See also John Stuart Mill, "Considerations on Representative Government," in *On Liberty and Other Essays*, ed. John Gray (Oxford: Oxford University Press, 1991 [1862]).
5 See Neil Vidmar, "The Canadian Criminal Jury: Searching for a Middle Ground," *Law and Contemporary Problems* 62 (1999): 141; Ethan J. Leib, "A Comparison of Criminal Jury Decision Rules in Democratic Countries," *Ohio State Journal of Criminal Law* 5 (2008): 636.
6 See, for example, Brown, "Survey Article."
7 Elizabeth Garrett, "Hybrid Democracy," *George Washington Law Review* 73 (2004): 1096-130.
8 See, for example, Bruce Ackerman, *We the People: Foundations* (Cambridge, MA: Belknap Press, 1991).
9 Edmund S. Morgan, *Inventing the People: The Rise of Popular Sovereignty in England and America* (London: W.W. Norton, 1988).
10 Ibid.
11 Ibid., 14.
12 Benjamin Barber, *Strong Democracy: Participatory Politics for a New Age* (Berkeley: University of California Press, 1985).
13 Ibid., 145.
14 Jean-Jacques Rousseau, *The Social Contract and Other Writings*, trans. Victor Gourevitch (Cambridge: Cambridge University Press, 1997).
15 David Plotke, "Representation Is Democracy," *Constellations* 4, 1 (1997): 19. Plotke notes that representation is intrinsic to democracy and that the opposite of representation is not participation but exclusion.
16 Hannah Fenichel Pitkin, *The Concept of Representation* (Berkeley: University of California Press, 1967).
17 Bernard Manin, *The Principles of Representative Government* (Cambridge: Cambridge University Press, 1997).

18 Suzanne Dovi, *The Good Representative* (Oxford: Blackwell Press, 2007).
19 Manin, *Principles of Representative Government*, 83.
20 In other works, by contrast, Manin is keenly sensitive to the difficulties inherent in the notion of a popular will. See Bernard Manin, "On Legitimacy and Political Deliberation," *Political Theory* 15, 3 (1987): 338-68.
21 We do not mean to suggest that there are no attempts to look at political representation within an institutional context. See, for example, John Burnheim, *Is Democracy Possible? The Alternative to Electoral Politics* (Berkeley: University of California Press, 1985); Andrew Rehfeld, *The Concept of Constituency: Political Representation, Democratic Legitimacy, and Institutional Design* (Cambridge: Cambridge University Press, 2005); Richard Katz, *Democracy and Elections* (Oxford: Oxford University Press, 1997). Our own most recent effort to intervene in this literature and render representation through the lens of fiduciary obligation can be found in a string of recent publications: Ethan J. Leib, and David L. Ponet, "Fiduciary Representation and Deliberative Engagement with Children," *Journal of Political Philosophy* 20 (2012): 178; David L. Ponet and Ethan J. Leib, "Fiduciary Law's Lessons for Deliberative Democracy," *Boston University Law Review* 91 (2011): 1249.
22 Brian Seitz, *The Trace of Political Representation* (New York: SUNY Press, 1995), 24-25.
23 Some recent treatments of democratic representation help bridge the normative-institutional gap. Nadia Urbinati, *Representative Democracy: Principles and Genealogy* (Chicago: University of Chicago Press, 2006); Nadia Urbinati and Mark E. Warren, "The Concept of Representation in Contemporary Democratic Theory," *Annual Review of Political Science* 11 (2008). For a helpful historical, institutional, and normative look at the idea of a constituency, see Rehfeld, *Concept of Constituency*. For a strong normative analysis that captures the many axes of democratic representation, see Jane Mansbridge, "Rethinking Representation," *American Political Science Review* 97, 4 (2003): 515-28.
24 For more on the absence of evaluative criteria in contemporary treatments of representation, see Suzanne Dovi, "Preferable Descriptive Representatives: Will Just Any Woman, Black, or Latino Do?," *American Political Science Review* 94, 4 (2002): 729-43; Dovi, *Good Representative*.
25 Leib, *Deliberative Democracy*, 93-98. See also Simon Threlkeld, "A Blueprint for Democratic Law-Making: Give Citizen Juries the Final Say," *Social Policy* 28, 4 (1998): 5-9.
26 John Gastil, *Back by Popular Demand: Revitalizing Representative Democracy Through Deliberative Elections* (Berkeley: University of California Press, 2000), 174. For jurors' positive attitudes, see Shari Seidman Diamond, "What Jurors Think: Expectations and Reactions of Citizens Who Serve as Jurors," in *Verdict: Assessing the Civil Jury System*, ed. Robert E. Litan (Washington, DC: Brookings Institution Press, 1993), 285.
27 *Apodaca v. Oregon*, 406 U.S. 404, 410 (1972).
28 Akhil Amar, *The Constitution and Criminal Procedure: First Principles* (New Haven: Yale University Press, 1997), 162.

29 Ibid., 165.
30 Alexis de Tocqueville, *Democracy in America*, ed. J.P. Mayer, trans. George Lawrence (New York: Harper Collins, 1969), 273-74.
31 Ibid., 272.
32 Dennis J. Devine, Laura D. Clayton, Benjamin B. Dunford, Rasmy Seying, and Jennifer Pryce, "Jury Decision Making: 45 Years of Empirical Research on Deliberating Groups," *Psychology Public Policy and Law* 7, 3 (2001): 622-727.
33 But see *Allen v. United States*, 164 U.S. 492 (1896) (allowing judges to charge a deadlocked jury with a firm instruction to work towards a verdict through deliberation).
34 See *Clark v. United States*, 289 U.S. 1, 13 (1933). However, juror isolation is not total. Media attention, for instance, might guide a juror's reasoning. See Neil Vidmar and Valerie Hans, *American Juries: The Verdict* (Amherst: Prometheus Books, 2007), 112.
35 For an argument that one could achieve deliberation in the jury without requiring unanimity, see Ethan J. Leib, "Supermajoritarianism and the American Criminal Jury," *Hastings Constitutional Law Quarterly* 33, 2-3 (2005): 141-96.
36 Cass R. Sunstein, "Deliberative Trouble? Why Groups Go to Extremes," *Yale Law Journal* 110, 1 (2000): 71-119.
37 Tali Mendelberg, "The Deliberative Citizen: Theory and Evidence," in *Political Decision Making, Deliberation, and Participation*, ed. Michael X. Delli Carpini, Leonie Huddy, and Robert Y. Shapiro (Stanford: JAI Press, 2002).
38 For an argument "against deliberation" due to the effects of gender, race, and class bias, see Lynn Sanders, "Against Deliberation," *Political Theory* 25, 3 (1997): 347-76.
39 Sunstein finds that "group polarization is among the most robust patterns found in deliberating bodies." See Cass R. Sunstein, "The Law of Group Polarization," *Journal of Political Philosophy* 10, 2 (2002): 177. Shari Seidman Diamond has been doing the most to understand what is really going on within the black box of the jury of late. She is quite convinced of the need for careful attention to incentivize deliberation through institutional design rules and, for this reason, supports unanimity.
40 It is worth noting that processes of direct democracy lack such attributes. See Leib, *Deliberative Democracy*.
41 U.S. Const. amend. VI.
42 Jeffrey Abramson, *We, the Jury* (Cambridge, MA: Harvard University Press, 1994).
43 See Richard A. Primus, "When Democracy Is Not Self-Government: Toward a Defense of the Unanimity Rule for Criminal Juries," *Cardozo Law Review* 18, 4 (1996): 1417-57.
44 Ian Shapiro, *Democratic Justice* (New Haven: Yale University Press, 1999).
45 U.S. Const. amend VI.
46 See *Holland v. Illinois*, 493 U.S. 474 (1990).
47 315 U.S. 60 (1942).
48 329 U.S. 187 (1946).
49 328 U.S. 217 (1946).
50 347 U.S. 475 (1954).

51 28 U.S.C. §§ 1861-69, 1871 (1994). For a classic investigation into the uncertain commitment to representative panels, see Jon Van Dyke, *Jury Selection Procedures: Our Uncertain Commitment to Representative Panels* (Cambridge, MA: Ballinger, 1977).
52 28 U.S.C. § 1861.
53 See Manin, *Principles of Representative Government*, 21.
54 On the merits of proportional representation, see David L. Ponet, "Multiculturalism and the Challenges of Political Representation," Columbia University, Ph.D. Dissertation, 2006.
55 28 U.S.C. § 1866(g). But see Vidmar and Hans, *American Juries*, 77. The authors write: "A substantial number [of summonses] are not returned. In some urban jurisdictions, fewer than 20 percent of the citizens who are summoned initially ever serve. This poor response rate has been identified as the biggest cause of non-representative juries."
56 730 F.2d 475 (7th Cir 1984).
57 Ethan J. Leib, "Pragmatism in Designing Popular Deliberative Institutions in the United States and China," in *The Search for Deliberative Democracy in China*, ed. Ethan J. Leib and Baogang He (New York: Palgrave Macmillan, 2006).
58 Payment of jury fees and expenses are federally mandated by 28 U.S.C. § 1871 but are rather paltry. The jury system can "afford" to be this cheap because it is mandatory. Precisely because others cannot compel service, they rely on far more generous compensation and reimbursement. See, for example, Bruce Ackerman and James Fishkin, *Deliberation Day* (New Haven: Yale University Press, 2004).
59 419 U.S. 522, 530-31 (1975) (citing *Thiel v. S. Pac. Co.*, 328 U.S. 217, 227 (1946)) (Frankfurter, J., dissenting).
60 169 F.3d 459, 466 (7th Cir. 1999).
61 See John Gastil's path-breaking research, http://www.la1.psu.edu/cas/jurydem/.
62 Abramson, *We, the Jury*, 252
63 Frank Michelman, "How Can the People Ever Make the Laws? A Critique of Deliberative Democracy," in *Deliberative Democracy: Essays on Reason and Politics*, ed. James Bohman and Willian Rehg (Cambridge, MA: MIT Press, 1997), 146-47.
64 Tocqueville, *Democracy in America*, 273 and 75.
65 Abramson, *We, the Jury*, 11; Vidmar and Hans, *American Juries*, 340.
66 Harry Kalven and Hans Zeisel, *The American Jury* (Chicago: University of Chicago Press, 1966)
67 Ibid., 258.
68 Ibid., 286.
69 Ibid., 301.
70 Ibid., 308.
71 Ibid., 313.
72 Ibid., 318.
73 Ibid., 339. See also Vidmar and Hans, *American Juries*, 341.
74 Mark E. Warren, "Citizen Representatives," in *Designing Democratic Renewal*, ed. Mark E. Warren and Hilary Pearse (Cambridge, UK: Cambridge University Press, 2008); Brown, "Survey Article," 210-11.

75 Even in the context of legislative or electoral representation, accountability is always imperfect and attenuated. Representatives do not always seek reelection, which may undermine electoral accountability. See Ethan J. Leib and David L. Ponet, "Representation in America: Some Thoughts on Nancy Pelosi, Gavin Newsom, Tim Johnson, and Deliberative Engagement," *The Good Society* 16, 1 (2008): 3-7. On the limits of accountability, see John Dunn, "Situating Democratic Accountability," in *Democracy, Accountability, and Representation*, ed. Bernard Manin, Adam Przeworski, and Susan Stokes (Cambridge: Cambridge University Press, 1999).

76 Amy Gutmann and Dennis Thompson, *Democracy and Disagreement* (Cambridge: Harvard University Press, 1996), Chap. 4.

77 Leib, "A Comparison."

78 Abramson, *We, the Jury*, 51.

79 As Abramson makes clear, there is also an "interest group" undercurrent to much jury law, which tends to underwrite a form of accountability that flows from a juror to his or her group interest. See ibid., 8.

80 For more on this aspect of the design, see Warren, "Citizen Representatives."

81 Ibid.; Jane Mansbridge, "Representation Revisited: Introduction to the Case against Electoral Accountability," *Democracy and Society* 2, 1 (2004): 1-13.

13 Supplementary Democracy? Democratic Deficits and Citizens' Assemblies

AMY LANG AND MARK E. WARREN

Over the last two decades, growing concerns about democratic deficits in the developed democracies have prompted widespread experimentation with new citizen engagement institutions such as citizen juries and panels, advisory councils, stakeholder meetings, lay members of professional review boards, representations at public hearings, public submissions, citizen surveys, deliberative polling, deliberative forums, focus groups, and advocacy group representations.[1] On its face, the sheer variety and innovative qualities of these new political venues and institutions suggests a major transformation in democratic governance.[2] But comparative assessment of the strengths and weaknesses of different public engagement tools for redressing distinct kinds of democratic deficits is in its infancy.[3]

In this chapter we aim to advance this assessment in two ways. First, using the American and Canadian political systems as our examples, we identify the kinds of democratic deficits the systems are likely to generate. Each country's political system is prone to different kinds of deficits, for different reasons. Both, however, have structural features that limit their capacities to represent and advance citizen interests and demands. In addition, we identify democratic deficits likely to plague referendums, one common response to deficits in representative democracy. Second, we outline the capacities of a particular type of new institution – the citizens' assembly (CA) – to supplement our received institutions in ways that address democratic deficits. We focus on three institutional features – random selection, learning and deliberation, and empowerment – that set the CA model apart from other kinds of public engagement processes. Owing to these features, we argue, CAs have capacities to supplement existing institutions in ways that directly address some areas of democratic deficit. However, we suggest that the CA design has a more limited capacity to address deficits caused by issue complexity and jurisdictional conflicts and vacuums.

Defining Democratic Deficits

We define a democratic deficit as a misalignment between citizen demands and the capacities of existing political institutions to respond to those demands. We take citizen distrust of and disengagement from traditional political institutions – a well-documented trend in the United States and Canada – as evidence for the existence of a deficit.[4] Scholars have offered a variety of explanations for this phenomenon, including the poor performance of political institutions;[5] the increasing capacities of new generations of better educated, more informed, less deferential citizens to be critical of those institutions;[6] a fundamental popular distaste for the conflict-ridden messiness of politics; and a general disinterest in public policy debates.[7] While scholars disagree about the causes of distrust and disengagement, these arguments have in common the idea that political institutions are failing to connect citizen concerns with collective decision making in legitimate and effective ways.

We take this evidence as suggestive. Our key method here is primarily theoretical and speculative, focused on those features of political institutions in the United States and Canada that are likely to produce particular kinds of democratic deficits. To define these kinds, we ask a normative question: what should democratic institutions do? At the highest level of abstraction, we believe democratic institutions should be *inclusive* of those affected, *deliberative* in the making of law and policy, and *accountable* for the results.

Democratic institutions should, minimally, serve to include the interests, perspectives, and arguments of those affected by collective decisions. Inclusion depends on political institutions that can respond to a variety of intermediary institutions that thematize and channel citizen demands into formal decision-making structures. Intermediary institutions, including political parties, lobby groups, social movement organizations, policy networks, and innovative public participation forums, act as the connective tissue of democracy, connecting decision-makers to the publics affected by decisions and the policies that result from them. Thus, *inclusion-based* deficits may result from weaknesses in these connections. Intermediary institutions that are strong on "thematizing" may be weak on "channelling" and vice versa. Social movement organizations and broad policy networks may adequately capture the range of concerns and interests in the public sphere but may have little capacity to channel those demands through decision-making processes. Political parties and lobby groups may be strong on channelling capacity but may only be weakly connected to broader public demands. As we discuss below, formal political institutions partly shape the channelling capacity of intermediary institutions by privileging particular kinds of resources and organizational forms. In this way, they can produce systematic exclusions, which, in turn, result in democratic deficits.

Second, democratic institutions should have the capacity to integrate citizen demands into proposals and decisions and to provide public rationales for decisions. That is, they should have the capacity for the deliberative formation of decisions. As we argue below, formal political institutions in Canada and the United States increasingly lack the ability to escape their structural adversarialism. Both create incentives that place a premium on winner-take-all politics rather than on deliberative decision making, resulting in *deliberative* deficits. Citizen distaste for this kind of politics is evident in their complaints about the adversarial, or polarized, culture of politics.[8]

Finally, democratic institutions should be accountable to citizens. Institutions should offer citizens mechanisms that enable them to hold elected officials accountable for a variety of actions, including the representation of plural interests, deliberation that seeks to weigh and integrate diverse concerns, and the production of public policy that is demonstrably in the public interest.[9] As we suggest below, American and Canadian political institutions have differing strengths and weaknesses with respect to representation and policy accountability, producing distinctive kinds of accountability deficits. While both the American and Canadian electoral systems allow citizens to use the vote to hold elected officials accountable for their performance, the Canadian system enables citizens to vote a government out of office. Even though the Westminster system is superior in this respect to the American system because it empowers strong, retrospective accountability, it is unable to connect citizen approval or disapproval to specific policies or performances. Indeed, moments of policy accountability – triggered by confidence votes – are decided by the elites of political parties, not by the voting public.

Democratic Deficits in Canadian and American Political Institutions

The Westminster parliamentary system used in Canada and its provinces as well as the presidential system used in the United States both have structural properties that exacerbate the gap between citizen demands, existing intermediary institutions, and political system responsiveness. But because the systems are different, the institutional causes of democratic deficits are also different.

In Canada, inclusion deficits are very likely the consequence of the Westminster parliamentary system. In comparison with other kinds of democratic systems, the Westminster system has higher barriers to entry. Because the system is based on single member, winner-take-all districts, competition at the district level tends to be limited to two major parties. And because Westminster systems unify powers, there are few institutional checks upon the legislative majority party, which, in turn, means that minority interests and perspectives have few institutional means for exercising influence. At the federal level, exaggerated legislative majorities are exacerbated by regionalism: no party in Canada today can aspire to more than about 40 percent of the popular vote. And yet parties work on the assumption that they will receive legislative majorities and will therefore have absolute control over the business of government.

Likewise, the elite-controlled Canadian Westminster system tends to privilege exclusive forms of social capital – tightly connected networks of trusted advisors. Centralized control means the system is not friendly to forum shopping by interest groups (in contrast to the American system). Governments may choose how widely to consult, and which actors to heed. Nominal consultation tends to be open-ended and widespread in Canada, but networks of influence are often much more limited than they are in the United States. A lack of transparency in the process for connecting consultation with policy undermines the credibility of consultation processes as legitimate and effective forums for the expression of demands. Canadian civil society organizations – particularly think tanks and other policy-focused organizations – also lack the independent funding available to American organizations, perhaps in part because Westminster political institutions provide fewer opportunities for organized advocacy and influence. And because many NGOs and community organizations have historically relied on the various levels of government for funding, they are weakly positioned as government watchdogs and agents of change.

The Westminster system is also relatively non-deliberative in its formation of policy. Responsible party government limits Parliament's role in agenda setting and policy making. Although at the federal level the Canadian system is formally bicameral, it is functionally unicameral and concentrates power in the hands of majority party leadership, although this power is tempered by the requirement of continued party caucus support (see White, Chapter 10, this volume). Even cabinet plays less of a role in channelling interests and deliberating about policy than it once did, with power now concentrated in the Prime Minister's Office.[10] Thus, the role of minority parties in Parliament – which often represent 60 percent or more of the electorate – is limited to oppositional debate. These qualities sharpen the adversarialism of the legislature, while precluding deliberative engagement of a representative continuum of public opinion.

Finally, an advantage of the Westminster system is that it produces strong retrospective accountability: if voters are unhappy with a government's performance, they have a clear agent to blame – namely, the majority party in Parliament. This kind of accountability, however, is relatively crude: the institutions do not allow for voters to differentiate among agents when holding them accountable, to simultaneously express approval of a government even if they disapprove of their representative or vice versa. A further problem is that voters are only able to hold their representatives to account periodically, in most instances when governments decide to call or force an election. Finally, voters have no means for holding elected representatives accountable for policy decisions that span levels of government. Policies are often the result of elite-brokered compromises among the prime ministers of the ten provinces. Voters may not know which level of government to blame; and, even if they do, they cannot oust the leaders of other provinces.

Political institutions in the United States are likely to generate democratic deficits for quite different reasons. With respect to inclusion, American institutions appear to do better than Canadian institutions. Most obviously, the American system is much less likely to produce governments that fail to garner a majority of votes than is the Canadian system. In addition, because political institutions have separate constituencies, citizens have multiple opportunities for representation – if not through the House or Senate then through the executive. Finally, because the American system separates powers, it provides multiple points of access for a variety of interests to be heard and to influence policy. On the surface, a directly elected executive, bicameral legislatures, and a strong judiciary would appear to create ample opportunities for citizens to engage with government to press their demands.

In practice, however, these multiple sites of influence create problems for democratic inclusion. The combination of weak parties and personalized politics, along with myriad congressional committees, hundreds of agencies with rule-making power, a strong and pluralized legal system, and separated powers, creates powerful incentives for a very large influence and advocacy industry in Washington. Intermediary groups could in principle function to connect broad social and public interests to policy making. Most (though not all) are organizations that rely on professional lobbyists and experts, and they lack credible representative connections to broad constituencies.[11] These qualities of the system multiply the value of organization and money as political resources, resulting in a system that is highly pluralistic but that also excludes those without these resources. Because citizens cannot vote for governments with clear policy agendas as they would in a parliamentary system, the American system is more open to influence by powerful interests, more prone to corruption, and less likely to respond to broad public interests.

With respect to deliberation, the American system is again more robust than the Canadian system. A system with separated powers depends more on bargaining and persuasion than does one with unified powers. The committee structure of Congress likewise provides more opportunities for deliberation and persuasion. Yet, because deliberative influences mix with undue access for special interests and brokered deals that are not transparent to the public, it is hard for citizens to tell whether policies are the consequences of deliberation about the public interest or non-transparent influences of interests with privileged access to decision-makers.

The American electoral system provides retrospective accountability between individual voters and representatives but not between voters and institutional performance. Owing to the separation of powers, citizens do not have the opportunity to vote governments into or out of office. The same features produce a system with multiple points of veto – that is, institutional positions that must agree to any proposed legislative change.[12] This means that democratic majorities have difficulty overcoming well-organized interests that are able to capture institutional veto points and use them to resist change. In addition, the separation of powers can lead to gridlock or veto cycles during which each site is controlled by different parties or factions. The result is often incremental or contradictory change that bears little resemblance to the preferences articulated by citizens and interest groups. What accountability exists is retrospective and weakly associated with policy decisions.

TABLE 13.1

Democratic ideals and institutional deficits

Normative dimensions of democracy	Institutional deficits	
	Canadian system	US system
Inclusion	Elite-centred exclusion, SMP electoral system produces minority majority governments	Pluralistic exclusion: agendas and outcomes biased towards well-resourced interests
Deliberation	Non-deliberative: policy making centralized in PMO's office; debate undermines deliberation in Parliament	Semi-deliberative, undermined by non-transparent brokerage
Accountability	Unified, retrospective accountability	Dispersed, retrospective accountability

We are arguing, then, that the American and Canadian political systems are both plagued by democratic deficits. The deficits are similar in the broad sense that they both involve disconnections between citizens and institutions. However, in so far as the sources are institutional, it is likely that the Canadian and American systems suffer distinct pathologies. The deficits in Canada result from a political system that is structurally exclusive, non-deliberative, and overly centralized to the point of authoritarianism, while also hamstrung by regional factionalization. The centralized nature of the Westminster system privileges interests that can mobilize exclusive social networks that connect interests to those actors in power. The deficits in the American system include fragmentation due to the separation of powers and penetration of the system by well-resourced interests. Table 13.1 summarizes the patterns of deficit.

Supplementary Democracy?

The key features of American and Canadian political institutions that generate democratic deficits are not likely to change. Even in deficit, they work well enough to avoid the broad constituencies and leadership necessary for re-engineering – with some possible exceptions in Canada in the area of electoral system reform. That said, democracies today are more like ecologies than "systems," and, as such, they can be patched, repaired, nudged, and reformed in ways that fall short of the difficult business of institutional redesign. The advantage of relating (if only theoretically) the unsatisfied demand for democracy to particular dimensions of institutional deficits is that we can also identify the places in which patches and repairs are likely to do the most good. Following this idea, we might conceive of the new experimentalism as *supplementary democracy*; and we might judge these supplements by asking whether they have capacities to address specific deficits. Because most such patches and repairs are ad hoc, brought into existence by specific problems of governance, they tend to be targeted at particular policies or issues: they are tools for specific jobs rather than broad transformations of the political system. Yet, considered as a whole, these developments could dramatically transform the functioning of existing democratic institutions, even if they do not alter their form.[13]

One kind of response to these democratic deficits is to turn some decisions directly over to voters. In the relatively more populist United States, direct democracy in the form of initiatives and referendums has long been popular, particularly in the western states. In Canada, with its history of deference to elites, referendums are rare, though there have been some important recent instances, such as the national referendum on the Charlottetown Accord; provincial referendums on electoral system reform in Prince Edward Island, British Columbia, and Ontario; and the referendum on the harmonized sales tax in British Columbia.

Referendums, however, can produce their own kinds of democratic deficits. With respect to inclusion, referendums are subject to control of the agenda by interests that are well enough organized and funded to place a proposal before the voters. In the United States, agenda setters are usually hidden, and, as they are exposed, voters come to distrust referendums. In Canada, the identities of agenda setters are known, but the process of agenda setting has been closed. Voters know but distrust the agenda setters. For example, in the case of the Charlottetown Accord, the agenda was elite-brokered behind closed doors, and, not surprisingly, voters distrusted the source and rejected the proposal.[14] More recently, British Columbians forced a referendum on a tax reform – the harmonized sales tax (HST)– that was most certainly good policy but was introduced suddenly and without public deliberation. The voters rejected the HST, a decision that reflected a broad distrust of the government's motives.

Although referendums can instigate healthy public deliberation, the proliferation of referendums in states such as California has led to so much information overload that few voters are able to familiarize themselves with the proposals. Moreover, particularly when issues are unfamiliar to voters, referendums are subject to the manipulation of public opinion by well financed interests who are able to dominate the information received by the public. As we discuss below, referendums can also be undermined by a lack of public deliberation, as was the case in the British Columbia and Ontario referendums on electoral reform.

Referendums are strong in terms of policy accountability. Although voters may not control the agenda (and, thus, representation of their interests in the formulation of policy), they do have an opportunity for a focused "yes" or "no" decision.[15] But this form of accountability suffers from a problem that mirrors those of Westminster systems: voters may have a strong moment of empowerment, but it is often unconnected to what should be a deliberative process of forming and assessing the proposal.

Can Citizens' Assemblies Redress Democratic Deficits?

We believe another kind of democratic supplement – the citizens' assembly – could play a key role in addressing some of the deficits identified above, including those associated with initiatives and referendums. CAs are randomly selected, deliberative bodies charged with formulating recommendations, policies, or referendum agendas. CAs are not cure-alls: they are costly and time-consuming, they require specific mandates and authorization, and they must address issues that admit of relatively clear recommendations or agendas. That said, CAs have some strengths in precisely those areas in which Canadian and American political institutions are weak and initiatives insufficient: inclusive representation, sustained deliberation focused on public interests, and accountability. And, interestingly, though the causes of American and Canadian deficits are quite distinct, there are reasons to believe that the CA model provides some remarkably broad solutions, assuming a fit between the issue and the process.

The CA model was developed in British Columbia in 2003 at the behest of the sitting provincial Liberal government.[16] After two elections that returned arbitrary results – one that awarded the government to the party that lost the popular vote, and one that virtually eliminated the opposition party – the Liberals made good on a promise to hold a "citizens' assembly" to address the question of whether British Columbia should reform its electoral system. Once constituted and funded by the government, a CA secretariat invited 160 near-randomly selected citizens – one woman and one man from each electoral district and two members of First Nations – to learn about electoral systems, hold public hearings, and, finally, deliberate on what system would be best for British Columbia. The government empowered the CA by precommitting to put its recommendation to a public referendum.

The BC CA convened at regular intervals from January to November of 2004 – a period of eleven months – and concluded that a single-transferable-vote system was preferable to the existing single-member-plurality system. The BC public was given the opportunity to vote on this proposal in a May 2005 referendum. While the proposal received strong support – 57 percent of the vote overall and over 50 percent in all but two ridings (electoral districts) – it fell short of the required 60 percent set by the government as the threshold for passing the proposal into law. Based on the strength of public support, the Province of British Columbia held a second referendum in May 2009. While some public funding was available for yes and no campaigns, this second referendum received less media coverage and generated more adversarial advertising, while the agenda setter – the BC CA – disappeared from public view. These factors may have contributed to voters' decisive rejection of the proposal for electoral reform in the second referendum.[17] The model has been replicated in Ontario and the Netherlands, and proposals inspired by the CA model are under review in several American states. The State of Oregon used a CA-like process in the 2010 general election to experiment with providing voters with guidance on two of the measures on the ballot.

The CA process belongs to a class of new collaborative and deliberative institutions that empower citizens to engage in political decision making. It is similar to the process used in participatory budgeting, Chicago police oversight boards, and environmental stakeholder groups.[18] But it is distinct from other public engagement processes in three important ways.

First, CAs are constituted through a process of near-random selection, comparable to a deliberative poll.[19] Significantly, and unlike many deliberative processes, the assembly process *excludes* stakeholders – in these cases, elected politicians and organized political interests. In this respect, CAs are comparable to juries: other advocates present their cases to the body, but the body is constituted and operates at some distance from directly interested parties. In the BC CA, these exclusions were justified on the grounds that stakeholders had a conflict of interest as they owed their professions to the current electoral system. Owing to this near-random selection process, CAs look very much like the populations from which they are drawn. They are descriptively representative, while holding no partisan interests that might

TABLE 13.2

Referendums and citizens' assemblies compared

Dimensions of democracy	Outcomes of supplementary institutions	
	Referendums and ballot initiatives	Citizens' assemblies
Inclusion	Pluralistic exclusion: agendas set by well-resourced interests (US) or elites (Canada)	Inclusive, agenda-setting
Deliberation	Inattentive citizens, low information, advantages for organized interests	Information-rich, robust deliberation
Accountability	Unified, retrospective accountability	Unified, prospective accountability

compromise their search for the public interest. Thus, CAs have *inclusive* qualities found in neither formal political institutions nor in many of the new democratic supplements, namely, a claim to represent an inclusive public interest rather than the sum of organized interests.[20]

Second, the relatively long duration of the CA process gives participants sufficient time to learn and reflect on their preferences in depth. The acquisition and mastery of technical information and understanding of their own and others' values enables participants to make sophisticated recommendations that formulate and capture the nuances of their preferences. In other words, the CA has *deliberative* qualities that are unusual in formal political institutions or in short-duration institutions such as public hearings or even deliberative polls. Finally, the fact that the CA process is accompanied by a public referendum raises the stakes of participation compared to what we find in short and unempowered public engagement exercises. The referendum provides a single point of *accountability* that creates important incentives for CA members to anticipate public judgment, which, in turn, encourages them to integrate their diverse concerns into a consensus recommendation. Table 13.2 compares the democratic outcomes of CAs with traditional ballot initiatives and referendums. The following sections provide more detail on how CAs might address these three areas of deficit.

Inclusion

CAs address deficits of inclusion in two ways. First, they expand the demographic pool of those included in the process of deliberation and decision making through near-random selection. Even if participants do not engage in active representation or advocacy on behalf of particular interests, their presence means that a broader set of values and life experiences is brought to bear on decisions that are made in the CA. CAs also enhance inclusion by providing extensive learning and by practising deliberating in a non-adversarial setting, features that empower the demographically diverse array of participants to become active advocates for distinct concerns, themes, and points of view. The result is active deliberation about ideas and concerns that might be excluded from political institutions that limit policy debates to those with high levels of political resources and experience.

In the BC and Ontario CAs on electoral reform and the Dutch Bürgerforum on electoral reform, participants were randomly invited from voter lists to participate in a lottery to become a CA member. Because those who received invitations had to agree to allow their names to be entered into a second lottery that would constitute the actual CA, the process incorporated an element of self-selection: only those willing to serve entered the second round. However, the organizers sought to anticipate the impact of economic circumstance on self-selection by paying participants a modest per diem. They also covered logistical costs, including travel, hotel, and child care. This level of support probably mitigated the effects of income disparity and family status on self-selection.

The resulting assemblies were not perfect demographic snapshots of the population: they overrepresented those with English-language skills, European heritage, stable housing, higher education, and community participation experience.[21] However, the assemblies were much more demographically inclusive than were existing municipal, provincial, or federal legislative bodies. In particular, gender parity in the BC and Ontario assemblies enabled women to be at the centre of deliberations and decision making, with women emerging as opinion leaders and negotiators at key moments of each CA's deliberations. Owing to these design features, the CA stands up relatively well to the test of inclusion of groups that are typically excluded or underrepresented within current political institutions, a finding that replicates observations of other collaborative citizen governance forums.[22]

Second, CAs enhance inclusion by empowering this near-representative sample to develop and express a variety of informed opinions.[23] The assemblies were designed to transform citizens into experts – first by including a significant period for learning about the issues and then by enabling members to learn from the public and from one another in subsequent stages of public interactions and CA deliberations.[24] Because the CAs excluded stakeholders, they were able to represent latent and unformed public interests of the kind that would have been suppressed by a body composed of intensely held and vested interests. Thus, these bodies had the opportunity to form and represent a *public* opinion that was very likely different from the recommendations that would have resulted from bargaining among intensely held interests – the form of representation that is more likely within elected legislatures and participatory processes such as public hearings and stakeholder meetings.

The BC and Ontario processes accomplished these transformations by equipping participants with the skills and the sense of self-efficacy to express their preferences in deliberation with one another, ensuring that those not accustomed to competitive political debate were heard. The preferences voiced by participants were not simple repetitions of what they had been taught by expert presenters. In contrast to electoral systems scholars, for example, both the BC and Ontario assemblies emphasized voter choices as a key criterion for choosing an electoral system.[25] The BC CA members further emphasized voter power over candidates as a key criterion for evaluating electoral systems, while the Ontario CA members privileged simplicity as a criterion. These criteria were important deciding factors in the systems chosen in each CA. Over the course of the CA processes, many participants gained the confidence to speak out to their communities and to the media on the issue of electoral reform. During the BC referendum campaign, members from the BC CA became active spokespersons for the BC single transferable vote system (BC-STV: the system designed by the BC CA), with several becoming active in national electoral reform organizations. In the final analysis, the CAs transformed lay citizens into sophisticated and confident experts who represented a diversity of public opinion. In doing so, they mitigated a common dimension of exclusion: the cleavage between citizens and experts.[26]

Deliberation

Because CAs are designed to include a broad array of interests and perspectives, perhaps the most interesting and difficult question is whether they can transform this diversity into a single, actionable, near-consensus position with a credible claim to represent the public interest. In this respect, the CA is a kind of political body that is quite different from current institutions.

Neither the American congressional system nor the Canadian Westminster system is flexible enough to generate consensus even when there are overlapping or convergent interests. In both systems, legislators face accountability pressures – to their constituents, their funders, and their parties – that too often call for adversarial rather than deliberative and collaborative politics. The strength of these pressures often outweighs incentives to engage in deliberative and collaborative problem-solving with other legislators.

In contrast to formal political institutions, the CA model places a premium on learning, deliberation, and effective problem-solving. Although CAs formally use majority voting, they are essentially collaborative institutions. Participants have strong incentives to reach super-majorities or full consensus. A supermajority or full consensus recommendation from a near randomly selected body would be a credible signal to the broader public that the CA has addressed the diverse concerns of its members in its final recommendation.

At least this is the idea. The challenges facing consensus decision makers are well known: seeking consensus may involve suppressing important conflicts of interest.[27] As Jane Mansbridge argues, groups that become ideologically committed to consensus decision making often have a difficult time switching to other decision-making techniques that recognize and legitimate divergent interests, such as bargaining, turn-taking, majority rule, and proportional distribution of benefits.[28] These difficulties can lead to processes that involve manipulation and the exertion of social pressure to force a minority to go along with the majority position.

Recognizing this challenge, deliberation practitioners have worked to frame the goal of deliberation as problem-solving rather than as achieving consensus.[29] By positioning participants as primarily problem-solvers rather than consensus-seekers, citizen deliberators become responsible for producing legitimate and effective recommendations that accommodate multiple interests and concerns. Using this framework, the process of deliberation looks less like a drive for agreement at the expense of some, and more like principled negotiation that seeks to produce agreements that address a variety of distinct concerns.[30]

This problem-solving approach was used effectively by the organizers and participants of the two Canadian CAs. In both CAs, some participants became active advocates for particular interests that potentially conflicted with one other. In both cases, other participants in each CA took on the role of "problem-solvers" who worked to find positions that addressed the conflicting interests raised over the course of each CA. For example, in the BC CA, advocates for rural representation insisted that rural constituencies' needs had to be met in a new electoral system, even though these constituencies were a proportionately much smaller part of the population than that comprised by urban constituencies. Problem-solvers within the BC CA worked to assure these rural advocates that the STV system favoured by many was as capable of meeting rural interests as was the status quo, which many rural CA members had initially preferred. Although some members of the CA were not open to addressing all the concerns raised by advocates within the assembly, notably women's representation,[31] there is limited evidence that the members of the BC CA used social pressure to suppress disagreements. Those who felt their points of view had not been sufficiently addressed by others did not appear to feel this undermined the process as a whole.[32]

In the Ontario CA, three distinct factions developed, each advocating a potentially contradictory principle for choosing a new electoral system. One group was concerned about limiting the increase to the size of the legislature, believing the Ontario public would not accept a system that gave them "*more* politicians." A second group favoured maximizing the amount of proportionality within their proposed system. A third group was vocal about maintaining the province's level of local representation – something of particular importance to CA members from rural areas. Each of these strongly held preferences made it difficult to create a system that fully met the preference of another camp. A mixed-member proportional (MMP) system that maximized proportionality and local representation would necessarily mean increasing the size of the legislature. An MMP system that maximized proportionality but kept the size of the legislature the same would mean cutting the number of local seats in half. A system that maximized local representation while limiting the number of seats meant that proportionality would be limited.

The impasse was resolved when a few key problem-solvers in the Ontario CA worked to develop an MMP proposal that balanced these concerns, producing a compromise that gave each faction some portion of what it wanted. The proposed system would increase the size of the legislature from 107 to 129 seats, with 90 seats allocated to local representatives and the remaining 39 seats allocated according to the proportion of votes received by each party. This proposal would not raise the total number of seats beyond historic levels, would not significantly reduce local representation in rural areas, and allowed for enough party seats to produce proportional representation most of the time.

Thus, the fear that collaborative institutions would suppress real conflicts of interest was not borne out in the case of the two Canadian CAs. Each CA had to produce a recommendation that met competing – and at times conflicting – interests. In the end, this process led to a remarkable degree of support for the proposed electoral systems, with each CA voting over 80 percent in favour of the recommended system and voting 90 percent or over in favour of putting the proposals to a public referendum.

Accountability

The American political system is particularly weak with respect to accountability to citizens. It is true that politicians may be voted out of office as individuals. But American voters have little control over the system as a whole and the policies it produces. Discontent must build to a very high level before voters are able to remove a sufficient number of politicians to shift policy.[33] The Canadian system provides stronger retrospective accountability, but it only does so in the manner of a referendum on the government's overall performance.

In contrast, the CA model provides collective, prospective, and policy-specific accountability. The BC and Ontario CAs replicated for the public as a whole the vote of confidence in Westminster systems. Because they were empowered to set referendum agendas, the CA members were oriented prospectively towards their collective responsibility: they crafted their proposals knowing that they would be judged by the public. Individual CA members are not accountable to specific constituents, and this freed them to ask, simply: What policy is in the public interest? What policy will the public accept?

The accountability defect in these particular CA models had to do with public awareness of their proposal and the referendum: by the time of the first referendum in British Columbia, for example, scarcely 60 percent of voters were aware of the issue; the level of awareness in Ontario was somewhat higher.[34] However, evidence from the BC referendum surveys suggests that citizens who knew about the BC CA tended to view the assembly as representative of their interests, which, in turn, led them to view it as trustworthy. The more citizens knew about the assembly, the more likely they were to view it as keeping in view the interests of "average" members of the public. Projected levels of trust in the BC CA far exceeded typical levels of trust in elected legislatures – a remarkable achievement for a "political" body.[35] These results suggest that the real challenge for the CA model of accountability lies in the transfer of knowledge developed within the mini-public of the CA into the broader public, not in its capacity to produce publicly acceptable proposals.

There is, however, a second important sense in which accountability is at work in the CA model. As suggested above, owing to the initial process of constitution, citizens in British Columbia placed a relatively high degree of trust in the BC CA. The general public voted for the CA proposal not necessarily because they understood it but because they judged the CA to be insulated from special interests and to represent the public interest. For these citizens, direct accountability via the referendum was mediated by the BC CA itself. Their vote reflected a trust-based judgment about the interests represented by the assembly – namely, that the interests of citizens were encapsulated in the interests of the assembly. The important lesson here is that, under some circumstances, direct accountability can be replaced (or supplemented) by institutions that are designed to be trustworthy owing to their credible capacity to represent public interests.[36]

Further Applications of the Citizens Assembly Model

Citizens Assemblies on Ballot Initiatives

With the benefits of enhanced inclusion, deliberation, and prospective accountability in mind, scholars and democratic reformers have proposed that CAs be used to sidestep democratic deficits in referendums and ballot initiatives, in effect supplementing direct democracy with a process that is more representative of interests and perspectives and more deliberative with regard to agenda setting. For example, John Ferejohn has proposed that CAs be used to avoid the problems of capture of initiative processes by public officials or well-resourced interests.[37] In his proposal for the state of California, a CA would be called to review and amend any initiative. It would be demographically representative, have the power to call witnesses, and be given the time to develop sufficient expertise to draft a proposal that would be put forward to the public. He argues that convening a CA would increase the likelihood of the initiative's passing because the CA's modifications would make it closer to the median voter's wishes. It would also deter special interests from abusing the initiative process by proposing and advocating for initiatives that address only their narrow interests.

In a similar vein, democratic reformers Ned Crosby and Pat Benn established the Citizens' Initiative Review (CIR) organization in Washington

State. The CIR builds on Crosby and Benn's work using citizen juries to deliberate on policy issues.[38] The proposed CIR process is smaller in scale and duration than is the CA process, with twenty-four randomly selected jurors meeting over the course of five days to hear arguments for and against proposed initiatives. But the spirit and purpose of the CIR is similar to Ferejohn's proposal. Theoretically, these proposals for "initiative assemblies" promise to address the representative and deliberative deficits in ballot initiatives. The State of Oregon adopted this model, called the Oregon Citizens' Initiative Review, for two measures on the 2010 general election ballot.[39]

CAs and Legislative Impasse

In addition to supplementing referendums and ballot initiative processes, the CA model also has the potential to supplement legislative decision making. Broadly, when legislative actors lack the political will or the institutional capacity to produce policy that is inclusive, deliberative, and accountable, then a CA may be able to provide a useful supplement.

Table 13.3 illustrates the variety of issue types for which CAs may overcome legislative impasse. The rows represent the three criteria that we have used throughout the chapter: inclusion, deliberation, and accountability. The columns specify particular kinds of legislative impasse, and the cell content indicates whether we think a CA process would exceed (+), match (0), or do worse (−) than a legislative process on the three normative dimensions.

The first two types of issues noted in Table 13.3 are those with which legislators want to avoid grappling, either because they face a conflict of interest (as in the case of electoral reform) or because there is no popular choice (as in the case of where to site an incinerator or any other NIMBY

TABLE 13.3

Citizens' assemblies and legislative impasse

Dimension of democracy	Legislative issue avoidance		Protracted conflict	Issue complexity	Jurisdictional incapacity	
	Conflict of interest	No popular choice			Conflict	Vacuum
Inclusion	+	+	+	+	+	+
Deliberation	+	+	+	0/−	+	+
Accountability	+	+	+	0	0	0

issue). For both of these types of issues, for the reasons detailed above, we believe a CA is likely to produce a better decision than are legislatures.

Where there is a conflict of interest, CAs are likely to be more inclusive of the public sentiment about an issue and to engage in deliberation that is more public-spirited than are legislatures. They produce policy-specific recommendations with a view to having to justify these publicly, which improves accountability. Their weakness is that legislators, because of conflict of interest, may not be willing to pass the recommendation of a CA or, having been cut out of the process, may be inclined to kill it with neglect, as some argued was the case with the poorly managed public education campaigns in Canadian referendums on electoral reform. For these reasons, we give a CA about the same odds as a legislature with regard to putting together a proposal that will be passed.

Where there is no popular choice, a CA is again likely to be more inclusive of the range of public opinion than is a legislature. It is likely to be more deliberative about the public good because the participants' careers do not depend on being elected, and it is likely to be more accountable than a legislature. We think that the chances of a CA recommendation's being passed is slightly higher in this situation than in a situation involving conflict of interest. This is because, while legislatures may have political interests in solving a problem that has no popular choice, a CA may provide the kind of substantive legitimacy that a legislature cannot generate on its own.

Finally, where there is protracted partisan conflict, we think a CA process is likely to improve the inclusion of interests and values in decision making, enhance deliberation by voicing a variety of interests and positions in addition to partisan claims, and be better able to produce policy recommendations that are in the public interest than are legislators invested in partisan gains.

We believe, however, that there are other types of legislative impasses for which a CA process holds promise but also faces serious challenges. When issues are extremely complex, CAs may be more inclusive than legislatures but may not be able to deliberate better than a legislative committee or ministry policy advisors. The constraints will be those of time and resources rather than expertise. Except in unusual circumstances, paid legislators and volunteer assembly members occupy the role of policy generalists tasked with identifying the fit between policy options and public values. However, paid legislators have access to more time, staff, and research support than do CA participants, and this may aid deliberation. Because of a lack of time and resources, volunteer assembly members may not produce a recommendation that appropriately maps complex decisions onto the public interest and, therefore, may fail in the kind of prospective accountability that characterized the BC and Ontario CA recommendations.

In addition, there are many issues in which legislators lack jurisdictional capacity either because two or more jurisdictions are in conflict over the regulation of an issue or because there is a jurisdictional vacuum (as in the case of cross-border resource management). In these cases, CAs are likely to be more inclusive than are the institutions that exist and will produce better, more public-spirited deliberation, as long as the issues are not too complex. Accountability will be about the same as with legislatures because, even though a CA will have to provide a public accounting of its proposals, cross-jurisdictional mechanisms for citizens to ratify or reject a CA proposal are politically difficult to design. In the case of jurisdictional conflict, we doubt that a CA would deliver a recommendation that would be so good that it would override jurisdictional conflicts. Nonetheless, where there are jurisdictional vacuums, CA recommendations could create some momentum for change.

Conclusion

We argue that deliberative and collaborative citizen institutions like CAs on electoral reform have the potential to redress democratic deficits by improving the connection between citizens' interests and government policy making and other outputs. CAs are new institutions that may help citizens to formulate and advance their concerns. They also may do a better job than adversarial representative institutions at integrating a wide variety of interests and concerns into public policy. And they promise a novel and robust direct form of democratic accountability. CAs are not cure-alls: they require time and money. They will be less effective when stakeholders hold (and choose to exercise) veto powers over CA proposals. And because they are policy-focused, they are probably best convened in those areas in which policy trade-offs can be defined in ways that admit of relatively clear public judgment.

For these reasons, CA processes are most likely to be valuable to democracy not as stand-alone institutions but rather as supplements to existing democratic institutions. Along with other scholars, we believe CAs would substantially improve referendums and ballot initiative processes. CAs are likely to produce referendum proposals that do better on the criteria of inclusion and deliberation than do existing initiative processes, which allow lobby groups or public officials to frame the question and set the terms of public debate. Where political actors have vested interests in a referendum issue, CAs are likely to produce referendum questions that better encapsulate the public interest. CAs should also function as useful supplements to the legislative process at moments of impasse. In situations of legislative issue avoidance, protracted partisan conflict, issue complexity, and jurisdictional conflict or vacuum, a CA's deliberations would encapsulate a broader array of concerns and would be more likely to produce recommendations in the public interest.

The CA concept faces challenges of implementation, empowerment, and connection to the general public. CAs are expensive and time-consuming. This fact alone suggests that they should be considered scarce resources and used only when they can be targeted at relatively clearly defined democratic deficits. CAs also face political problems: they usurp political actors' control over policy, which creates disincentives to formally empower them. Even where they are formally empowered, as was the case in British Columbia and Ontario, it remains unclear as to how best translate CA proposals into broader public debate, particularly within contexts of political and media inattention or hostility. These experiences underscore the need for improved means of connecting CA deliberations with the general public. Improved communications strategies during CA deliberations as well as clear plans for dissemination of their recommendations should be part of any future CA design. That said, two key features – random selection combined with learning and deliberation over a long period of time – enable the CA model to address a remarkably wide spectrum of democratic deficit problems, and to do so within systems that generate deficits for quite different reasons.

NOTES

We thank John Gastil, whose presentation at the May 2008 University of British Columbia conference entitled "When Citizens Decide: The Challenges of Large-Scale Public Engagement" inspired us to expand our discussion of citizens assemblies as institutional supplements to include problems of legislative impasse, jurisdictional vacuum, and issue complexity.

1 Bruce Cain, Russell Dalton, and Susan Scarrow, eds., *New Forms of Democracy? The Reform and Transformation of Democratic Institutions* (Oxford: Oxford University Press, 2003); John Gastil and Peter Levine, eds., *The Deliberative Democracy Handbook: Strategies for Effective Civic Engagement in the Twenty-First Century* (San Francisco: Jossey-Bass, 2005); Graham Smith, "Beyond the Ballot: 57 Democratic Innovations from around the World," (London: The Power Inquiry, 2005); Graham Smith, *Democratic Innovations: Designing Institutions for Citizen Participation*

(Cambridge, UK: Cambridge University Press, 2009); Archon Fung, "Democratizing the Policy Process," in *The Oxford Handbook of Public Policy*, ed. Robert Goodin, Michael Moran, and Martin Rein (Oxford: Oxford University Press, 2006).

2. Mark E. Warren, "A Second Transformation of Democracy?" In Cain et al., *New Forms of Democracy?*, 223-49.
3. Fung, "Democratizing the Policy Process"; John Gastil, *Political Communication and Deliberation* (Los Angeles: Sage, 2008); Smith, *Democratic Innovations*.
4. Elisabeth Gidengil, André Blais, Neil Nevitte, and Richard Nadeau, *Citizens* (Vancouver: UBC Press, 2004); Susan J. Pharr and Robert D. Putnam, *Disaffected Democracies: What's Troubling the Trilateral Countries?* (Princeton: Princeton University Press, 2000).
5. Pharr and Putnam, *Disaffected Democracies*; Russell J. Dalton, *Democratic Challenges, Democratic Choices: The Erosion of Political Support in Advanced Industrial Democracies* (Oxford: Oxford University Press, 2004).
6. Neil Nevitte, *The Decline of Deference: Canadian Value Change in Cross-National Perspective* (Peterborough, ON: Broadview Press, 1996); Ron Inglehart, *Modernization and Postmodernization: Cultural, Economic and Political Change in 43 Societies* (Princeton: Princeton University Press, 1997); Jane Mansbridge, "Social and Cultural Causes of Dissatisfaction with US Government," in *Why People Don't Trust Government*, ed. Joseph S. Nye, Philip Zelikow, and David C. King (Cambridge, MA: Harvard University Press, 1997); Pippa Norris, ed., *Critical Citizens: Global Support for Democratic Governance* (Oxford: Oxford University Press, 1999); Dalton, *Democratic Challenges*.
7. John R. Hibbing and Elizabeth Theiss-Morse, *Stealth Democracy: Americans' Beliefs about How Government Should Work* (Cambridge/New York, UK/NY: Cambridge University Press, 2002).
8. Ibid.
9. Mark E. Warren, "Citizen Representatives," in *Designing Democratic Renewal*, ed. Mark E. Warren and Hilary Pearse (Cambridge, UK: Cambridge University Press, 2008).
10. Donald Savoie, *Governing from the Centre: The Concentration of Power in Canadian Politics* (Toronto: University of Toronto Press, 1999). See White (Chapter 10, this volume) for a review and refinement of this thesis.
11. Theda Skocpol, "Advocates Without Members: The Recent Transformation of American Civic Life," in *Civic Engagement in American Democracy*, ed. Theda Skocpol and Morris P. Fiorina (Washington, DC/New York: Brookings Institution Press/Russell Sage Foundation, 1999); Theda Skocpol and Morris P. Fiorina, "Making Sense of the Civic Engagement Debate," in Skocpol and Fiorina, *Civic Engagement in American Democracy*.
12. George Tsebelis, *Veto Players: How Political Institutions Work* (Princeton: Princeton University Press, 1995).
13. Mark E. Warren, "A Second Transformation of Democracy?," in *New Forms of Democracy? The Reform and Transformation of Democratic Institutions*, ed. Bruce Cain, Russell Dalton, and Susan Scarrow (Oxford, UK: Oxford University Press, 2003).

14 Richard Johnston, André Blais, Elisabeth Gidengil, and Neil Nevitte, *The Challenge of Direct Democracy: The 1992 Canadian Referendum* (Montreal and Kingston: McGill-Queen's University Press, 1996).
15 Shaun Bowler and Todd Donovan, *Demanding Choices: Opinion, Voting, and Direct Democracy* (Ann Arbor: University of Michigan Press, 1998).
16 Warren, "Citizen Representatives."
17 Some observers view the referendum defeats in British Columbia and Ontario as evidence of the failure of the Citizens' Assembly model. We view these defeats as failures of the referendum processes associated with these particular cases – through a high threshold for success and relatively low public information and discussion of the proposal. Experience elsewhere (such as New Zealand) suggests that publics who are provided with ample time and resources to learn about and discuss proposals for electoral reform may endorse them in a referendum process. See J.H. Nagel, "What Political Scientists Can Learn from the 1993 Electoral Reform in New Zealand," *PS: Political Science and Politics* 27, 3 (1994): 525-29.
18 Archon Fung and Erik Olin Wright, eds., *Deepening Democracy: Institutional Innovations in Empowered Participatory Governance*, vol. 4, The Real Utopias Project (New York, NY: Verso, 2003).
19 James Fishkin, *The Voice of the People: Public Opinion and Democracy* (New Haven: Yale University Press, 1995); Robert C. Luskin, James S. Fishkin, and Roger Jowell, "Considered Opinions: Deliberative Polling in Britain," *British Journal of Political Science* 32, 3 (2002): 455-87.
20 Mark E. Warren and Hilary Pearse, eds., *Designing Deliberative Democracy: The British Columbia Citizens' Assembly* (Cambridge, UK: Cambridge University Press, 2008); Michael Rabinder James, "Descriptive Representation in the British Columbia Citizens' Assembly," in Warren and Pearse, *Designing Deliberative Democracy*.
21 Warren and Pearse, *Designing Deliberative Democracy*.
22 Fung and Wright, *Deepening Democracy*; Archon Fung, *Empowered Participation: Reinventing Urban Democracy* (Princeton, NJ: Princeton University Press, 2004); Gianpaolo Baiocchi, *Militants and Citizens: The Politics of Participatory Democracy in Porto Allegre* (Palo Alto, CA: Stanford University Press, 2005).
23 James, "Descriptive Representation."
24 Hilary Pearse, "Institutional Design and Citizen Deliberation," in Warren and Pearse, *Designing Deliberative Democracy*.
25 André Blais, R. Kenneth Carty, and Patrick Fournier, "Do Citizens' Assemblies Make Reasoned Choices?," in *Designing Deliberative Democracy*, ed. Mark E. Warren and Hilary Pearse (Cambridge, UK: Cambridge University Press, 2008).
26 Ibid.; Pearse, "Institutional Design and Citizen Deliberation."
27 Joyce Rothschild-Whitt, "The Collectivist Organization: An Alternative to Rational-Bureaucratic Action," *American Sociological Review* 44, 4 (1979): 509-27; Anna Snyder, "Critiquing Consensus: An Analysis of Process Designed for Non-Governmental Collaboration," *Research in Social Movements, Conflicts and Change* 24 (2003): 31-60.
28 Jane Mansbridge, *Beyond Adversary Democracy*, 2nd ed. (Chicago: University of Chicago Press, 1983).

29. Alison Kadlec and Will Friedman, "Deliberative Democracy and the Problem of Power," *Journal of Public Deliberation* 3, 1 (2007): Article 8.
30. Roger Fisher, William Ury, and Bruce Patton, *Getting to Yes: Negotiating Agreement without Giving In*, 2nd ed. (New York: Penguin Books, 1991).
31. Amy Lang, "Agenda-Setting in Deliberative Forums: Expert Influence and Citizen Autonomy in the BC Citizens' Assembly," in *Designing Democratic Renewal*, ed. Mark E. Warren and Hilary Pearse (Cambridge, UK: Cambridge University Press, 2008).
32. Amy Lang, "But Is It For Real? The British Columbia Citizens' Assembly as a Model of State-Sponsored Citizen Empowerment," *Politics and Society* 35, 1 (2007): 35-70.
33. Walter Dean Burnham, *Critical Elections and the Mainsprings of American Politics* (New York: W. W. Norton, 1970).
34. Fred Cutler and Richard Johnston, with R. Ken Carty, André Blais, and Patrick Fournier, "Deliberation, Information and Trust: The British Columbia Citizens' Assembly as Agenda Setter," in *Designing Democratic Renewal*, ed. Mark E. Warren and Hilary Pearse (Cambridge, UK: Cambridge University Press, 2008).
35. Ibid.
36. Warren and Pearse, *Designing Deliberative Democracy*; Cutler et al., "Deliberation"; Michael K. Mackenzie and Mark E. Warren, "Two Trust-Based Uses of Minipublics in Democratic Systems," in *Deliberative Systems*, ed. Jane Mansbridge and John Parkinson (Cambridge, UK: Cambridge University Press, 2012).
37. John Ferejohn, "Conclusion: The Citizens' Assembly Model," in *Designing Deliberative Democracy*, ed. Mark E. Warren and Hilary Pearse (Cambridge, UK: Cambridge University Press, 2008).
38. Ned Crosby and Doug Nethercut, "Citizens Juries: Creating a Trustworthy Voice of the People," in *The Deliberative Democracy Handbook*, ed. John Gastil and Peter Levine (San Francisco, CA: John Wiley and Sons, 2005).
39. John Gastil and Katie Knobloch, "Evaluation Report to the Oregon State Legislature on the 2010 Oregon Citizens' Initiative Review." Unpublished report, University of Washington, Seattle, WA. Viewed online 13 June 2011 at http://faculty.washington.edu/.

14 Reflections on the Democratic Deficit in Canada and the United States

SIMONE CHAMBERS AND PATTI TAMARA LENARD

What then can we conclude from the studies contained in this volume? Four questions that come to mind are these: Is there a democratic deficit? How serious is it? What insight into the democratic deficit can be gained by studying Canada and the United States from a comparative perspective? What can we do about it? Not surprisingly, *Imperfect Democracies* does not offer simple answers to any of these questions. Yet the debates raised by the contributors suggest that valuable insights can be gained by comparing the meaning and practice of democracy in two neighbours characterized by distinctive political systems but with a common commitment to liberal democratic values. These four initial questions serve to frame some broad lessons provided by the preceding fourteen chapters. We conclude that: (1) there is a deficit, (2) it is bad enough to warrant serious concern, (3) comparison sharpens the analytic tools used to identify the sources of the deficit, and (4) reducing the deficit calls for reimagining and reinvigorating the relationship between citizen and government.

A Question of Perspective: Deficit According to Whom?

As the introductory chapters to *Imperfect Democracies* observe, it is impossible to deny that citizens of both Canada and the United States express dissatisfaction with key aspects of democratic rule. Surveys in both countries point to a widespread belief that political actors are not responsive to citizens' needs but, rather, are beholden to special interests; that there are no effective mechanisms by which political actors are held accountable; and that citizens have little or no influence on the political process. Although low and dropping voting turnout is almost always lumped in with, and interpreted as an indicator of, a democratic deficit, subjective opinion rather than objective behaviour is the primary evidence of democratic deficit.

The data presented in the early chapters suggest two quite different stories as possible explanations for citizen discontent. While there may be elements of truth in both stories, the one that is emphasized will make a significant difference when it comes to the assessment of democratic weaknesses and proposed remedies to them. In the first story, the source of the "citizen-level" democratic deficit reflects a failure of democratic institutions to live up to their potential. This story presses us to look at the ways in which political institutions and actors have failed to be responsive and accountable to citizens. Here, the assumption is that citizens' perceptions reflect a genuine diminishing of institutional and elite responsiveness and accountability. This interpretation of the data would naturally spur studies that attempt to measure institutional decline or failure, independent of citizens' perceptions. If institutional weakness is a central cause of citizen dissatisfaction, we have good reason to consider reforming democratic institutions as a way to decrease the democratic deficit.

The second story attributes high levels of dissatisfaction to rising (or changing) expectations rather than to diminishing performance. In this story, citizens may be dissatisfied because they expect more of their democratic institutions; they may, as a result of increased understanding of the workings of democratic institutions, take an increasingly "critical" attitude towards them and respond by demanding more from them.[1] If citizens have set the bar higher – for example, by demanding greater responsiveness or opportunities to participate – then we might assess the democratic deficit differently. Indeed, we may well conclude that democracy is, in an important sense, getting stronger rather than weaker. We might conclude that, historically, citizens were unable or unwilling to pay close attention to the quality of democratic governance (perhaps in part as a result of lower levels of education) or simply that they were too preoccupied with their private lives to do so, whereas citizens in contemporary democracies are more able and willing to attend to democratic politics. This additional attention may have generated widespread dissatisfaction with democratic politics as it is presently practised. Indeed, Neil Nevitte and Stephen White's data suggest that there is some truth to this observation: at present, those who participate actively in politics are more likely to report dissatisfaction in the political system than are those who generally abstain from political participation. This suggests the possibility that attempts to improve political access (see below), with the aim of improving political voice, will paradoxically appear to generate political dissatisfaction.

It may equally be the case that changing citizen attitudes can be traced to broad cultural shifts in the ideals of democracy. For example, over the last twenty years, the public may have moved from a general Burkean model of political representation, which allows for and encourages a deferential relationship between elites and citizens, to a more consultative model in which elites are expected to check in with, and respond to, citizens rather than simply look out for their best interests at a certain degree of remove. Whether it is rising expectations, or merely shifting expectations, we may have reason to celebrate the democratic deficit as an indication of an engaged and critical public. The very fact that citizens register the existence of a democratic deficit, and voice their concern about it, suggests that they have come to think of themselves as able to work towards its elimination. This explanation may appear to conflict with turnout data, which, as we observed, indicate that fewer and fewer Canadians and Americans are turning out to the polls. Rather than focus on voter turnout, those who focus on higher expectations often point to increases in unconventional modes of political activism, including protests, letter-writing campaigns, and online forms of political participation as indicators of political engagement.

Measuring, Comparing, and Reducing the Deficit

As the introduction and first chapter of *Imperfect Democracies* notes, many of the cross-national indices and diagnostic tools used to conduct large-scale comparisons of democratic performance are not very helpful for studies of the democratic deficit in Canada and the United States. Pippa Norris scans the best known methods we have for evaluating the quality of democratic practice – methods that focus on the existence and functioning of democratic institutions – and expresses scepticism with respect to the value of these indices in the Canadian and American cases. Canada and the United States both score highly and thus appear nearly indistinguishable from each other and from other advanced democracies. These large cross-national studies deploy indicators of democratic health that are, after all, rather blunt instruments.

In general, Norris's conclusions suggest, the more global and inclusive the diagnostic tool, the more difficult it is to determine solutions to identified problems. A failure to hold regular, let alone fair, elections is pretty good evidence that democracy is failing, but it tells us nothing about how to revive elections in any particular case. Context is thus essential to determining what kinds of solutions will be effective in a given political environment. As David Beetham suggests: "The deeper one's analysis of an individual country, the more it is the specific features of that country's institutions, political culture, and historical evolution that assume importance in assessing its democratic condition and explaining differences in people's views about it."[2] In other words, two countries can suffer from a similar deficit, but additional contextual considerations may suggest vastly different remedies. This complicates the process of measuring, comparing, and reducing the democratic deficit. It does not mean, however, that, as we move from large studies to country-specific solutions, comparison becomes less relevant or useful; rather, comparative analysis highlights the importance of measuring democracy, at both the institutional and attitudinal levels, as well as of catering democratic reforms to what these evaluations reveal.

Take, for example, the differences between the central objections to democracy as it is practised in Canada as compared to the United States. As Robert Boatright observes, Americans conceive campaign contributions to be an essential aspect of political participation in their democratic system (he points to the widespread celebration of Barack Obama's success in raising money from small-scale donors). Yet permitting wealthier Americans to donate as much as they might like can drown out the voices of less wealthy Americans, who also try to influence political actors and policies via contributing to specific campaigns. The recent Supreme Court decision, permitting corporations to donate extensively to election campaigns, only serves to exacerbate this concern. On the other hand, Canadians are critical, as David Docherty observes, of the ways in which the Westminster system produces inadequately representative government. In other words, whereas Americans express concern with respect to *access* to the political system, Canadians express concern with respect to the *results* of the democratic process. Both these complaints reflect worries about the fundamental equality that underpins democratic practice; however, Canadians and Americans worry about equality violations at different points in the democratic process. The distinctive sources of dissatisfaction, therefore, suggest the importance of country-specific reforms. And the reform proposals considered over the course of this volume reveal the importance of country-specific solutions to the democratic deficit.

Democratic Reform versus Democratic Innovation

There are two very general approaches to remedies for the democratic deficit. One focuses on improving existing institutions, while the other seeks out new and innovative institutional forms to supplement existing institutions. The natural place to begin if interested in reforming existing institutions is with elections, especially with voting. Michael McDonald's chapter highlights the two-step voting process in the United States: citizens must formally register before they are permitted to vote (whereas in most countries, including Canada, this "registration" is carried out by the government). Thus, resolving the democratic deficit, in so far as it is located in the large number of Americans who do not vote, focuses not only on enticing Americans to vote but also on facilitating voter registration in the first place. McDonald concludes his chapter by offering several modifications to the registration procedure (e.g., same-day voter registration) and suggests that, although these reforms may not radically increase the proportion of Americans who participate in politics, they highlight the existence of arenas in which the complex American electoral system is amenable to democracy-enhancing changes. The existence of these arenas can serve as opportunities to experiment with democratic change. It may be that Canadians are critical of the American system's decentralization and the consequent large variation in rules across states and local jurisdictions; however, McDonald treats this variation as an opportunity to experiment with reforms, without having to initiate national-level electoral change. Certainly, some of these "minor" shifts in registration and voting procedure are more likely to find local- and state-level support than are more radical shifts in American democratic structures. While there is always talk about getting rid of the Electoral College and one can even hear some wishful talk about proportional representation, the American political and constitutional context makes such national-level reforms very difficult.

The challenges of reforming democratic procedures are also apparent in Canada, as John Courtney observes in his account of the very long history of electoral reform or, rather, attempts at electoral reform in Canada. As McDonald's and Courtney's chapters both suggest, electoral reform stands at the centre of the two views of the democratic deficit mentioned earlier: one focusing on citizen attitudes and the other focusing on the democratic credentials of political institutions. On the first view, the case for electoral reform is championed because it will bring citizens to the polls. On the second view, electoral reform is championed because it will make democratic institutions more representative. Proposals for electoral reform are thus championed for reducing both possible sources of the democratic deficit: the hope is that an electoral process that is widely believed to produce a representative outcome will encourage citizens to return to the polling booth. However, as there is still no single, clear, or agreed-upon answer to the question "why don't people vote?" the argument that electoral reform will have a significant effect on voting levels is perhaps more wishful thinking than well-founded hypothesis. With regard to the democratic deficit, it is much more sensible to defend electoral reform as directly enhancing some agreed-upon democratic value (e.g., representativeness or equality) even if it does not bring citizens flocking to the polls.

The contributors to *Imperfect Democracies* are careful to indicate the relationship between particular sources of democratic dissatisfaction and the ways in which proposed reforms are able to offer resolution. First, we might aim, for example, to reform democratic institutions in terms of improving the *accountability* of political actors. Consider here the debates concerning the perceived absence of accountability of the executive in both Canada and the United States. Both Graham White and Daniel Tichenor ask us to consider whether reforms to the executive are essential to generating genuine accountability of the most powerful office in both democracies. For White, there are reasons to believe that the centralization of power in the Canadian executive, and the secrecy associated with the decisions made therein, are exaggerated. Tichenor concurs with respect to the American case and offers many reasons to believe that the presidential prerogative, deployed most publicly during wartime, is subject to checks and balances that are frequently under-appreciated. These two chapters raise some very interesting questions about the relationship between democracy and executive power. They both take as their starting point the assumption that checks and balances, institutional accountability, and transparency are the hallmarks of strong democratic limits on the executive. They reject the populist view that sees democracy embedded within a more direct relationship between the executive and the electorate. This populist view is especially strong in the United States, where presidents are directly elected, but it is certainly not absent in Canada. For example, prime ministers' polling numbers often determine what they will do, and Stephen Harper's 2008 election campaign made an explicit appeal to voters, as though they were responsible for directly electing the prime minister.

For White and Tichenor popular mandates do not promote and protect democracy; instead, institutional safeguards play that role. Yet popular mandates and institutional safeguards are connected. Transparency is especially important in both the Canadian and American systems to ensure that citizens – both those who did and those who did not vote for the incumbent – are able to assess the exercise of executive power and call to account those who move in unmandated, or even unconstitutional, directions. The comparison of the two systems also draws our attention to the ways in which executive power naturally expands rather than contracts. White and Tichenor agree that powerful executives do not in and of themselves create a democratic deficit, even as they both highlight the need for vigilance against the natural tug of efficacy over accountability.

Reforming existing institutions is an essential ingredient in any plan to tackle the democratic deficit, but designing new institutions and finding new ways to invigorate the system is also a strategy that plays out in this debate. Scholars are increasingly focusing on studying and designing new forms, venues, and institutions of citizen participation. Old-fashioned voting is still important, and basic questions about who is entitled to vote are not fully resolved, as Patti Tamara Lenard and Daniel Munro suggest. Non-citizen permanent residents can remain disenfranchised for an extended period of time, and Lenard and Munro marshal arguments in favour of extending them at least the municipal vote. Yet voting is by no means the only way that citizens can become politically active. Some scholars suggest that we ought to move towards generating environments in which citizens can play a more significant role in democratic politics. The deficit, they imply, is a direct result of under-emphasizing the ways in which citizens can be more directly involved in political activity, indeed in political decision making. This strategy can be seen, for example, in attempts to investigate the democratic potential of electronic media, including internet voting, political blogging, tweeting representatives, and much more. The democratic deficit is particularly apparent in young citizens who are entering (or failing to enter) the democratic sphere for the first time. For this group, relatively minor reforms to traditional democratic institutions may not be enough to give them the sense of political efficacy necessary to reduce the democratic deficit.

Perhaps the most successful and powerful democratic innovations of the last fifteen years are represented by attempts to implement deliberative forms of democracy, represented in this volume in the chapters by Mark Warren and Amy Lang, as well as by Ethan Leib and David Ponet. In both Canada and the United States, deliberative initiatives and experiments are flourishing across the political perspective at all levels, with the exception of the national level. Despite some very innovative suggestions for national-level deliberation, for example, a deliberation day proposed by Bruce Ackerman and James Fishkin and a national-level deliberative assembly proposed by Ethan Leib, most actual experiments in deliberative democracy can be found at the subnational level. Perhaps uniquely, attempts to incorporate deliberative institutions – in the form of citizen juries, citizen assemblies (CA), participatory budgeting, or deliberative polls – offer us *new* institutions that "supplement," in Amy Lang and Mark Warren's formulation, existing representative democratic institutions. These new institutions are intended to improve inclusiveness and representativeness, as well as the perception of inadequate accountability, by generating new environments within which citizens can actively participate in meaningful politics. Most important, the policy choices and political decisions produced via participation in these institutions reflect citizens' informed opinions and preferences.

Reform and innovation are clearly responses to the democratic deficit. Yet the rhetorical *claim* to be pursuing reform and innovation is also a frequent response to that deficit. Both Canada and the United States have seen significant public acknowledgment that there is a democratic deficit that must be addressed. In Canada, every province has launched some form of democratic renewal initiative, and the federal government has had a minister in charge of democratic renewal since 2003. On his first day in office Barack Obama issued an open government directive that called on all administrative agencies to address its three pillars: transparency, participation, and collaboration. The claim to be concerned with democratic renewal is democratically popular, and Obama's apparent capacity to engage citizens in politics was heralded as a sign of his genuine commitment to democratic reinvigoration in the United States. Yet, just as there is an important line between focus group research and genuine democratic consultation, so, too, there is an important line between identifying a policy area and following through on any actual policy initiative. By the time he stood for re-election in 2012, talk of democratic renewal was nearly absent from the American administration's talking points. In Canada, there are no plans to mount another citizens' assembly, despite scholarly and popular enthusiasm for these types of democratic innovation. There is, it seems, a real risk that government-sponsored democratic renewal might itself suffer from a democratic deficit.

Democratic Vote and Democratic Voice

Because we think that deliberative democracy is a new and potentially productive response to the democratic deficit, in this section we take up the issues that surround these innovative experiments in more detail. The concern to improve inclusiveness, and to devise institutions capable of doing so, occupies both democratic theorists and practitioners. While formally complete, the first wave of democratization, in which the franchise was extended to include every competent adult, regardless of gender, race, or wealth, has not always produced the substantive inclusiveness for which one might have hoped. Not only are there lingering questions with respect to who gets the vote, as can be seen in Lenard and Munro's discussion of new immigrants, as well as serious questions about the fairness of the vote (see McDonald's chapter), but the power and effectiveness of the vote is an ongoing and open question as well. From social choice arguments regarding the irrationality of voting to institutionalist arguments downplaying (if not completely sidelining) the median voter in favour of institutional constraints as the explanatory variable in elite policy choice,[3] the one-person-one-vote model of citizen empowerment has come under attack from many sides. These lingering questions have led to a move to consider more deeply the role, beyond the vote, that citizens can and should play in democratic communities. Theorists of deliberative democracy have adopted a more reflective attitude towards the relationship between democratic citizens and the state that governs them, an attitude that has propelled a strong interest in identifying when we can say that citizens have not simply a right to vote but also a right to have their voice heard in a significant way.

It is the tension between vote and voice – the frequency with which one's vote does not translate into genuine political influence – that motivates many deliberative democrats to offer new institutional mechanisms by which to increase the "voice" of democratic citizens in the political sphere. The institutional innovations suggested by deliberative democrats in general – as defended by Leib and Ponet's assessment of the lessons we might learn from attending to the details of "representation" in American juries as well as by Lang and Warren's specific assessment of the CAs in British Columbia and Ontario – are intended to improve the voice of citizens in their democratic community.

Deliberative democracy in general and CAs in particular are not meant to undermine or replace the representative democratic system; rather, they add another layer to traditional forms of representative democracy. If they are well designed, they can enhance the democratic legitimacy of the system.

As a self-consciously deliberative institution, the CA was an innovative addition to Canadian democracy in two senses. First, it offered an inventive solution to an endemic problem: finding a democratic way in which to change the rules of democracy. In general, electoral reform is difficult; the elected representatives who are empowered to change the rules are also stakeholders in the process. The most common solution to the problem is the appointment of a blue-ribbon panel of experts. However, these panels often have little or no perceived democratic legitimacy among citizens, beyond the formal legitimacy of being constituted and empowered by a democratic authority. The CAs were able to combine democratic credentials with a claim to impartiality that seemed exactly right for the question at hand. Rather than elites appointed by elites, the assemblies were drawn from random samples of the electorate and could be said to represent ordinary citizens from all walks of life.[4] The CA, as developed in both Ontario and British Columbia, were impartial in the sense that those participating had no personal stake in the outcome. The CAs were innovative in a second sense as well. They revealed that carefully designed institutions can indeed involve citizens in complex political issues and that the experience of participation can breed an interest, and willingness to participate further, in politics.

In what sense are the Canadian experiences with the CAs successfully responding to the democratic deficit? We believe that, from an institutional as well as from a citizen perspective, they enhanced the quality of democracy, despite the fact that the recommendations of both assemblies failed to be ratified in a referendum. They were successful in three respects. First, there is good evidence that citizens, once they had information about the assemblies, trusted them; here, therefore, we can see one dimension of the democratic deficit (i.e., distrust of decision-making institutions and the individuals who control them) shrinking. For those citizens who knew something about the assembly the perception was positive: as Lang and Warren observe, citizens generally believed that assembly members had done a good job in representing their interests and, therefore, thought of the CA itself as trustworthy. Ultimately, the problem was not one of extending trust (or not) but, rather, that too few citizens knew about the CA to begin with. As Lang and Warren suggest, therefore, a significant challenge posed by CA models of political decision making in general "lies in the transfer of knowledge developed within the mini-public of the CA into the broader public, not in its capacity to produce publicly acceptable proposals."[5]

The second dimension along which we can say that the initiative successfully reduced the deficit concerns the subjective attitudes of participants. The CA experience had a profound effect on citizen participants. It generated among those who participated a genuine sense that their agency mattered.[6] This sense of agency was reflected in the large number of assembly members, for example, who actively participated in the dissemination of information about the proposal, even after their formal role was complete. Moreover, assembly members' conception of themselves as empowered to influence Canadian political life did not seem to depend on whether the proposal was adopted by referendum; rather, participants reported an increased sense of themselves as political actors more generally – that is, as more generally capable of making their voice heard in a significant way. Almost all of them expressed an interest in continuing to participate actively in politics. The self-reported sense of political efficacy and commitment to further political activism on the part of assembly members reinforces earlier scholarship that suggests that citizens' face-to-face experience with political actors (e.g., in the form of politicians who go door-to-door soliciting votes and engaging citizens in political discussion or members of NGOs who aim to "get-out-the-vote" by going door-to-door) is positively correlated with their turning out to vote.

The final dimension along which we can say that the CA was a success involves the fact that the quality of deliberation, both from a substantive and a procedural perspective, was very high. Comparing the debate within the CAs to, for example, parliamentary debates or debates in the House of Representatives, one cannot help but be impressed with the serious, respectful, and knowledgeable ways in which citizens pursued and struggled with difficult problems. As an institution of democratic deliberation, the CA can only receive high marks.

In sum, we can see that CAs and similar initiatives serve to enrich democracy along a number of dimensions. It is not, however, a cure-all, and, in certain respects, it falls very short of a full response to the democratic deficit. Most obvious is that only a very small number of citizens (160 in British Columbia and 103 in Ontario) participated in these forums. Thus, although these citizens emerged from the experience with an invigorated sense of democratic efficacy and potential, they are not even a drop in the bucket when it comes to the general problem of citizen disappointment with democratic institutions. In any case, the sense of empowerment experienced by the participants was a side benefit, rather than the primary goal, of the experiment. Indeed, it would have been an awful lot of money to spend to make 263 citizens feel good about democracy. As one commentator noted, the CA model is the "Rolls Royce" of democratic innovation.[7]

While it can perhaps give us a window into what sorts of political initiatives are needed to enhance the sense of efficacy on the part of citizens, it seems clear that any initiative that attempts to include large numbers of citizens will have to look very different than the CA. As scholars concerned with the democratic deficit, we need to pay attention to which aspect of the deficit can be remedied by institutional innovation of the kind presented by the CA model. As instantiated in the Canadian case, CAs appeared to generate a sense of agency among participants, and citizens familiar with the institution generally trusted its proposals. Moreover, it seems that the CA model can produce democratically legitimate proposals for change.

Another question is whether CAs are appropriate in other policy areas. Electoral reform does appear to be a special case requiring extraordinary procedures. Yet deliberative mechanisms, some of which are modelled on CAs, feature among a growing number of initiatives designed to include citizens in political decision processes both big and small. The proposed, and implemented, deliberative institutions vary considerably in their structure in order to meet particular challenges and to answer specific questions.[8] So the CA may not suit all occasions, and other forms of deliberative consultation or polling may prove to be more effective in different political and social environments. The central insight of deliberative democracy – that citizens can and do contribute in productive ways to the resolution of political dilemmas – is increasingly being recognized.

Conclusion

What conclusion can we draw from this study? First and most obvious, no democracy is perfect. Perfection escapes us for many reasons, from the banal observation that all human endeavours are fallible to the more methodological observation that there are so many competing indicators of success that it is hard to know, or agree upon, what counts as success. Yet the title of this book and the chapters contained within it do not reflect the limitations of human reason and social science so much as they reflect the aspiration to do better. As the title implies and as the introduction notes, we in stable democracies should not be resting on our laurels. There is still much work to do, and the division between stable and transitional, old and new, and even authoritarian and democratic regimes is breaking down in all sorts of ways.[9] Thus, to describe Canadian and American democracies as "imperfect" points us to the *process* of perfecting, a process that is not likely to reach a conclusion.

The lens through which all the contributors view the imperfections of democracy is the "democratic deficit" – a metaphor that implies that we need to make up a shortfall, that we need to find the resources and human and social capital to move forward with our democratic project. While apt, this metaphor can be misleading if it implies that we can, or ought to, balance the books. Whether the deficit is understood, on the one hand, as institutions that fall short of democratic ideals or, on the other, as institutions that fall short of citizen expectations, it would be wrong-headed to think that either shortfall could (or indeed should) ever be fully made up. It is not an entirely bad thing if our ideals and expectations outrun our institutions. Yet, at certain points, the shortfall threatens bankruptcy, and we need to ask whether we have reached that point. The chapters in *Imperfect Democracies* tell us that so-called stable democracies are riddled with fault lines (to switch from an economic to a seismic metaphor). The democratic deficit is real, and while it does not yet signal system failure, it at least signals the need to study, understand, and remedy the multiple and complex ways our democratic institutions can and do fall short.

Imperfect Democracies takes up the question of democratic deficit in a comparative perspective by bringing together work on Canada and the United States. Thus, to the question "is there a deficit?" we can add the natural follow-up, "who is doing better?" Indeed, the question "who is doing better?" is deeply embedded in the field of comparative democratic studies. It is reflected in a driving interest to measure democracy and freedom. As we noted earlier, Norris's contribution to this volume gives a clear picture of many of the instruments at our disposal. We love to rank, and sometimes ranking can be very helpful. However, in this case ranking does not provide us with any meaningful insight: comparing Canada and the United States requires a more substantive approach to evaluating democracy than most global indices can offer. Any detailed and comprehensive comparison will take up multiple and sometimes cross-cutting lines of analysis, as the contributors to this volume demonstrate.

In sum, the contributions to *Imperfect Democracies* together raise important questions that ought to guide future research into the nature of democratic dissatisfaction and the ways in which it can be mitigated. It seems clear that we need to think more about the general conditions (across industrialized democracies) that appear to correlate with democratic dissatisfaction and the ways in which specific countries possess the institutional capacities (whether the goal is to reform existing institutions or to generate new ones) to resolve this dissatisfaction. Country-specific comparisons of the type carried out by the contributors to this volume reveal widespread dissatisfaction in both Canada and the United States, despite the very large differences in legislative and executive institutions and despite considerable differences in the electoral systems. Institutional explanations are insufficient to account for the democratic deficit, and this is, in itself, an important observation. Moreover, while the comparisons carried out in *Imperfect Democracies* reveal a range of possible solutions to the democratic deficit, they also suggest that solutions in one country will not translate automatically to solutions in another. For example, Canada twice introduced a CA to address the democratic deficit in electoral reform, whereas attempts to do the same in the United States have not met with much enthusiasm. A ballot initiative in California to construct a citizen redistricting commission found support from just over 50 percent of voters in 2008 but remains controversial, and was nearly overturned in the 2010 elections. Clearly, more work must be done to assess where, and when, institutional solutions translate effectively from one environment to another. Additionally, this research must correlate with evaluations of the specific source of dissatisfaction. While both Canada and the United States face sinking levels of trust in political elites, the variations in institutional structure and political culture (and therefore in political hurdles to democratic reform) suggest that we need to be careful in proposing "cross-national" solutions. There is no simple solution, it seems clear, but the comparative work – with a dual focus on institutional and normative questions – offers important insights that are worth further exploration.

NOTES

1 Pippa Norris, ed., *Critical Citizens: Global Support for Democratic Governance* (Oxford: Oxford University Press, 1999).
2 David Beetham, Chapter 3, this volume, 88.
3 Paul Pierson, *Politics in Time: History, Institutions, and Social Analysis* (Princeton: Princeton University Press, 2004); William H. Riker, *Liberalism against Populism: A Confrontation between the Theory of Democracy and the Theory of Social Choice* (San Francisco: W.H. Freeman, 1982).
4 For more on the representativeness of the citizens' assembly model, see Lang and Warren (Chapter 13, this volume) as well as the contributions to Mark E. Warren and Hilary Pearse, eds., *Designing Deliberative Democracy: The British Columbia Citizens' Assembly* (Cambridge, UK: Cambridge University Press, 2008).
5 Lang and Warren, Chapter 13, this volume, 307.

6 The suggestion to consider the benefits of the citizens' assembly (as well as other institutional innovations intended to enrich the practice of democracy) from an institutional and a citizen perspective is Jane Mansbridge's.
7 James Snider made this observation in his concluding comments to the workshop that gave rise to this volume.
8 For a recent review of attempts to implement deliberative democracy in practice, as well as the principles that underpin deliberative democratic efforts, see Simone Chambers, "Deliberative Democratic Theory," *Annual Review of Political Science* 6 (2003): 307-26.
9 Robert A. Pastor, "Improving the US Electoral System: Lessons from Canada and Mexico," *Election Law Journal* 3, 3 (2004): 584-93.

Contributors

David Beetham is Professor Emeritus, University of Leeds, Visiting Fellow, Human Rights Centre, University of Essex, and Associate Director, Democratic Audit. His current research and publications are in the fields of political legitimacy, democracy assessment, and the relation between democracy and human rights.

Robert G. Boatright is Associate Professor of Political Science at Clark University. He is the author of *Interest Groups and Campaign Finance Reform in the United States and Canada* (2011) and he is currently completing a book on congressional primary challenges.

Simone Chambers is Professor of Political Science at the University of Toronto. Her primary areas of scholarship include political philosophy, ethics, democratic theory, constitutionalism, and citizen participation.

John C. Courtney is Senior Policy Fellow of the Johnson-Shoyama Graduate School of Public Policy and Professor Emeritus of Political Science at the University of Saskatchewan. A former President of the Canadian Political Science Association, his research interests include Canadian parties, elections, leadership selection, and electoral boundary readjustments.

David C. Docherty is President of Mount Royal University in Calgary. He holds a PhD from the University of Toronto and spent seventeen years in various teaching and administrative capacities at Wilfrid Laurier University. His two primary areas of research interest are political careers and the Canadian parliamentary process.

Amy Lang is a policy consultant specializing in citizen engagement for the City of Toronto. Prior to joining the City, Amy completed her dissertation and postdoctoral fellowship research evaluating the Citizens' Assemblies on Electoral Reform in British Columbia and Ontario. Her research has been published in *Politics & Society* and several edited volumes.

Ethan J. Leib is Professor of Law at Fordham Law School. He is a political theorist and lawyer with interests in deliberative democracy, institutional design, and the jury. His latest book is *Friend v. Friend: The Transformation of Friendship and What the Law Has to Do with It* (2011).

Patti Tamara Lenard is Assistant Professor of Applied Ethics at the Graduate School of Public and International Affairs at the University of Ottawa. She is the author of *Trust, Democracy and Multicultural Challenges* (2012).

Michael McDonald is Associate Professor of Government and Politics in the Department of Public and International Affairs at George Mason University and a Non-Resident Senior Fellow at the Brookings Institution.

Daniel Munro is a Principal Research Associate at the Conference Board of Canada and lecturer in the Graduate School of Public and International Affairs at the University of Ottawa. His research interests include innovation and education policy, institutional design, and the theory and practice of democratic citizenship.

Pippa Norris is the McGuire Lecturer in Comparative Politics at Harvard University and Laureate Fellow and Professor of Government and International Relations at the University of Sydney. Related publications include *Cosmopolitan Communications* (2009), *Democratic Deficit* (2010), and *Making Democratic Governance Work* (2012).

Neil Nevitte is a professor in the Department of Political Science and at the School of Public Policy and Governance at the University of Toronto. His research interest and publications are mainly in the areas of political participation and value change, and he is the principal investigator of the World Values Surveys (Canada) and past co-investigator of the Canadian Election Study.

David L. Ponet is a parliamentary specialist at UNICEF where he serves as the organization's point person for engagement with parliaments around the globe. He earned his BA in political philosophy from Yale University and his MA, MPhil, and PhD in political science from Columbia University.

Richard Simeon is Professor Emeritus of Political Science and Law, University of Toronto. Simeon's research and writing has focused on Canadian politics and public policy, with a special emphasis on federalism, the constitution, and intergovernmental relations. More recently, Simeon has explored broader issues in contemporary governance, both in Canada and comparatively. His current work focuses on federalism, democracy, and constitutionalism in divided societies.

Daniel J. Tichenor is the Philip H. Knight Professor of Social Science and Senior Faculty Fellow at the Wayne Morse Center of Law and Politics at the University of Oregon. He is the author of numerous publications on American political institutions, public policy, social movements, immigration, and citizenship.

Mark E. Warren teaches political theory at the University of British Columbia, where he holds the Harold and Dorrie Merilees Chair for the Study of Democracy. He is currently working on a project entitled *Participedia* (www.participedia.net), a website that catalogues, maps, and collects data on new democratic processes.

Graham White is Professor of Political Science at the University of Toronto, Mississauga. His principal research interests are Canadian legislatures, cabinets, and bureaucracies, especially at the provincial and territorial level, and the politics of the Canadian Arctic. He is a former President of the Canadian Political Science Association and is currently English-language co-editor of the *Canadian Journal of Political Science*.

Stephen E. White is a Post-doctoral Fellow on Diversity and Democratic Citizenship with the Centre for the Study of Democratic Citizenship at Concordia University. His research interests include Canadian and comparative public opinion, parties and elections, and immigrant political attitudes and behaviour.

Lisa Young is Professor of Political Science at the University of Calgary. Her research focuses primarily on Canadian political parties and election finance. She has authored/co-authored several journal articles and books, including *Rebuilding Canadian Party Politics* and *Advocacy Groups,* and co-edited *Money, Politics, and Democracy: Canada's Party Finance Reforms.*

Index

9/11 events: as peak of support for US government, 26, 34; as peak of trust in European governments, 43; and US president's prerogative powers, 206; and War on Terror, 207
501(c) organizations (US), 175
"527" organizations, 168, 171

Abramson, Jeffrey, 278, 281-82
accountability: citizens' assembly, 301, 306-7; Congress (US), 296, 297; deliberative or discursive, 284; of democratic institutions, 293; external, 284; House of Commons (Canada), 190-91, 199-200; indirect, and US jury system, 282-84; norms of, and representation theory, 273; Parliament (Canada), 190-95; populist view, as direct relationship between executive and electorate, 320-21; Presidency (US), no direct accountability to Congress, 192; Presidency (US), prerogative power as limit on democratic accountability, 204-22, 320; referendums, 301, 307; retrospective, in elections in Canadian political system, 306; trustee, 284; as weak in US political system, 306; Westminster cabinet-parliamentary system, 232, 295, 297
Accountability Act (Canada, 2006), 141
ACT. *See* America Coming Together (ACT)
advertising, effect on voter turnout, 143-45
AFL-CIO. *See* American Federation of Labor-Congress of Industrial Organizations (AFL-CIO)
African Americans, underrepresented in US Congress, 186
African Canadians, underrepresented in Canadian Parliament, 186
Almond, Gabriel, 27-28, 31
Amar, Akhil, 276
America Coming Together (ACT), 169

American Association of Retired Persons (AARP), 177
American Federation of Labor-Congress of Industrial Organizations (AFL-CIO): on BCRA effect on discussion of issues in election campaigns, 177; issue advocacy advertising by, 164; political financing, effects of BCRA on, 175; voter mobilization by, 169
American Immigration Voting Project, 248
American National Election Studies (ANES), 31, 32-35, 162
American Political Science Association, 200
Americans for Job Security, 170
Americans Working for Real Change. See The Coalition: Americans Working for Real Change
Aristotle, 281-82
Australia: citizen commitment to democracy, 59; citizen evaluation of democratic performance, 61, 63; dissatisfaction with democratic performance, country comparison, 69, 70
Austria, survey result of trust in government, 41, 42, 44, 45
Axworthy, Tom, 236
Ayers, Bill, 178

back-burner elections, 121-25
Baird, John, 238
Bakvis, Herman, 227
Ballard v. United States (US, 1946), 279
banks, survey of US citizen confidence in, 38-39
Barber, Benjamin, 272
Bauböck, Rainer, 255
Beetham, David, 318
Belgium, survey result of trust in government, 40, 41, 42, 43, 44, 45
Belz, Herman, 213

Benn, Pat, 307, 308
Bennett, W.A.C., 233
Beschloss, Michael, 206
Biddle, Francis, 218
Bipartisan Campaign Reform Act (BCRA) (US, 2002): campaign contributions, and issues of transparency and corruption, 174-75; changes in campaign financing, 165; goals of, 161-62; impact of, 170-78; and increase in person-to-person voter mobilization, 171-72, 175-76; lack of influence on competition in elections, 176-77; organized third-party advertising, effects on, 169-70, 171; political parties, effects on, 166-68, 171; and public discourse in elections, 177-78; reforms, and public sentiment about elections, 178
Blair, Tony, 85, 86
Bloc Québécois Party (Canada): federal election results, 122, 124; importance of public funding, 155; and multi-party system in Canada, 124, 193; regional support, 130
Boatright, Robert, 318
Booth, William James, 250
"bowling alone" thesis (Putnam), 121
Breaking the Bargain (Savoie), 227
Britain. See United Kingdom
British Columbia Citizens' Assembly. See citizens' assembly, BC
Brodie, Ian, 237, 238
Brown, Gordon, 85
Bryce, James, 229-30
Buckley v. Valeo (US, 1976), 163, 165
Burleson, Albert, 215
Bush, George H.W. (father), 206, 208
Bush, George W. (son): and citizen trust in US government, 34; election of, 103; expansion of presidential power, 206-7
business. See companies

Business Roundtable, 177
Business-Industry PAC, 170

Cabinets and First Ministers (White), 240, 243
California citizens' assembly, 270, 328
campaign financing. *See* political financing, Canada; political financing, US
Canada: citizenship application, wait period, 262; democracy, international ranking, 1, 7; democracy, progress in human rights, 230; democratic audit, 5-6; democratic deficit issues, 3, 120-21; multi-party system, 7. *See also* citizens, Canada; electoral system, Canada; names of political parties and politicians; Parliament (Canada); political financing, Canada; Prime Minister's Office (Canada); voting, Canada; Westminster cabinet-parliamentary system
Canada: An Actual Democracy (Bryce), 230
Canadian Alliance Party, 146
Canadian Charter of Rights and Freedoms (1982): and changes in electoral law, 140; no Canadian human rights codes prior to, 230; as restriction on government's scope for action, 233; and widening of franchise, 113, 117
Canadian Democratic Audit: and democratic deficit, 23; and election financing, 138-39; purpose, 5-6; ranking system, 7; role of backbenchers, 243
Carens, Joseph, 250
Carter, Jimmy, 206
Carter, John Franklin, 217
Chamber of Commerce (US), 170, 175
Charter of Rights and Freedoms (Canada, 1982). *See* Canadian Charter of Rights and Freedoms (1982)
Chinese, franchise in Canada, 113, 117
Chrétien, Jean, 188-89, 236
citizens: "citizen representatives," and reform of democratic deficit, 17-18; "critical citizens," and political engagement, 70-71; democratic institutions, dissatisfaction with, 1-2, 7-8, 9, 12, 53, 292-93; democratic institutions, increase in expectations of, 18-19, 316-17; demographic factors, and dissatisfaction with democratic performance, 67; elite and mass publics, divergence in views of democratic deficit, 79-80, 87; engagement institutions, to address democratic deficit, 291; non-citizen residents, voting restrictions as democratic deficit, 248-64; political leaders, decline of trust in, 2; political participation, decline in, 9, 10, 12, 29, 53; representation, and US jury selection, 269-85; "right" and "left" political leanings, and evaluation of democratic performance, 68; values, and expectations of democratic performance, 64-67; values, as factor in dissatisfaction with democratic performance, 68-73, 78-79; youth, and democratic deficit, 321. *See also* citizens' assembly (CA); citizens, Canada; citizens, US
citizens' assembly (CA): accountability, 301, 306-7, 308; Canada, no plans for future mounting of, 322; challenges of implementation, 311; deliberation, 301, 303-6, 308, 310, 325; and democratic deficits, potential for redressing, 291, 310; as democratic supplement, 299, 310, 323-26; inclusion, 301, 302-3, 308-10; institutional features, 291-92;

Index 337

international interest in, 270; lack of awareness of, by general public, 324; member near-random selection process, 302; members, near-random selection process, 300-1; model, applications of, 307-10; model, developed in BC, 299-300; participants, effect on, 325-26; problem-solving approach, 304-5; purpose, 300; and referendums, 307-9, 311; as representing public, not stakeholders, 300, 303, 309, 310; strengths, 299; trusted by informed citizens, 306, 307. *See also* citizens' assembly, BC; citizens' assembly, California; citizens' assembly, Ontario

citizens' assembly, BC: deliberation process, 299-303; as model for citizens' assembly, 299; recommendation of STV voting system, 128, 129, 303; referendum on electoral reform, 299, 302

citizens' assembly, California, 270, 328

citizens' assembly, Ontario, 305

citizens, Canada: civil service, decline of confidence in, 55; companies, decline of confidence in, 55; concern about inadequate political representation, 318; and country comparison of evaluation of democratic performance, 69-70, 71, 72; courts, decline of confidence in, 55; democracy, commitment to, 12, 59; democracy, view of essential characteristics of, 57, 58; democratic institutions, decline of confidence in, 120, 121; evaluation of democratic institutions, 25; evaluation of democratic performance, 61, 63; legislature, decline of confidence in, 54; media, decline of confidence in, 54, 55; parliament, decline of confidence in, 55; political engagement, and campaign donations, 145; political participation, decline in, 141, 143; unions, decline of confidence in, 55. *See also* citizens' assembly (CA); democratic deficit, Canada

Citizens for Better Medicare, 169

Citizens' Initiative Review (CIR), 307-8

Citizens United v. FEC (US, 2010), 162, 165, 171, 172, 174, 175, 177

citizens, US: BCRA political financing reforms, as unlikely to influence sentiment about elections, 178; campaign financing, as not pressing issue for, 161; civil service, decline of confidence in, 55; companies, decline of confidence in, 55; Congress, decline of confidence in, 55, 182; courts, decline of confidence in, 55; democracy, commitment to, 12, 59; democracy, view of essential characteristics of, 57, 58; democratic institutions, decline of confidence in, 55; democratic institutions, dissatisfaction with, 25, 26-29; democratic institutions, multiple points of access for representation, 295; democratic performance dissatisfaction, sources, 67-69; democratic performance evaluation, 32-39, 60, 61, 62, 63; democratic performance evaluation, country comparison, 69-70, 71, 72, 73; interest groups, disapproval of power of, 162, 318; justifications for extending franchise to non-citizen residents, 251-56; legislature, decline of confidence in, 47, 54; media, decline of confidence in, 54, 55; presidency/executive branch, support for, 47; proposal for incentives to make political contributions by, 173, 174; Supreme

Court, support for, 47; unions, decline of confidence in, 55
Citrin, Jack, 32
The Civic Culture (Almond and Verba), 27-28, 31
Civil Rights Commission (US), 255
civil service, citizen decline of confidence in, 55
Clay, Henry, 209
Clinton, Bill, 34, 192, 206
Clinton, Hillary, 173
The Coalition: Americans Working for Real Change, 169
Common Cause, 6
companies: citizen decline of confidence in, 38-39, 54, 55; issue advocacy advertising, in US election campaigns, 169-70; political donations, and political influence, 153
Conference Board of Canada, 182
Congress (US): accountability, 296, 297; benefits of confrontational nature of legislature, 187; citizen support, erosion of, 47; codification of randomness of jury selection, 279; committee system, 199; competition for, not influenced by BCRA, 176-77; Congressional Budget Office, 191, 192; critique of perceived excesses in partisanship, 183; deliberation, 296, 297; democratic deficits, 201, 295-97; as effective check on presidential power, 182; geared more to local than pan-American policies, 198; inclusion, 295-96, 297; institutional difference, compared with Canadian Parliament, 183; legislative gridlock, 183; legislative power, compared with Canadian Parliament, 186-87; legislative process, and dispersal of power, 189-90, 200; loss of public confidence in, 182; member pressures, by local electorate, 201; member success as legislative entrepreneurs, 187; members, as full-time fundraisers, 201; members, independence of, 200; as model of liberal democratic legislature, 181; party discipline, compared with Canadian Parliament, 192, 200; party unity and membership control, increase in, 189; political donors and political influence, 153, 201, 296; survey of US citizen confidence in, 37-38. *See also* House of Representatives (US); names of parties and politicians; political financing, US; Senate (US)
Conservative Party (Canada): attack advertising outside election writ period, funded by individual contributors, 153; electoral system reform, to disadvantage of minority parties, 140-41; fundraising by, 146-47; regionalization of support base, 130. *See also* Progressive Conservative Party (Canada)
Contract with America, 192
Court Government (Savoie), 227, 238
courts, citizen decline of confidence in, 55
Crerar, T.A., 122
Croly, Herbert, 216
Crosby, Ned, 307, 308
Cross, William, 5-6, 7, 23
Cullell, Jorge Vargas, 3

Dahl, Robert, 4, 252
Dalton, Russell J., 10, 29
Davis, Bill, 235
Dean, Howard, 166, 173
Debs, Eugene, 215
deliberation: by citizens' assembly (CA), 301, 303-6, 308, 310, 325; by Congress (US), 296, 297; initiatives designed to include citizen decision-making, 326; by jury system (US), 276-77; in Westminster

Index

cabinet-parliamentary system, 294-95, 297
democracy: assessment standards, 229-30; Canada, international rankings, 1, 7; citizen values, and expectations of democratic performance, 64-67; compared with ecologies, 297; conceptions of, 56-57; deliberative, 4, 269-70; and economic and legal order, 57, 58; and economic redistribution, 57, 58; evaluating quality of practice of, 317-18; ideal, characteristics, 2, 4, 5; as imperfect, 2-3, 326; liberal, 3; nations' commitment to, 59; participatory, 4, 269-70; procedural, 56-57, 58, 68; redistributive, 68; referendums, 298-99; representative, 4, 271-72; and right to vote, 250; salience, 59-60, 61, 63; supplementary, 298; tension between vote and voice, 323. *See also* democratic audit; democratic deficit; democratic institutions; democratic reforms
democratic audit: IDEA methodology, 4-5; purpose, 5. *See also* Canadian Democratic Audit; democratic deficit
Democratic Challenges, Democratic Choices (Dalton), 10
democratic deficit: assumptions in examination of, 51-52; characteristics, 53; as citizen or institutional deficit, 8; and civic disengagement, 25; comparison between Canada and US, 23-47, 53, 292-97; country-specific reforms, necessity for, 318; definition, 76, 228-29, 292, 327; dissatisfaction with democratic performance, consequences, 70-71, 73; dissatisfaction with democratic performance, findings, 67-70; dissatisfaction with democratic performance, hypotheses, 62-67, 63, 327, 328; gap between theory and practice, 1-2; as perceived by public, 315-16, 321; political salience of, 10, 79; reform approaches, 17-19; sources, 11-12. *See also* citizens; democracy; democratic audit; democratic deficit, Canada; democratic deficit, European Union; democratic deficit, US; democratic institutions, Canada; democratic institutions, US; electoral systems; voting
democratic deficit, Canada: comparison with US, 23-47, 53, 292-97; definition, 226; "governing from the centre" thesis, 227; issues, 120-21; as perceived by public, 315-16; reduction measures, 241-44
democratic deficit, European Union, 24
democratic deficit, US: comparison with Canada, 23-47, 53, 292-97; as perceived by public, 315-16; president's wartime prerogative powers, 204-22; specific concerns about, 3, 162
democratic distress. *See* democratic deficit
democratic institutions: accountability, 293; citizen decline of confidence in, 55-56; citizen dissatisfaction with, 1-2, 7-8, 9, 11, 25, 53, 316; citizens' assembly, as supplement to, 299, 310, 323-26; comparison, Canada with US, 7-9; deliberation, 293; inclusion, 292-93; reform, through innovations, 17-19; views of elite and mass publics, 79-80, 87. *See also* citizens; citizens' assembly (CA); Congress (US); democratic deficit; democratic institutions, Canada; democratic institutions, US; legislatures; Parliament (Canada); Westminster cabinet-parliamentary system

democratic institutions, Canada: citizen decline of confidence in, 55; compared with US, 7-9. *See also* Parliament (Canada); Prime Minister's Office (Canada); Westminster cabinet-parliamentary system

democratic institutions, US: compared with Canada, 7-9. *See also* Congress (US); House of Representatives (US); Presidency (US); Senate (US)

Democratic Party (US): campaign committee fundraising (2000-10), 167, 168, 171; political financing reforms, 163

democratic reforms: and democratic innovation, 319-22. *See also* citizens' assembly (CA); democratic deficit

Denmark: required residency period, and non-citizen voting rights, 249; survey result of trust in government, 41, 42, 43, 44, 45

DeWitt, John L. (Lieutenant General), 217

Dion, Stéphane, 239-40

Disaffected Democracy (Pharr and Putnam), 2

DISCLOSE Act (US), 172

Diversity Management and Community Engagement Unit (Toronto), 257

Divided We Fail coalition, 177, 178

Docherty, David, 318

Donovan, William, 217

Durbin, Dick, 173

East Germany. *See* Germany

elections. *See* electoral systems; franchise; political financing, Canada; political financing, US; voting

Elections Act (Canada): amendments on election financing (1974), 139; amendments on election financing (2004, 2006), 153; registered party status, 150-51

Electoral Assistance Commission (EAC) (US), 92

Electoral College (US), 92, 103, 319

electoral system, Canada: back-burner vs. front-burner elections, 121-25; Bill C-24 (2003), 140, 141; as centralized and uniform, 118; debates on replacing FPTP system by elites, 128-29, 132; and democratic deficit, 13-17; elections, back-burner vs. front-burner, 121-25; electoral district redistributions, 114-15, 117, 124; fixed election dates, as reform measure, 198-99, 241; lack of public debate on, 132-33; Office of Chief Electoral Officer, 113-14, 117; parliamentary debates on replacing FPTP system, 125-28; parties and regional representation, 130-31; provincial issues, 125-26, 130; reforms, and citizens' assembly, 299-303, 328; reforms, effect on core democratic values, 157; reforms, since Confederation, 112-17; reforms, to enhance democratic value, 319; single-member plurality (SMP) vs. proportional representation (PR), 118-20, 131, 132, 133-34. *See also* franchise, Canada; political financing, Canada; voting, Canada

electoral system, New Zealand, 83

electoral system, US: decentralization of, 92-93, 102; and democratic deficit, 13-17; electorate participation, 91-105. *See also* political financing, US; voting, US

electoral systems: majoritarian, 8; mixed-member proportional (MMP), 129, 305; proportional representation (PR), 8, 118-20, 133-34; and representation theory, 274; single transferable vote (STV), 82, 128, 129, 132; single-member plurality (SMP), 118-20, 133-34, 151. *See*

also political financing, Canada; political financing, US; representation theory; voting
Emerson, David, 238
Employee Free Choice Act (US), 175
Equal Protection Clause (US), 251
Espionage Act (US, 1917), 215, 216
Eurobarometer, 39-40
European Convention on Human Rights, 84
European Union: citizenship application, wait period, 262; countries with public satisfaction with democracy, 26; "critical citizens," and democratic deficit, 24, 25; Eurobarometer, 39-40; national governments, survey of citizen trust in, 40-43; nationalism, as relatively strong and stable, 46; non-citizen residents, and franchise, 249, 262; and origins of term "democratic deficit," 76; parliaments, survey of citizen trust in, 43-46; standards framework for democracy assessment, 77. *See also* names of specific countries
"Eviction Free Zone" (US), 255
Executive Order 9066 (US, 1942), 217, 218

Farber, Daniel, 211
FEC v. Wisconsin Right to Life (US, 2007), 165, 177
Federal Election Campaign Act (FECA) (US, 1972), 163-64, 165
Federal Election Commission (FEC) (US), 162, 165, 168
Feingold, Russell, 165, 172, 173, 189
Ferejohn, John, 307, 308
Figueroa v. Canada (Attorney General) (2003), 150
Finland: citizen commitment to democracy, 59; citizen evaluation of democratic performance, 60, 61, 63; dissatisfaction with democratic performance, country comparison, 69, 70; required residency period, and non-citizen voting rights, 249; survey result of trust in government, 40, 41, 42, 44, 45
First Nations (Canada): better represented in Senate than House of Commons, 186; franchise, 113, 117, 230; as member of BC citizens' assembly, 299
first past the post (FPTP) voting system, 118-20, 133-34, 232. *See also* single-member plurality (SMP) voting system
Fisher, Louis, 206
Flaherty, Jim, 238
Ford, Gerald, 205
Fortyn, Pim, 78
FPTP (first past the post) voting system, 118-20, 133-34, 232
France: citizen commitment to democracy, 59; citizen decline of confidence in parliament, 53-54; citizen evaluation of democratic performance, 61, 63; survey result of trust in government, 41, 42, 43, 44, 45
franchise: "all affected principle," 251-56; for non-citizen residents, 251-56, 321, 323; psychological benefits to extending franchise to immigrants, 264
franchise, Canada: and Charter of Rights and Freedoms (1982), 113, 117; First Nations, 113, 117, 230; history, 112-13, 117, 118, 131; restrictions for non-citizen residents, as democratic deficit, 15, 248-49, 256-59
franchise, European Union, and non-citizen residents, 249, 262
franchise, US, and non-citizen residents, 15, 251-56
Franks, C.E.S., 198
Freedom House, democracy rankings, 1

Freedom of Information Act (UK), 85
The Friendly Dictatorship (Simpson), 228
front-burner elections, 121-25
Frost, Leslie, 233
Fuchs, Dieter, 64, 72

Gallup poll, 43
Garrett, Beth, 272
General Social Survey (GSS) (US), 31, 36-39
Genovese, Michael, 205
Germans, in US: internment, during WWI, 214; selected relocation, during WWII, 218-19; trial of eight saboteurs, during WWII, 217
Germany: citizen commitment to democracy, 59; citizen decline of confidence in parliament, 54; citizen evaluation of democratic performance, 61, 63; survey result of trust in government, 41, 42, 44, 45
Gingrich, Newt, 192
Glasser v. United States (US, 1942), 279
Glasson, Thierry, 2
Global Democracy, democracy rankings, 1, 7
Goldenberg, Eddie, 236
Good, Kristin, 257
Gore, Al, 103
The Governance of Britain (UK "green paper"), 85
Governing from the Centre: The Concentration of Power in Canadian Politics (Savoie), 227, 228, 237, 238
government: erosion of competence under globalization, 87; rising popular expectations of, 87. *See also* democratic institutions
Graham v. Richardson (US, 1971), 255
Granatstein, Jack, 240
Grant, Ulysses S. (General), 212
Great Britain. *See* United Kingdom

Greece, trust in government, 41, 42, 44, 45
Green Party (Canada): campaign donations to, 147; public financing, and growth of, 151-52, 155; status of, 157
Gregory, Thomas, 215-16
Guantanamo Bay prison, 219, 221

Hamilton, Alexander, 101
Hardin, Russell, 32
Hargrove, Erwin, 217
Harper, Stephen: autocratic management style, 237, 238-39; calling of early election to advance political agenda, 241; election campaign (2008), direct appeal to voters, 320-21; instructions for MPs on stonewalling parliamentary committees, 242; relations with media, 238
Harper vs. Canada (Attorney General), 148
Harris, Mike, 233
Harris poll, 43
Harrison, William Henry, 209-10
Hayduk, Ron, 248, 254
Help America Vote Act (HAVA) (US), 92, 104
Hernandez v. Texas (US, 1954), 279
Holmes, Oliver Wendell, 216
Hoover, J. Edgar, 218
House of Commons (Canada): accountability, 190-91, 199-200; adversarial system, 187, 190-91; backbenchers, and democratic deficit, 243-44; committees, 191, 193, 194, 199; executive control and centralization of power, 181, 187-89, 190; lack of inclusion of minorities and recent immigrants, 185; private members' bills, 181, 187, 190; as providing conditions for collectivist, national policies, 198; Question Period, 190-91, 199, 242; seat protection for less

populous provinces, 184-85; Speech from the Throne, 191; turnover, greater than US Congress, 185; variance in population of districts, 184, 185; women, underrepresentation of, 149, 150, 185
House of Representatives (US): committee system, 193-95; elections, 102; party loyalty, role of, 193; state seats, vary with population changes, 184
Howe, Daniel Walker, 209
Human Rights Act (UK), 85

IDEA. *See* International Institute for Democracy and Electoral Assistance (IDEA)
immigrants: and all-affected principle, as justification for extending franchise to non-citizen residents, 251-56; alternative means of participation in decision-making process, 260-61; fairness, and rewards of citizenship, 261-62; franchise, for non-citizen residents, 321, 323; non-citizens, voting restrictions as democratic deficit, 248-64; psychological benefits to extending franchise to, 264; residency requirement for citizenship application, 262-63
immigrants, US: distinction between economic and political rights, 251; illegal, rights of, 250-51; vulnerability to exploitation, 254, 255-56
Immigration and Settlement Policy Framework (Toronto), 257
Imperial Presidency (Schlesinger), 206
inclusion: citizens' assembly, 301, 302-3, 308-10; Congress (US), 295-96, 297; democratic institutions, 292-93; of minorities and recent immigrants, lacking in House of Commons (Canada), 185; Westminster cabinet-parliamentary system, 294, 297
Inclusive Cities Canada, 258
Industrial Workers of the World, 215
insurance companies, advocacy advertising, in US election campaigns, 170
International Institute for Democracy and Electoral Assistance (IDEA): democratic assessment framework, 88; international standards for democracy assessment, 76-77; methodology for context-specific democratic audits, 4
Inuit, franchise in Canada, 113, 117
Ireland: evaluation of public institutions and democratic performance, 81-82, 87; survey result of trust in government, 40, 41, 42, 44, 45
Italians, selected relocation during WWII by US, 218
Italy: alienated political culture, 28; citizen commitment to democracy, 59; citizen evaluation of democratic performance, 61, 63; survey result of trust in government, 40, 41, 42, 44, 45

Jackson, Andrew, 209
Japan: citizen commitment to democracy, 59; citizen evaluation of democratic performance, 61, 63; dissatisfaction with democratic performance, country comparison, 69, 70
Japanese Canadians, franchise, 113, 117
Japanese, US internment during WWII, 208, 214, 216-19
Johnson, Andrew, 212
Jury Selection and Service Act (US), 279
jury system (US): accountability, indirect, 282-84; civic responsibility, 280-81; and 'collective wisdom,' 282; cross-sectionality, 279-80; deliberation, 276-77; impartiality,

278-79; implicit theory of "citizen representation," 270; legitimacy, 281-82; as mandatory, 280, 281; primary function of, 276; and representation theory, 273; as useful model for citizen political representation, 275, 276

Kalven, Harry, 282
Kenny, Colin, 197
Kerry, John, 166
Keyssar, Alexander, 249
Kini, Tara, 255
Klein, Ralph, 233
Klingemann, Hans-Dieter, 72

Lammers, William, 205
Lange, David, 84
Lawrence Stephen, 78-79
legislatures: accountability role, 190-95; citizen decline of confidence in, 54; impasse, and role of citizens' assembly in decision making, 308-10; legislation role, 186-90; representation role, 183-86. *See also* Congress (US); House of Commons (Canada); House of Representatives (US); Parliament (Canada); Senate (Canada); Senate (US); Westminster cabinet-parliamentary system
Liberal Party (Canada): campaign donations to, 147; electoral system reforms (Bill C-24), 140, 141; federal election results, 122, 123, 124; inability to respond to Conservative attack advertising, due to lack of funds, 153; public funding, effect of removal on, 146-47; public funding, importance of, 155; regional support for, 130
Lincoln, Abraham, 207, 208, 209-13
Lipset, Seymour Martin, 200
Lusitania (ship), 214
Luxembourg, survey result of trust in government, 40, 41, 42, 44, 45

Maastricht Treaty, on voting rights of non-citizen residents, 249
Macdonald, John A., 115-16
Mackenzie, Alexander, 116
Madison, James, 205
Manin, Bernard, 273-74
Mansbridge, Jane, 284, 304
Maori people (New Zealand), 83
May, Elizabeth, 152
Mayer, Kenneth, 221
Maytree Foundation, 257, 258
McCain, John, 165, 173, 189
McCarren-Walter Act, 1952, 217
McClellan, George (General), 212
McConnell v. FEC (US, 2003), 165
McGuinty, Dalton, 258
media: citizen decline of confidence in, 54, 55; electronic, democratic potential of, 321
media, Canada: and debate on voting system, 128; Prime Minister Harper's relations with, 238; and public image of prime ministers, 235-36; reports on cabinet decisions, 234, 235
Mendelberg, Tali, 277
Merryman, John, 211
Military and Overseas Voter Empowerment Act (US), 104
Miller, Arthur, 32-33
Miller, David, 257-58
Miroff, Bruce, 205
Mississauga, and voting rights of non-citizen residents, 257, 263
mixed-member proportional (MMP) voting system, 129, 303, 305
MMP voting system. *See* mixed-member proportional (MMP) voting system
Modern Democracies (Bryce), 229-30
Morgan, Edmund, 272
Morley, Terry, 240
"Motor Voter," 98
MoveOn.org, 6

Nadeau, Richard, 2

National Association of Secretaries of State (NASS) (US), 92-93
National Federation of Independent Businesses (NFIB) (US), 170, 177
National Popular Vote Plan (US), 103
National Progressive Party (Canada), 122, 123
National Unity Party (US), 212
National Voter Registration Act (NVRA) (US), 97, 98, 104
NDP. *See* New Democratic Party (NDP) (Canada)
Neely, Mark, 212
Netherlands: citizen commitment to democracy, 59; citizen decline of confidence in parliament, 54; citizen evaluation of democratic performance, 61, 63; citizens' assembly, 302; findings of IDEA democracy assessment, 77-78; survey result of trust in government, 41, 42
Neustadt, Richard, 206
Nevitte, Neil, 316-17
New Democratic Party (NDP) (Canada): campaign donations to, 147; federal election results, 122; support for, 130
New Zealand: citizen evaluation of public institutions and democratic performance, 82-84, 87; electoral system, 83; required residency period, and non-citizen voting rights, 249
Norway, required residency period and non-citizen voting rights, 249

Obama, Barack: administrative challenges of, 205, 220-22; decline of federal campaign funding, 166; on democratic renewal, 322; on democratic rights during presidential campaign, 219-20; fundraising by, 173, 318; on open government, 6

Occupy Canada movement, 25
Olson, Culbert, 217, 218
O'Malley, Eion, 240
One Resident, One Vote (OROV) coalition, 258-59
Ontario: citizens' assembly, 303; referendum on electoral reform, 299, 300, 302
Ontario citizens' assembly, 305
Open Government Initiative, 6
Oregon Citizens' Initiative Review, 308
The Ottawa Men (Granatstein), 240

PACs (political action committees). *See* political financing, US
Paine, Thomas, 207
Palin, Sarah, 220
Parliament (Canada): accountability, 190-95; committees, 191, 199; critique of perceived excesses in partisanship, 183; democratic deficits, 294-95, 297; executive domination of, 16-17, 120, 199, 200; fundamental institutional difference compared with US Congress, 183; legislative process, 187-89; minority governments, 243; as model of liberal democratic legislature, 181; Parliamentary Budget Office, 191-92; public confidence in, 182; representation, 183-86; Speech from the Throne, 191; strengthening, to reduce democratic deficit, 242-43. *See also* House of Commons (Canada); Prime Minister's Office (Canada); Senate (Canada)
participation, political. *See* citizens
Pastor, Robert, 8
PCTC. *See* political contribution tax credit (PCTC) (Canada)
The People's House of Commons (Smith), 242
Perlin, George, 121
Pettit, Philip, 254

pharmaceutical companies, issue advocacy advertising in US election campaigns, 169-70
Pharr, Susan, 2
Pitkin, Hannah, 273, 285
political action committees (PACs). *See* political financing, US
political contribution tax credit (PCTC) (Canada), 140, 145, 155, 174. *See also* political financing, Canada
political financing, Canada: campaign financing regulations, 15, 188-89; and citizen engagement, 145; compared with US, 157; donations disclosure, 139-40; election spending, and effect of advertising on voter turnout, 143-44; election spending, limits on, 139, 157; elections, and "third-party" advertising, 140, 148; fundraising, importance of, 146-47, 157-58; history, 115-16, 118, 138-39; individual contributors, and citizen political engagement, 145; individual contributors, as only legal source of funding, 146, 153, 154; individual contributors, characteristics, 154; and party responsiveness to donors, 152-56; per-vote public subsidies for political parties, 140-41, 150-52, 154; political contribution tax credit (PCTC), 140, 145, 155, 174; as potential barrier to election of women, 149; regulation of, 15, 138-57
political financing, US: 501(c) organizations (US), 175; "527" organizations, 168; campaign contributions, implications of wealthy donors, 318; compared with Canada, 157; elections, and "third-party" advertising, 148; fundraising by candidates for Congress, 173, 201; fundraising by PACs, 163, 164, 165, 168, 170, 171, 173, 175; and "issue advocacy" advertising, 164; McCain-Feingold reforms, 165, 189; presidency campaign fundraising, 165-66, 168, 172-73; reform, effects of, 166-70; reform, history of, 163-66; self-financing of bid for elected office, 150; television coverage reform proposals, 173. *See also* Bipartisan Campaign Reform Act (BCRA) (US, 2002)
political institutions. *See* Congress (US); democratic institutions; Parliament (Canada)
Polk, James, 210
Portugal, survey result of trust in government, 40, 41, 42, 43, 44, 45
Prentice, Jim, 238
Presidency (US): campaign fundraising, 165-66, 168; citizen support for, 47; competition for, not influenced by BCRA, 176; impeachment, as only way to unseat incumbent, 189; Lincoln, prerogative power during Civil War, 209-13; national security, as first priority set by US Constitution, 207; no direct accountability to Congress, 192; persuasive role in passing legislation, 189-90; prerogative power, as limit on democratic accountability, 204-22, 320; Roosevelt, and Japanese internment during WWII, 216-19; Wilson, prerogative power and national security during WWI, 213-16. *See also* Bush, George H.W. (father); Bush, George W. (son); Carter, Jimmy; Lincoln, Abraham; Obama, Barack; Reagan, Ronald; Roosevelt, Franklin Delano; Wilson, Woodrow
"President and Parliament" (Smith), 227
Presidential Funding Act (US, 2007), 172-73

Presidential Power (Neustadt), 206
Prime Minister's Office (Canada): centralized concentration of political power, 295, 320; leadership reviews, as recommendation for reducing democratic deficit, 241-42; as longest serving in Anglo-Celtic world, 240; rated as most powerful in international comparison, 228
private members' bills (Canada), 181, 187, 190
Progressive Conservative Party (Canada): back and front-burner federal election results, 122, 124; merger with Canadian Alliance and Reform Party, 146. *See also* Conservative Party (Canada)
proportional representation (PR): as generating less disaffection than majoritarian systems, 8; voting system, 118-20, 133-34
Putnam, Robert, 2, 121

Randall, James, 212
Reagan, Ronald, 33, 206
referendums: accountability, 301, 307; Canada, voter information issues, 132; citizens' assembly, potential assistance for, 307-9; deliberative qualities, 301; inclusive qualities, 301; US, voter distrust of agenda setters, 298-99
Reform Party (Canada), 122, 124
representation theory: contemporary, 273-75; democracy, and representation, 271-73; descriptive representation, 283; and norms of accountability, 273; tension between vote and voice, 323; US jury system, as useful model for citizen political representation, 275, 276-85. *See also* jury system (US)
Republican Party (US): campaign committee fundraising (2000-10), 167, 168; political theory, central concern with freedom, 254
Revenue Act (US, 1971), 163
The Right to Vote (Keyssar), 249
Roosevelt, Franklin Delano: and Japanese internment during WWII, 216-19; wartime leadership of, 207, 208
Roosevelt, Theodore, 222
Rosenthal, Steve, 177
Rostow, Eugene, 219
Rousseau, Jean-Jacques, 272
Royal Commission on Electoral Reform and Party Financing (Canada, 1991), 149
Rubio-Marin, Ruth, 248, 251, 255-56
Russell, Peter, 243

Sample, John, 161
Savoie, Donald: on "court government," 238; on "governing by bolts of electricity," 235; "governing from the centre" thesis, 227-28, 237; Stéphane Dion on works of, 239-40; on Trudeau's conversion to austerity program, 236
Schlesinger, Arthur, 206
Sedition Act (US, 1918), 216
Seitz, Brian, 274
Senate (Canada): lack of public support for, 196, 197; as less partisan, deliberative body, 196-97; members, appointment of, 195-96; members, question of election of, 197-98; representation of demographic profile of Canada, 186; seat distribution based on regional distribution, 185
Senate (US): elections, 102; equal seat distribution among states, 185; members, election of, 195; as preeminent democratic chamber, 196
Service Employees International Union (SEIU), 177

Seward, William, 213
Shapiro, Ian, 2
Sharp, Mitchell, 235-36
Siemiatycki, Myer, 258
Simpson, Jeffrey, 228, 240
Sinclair, Upton, 216
single transferable vote (STV) voting system, 82, 128, 129, 132, 300, 303
single-member plurality (SMP) voting system, 118-20, 133-34, 151
Smallwood, Joey, 233
Smith, David, 242
Smith, Denis, 227
SMP voting system. *See* single-member plurality (SMP) voting system
South Asia, ranking of components in democratic assessment, 88
Spain, survey result of trust in government, 41, 42, 44, 45
STV voting system. *See* single transferable vote (STV) voting system
Sunstein, Cass, 277
Supreme Court (US), citizen support for, 36, 47
Sweden: citizen commitment to democracy, 59; citizen evaluation of democratic performance, 60, 61, 63; dissatisfaction with democratic performance, country comparison, 69, 70; required residency period, and non-citizen voting rights, 249; survey result of trust in government, 40, 41, 42, 43, 44, 45
Swift Boat Veterans for Truth, 178

Taney, Robert B. (Chief Justice), 211
Task Force on Access and Equality (Toronto, Canada), 257
Taylor, Charles, 264
Taylor, Matthew, 154
Taylor v. Louisiana (US, 1975), 280
Tea Party (US), 25, 29
Thiel v. S. Pac. Co. (US, 1946), 279
Tocqueville, Alexis de, 276

Toronto: "Diversity Our Strength" motto, 256-57; immigrant population, 256; and non-citizen resident voting, 256-59
Toronto Region Immigrant Employment Council, 257
Transparency International, democracy rankings, 1
Trilateral Commission, 28
Trudeau, Pierre Elliott, 234, 235, 236-37
Two Cheers for Minority Government (Russell), 243

Unionist Party (Canada), 122, 123
unions: BCRA, and increase in person-to-person "ground war" tactics in swing states, 172; citizen decline of confidence in, 55; issue advocacy advertising, in US election campaigns, 164, 169; political donations, and political influence, 153
United Kingdom: citizen commitment to democracy, 59; citizen evaluation of democratic performance, 61, 63, 84-87; criminal case mismanagement, as democratic deficit, 78-79; plurality election system, and democratic deficit, 79-80; survey result of trust in government, 40, 41, 42, 43, 44, 45
United Seniors Association, 169-70
United States: democratic audit, 6; democratic institutions, compared with Canada, 7-9; government, legislative gridlock caused by dispersal of power, 16; government, measurement of trust in, 30, 31, 32-39; government, president's prerogative powers, 17; in international democracy rankings, 1; jury selection, and citizen representation, 269-85; presidential/congressional system, power shifts

between, 7; two-party system, 7; voting rights of non-citizen residents, 249-56. *See also* American National Election Studies (ANES); names beginning with US

United States v. Gometz (US, 1989), 280

United States v. Raszkiewicz (US, 1999), 280

Van Deman, Ralph (General), 218
Vander Zalm, Bill, 235
Verba, Sidney, 27-28, 31
voting: absentee ballots, 99, 100; decline in voter turnout, 53; early voting, 99-100, 101; mail balloting, 99, 100, 101; polling place locations, 99, 101-2; as privilege, 91, 93, 95; referendums, 133; as right, 91, 93, 95-96, 250; tension between vote and voice, 323; US, all-affected principle, 251-54; US, low participation in, 91-92; "vote value," varies in Canada, 115. *See also* electoral systems; franchise; names of specific countries; representation theory; voting, Canada; voting, US

voting, Canada: based on party and leader, not individual candidates, 185-86; franchise, history, 112-13, 117, 118, 131; franchise, restrictions for non-citizen residents, 15, 248-49, 256-59; low voter turnout, 120, 135; majority governments, and FPTP voting system, 232; referendums, 133; voter registration, 116-17; voter turnout, theories on decline in, 143-45

Voting Rights Act (VRA) (US), 92, 96, 101-2, 104

voting, US: based on personal characteristics of candidates, 185; convenience voting options, 98-102; electorate mobilization, 103-5; electorate participation, 93-95, 102; history, 95-96; improving voter participation, 104-5; low participation rates, 91-92; presidential elections, 94-95, 96; registration process, 13, 93, 95-98, 104, 319; restrictions for non-citizen residents, 248, 249-56

Warren, Earl, 217, 218
Warren, Mark E., 284
The Way It Works (Goldenberg), 236
Webster, Daniel, 209
Weed, Thurlow, 213
West Germany. *See* Germany
Westminster cabinet-parliamentary system: accountability, 232, 295, 297; cabinet monopoly, regarding bills and issues of finance, 231; cabinet secrecy, 234; centralized executive concentration of power, 7, 233-41, 294, 295; deliberation, 294-95, 297; democratic deficits, 294-95, 297; few opportunities for organized advocacy and influence by NGOs, 294; first ministers, constraints on, 232-33; first ministers, increasing concentration of power by, 231, 233-41; inclusion, 294, 297; lack of checks on legislative majority party, 294; limits on government action, 233; majority governments, and FPTP voting system, 232; majority governments, and strong party discipline, 231; minority governments, 231, 232; as non-deliberative in formation of policy, 294-95; provincial premiers, autocratic reputations of, 233

Whelan, Eugene, 235
White, Stephen, 316-17
Wilson, James, 205
Wilson, Woodrow, 207, 208

Wisconsin Right to Life case. *See FEC v. Wisconsin Right to Life* (US, 2007)
women: better represented in Senate than House of Commons, 186; Canada, franchise, 113, 117, 230; gender parity in citizens' assemblies, 302; political financing, as potential barrier to election, 149-50
World Audit, democracy rankings, 1
World Values Survey (WVS): Canadian and US citizens, on democracy, 11-12; on eroding confidence in parliaments, 43; and examination of democratic deficit, 52-73; on public's loss of confidence in US Congress, 182

Young, Walter, 240

Zeisel, Hans, 282